F

DO

FLAUBERT'S *TENTATION*

Flaubert's *Tentation*

Remapping Nineteenth-Century
French Histories of Religion and Science

MARY ORR

OXFORD
UNIVERSITY PRESS

OXFORD

UNIVERSITY PRESS

Great Clarendon Street, Oxford OX2 6DP

Oxford University Press is a department of the University of Oxford.
It furthers the University's objective of excellence in research, scholarship,
and education by publishing worldwide in

Oxford New York

Auckland Cape Town Dar es Salaam Hong Kong Karachi
Kuala Lumpur Madrid Melbourne Mexico City Nairobi
New Delhi Shanghai Taipei Toronto

With offices in

Argentina Austria Brazil Chile Czech Republic France Greece
Guatemala Hungary Italy Japan Poland Portugal Singapore
South Korea Switzerland Thailand Turkey Ukraine Vietnam

Oxford is a registered trade mark of Oxford University Press
in the UK and in certain other countries

Published in the United States
by Oxford University Press Inc., New York

© Mary Orr 2008

The moral rights of the author have been asserted
Database right Oxford University Press (maker)

First published 2008

All rights reserved. No part of this publication may be reproduced,
stored in a retrieval system, or transmitted, in any form or by any means,
without the prior permission in writing of Oxford University Press,
or as expressly permitted by law, or under terms agreed with the appropriate
reprographics rights organization. Enquiries concerning reproduction
outside the scope of the above should be sent to the Rights Department,
Oxford University Press, at the address above

You must not circulate this book in any other binding or cover
and you must impose the same condition on any acquirer

British Library Cataloguing in Publication Data

Data available

Library of Congress Cataloging in Publication Data

Orr, Mary, 1960–
Flaubert's Tentation : Remapping Nineteenth-Century French Histories of Religion
and Science / Mary Orr.
p. cm.
Includes bibliographical references and index.
ISBN 978–0–19–925858–1
1. Flaubert, Gustave, 1821–1880. Tentation de saint Antoine. I. Title
PQ2246.T5O77 2008
843'.8–dc22 2008024317

Typeset by SPI Publisher Services, Pondicherry, India
Printed in Great Britain
on acid-free paper by
Biddles Ltd., King's Lynn, Norfolk

ISBN 978–0–19–925858–1

1 3 5 7 9 10 8 6 4 2

Acknowledgements

Although I have been teaching BA final year special subject courses on Flaubert since 1990, the *Tentation de saint Antoine* has never featured. It was not until October 2004 and the invitation of Professor Allan Pasco to give a research lecture at the University of Kansas on the *Tentation*'s hagiographical intertexts that I also had my first opportunity to teach the text. It is therefore thanks to Allan's intellectually curious MA and Ph.D. students, the searching questions of his colleagues, and his hospitality during my visit that the dialogic shape and structure of this book were crystallized. But the Kansas lecture could not have been given without prior research support, and a particularly memorable, probing, and stimulating discussion in London in 2003 with Professor Malcolm Bowie. In spite of his myriad commitments as Marshal Foch Chair of French at Oxford, Malcolm wrote the reference which secured a British Academy Small Grant to undertake research on the *Tentation*'s rich theological materials in Paris in February–May 2004. Malcolm's untimely death means that his strategic roles in this book can only be acknowledged in print. Oxford also provided the second key supporter of this book, Dr Adrianne Tooke, whose interdisciplinary breadth and enrichment of Flaubert scholarship have been the gold standard for this study. Her reference enabled the securing of an *AHRC* Leave Scheme Award to match the semester's research leave granted by the University of Southampton in 2006–7. In thanking Adrianne, I would also like to thank both Southampton and the *AHRC* for the institutional and financial support which brought this book to completion.

Debate and dialogue have been fundamental to this project from its earliest inception to its birthing. Especial thanks go to my two Ph.D. students on Flaubert, Dr Andrew Cuthbert (Exeter) for those many hard questions on the Trinity and Flaubert's theology, and Michael Seabrook (Southampton) for requiring me to come up with better definitions of Flaubert's Romanticism. Andrew Cuthbert is also one of the two people who have been extraordinarily generous with their time in reading the completed manuscript. The other is Professor Lawrence M. Porter, whose Flaubert encyclopedism and intellectual largesse is an inspiration and hence aspiration for this book. His suggestions for revisions have undoubtedly improved the end result. Remaining errors and blind spots are my own.

The final stages of production have all been helped by Jacqueline Baker and her team at OUP. I would also like to thank Professor Eelco Rohling of the National Oceanography Centre, University of Southampton for permissions to use his photographs of microfossils to illustrate the cover.

This book is dedicated to Neil. As its resident geologist and intrepid photographer of all things Flaubertian, thank you for living unstintingly with its writing for too much of the last four years.

Contents

Sources, Abbreviations, and Reference Matter

Flaubert's fictional Saint Antoine owes much to the life of St Anthony the Great of Egypt (AD 250–356). To distinguish the two figures throughout this book, I use 'Antoine' when referring to Flaubert's protagonist and 'St Anthony' when referring to his precursor.

Unless otherwise stated, all references in this book to Flaubert's *La Tentation de saint Antoine* (henceforth *Tentation*) are to the final revision published in 1874. Although its several versions are found in Flaubert's *Œuvres complètes* edited by Bernard Masson (Paris: Seuil, 1964, 2 vols.), I use and quote throughout this book from Claudine Gothot-Mersch's unsurpassed critical edition of the 1874 text (Paris: Folio, 1983, henceforth *Tent*, followed by the page reference), because it offers newcomer and specialist readers alike an accessible and portable compendium of all the supporting erudition needed to enhance further study of Flaubert's text. All references to Flaubert's *Correspondance* are to the Bibliothèque de la Pléiade edition by Jean Bruneau, using the format *Corr* followed by the volume number and then the page reference.

One of the main arguments of this book is the accessibility of the *Tentation* to the modern reader, in spite of its renown as a text of almost overwhelming authorial and critical erudition. To counter this negative reputation while offering pointers for further investigation, this book banishes all secondary reference matter to endnotes, and in these uses the author: date system. Secondary works quoted severally in the main text are then given an abbreviation in an endnote following their first occurrence. This abbreviation and a page number then follow subsequent references. The bibliography of works consulted (primary and secondary works) gives full details of all works cited. Secondary works are listed under the following subsections: 'nineteenth-century texts consulted', 'non-nineteenth-century texts consulted', 'electronic resources'. These follow a section listing secondary criticism specifically about the *Tentation*. Only this section of the bibliography includes works not directly cited in this study.

B   Jan Bondeson, *The Feejee Mermaid and Other Essays in Natural and Unnatural History*. Ithaca, NY: Cornell University Press, 1999.

Corr   Gustave Flaubert, *Correspondance,* ed. Jean Bruneau. 4 vols. Paris: Bibliothèque de la Pléiade, 1973–98.

DH François-André-Adrien, *Abbé Pluquet, Mémoires pour servir à l'histoire des égarements de l'esprit humaine par rapport à la religion chrétienne, ou dictionnaire des hérésies, des erreurs et des schismes.* 2 vols. Besançon: Chez Petit, 1817.

EC Henry Chadwick, *The Penguin History of the Church: The Early Church.* London: Penguin, 1999.

École 2 *Histoire de l'école d'Alexandrie comparée aux principales écoles contemporaines.* Vol. ii. Paris: Hachette, 1844.

GA Apuleius, *The Golden Ass.* trans. and introd. Robert Graves. London: Penguin, 1950.

HCEA Étienne Vacherot, *Histoire critique de l'école d'Alexandrie.* 3 vols. Paris: Librairie Philosophique de Ladrange, 1846–54.

LD Jacques de Voragine, *La Légende dorée.* Paris: Éditions du Seuil, 1998.

LP René Descharmes (ed.), *Alfred Le Poittevin: Une promenade de Bélial et Œuvres inédites.* Paris: Les Presses Françaises, 1924.

Magie L. F. Alfred Maury, *La Magie et l'astrologie dans l'antiquité et au moyen âge: étude sur les superstitions païennes qui se sont perpétuées jusqu'à nos jours.* Paris: Didier et Cie, 1860.

OC Gustave Flaubert, *Œuvres complètes*, ed. Bernard Masson. 2 vols. Paris: Seuil, 1964.

StJ Jean Miniac (ed. and trans.), *Saint Jérôme: vivre au désert: vies de Paul, Malchus, Hilarion 375–390.* Grenoble: Éditions Jérôme Millon, 1992.

Tent Gustave Flaubert, *La Tentation de saint Antoine*, ed. Claudine Gothot-Mersch. Paris: Gallimard, 1983.

VA G. J. M. Bartelink (ed.), *Athanase d'Alexandrie: Vie d'Antoine.* Paris: Éditions de Cerf, 1994).

VJ Ernest Renan, *Vie de Jésus (version intégrale).* Paris: Arléa, 1992 (reprint of the 13th edn published in 1864 by Michel Lévy).

W Timothy Ware, *The Orthodox Church.* New edn. London: Penguin, 1993.

Introduction

Whatever exists has already been named, and what man is has been known... The more the words, the less the meaning, and how does that profit anyone?... No-one can comprehend what goes on under the sun. Despite all his efforts to search it out, man cannot discover its meaning. Even if a wise man claims he knows, he cannot really comprehend it.... 'Meaningless! Meaningless!' says the Teacher. 'Everything is meaningless!'... Of making many books there is no end, and much study wearies the body.[1]

In spite of the fame and lasting success of Flaubert's *Madame Bovary* after acquittal at its public trial for offences to religion and public morality in 1857, Flaubert's life as a writer is epitomized by biographers and literary critics as one of suffering for his art.[2] Causes for this suffering include circumstance, illness, or personal afflictions such as perfectionist redrafting and the pain of writer's block. Critics' block is rarely discussed, however, although Flaubert encountered it long before the famous trial of *Madame Bovary* at the very outset of his writing career.[3] Prior to launching the *Tentation de saint Antoine* as his first major work on the public, he read it aloud over four days in September 1849 to Louis Bouilhet and Maxime Du Camp, his closest friends and lifelong critics. If Du Camp was expecting Flaubert to recraft the exemplary life of St Anthony the Great of Egypt as a psychological study, Bouilhet anticipated instead a reconstruction of third-century AD Alexandria, knowing that Flaubert would be strongly attracted to the strange melting pot of the saint's historical times. Neither expectation was fulfilled. For both critics, the *Tentation*'s worst faults—its characterization, subject matter, exaggerated style, lack of originality—were summed up in an intertextual reference: the *Tentation* was an exaggerated recasting of Edgar Quinet's *Ahasvérus* (1834). Flaubert had in effect produced a rather derivative 'mystère'.[4] Bouilhet pronounced the ultimate verdict: 'Nous pensons qu'il faut jeter cela au feu et n'en jamais reparler.'[5]

In the history of the book, texts deemed sacrilegious have often been banned and also publicly burned, like martyrs, heretics, and witches. Their outrage is to have challenged the authority and rule of the (divine) order of things by presenting dangerously conflicting, or alternative, truth statements about authorities. (Anti-)religious texts thus qualify most obviously for book burning in times of particularly intense ideological change and persecution, such as the Reformation or Counter-Reformation. Works treacherous to the status quo are, however, no pre-modern or solely religious phenomenon. Early and mid-nineteenth-century France witnessed similarly stringent and public displays of political censorship in spite (or perhaps even because) of its Revolution to end former orders of absolutism. The first Republic's avowed separation of State from Church (of Rome) was overturned in the first Empire after Napoleon I signed the Concordat in 1801, but this made the State no less vigilant concerning acts of 'heresy' haboured in dangerous secular books. The most famous example was Napoleon's confiscation and then burning of Germaine de Staël's *De l'Allemagne* in 1810 after he ordered her into exile. Her crime was high treason for what he saw as her negative portrayal of France in her comparative critique of vibrant German life, thought, letters, and religion.[6] Napoleon's inquisitorial tactics failed (as did his expansionist military campaigns before and after the *De l'Allemagne* débâcle), and were foiled by powers and natural forces greater than those he had bargained for. Germaine de Staël evaded his censorship by having another copy of her *De l'Allemagne* published in London during her exile there in both French and English. The scandal of its burning in France was no small part of its resounding international success.

For Flaubert in 1849, the private scalding of his friends' judgements and definitive exclusion of his *Tentation de saint Antoine* from the Republic of Letters was no less acutely felt,[7] although Bouilhet and Du Camp thought that they were saving Flaubert from worse public censure,[8] and of the kind he would indeed later experience with *Madame Bovary.* His response was to leave his *Tentation* project behind him, literally, by setting off in November 1849 for Egypt (Alexandria and then Cairo) and a tour in 1850 of the Middle East (Beirut,

Jerusalem, Nazareth, Damascus, Baalbek, Tripoli, Rhodes, Smyrna, and Constantinople), before returning to Croisset in June 1851 via Greece and Italy. Metaphorically, however, his *Tentation de saint Antoine* project was not so easily left at home. Flaubert was richly aware of St Anthony's Egypt on the initial stage of his journey,[9] just as he was unable to evade his two censors through exile from France. The journey was only possible thanks to Du Camp (who had won the commission of the Académie d'Inscriptions to photograph antiquities in Egypt and the Orient), while Flaubert's many letters recording what he saw on his *Voyage en Orient* had Bouilhet as their main addressee.[10] If this trip provided the inspiration and distancing effects necessary for writing the 'Normandy' novel of his return, *Madame Bovary* (written concertedly from 1851 to 1856), the 'Normandy' patterns of critical reception synonymous with the 1849 *Tentation* remained. Du Camp (now editor of the *Revue de Paris*) again censored Flaubert's text by suppressing episodes in the serialized version of *Madame Bovary* which came to be central to the famous public trial. While the 'heretical' Flaubert rather than his public prosecutors won the day, his defence as regards the merits of his art in *Madame Bovary* also defied the views of his private censors of 1849. At the very outset of his almost aborted public writing career Flaubert had learned through his 1849 *Tentation* a deeper lesson, to be resilient to writing what others deemed 'acceptable' books.

Resilience is very much the watchword of the *Tentation*. Flaubert defied Bouilhet's recommendation to burn it and never speak of it again. He returned to the work three times throughout his life,[11] and even called it the '*œuvre* de toute ma vie'.[12] Following the famous model of St Anthony the Great, Antoine epitomizes this character trait as the *Tentation*'s otherwise unpromising main protagonist. The many temptations and attacks on his flesh, mind, and spirit (which form episodes in the assault on his core beliefs) constitute the plot of Antoine's resistance and eventual overcoming. Resilience is then the theme and moral of the work. Where attack and persecution (religious or artistic) can act to strengthen the faith of true believers, painful censure or public censorship may serve to sharpen a critical spirit. Flaubert thus understood the resilience of saints and martyrs to death if necessary in pursuit of their cause, which for him was art. The beginning and ending of the concerted *Bovary* period with its private and public trials also mark Flaubert's work on a revision of the 1849 *Tentation*: he read some fragments to Bouilhet in 1851 and published revisions of strategic scenes in *L'Artiste* in 1856–7.[13] The crushing blow of his friends' adverse criticism had not blocked the work of writing, or eventual committing of the *Tentation* to print and a general public. The published fragments were nonetheless an incomplete revision of the whole, aborted this time by Flaubert's own self-critical dissatisfaction with his project, and his decision to revisit the Mediterranean, this time Carthage. Ostensibly, authentic detail was needed in order to write *Salammbô* (published in 1862, the manuscript again entrusted to Du Camp), but this historical novel about the fall of the Carthaginian empire turned into a diptych on France of 1820–48,[14] in the shape of *L'Éducation sentimentale* (read and annotated by Du Camp, published in November 1869). Bouilhet's death in July 1869 ended his lifelong commitment as sounding-board for Flaubert's writing and his 1849 judgement of the *Tentation*. The same year Flaubert returned to the *Tentation*, but as a thoroughgoing reworking, completed in 1872 but not published until 1874.[15] His final wrestling with the demons of writer's (and critics') block saw the exceptionally rapid completion thereafter of the *Trois Contes* (1876).

When the 1874 *Tentation* was published, Flaubert may have defied his private critics of the 1849 version, but he had to face the consequences of not heeding the warnings lying behind their earlier protective censure. Resilience to the text also characterizes the responses of readers and critics then and since. Most are resoundingly dismissive of the work, both for itself and within nineteenth-century French letters.[16] Even the strong advocates of Flaubert's other works who thereby seek justification for redeemable features in the *Tentation* have found it resilient to satisfactory interpretation, literary classification, and aesthetic interest, let alone reader satisfaction. Instead, it is the *Tentation*'s diptych, the unfinished *Bouvard et Pécuchet*, which receives the critical plaudits. As the no less difficult and erudite work of Flaubert's whole life, critics see in it both a rambunctious social satire and a Flaubert who is the first modern/Modernist novelist in the class containing Proust, Joyce, or Perec.[17] For the small cohort of dedicated *Tentation* scholars, Flaubert's own judgement of his work as the 'œuvre de toute ma vie' has largely been the redeeming feature. However, instead of seeking to demystify Flaubert's gnomic remark and the text by opening it up to a wider public, these critics have paradoxically made of the *Tentation* an exclusive domain for specialist source or genetic studies. By glaring contrast with Flaubert's other works, there are therefore no short guides, general introductions, or student commentaries on the *Tentation* in either French or English.

This book proposes to change such critical resilience by arguing the case that Flaubert had good reason not to change his belief in the importance of writing the *Tentation*, and with its general public readership in view. If the potted account above of its critical genesis—in its several versions and set against the backdrop of Flaubert's life—will be familiar to the specialist, the story of its critics' blocks even thus far offers a different optic on the text in its biographical and critical contexts for expert and newcomer alike. A way of looking afresh at the accepted story crystallizes the main object of this study, to prize/prise the *Tentation*, along with the best works of its critical reception, out of fixed modes of approaching its reading. In the first sense of the word, 'prize', 'to esteem', this study ultimately proposes a first book-length monograph in English on the 1874 *Tentation* in the text's wider contexts,[18] because Flaubert's forgotten work merits much greater exposure for itself, and for its creative account of a plethora of 'heretical' ideas—religious, scientific, aesthetic—in the air of nineteenth-century France. These remits are an initial response to the basic question why the text was so important to Flaubert. The second sense of the verb 'prize', 'to extricate' or 'to dislodge', presents the larger *critical* challenge for any new study of the *Tentation*. Flaubert's work has consistently been lambasted for its crushing and prohibitive weight of erudition, and its most worthy French advocates, Seznec, Gothot-Mersch, and Séginger, leave a further wealth of erudite scholarship about Flaubert's erudition, which ultimately blocks the text itself from view, especially for interested newcomers.[19] In what follows in this book, the epigraph from Ecclesiastes encapsulates the check and balance to the paradox of reading the *Tentation* for all its erudition, and on two counts. The first, following Flaubert's own problems in finding the overall 'plan' and running threads in his vast reading that would pull it together,[20] pertains to finding meaningful ways of talking about how the *Tentation* treats the imponderable questions that humankind has faced from time immemorial. The second is the problem of finding a working method that captivates new and specialist reader alike. What specialists seem to forget is that Flaubert's *Tentation* is the aesthetic expression of his vast erudition. To allow the text's critical story to stand out in this book, the vast library of secondary critical work which informs the *Tentation* has been relegated to the place of its necessary reference matter (endnotes, bibliography) to aid further study. At the same time, chapters below will not fail to highlight important critical approaches and insights into specific episodes or the *Tentation* as a whole, but will regard these as (starting) blocks rather than as final authorities. New and specialist readers will in consequence engage with the *Tentation* from a different perspective, to rediscover forgotten contributions confined to very specialist corners of the Flaubert archive, challenge received ideas, and make connections in what has hitherto been unconnected. If the problems of Flaubert's age are at stake in his *Tentation*, some of the conclusions of this study will necessarily return to core debates around what the *Tentation* is about and why Flaubert revised but did not change its form. Was it indeed the 'œuvre de toute [s]a vie'? Can Flaubert's canonical place in nineteenth-century French literature, especially his craft as among France's most important realist novelists, be justified in the light of this fantastical text?

The interest of this study is therefore not in finding some new approach to Flaubert or his *Tentation* that will explain the text through further layers of glittering erudition or critical theory.[21] Rather, it is the powerfully unassuming ending of the text that provides a harder model for open critical work that may be closer to Flaubert's own. Antoine 'simply' returns at dawn to his daily work of prayer, to the reality of the human condition and its expression, summed up in the well-known words from Ecclesiastes: 'there is nothing new under the sun.' As a lesson in attention to common experience, the *Tentation* is not a virtuoso text about nothing, but an invitation to look at the real writ large but passed unnoticed, and explored through concerted deployment of different angles of vision. Ever the attacker of cliché and received ideas, it is Flaubert's disorientation of the acceptable and familiar that will be at stake. This is a text which, like his *Salammbô*, appears utterly alien and alienating, but which may in fact say something telling about the too familiar. To these ends, this book will relate seven alternative stories about the seven tableaux which comprise it as part of the bigger history that encompasses them. First, the major critical positions and (starting) blocks that serve this book must be addressed so that the parameters for attentive (re)reading can be set out.

MODERN CRITICAL LEGACIES

If modern scholarly debates and specialist attempts to explain 'the fantastic library' of Flaubert's *Tentation* have benefited from various movements generated within literary critical studies more broadly,[22] all conform to a pattern of sub-disciplinary emphases within wider literary-critical frames. Author-centred literary analyses based on Flaubert's correspondence were superseded by psychoanalytic criticism; source study was recast by postmodern concern to challenge authorial intentions, and genetic criticism made the rich *avant-texte* of Flaubert's manuscripts and *brouillons* of all versions of the *Tentation* its own within New Critical modes of close reading. These twentieth-century approaches to the 1874 *Tentation*, however, differ very little from the initial reactions of Du Camp and Bouilhet to the reading of the first. Most frequently, the *Tentation* has been read as if through the eyes of Du Camp, as a psychological work. Sartre, following Freud, famously saw the *Tentation* as describing Flaubert's Œdipal complexes and the drives governing the whole of his *œuvre*, an approach building on Reik (and by one remove Allenspach), but inflected variously since by Bem, Dünne, Gendolla, Gothot-Mersch, and Porter.[23] Conversely, and following Bouilhet's expectation of some historical reconstruction of St Anthony of Egypt's life and times, Bowman has been a leading figure in his critical appraisals of the comparative religious debates represented by Flaubert's saint as concurrent in nineteenth-century France.[24] This line of enquiry builds on Seznec's still pivotal and unchallenged work on the 'heresies' in tableau four of the *Tentation*, but which Neefs and Séginger have further inflected to favour a syncretistic, pantheistic, but definitely anti-religious Flaubert.[25] Very belatedly, Orr and Pasco have read Flaubert's knowledge of church history as certainly anti-clerical, but also unusually 'un-Catholic' in his stance on the Trinity or Eastern Orthodoxy.[26] And the fear shared conjointly by Du Camp and Bouilhet about the literary originality and form of the *Tentation* as a derivative version of Quinet's *Ahasvérus* constitutes a third major critical reaction to the text.[27] Source hunting and Flaubert's exegesis of his vast and erudite reading perturbed and challenged pre-1970s critics in the main.[28] Post-1970s criticism worried much more about the relativism of the bricolage of intertexts that constitute the *Tentation*, whether the indigestible reference libraries which add up to a confusion of authorities, the niceties of genetic cross-fertilization, or the larger generic problems that the final version of the text presents as some syncretistic patchwork.[29] Is it a drama of undecidable fictional representation, a fantasy, or a hallucination?[30] Does the *Tentation* play with a combination of physiological and psychic symptoms in equal measure and in ways which attest to a medical realism?[31] As Du Camp and Bouilhet found initially, the main problem for critics following one particular critical line of enquiry, let alone any combination of the three, is that the text refuses to sit neatly within disciplinary or sub-disciplinary frames of critical investigation just as it defies classification within periods of Flaubert's *œuvre*. Where critics resort to the *œuvres de jeunesse*, particularly *Smarh*, to discuss the subtitle Flaubert gave to the first version of the text—'un vieux mystère'—the form of the third version exceeds this sub-genre not least by omitting reference to any such categorization or demarcation of form in a subtitle. Elision of the *Tentation* with Flaubert's fixation with ambiguous saints in the *Trois contes* fails to explain the marked differences in scope between these late works.

It is perhaps those tacit expectations about the scope of the *Tentation* as within 'acceptable' bounds that have been the critical stumbling block that Bouilhet and Du Camp first personified. To judge the text as they did on assumptions about its depth (psychology), accuracy (history), or form (a recognizable literary or generic tradition), discloses their *un-self-critical* expectations derived from their intimacy with Flaubert as friend and contemporary above budding writer who was, as Bouilhet's ultimate verdict implies, too heretical for (their) comfort. In spite of the seeming advantages of greater distance, modern critics' blocks are similarly erected, although they pass as more 'impersonal' by means of 'critical' or 'textual' theories such as deconstruction.[32] The underlying methodology of recent critical assumptions about the *Tentation* has thus erred in the opposite direction to assuming too much intimacy or appealing to the mind/life of the author: to avoid the intentional fallacy, Flaubert's impersonality and the undecidability of his works are rigorously upheld.[33]

Such censorship of 'appropriate' critical method bespeaks the kind of ideological climate that only a text such as the *Tentation* swimming so overtly against prevailing mainstreams can directly confront. Current work in nineteenth-century French literary and cultural studies inclines largely to understanding the period as post-Enlightenment, secular, troubled, or inspired according to its political pendulum swings by the implications of positivism, socialism, and Darwinism (in its French, Lamarckian, form as 'transformisme').[34] Through Foucauldian, New Historical, or gender studies lenses, focus has therefore concentrated with no small effect on literary-cultural investigations of power and social inequalities, whether class, gender, or more recently race, but not on contentions of *religious* creed. By its very subject, the *Tentation* is an unavoidably religious and theological text at levels which cannot be ignored, or ultimately silenced, by the new codices of post-1970s, liberal post-humanist criticism. If high theory has circumscribed religious topics or enquiry as *ex cathedra* by its own doctrinal lights, biographical study has been deemed equally irrelevant, a relic of critical regions deemed *extra muros* because the author (like God previously) is dead.[35] Sectarianism of whatever form, religious or secular, is one of the pivotal issues that Flaubert's *Tentation* confronts and holds up to its own censure, not least in tableau four. The larger story of the text will demonstrate that heresies may not simply be a matter of recherché, fourth-century, theological debates.

A further kind of modern critical block deserves brief mention since it informs the different optic of this study. In the story familiar to Flaubert critics and nineteenth-century specialists recounted above, I made deliberate choices by foregrounding certain facts, while *not* mentioning those previously considered primary to understanding the genesis of the *Tentation*. Four omissions are particularly salient. The initial writing and eventual publication of the text are framed by the death of Flaubert's father (1846) and mother (1872) respectively. An essential continuity is the *Tentation*'s dedication to Flaubert's first 'accoucheur' before Bouilhet, Alfred Le Poittevin. His premature death—Flaubert was one of his pall bearers—occurred shortly before the fateful reading of the 1849 text. A third is the impact that Brueghel's painting of *The Temptation of St Anthony* had on Flaubert when he saw it in Genoa in 1845 as the 'source' for his first version of the subject.[36] Critical readings of the seven tableaux of Flaubert's final *Tentation* version have largely been more satisfactory when understood as visual art rather than as literary representation.[37] Finally, critics too frequently equate the ascetic saint with the reclusive author by naming Flaubert the 'hermit of Croisset'. To prize the *Tentation* out of very entrenched modes of appreciation, not least because they may have some pertinence, means rereading such facts or gaps in its critical legacies by first asking some seemingly very basic questions. Why was Flaubert the inveterate cynic, unbeliever, or ambivalent Catholic drawn to the story of St Anthony of Egypt in the first place,[38] let alone able to find in the subject such an attraction and inspiration that he refused to consign the first version to the flames, and rework it at crucial moments of his literary output? Does the 1874 *Tentation* then map Flaubert's life work (l'*œuvre* de toute sa vie') rather than merely its own genesis, since these moments coincide with public disapproval of his most historical works about nineteenth-century France, *Madame Bovary* (1856–7) and *L'Éducation sentimentale* (1869–70)? Why did Flaubert retain the 'mystère' genre for the 1874 *Tentation* when he had so successfully developed the realist novel for the ends of cultural and aesthetic critique (via his famous 'style indirect libre', impersonal authorial viewpoints, and art of the 'petit détail qui fait vrai')? And when he was so allergic to conclusions why, finally, did Flaubert feel impelled to complete and publish the *Tentation* project when the Devil in tableau six tells Antoine specifically that 'Il n'y a pas de but' (*Tent*, 210)?

REMAPPING LITERARY-CRITICAL AND GENERIC DIALOGUES

Flaubert's resistance to definitive statements or conclusions has been richly endorsed by postmodernist 'uncertainty', but this does not mean that such an approach is the final word about the *Tentation*, or that no answers can be found to the strategic questions just posed. Genetic criticism may contribute much to understanding some of the recon-structions of the final text, but it cannot answer speculative questions about the origination of its first ideas, or give reasons for radical change in the later drafts concerning the overall plan or characterization of Antoine as central protagonist. Critical focus on the impersonal and factual—the mass of evidence left by Flaubert's manuscripts, library, or correspondence—leaves a hugely descriptive, analytic and deductive, rather than synthetic and inductive, legacy. With an eye to redressing such critical imbalance, this book takes up the challenge of working by lateral thinking through the same evidence, but always regarding this as second to, and a check for, modes of reading inductively and synthetically that are suggested internally by the text itself. One of the *Tentation*'s main motors is indisputable, and so blindingly obvious that it has not been highlighted. Regardless of its particular form or expression ('*the*' temptation of the title), the very nature of temptation is intimately dialogic.[39] Temptation requires a tempter and a tempted on the one hand (protagonists in opposite 'faith' or ideological camps which prove not to be so neatly polarized). On the other, both parties play symbiotically to predominant but balancing character traits in the other. By knowing his or her antagonist's dearly held beliefs or codes of conduct, the Tempter arouses the natural curiosity and desire to know outside these in the tempted; the innate curiosity of the tempted is what stimulates the Tempter to prove once more a vaunting arrogance or superiority (intellectual, sexual, spiritual) by winning over the tempted. In short, temptation is a very strong, Don Juanesque, and serial mode of seduction of rival equals in a relationship based on attraction and resistance. It is this relationship that Flaubert exploits by choosing not to pluralize the subject as *Les Tentations de saint Antoine*, although critics constantly impute such an idea of the whole even for the 1874 version.[40] More importantly still, Flaubert saw in the dynamic of temptation a structure to shape his text centripetally—the intense, one-to-one 'dialogue' tableaux (two, three, and six) are vital to the renewing of the polyphonic textual energy of tableaux four, five, and seven of the final *Tentation*—and centrifugally for its wider 'lesson', how it may speak analogously about imponderable or universal things (beginnings, causes, concepts such as 'civilization', supreme values or beings). It is at this second level that the further motor of dialogic relation operates, where the one stands for (a) the whole (*pars pro toto*); (b) similar realities on different planes (micro- and macrocosm), or (c) distinguishes itself (in form rather than structure) from its similar others (morphology).

By borrowing as model the *Tentation*'s inherent insistence upon the dialogic, this book will look specifically at these three kinds of 'dialogue' at work in the individual tableaux, and between the parts and their sum, in chapters following the order of the text itself. By eschewing methods that have looked overly into but not out from the text,[41] this move brings us closer to elucidating what the overall 'plan' might be that Flaubert sought for the final version, and hence to offering an elaboration of its sum. However to arrive at this, a falsely dichotomized dialogue is set up between the two major orders of things in the two parts of this book, to reveal in larger structural form the internal motor of similarity/difference in protagonists just discussed. These two orders are Religion and Science, mapping back directly onto their mouth-pieces, Antoine and Hilarion/the Devil.[42] The distinction between Antoine's two main interlocutors will be unpacked in Chapters 3, 5, and 6 and the paradoxical similarities between Religion and Science will be scrutinized in Chapters 4, 5, and 7. Critical gaps (in the text, or secondary literature), or facts that remain unchallenged, can thus be reviewed by this book when comparative analogy (connection of the previously unconnected) and inductive reasoning (informed hypothesis) are assiduously applied to reading the *Tentation*. This method can then show further dialogic operations at work in the final version of the text (of interest to specialists), and open up new critical dialogue about it (of interest to new readers). As a test case for the critical leverage of this method, let us take the received wisdom about the nature of the text's genesis and beginnings central to source and genetic criticism: Flaubert's encounter with the Brueghel in Genoa was the 'visionary moment' inspiring his *Tentation*. But what if this encounter was a flash of *recognition* crystallizing Flaubert's much earlier predisposition to the subject of St Anthony?[43] How might an inductive, comparative approach adjudicate between 'fact' and our new hypothesis that neither genetic nor source criticism can resolve?

The major evidence is in black and white. In spite of the death of his lifelong friend and critic-'accoucheur' Bouilhet in 1869 while the final version of the *Tentation* was being rewritten, Flaubert dedicated the published 1874 *Tentation*, like the first, to Alfred Le Poittevin. Surprisingly, Alfred's initial and unshakeable connection with the *Tentation* has evinced only passing critical attention with regard to its significance for the final 1874 text.[44] Desporte's recent article on the circulation of memory by means of dedications between Flaubert and his significant others takes dedication to a subject a little further:

Gustave lui doit Rousseau, Lamartine, Vigny, tout un fonds de littérature romantique qui anime les écrits de jeunesse à la fin des années 1830; Gustave lui doit les moralistes et Montaigne; Gustave lui doit enfin Goethe, Byron, Quinet, Spinoza, Satan, la métaphysique et le goût du mysticisme, tout ce qui entre dans la composition de la *Tentation de saint Antoine*, tentative d'expression du tempérament de Flaubert, libération de son 'moi tout entier' et du fantôme d'Alfred.[45]

Insofar as Alfred is Flaubert's personal 'bibliothèque fantastique', or dialogic other in terms of this book, how does his essential psycho-critical influence translate into Flaubert's Antoine or the *Tentation* except in superficial terms? Investigation of Flaubert's early *Correspondance* during the initial writing of his first *Tentation* only adds other works the two were reading and discussing to this list, including various books of the Bible (particularly the Old Testament) and Chateaubriand's *L'Itinéraire*.[46] We will come back to Flaubert's extensive knowledge of the Bible in his uses of it throughout the *Temptation* in ensuing chapters. With regard to the fundamental question, why St Anthony?, more interesting are the subjects that Le Poittevin was treating in his own poetry, and the ways in which he was reworking quintessentially Romantic forms, particularly in his *Une promenade de Bélial*.[47] As more than models that the first *Tentation* might imitate, and by which his own creative voice might be found by contrast, Flaubert's text is his homage to Alfred's—hence the 1849 and 1874 dedications—but also Flaubert's literary response to their unfinished aesthetic dialogue caused by Alfred's early death.

In terms of chronology and shared history as further evidence, Flaubert's own early works were being published at the same time and in some of the same local journals as Le Poittevin's 'Satan', 'Ahasvérus', and 'L'Orient'.[48] Other undated poems by Le Poittevin treat subjects that will return in the *Tentation* (in its several versions)—'Heure d'angoisse', 'La Foi', 'Le Jeune Homme et la Bayadère', 'Les Lotophages'[49]—and are richly suggestive of the bigger themes which are preoccupying Le Poittevin and Flaubert (which they are discussing, not corresponding about), such as the relative place of Greek classical culture alongside the gods of other ancient civilizations, and whether there is a link or progression from one civilization to another.[50] With the benefit of hindsight, one of Alfred's poems, 'Le Stylite', distils in three main parts—'Les Pèlerins' (three stanzas), 'Le Saint' (five stanzas), 'Le Poète' (four stanzas)—the subjects which elicit the (first) *Tentation*'s dialogic response (*sponsum*). The penultimate stanza of the second part contains in line three an all-important reference:

> Si je descends, soudain m'assiège
> Confus et bruyant, le cortège
> Qui troublait Antoine aux déserts,
> La tentation déchaînée,
> Et Proserpine couronnée
> Avec les pompes des enfers.
>
>   (*LP*, 112–14)[51]

In this poem, the poet remains aloof, to keep his soul untrammelled by the 'real' world, but this position is more than the clichéd poet-elect of Romantic poetry. There is a 'high ascetic' and Neoplatonic metaphysics in evidence in the final stanza of this second section which flies in the face of the worldly and debauched Le Poittevin that critics paint of excess, hashish, alcohol, cynicism, even Satanism.[52]

> Laissez-moi donc sur ma colonne,
> Mes frères! Dieu lui-même ordonne
> De fuir quand on craint le danger.
> Des hauts lieux où nul bruit n'arrive
> Notre âme, dans le corps captive,
> Apprend mieux à s'en dégager.
>
>   (*LP*, 112–14)

We will be returning to these issues in Chapter 4 as richly indicative of some of the major decisions that Flaubert took in his final revisions of the *Tentation* of the so-called 'heresies'. The poem's tripartite and episodic or pseudo-epic journey, although quintessentially situated within staple Romantic modes for poetic expression, is developed further in Le Poittevin's *Une promenade de Bélial* as an artful metaphysical speculation. While *Ahasvérus* and *Faust* are two examples of this form which were very familiar to Le Poittevin (and of course Flaubert), more important for his conceptualization of *Bélial* was his attentive reading of Byron, especially *Don Juan* (1819) and *Cain: A Mystery* (1822).[53]

   Une promenade de Bélial is a 'mystery' in the tradition of Cazotte's *Le Diable amoureux* (1776), but what is peculiar to it is that although Le Poittevin directly links his Devil as Bélial to Milton's god of impure love, his central antagonist is a *mondain* and polished Don Juan, a libertine of the mind rather than an overtly supernatural figure. Bélial transports his two playthings, le duc and la duchesse Préval, in a 'carriage-time machine' so that they can review the past loves of contemporaries later seen at a Ball, and learn of the soul's 'pact', its transmigrations by three *hypostases*. Matter dominates Soul through instinct and carnal desires as the first *hypostasis*, but the Soul increasingly eschews this dominion in a second by denying things of the flesh. Conciliation of both principles is the final and highest, but the overall order is determined within all life. Bélial's is a 'hyper-rational' and Stoic mysticism, indebted to Plotinus, Spinoza, Swedenborg, and finely attuned to the two human protagonists; M. Préval is an Eclectic, Madame is a professing Catholic. The overriding 'temptation' appealing to both parties in the six unequal parts of the work is to find answers to simple questions set out in the mystère's playfully suggestive opening lines situated in Madame's boudoir: 'Je ne chercherai point à quoi qi'ils s'occupent... ni à quel propos ils parlèrent de la vie, se demandant d'où elle venait, ce qu'elle était et pourquoi on la recevait' (*LP*, 3). The response is Bélial's cynical commentary, constantly playing off the grounds of his victims' seemingly oppositional belief structures. Also illustrating the chilling economy and non-supernatural in *Bélial* is an example in the fourth part, where the Duvals are transported to the land of the dead:

Le règne effréné de la Matière amène la réaction de l'Esprit. ... C'est au sortir de l'athéisme que la France rouvrit les églises, et c'est après les festins de Vérus et les orgies d'Héliogabale que Jérôme fuyait dans le désert, *et que retentissait la Thébaïde des flagellations des solitaires.* ... Laissez faire les agents de change, les prostituées et les écrivains! Ils hâtent la fin du vieux monde, et préparent sans s'en douter l'aurore du nouveau. *La vie naît dans la pourriture: un jour de ces peuples pervertis sortiront des apôtres aussi héroïques que saint Paul et que saint Antoine.* (*LP*, 27–8, emphasis added)

Le Poittevin's creative impact on Flaubert's (final) *Tentation* can hardly be better promoted. But these lines further prepare scene five, which takes the Duvals to a Ball (in time actual to theirs), a comic interlude where they witness a geologist used to making speculations about nature, but now speculating (with much less surety) about a much more personal and real issue, whether his wife is being seduced by her dancing partner. From the Ball, the Duvals are taken to the Père Lachaise cemetery, where Bélial chastises them for their curiosity to see 'life'; yet once transported to the cold regions of the stratosphere from which they glimpse the speck of the earth, terror causes them to wish to return to their mortal coil. Flaubert's Antoine has a remarkably similar

experience and response in tableau six of the *Tentation*. When Bélial
leaves the couple with death 'en abîme' and departs himself, the mystery
ends (seemingly) where it started, but with the horror of life determined
outside grace now manifest. If the infamous ending of the final *Tentation*
asks in different key 'what is life and where does it come from?' to work
this same non-return to the beginning of the text, it also operates a non-
return to its own first version.

Flaubert's earliest dialogues with Le Poittevin about St Anthony
as a suitable subject for aesthetic, metaphysical, and theogical/anti-
theological speculations are, if not proved, at least convincingly
recuperated.[54] Moreover, this is no popular Antoine of medieval hagiography, complete with pig, Tau, and bells, but one fit for purpose for the
final *Tentation*. Flaubert's 'recognition scene' in Genoa standing before
Brueghel's *Temptation of St Anthony* comes after Le Poittevin wrote his
'Le Stylite' and on the heels of the completed *Bélial*. The genre and
ending of *Bélial*, however, also inform those of Flaubert's *Temptation*
(in its first and also final versions) and make the 1874 text a further,
late Romantic, example. We will discover the paradoxical realism of
Flaubert's 'mystère' in the sixth chapter.

Le Poittevin's uncompromising 'return' to beginnings (with the
naivety of unknowing destroyed) reworks similar subjects and motors
of plot from French 'Romantic' intertexts such as Goethe's *Faust*, but
in more sacrilegious vein. More important in terms of its anti- or
comparative-religious characters, plot, and décor is Byron's *Cain: A
Mystery*.[55] The first of its three acts takes place in 'the land without
Paradise' at 'sunrise' when Cain seeks to know the mystery of his being,
whereupon Lucifer only too happily obliges as the killing of Abel is
replayed, an action which unleashes the second act. In its first scene,
the 'Abyss of Space', and in scene ii, 'Hades', Cain is taken on a journey
to see the stages of creation prior to Eden or its Fall. Scene iii returns
Cain to 'The Earth near Eden as Act 1', but the act of murder has
changed the post-Edenic life of Adam, Eve, Adah, and Zillah, as also
for Cain, into a place 'without Paradise'. From the same inspiration
is Quinet's *Ahasvérus*, the text immediately located by Flaubert's first
critics as the richer intertext. Like *Bélial* or *Cain*, it leaves the reader
with the chill of the emptiness of 'pure' Eternity. After having taken the
reader through the four days of 'The Creation', 'The Passion', 'Death',
and 'The Last Judgement' respectively even Nothingness has no further

place. Its central protagonist, Ahasvérus, appears in the second, refuses to carry Jesus' cross because he does not accept that he is the Messiah, and is condemned to homeless wandering in the known worlds and underworlds of the civilizations of Christendom until Judgement Day. Like Goethe's Mephistopheles, Quinet's Ahasvérus is the spirit which continually denies Christ. Even when he is 'saved' by Rachel's love and faces Christ as his Judge, he uses this occasion to win his place as 'l'homme éternel', thus permitting a further journey as pilgrim of worlds to come, as the new second Adam.[56] Quinet also makes clear in the *finis* that his *Ahasvérus* is a 'mystère', a genre summed up by Byron's preface to his *Cain: A Mystery*

in accordance to the ancient title annexed to dramas upon similar subjects, which were styled 'Mysteries or Moralities'. The author has by no means taken the same liberties with his subject which were common formerly, as may be seen by any reader curious enough to refer to those very profane productions, whether in England, France, Italy or Spain.[57]

Byron's reference is to the extensive medieval tradition of the mystery which *Cain*, *Bélial*, *Ahasvérus*, 'modernize' only by locating the 'Passion' or the overcoming of evil in more overtly non-Christian settings, and by reducing the popular, fantastical aspects of Satan's 'diableries' or his attributes (cloven hoofs, horns). Satan the main protagonist-antagonist is therefore central to the mystery genre, and, far more importantly for Byron, places the profane (and pagan) undertow of 'Christianity' central stage. Flaubert's reworking of the subject of the *temptations* of St Anthony (the seven deadly sins) makes his text literally in the first version more faithfully a 'medieval' mystery (in Byron's sense), even if its final reworking of 1874 (where Flaubert's Satan is refracted as a kind of unholy trinity with Hilarion and Science) more overtly situates it alongside Byron's or Le Poittevin's 'modern' mysteries. We will be returning to Byron's *Cain* in a different context in Chapter 6 of this study. The relevance of a historical, critical, and personal St Anthony as dialogic subject of Flaubert's *Temptation* (for all three versions) has thus found more amplified justification. It is not Alfred, but his works and preoccupations, which inform the history of Flaubert's text, yet also distinguish it. Where Le Poittevin opted for anti-theological figures to puncture theology, Flaubert chooses instead indubitably theological figures to puncture the anti-theological. Let us now set out why, and

how this book will undertake to prove its case through its Religion/
Science frame.

REMAPPING FORMS AND KNOWLEDGE

Given the rich critical heritage that has come from Michel Foucault's
Les Mots et les choses: une archéologie des sciences humaines or his
L'Archéologie du savoir among others,[58] Foucault's interest in Flaubert's
Tentation as a 'bibliothèque fantastique' has had a fascinatingly counter-
productive result by leaving an overly Borgesian nightmare of erudition
for new readers, and more interestingly specialists, of the *Tentation* to
negotiate. If the *Tentation* significantly is the one work in the *œuvre* for
which we have extensive records of Flaubert's reading,[59] it is striking
how tiny a subsection of it even his most assiduous critics, including
Foucault, have demonstrably read. By and large the more 'arcane' and
'theological' works on Flaubert's list have been the most resoundingly
ignored. In this remapping of the *Tentation*, a larger number of works
from Flaubert's own reading, and the 'theology' in particular, will be
included and investigated, so that some of the modern secondary critical
freight that has stifled creative enjoyment of the text can be challenged
by nineteenth-century bibliographical evidence. But as will also emerge
in various chapters of this study, this reading list proves only indicative,
since it pertained to the second version of the text.[60] If these facts richly
explain the existence of critical blocks to the *Tentation*, they occlude
Flaubert's resilient, *creative*, response to his extensive and eclectic reading, magnified by the time he arrived at his final version. He was surely
hypersensitive to the dangers and 'temptation' of erudition culled from
others' authority and encyclopedism when 'copied' into creative writing,
as his unfinished novel *Bouvard et Pécuchet* (with its *Dictionnaire des
idées reçues*) amply attests in black-comic form. The *Tentation*'s critics
post 1970 have too frequently followed the two 'cloportes' by recopy-
ing, albeit within their own critical frames, the scholarly, encyclopedic
classical knowledge of Seznec, for example.[61] It is not this tactic that this
book replicates, nor even that of a Northrop Frye, choosing the rather
different metaphor for a synthetic criticism of parts and wholes in his
Anatomy of Criticism.[62] Rather it seeks to imitate critically Flaubert's
own solution to wearisome bookishness for the *Tentation*.[63] To guard

what is therefore intriguing about the plethora of knowledge on parade in the text, Flaubert resorts to two main 'realist' tactics. The first essentially minimizes the weight of erudition by limiting it to authenticating details, and then recomposing these via strategic mouthpieces. Delimiting the *dramatis personae* in number and extent of what they say, and editing the over-flowery style (Flaubert did take seriously some of Du Camp's and Bouilhet's candid criticism), then went hand in hand in Flaubert's revisions for the second and third versions, where further extensive research on all manner of scholarly topics and subjects further honed chosen characters' lines. The second tactic concerns having a singular viewpoint on this knowledge, the *unlettered* Antoine, whose naive curiosity determines the pathways into other branching forms of knowledge (abetted by his tempters), but whose responses are almost equally important before its (encyclopedic) hallucinatory effects. 'Quelle invention!' (*Tent*, 163) is an example.[64] Antoine's lack of final authority, dogmatism, or doctrinal prejudice makes him paradoxically more fit for purpose than his intransigent others. A saint only with the hindsight of church and literary history, Flaubert's more modest Antoine does not then come up with final answers on faith or beliefs, but a resolution to the temptation of knowledge articulated in the combined force of the Sphinx and the Chimera (key protagonists in all three versions). That a solution is to be had to the ultimate riddle of life is indeed a figment of the mad imagination, yet to be able to frame the riddle in the first place is part of the material, finite, grounded human condition and hence driver of the religious and scientific spirit.

So what is the larger purpose for which the arcane life and temptations of St Anthony the Great were deemed by Flaubert to be fit? Bouilhet's expectation that Flaubert would be strongly attracted to the strange melting pot of the saint's historical times intimates part of an answer (which fewest critics have taken up). When this is inflected by the saint's aesthetic import (elaborated above in Flaubert's dialogue with Alfred on the same subject), Flaubert was surely attracted to the big unanswered questions faced by St Anthony the Great of Egypt (250–356), because they were quintessentially the same big unanswered questions of nineteenth-century France. Flaubert's fictional Antoine and the *Tentation* should thus be read less as an intertextual (and genetic) reworking of other artistic representations of St Anthony, and more as a *critical* prism on key debates within the nineteenth-century French history of ideas of which, as a text also undertaken at cusp moments in French history (1848–9, 1869–70), it is fully part. In short, the main premiss of this book is that Flaubert's *Tentation* is an imaginative and 'fantastic' history of nineteenth-century France following Anne Green's pioneering work on *Salammbô* in similar vein.[65] The final *Tentation* is therefore its pendant: the *œuvre* 'de toute [sa] vie' is a *vita* of the emergence of modern Republican France. The distinguishing factor, however, is that this book will argue not for the *Tentation* as political allegory, but as enlightening bigger critical stories about French nineteenth-century history of beliefs in several disciplines—comparative religion, natural history, and science—through their literary remapping. As variation within the bigger whole (or species within a class) of Flaubert's *œuvre*, or its representative text (an order in zoological classification), depending on one's view of the relation of part to whole, the *Tentation* can then be justified critically as a way to introduce new, as well as specialist, readers to the wider intellectual melting pot of nineteenth-century France, but understood through a single paradigm and *creative* text rather than through literary-critical histories.[66]

To posit the *Tentation* as a literary critique and commentary on key debates of its own historical times then only further complicates previous critical impasses regarding the classification of its form, whether as theatre, fiction, or fantasy, let alone as a 'history'. Almost without exception, the *Tentation* has been assigned to the literature of the fantastic,[67] a 'mystère' following Goethe's *Faust* or Quinet's *Ahasvérus*.[68] However, when understood in the light of its main intertext, Athanasius' *Vita Antonii* and its medieval hagiographical heritage such as Voragine's *Légende dorée*, the *Tentation*'s 'historical' substructures suddenly appear. The *Vita Antonii* was not only the founding model of the inspirational genre of saints' lives (the hagiography), but also the *vita* as theological exemplum (a saint's trials, experience, or position in overcoming the 'world' illustrated points of doctrine and proper religious conduct), and hence *apologetics*.[69] Of even more vital ideological and theological valence, Athanasius proposed the *Vita Antonii* specifically as a *summa theologiae* regarding the authoritative position of the Christian Church of Alexandria in the teeth of counter truth claims by setting out and instituting what would become the founding statement of faith for Western Christendom, the Nicene Creed. The need for such a final decree on belief was driven by the powerful promotion of many rival and *similar* doctrines at the time, concerning the person and nature of Jesus in the Trinity (God the Father, God the Son, God the Holy Spirit). It was St Anthony the Great who played a strategic role in the stand against Arius and other heresiarchs vying for supreme authority in matters of (Christian) faith. Flaubert's *Temptation* directly follows various French digests of Athanasius' *Vita* for its own purposes, as the first chapter will show. Not least, it rewrites hagiography as commentary or modern summa of powerful beliefs and dogmas circulating inside and outside the institutions of nineteenth-century France, whether the French Catholic Church, the 'secular' academies, or the structures of economic and political power. Necessary distance on them can only be attained by the seemingly irrelevant, and often irreverent, vision of Flaubert's Antoine as modest successor to his great precursor. The *Vita Antonii* and medieval hagiography thus directly enable Flaubert in his *Tentation* to play several time frames off one another analogically, namely the early Church in fourth-century Egypt, medieval Christendom, and nineteenth-century France. If further evidence were needed for such a structure of parallel and inter-reflecting epochs, Flaubert will exploit and replicate these same time frames and the *vita* as fictional form in triplicate in his *Trois Contes*.

In providing some answers to why the 'life of Antoine' genre is fit for Flaubert's purpose as eyepiece on his (nineteenth-century) times, the larger ends of this fantastic history become clearer. Certainly in aesthetic terms Flaubert's use of the *vita* and summa as history paradoxically liberates the solely theological constraints of these genres, and widens the question of representing exemplariness to non-theological domains such as comparison of cultures and societies. Flaubert also exploits the summa and *vita* for their creative strategies of showing and telling: symbol and allegory, analogy and transposition, exemplum and singular detail, the world in micro- and macrocosm, metaphor and literal usage of words become his fantastical history of nineteenth-century France and also remake the Romantic *Gesamtkunstwerk* (the 'anatomy', 'library', or 'encyclopedia' in different guise). Moreover, by borrowing the *vita*'s moral and doctrinal constraints for nineteenth-century ends (the so-called fourth tableau 'of the heresies' sits *en abyme* in the *Tentation*), Flaubert is then better able to weigh by comparison and contrast powerfully persuasive and conflicting tenets, beliefs, doctrines, and truth statements including the scientific, to make summary statements about them by implication on completion of the seventh tableau. Concentrating open judgement in his Antoine is an economical way of interleaving several world views where world and word (authority texts), orthodoxy and heterodoxy, and the negotiation of authorities concerning them may be weighed in the balances of history. Flaubert's Antoine then sits in judgement on the times of his great precursor, St Anthony of Egypt, whose life and times were themselves a reflection on the great civilization of *ancient* Egypt. How these Egyptian constants crucially pertain to France will be outlined in Part I. Suffice it to say that ancient Egypt may prove to be in advance of modern nineteenth-century France, in spite of its exploration of and progress in the fields of comparative religion, philology, comparative anatomy, natural and hard science, medicine, and of course Egyptology.

The stakes have now been raised for the *Tentation* to be prised from highly specialist critical domains and debates and reread as a fictional summa of its own epoch. The temptation is then very strong not only to return to the weighty erudition of Foucault's 'bibliothèque fantastique', but also to extend and deepen its Enlightenment heritage as an 'archaeology' of knowledge, and thus re-enter and copy literary-critical encyclopedism that the fictional Bouvard and Pécuchet show to be sublime folly. Antoine's response to such folly just outlined represents the more modest proposal of this book which is encapsulated by the term 'remapping' in its title. While geography is an essential part of the context for individual tableaux—the Egypt of St Anthony is the constant site throughout as ensuing chapters will attest—the detailed mapping of territories, surfaces, or fields of knowledge in the *Tentation* is not what readers should expect to be 'remapped' in this book. If France's nineteenth-century explorations and colonization of the globe richly permitted an empirical and deductive filling in of gaps in knowledge in natural science, for example, or reclassification of bounds of knowledge because new information became available (as in comparative religion or early ethnography), this only produced an explosion of definitions, catalogues, and collections. The parades of knowledge in the tableaux of the *Tentation*, like specialist criticism hitherto on these, amply demonstrate the point.

To get behind and under these, by contrast, the remapping proposed here is more neatly spatio-temporal, inductive, and synthetic and builds on no less pertinent a nineteenth-century model of exploration of surfaces for intensely *practical* ends. Empirical observation of territories and things in them was only part of making sense of (and exploiting) the visible world under one's feet. Unlike the rather more dilettante or scholarly archaeological dig, excavations for the serious business of the Industrial Revolution—coal mines, canals, railways—allowed one William Smith to 'see' the hitherto hidden patterns of rock formations and their stratification, and thence use this knowledge to predict where further coal or other resources might occur in another part of the country with a seemingly different *surface* geology within the same necessary sandwich of strata. Viewed in cross-section, what appeared as isolated outcrops in different locations became ends of the same underground folds or exposed intrusions. Of perhaps even greater significance than this three-dimensional, inductive, kind of mapping of *similarity* within seeming difference was the discovery made by Smith (as also by Cuvier and Brogniart in the limestone quarries in the Paris basin in 1809–10[70]) that each stratum dated in geological time also explained the age of certain kinds of fossils found there but not in younger or older rocks. This supremely analogous, lateral, system of thinking requires huge attention to the observable details, but these remain details until they are put back into their beds of greater interconnecting significance. To uncover this significance requires a satisfactory hypothesis overarching and threading together the known secondary-order levels of classification or modes of interpretation. It is William Smith's geological map, a paradigm shift which 'changed the world' in its own time,[71] which is then the figurative model for the 'remapping' envisaged throughout this book. As literary-critical geology of nineteenth-century French knowledge, this book offers a blueprint for other critics to follow and refine by application to other *œuvres* because, like genetic, source, and comparative criticism, it appeals to empirical data that subsequent critics may check. In its very different method of interpretation, however, this book demonstrably and radically parts company from genetic criticism's genetico-'complexification' as explained so persuasively by Gothot-Mersch.[72] Remapping in its geological sense now provides that necessary inductive model of seeing and reading that justifies the contention of this study that the 'plan' underpinning Flaubert's final attempt at writing the *Temptation* can in fact be exposed, whereas source, genetic, and postmodern criticism blocks such explorations. Following Smith's geological remapping, the seven individual chapters on the seven tableaux taken sequentially also permit a view of their deeper cross-sectional structures. As a seven-layered stratification, the similarities within the seeming differences of surfaces can be uncovered by understanding the deeper metamorphic processing of religion and science. At the same time, the folding, fracturing, embedding, and resurfacing of deeper pasts and recurrent patterns with surprisingly similar cultural values to those of the surface present can also be explained, to align several times and spaces in ways which Green's more directly analogical reading of Carthaginian and nineteenth-century French history in *Salammbô* cannot encompass. Flaubert may then map the life and times of St Anthony onto ancient Egyptian civilization on the one hand, and as double-layered model by which to compare nineteenth-century times on the other. Geological mapping also helps to discover right questions to ask of second orders of things (religion in Part I, science in Part II) in the synthesis of an enfolded, dialogic 'binary' to disclose its underlying belief systems and principles. The overall shape and two-part structure of this book discussed above then follows with even neater logic. Against the confusions and critical obfuscations of the text, the integral and ultimate fusions of 'third-century AD' religion and science in the *Tentation*—by geological analogy, sedimentary and igneous rock types can both be metamorphic—proves and illuminates the fascinating cultural melting pots of Flaubert's times. Consequently, the seemingly fantastical, *religious* colours of the *Tentation* allow the retelling of an intensely realistic, scientific world. Digging around in the depths of nineteenth-century French history of ideas, beliefs, and convictions in Flaubert's *Temptation* will hopefully prove in this remapping of his text to be not the dusty world of the antiquarian—indeed this term could have a very positive sense if uttered by a Cuvier—but a creative exploration of the strata which ultimately underpin and shape nineteenth-century French civilization and culture in its colourfully disrupted republics of letters.

PART I

THINKING RELIGION(S)

The Egypt and Alexandria of the life and times of St Anthony the Great (AD 250–356) appear worlds apart from Flaubert's France and Paris in the nineteenth century, just as the theological controversies of the early Christian Church in the fourth century seem irrelevant to a post-revolutionary, secular, nineteenth-century France. To explain why Flaubert might then have become fascinated by St Anthony, the Introduction proposed that it was thanks to the big, unanswered questions raised by third- and fourth-century Alexandria's melting pot of cultures, new ideas, and ideologies that epitomize very similar issues emergent in nineteenth-century France. As fictional St Anthony, Flaubert's Antoine thus becomes a mouthpiece on debates about Authority and authorities in modern France, not only religious but also philosophical and scientific. To understand the parallel plotting of these histories and questions throughout the *Tentation*, the context that holds them in tension first needs to be set out, not least because Flaubert so carefully situates his Antoine at the beginning of each tableau, as he does during longer parades by means of different locations. By aligning key elements in St Anthony's religious life and lifetime with similar events and debates in Flaubert's France, ensuing chapters can better elucidate their specific significance and make connecting links more visible. This first part (introducing Chapters 1 to 4) pertains to religious debates whereas the second part concentrates on contentions in science (to frame Chapters 5 to 7). As the Introduction made clear, this over-separation of the two spheres then permits paradoxical similarities to be discovered through the experiences of manifold 'temptations' besetting a single, unifying protagonist throughout. The superlative father of monasticism for Western and Eastern Christendom, the Coptic St Anthony the Great of Egypt, is reinvested in Flaubert's no less singular Antoine.

THE EGYPT OF ST ANTHONY

The Antoine of the 1849 *Tentation* complete with the accoutrements of pig, Tau, and bell of traditional iconography and confronting the seven deadly sins is assumed to be at one with the subject of the Brueghel painting Flaubert saw in Genoa. It is not medieval Christian France involved in the Crusades in the Middle East against the Muslim 'Infidel' that the 1874 *Tentation* reconfigures, however, but a reconstruction of early Christian Egypt. We saw in the introduction how Alfred Le Poittevin's Anthony was no figment of superstition or popular religion either, but a figure of ideas through his life of contemplation in the desert, isolated from the populace, the city, and material culture. The temptations that face the 1874 Antoine are therefore much truer to Alfred's inspiration, since they are principally of the 'religious' mind. However, this will be defined by a double contradistinction: to the Neoplatonic philosophical thinking and syncretism inherent in Le Poittevin's Romantic depiction (summed up in the stylized desert setting of 'le Stylite'[1]) and to unquestioning, naive belief of a signed-up adherent. Antoine's curiosity and metaphysical enquiries throughout the *Tentation* firmly separate him from any passive acceptance of credal positions and beliefs authorized by the established Church.

The stylized desert opening of Flaubert's *Tentation* is a no less effective setting for Antoine's position as insider-outsider, his mindscape and landscape. Evoking the timelessness of icons and manuscript illuminations, the desert's inner and outer spaces with its shimmering surfaces and deeper significance will inter-reflect throughout the *Tentation*.[2] At the same time, this symbolic landscape has various recognizable temporal layers. Through meticulous attention to topography and church history, Flaubert sets his 1874 Antoine squarely within the specific desert milieu of fourth-century Egypt.[3] A chronology of its key dates, protagonists, and events as remapped in the *Tentation* can be found in

Appendix 1.[4] This historically specific optic (mirroring the historical viewpoints of St Anthony the Great as authentically as possible) allows direct and indirect comparison and contrast with those of nineteenth-century France. For example, the Church is not the Holy Catholic See of Rome since it has yet to be established as the head of Western Christendom, but the Alexandrian Church of Egypt from the fourth to the beginning of the seventh century, *from the time of* Anthony forwards. The *Tentation* fully exploits this seemingly simple, but key point of church history for its ironies, and for distinctly critical ends, as Chapter 2 will explore. Major Christian churches had been established in Rome, Antioch, Jerusalem, and Constantinople (each with their bishop or patriarch), but were under the jurisdiction of Alexandria and its Bishop—in this case Athanasius—within a confraternity of equal authorities (rather than as a hierarchy of bishops and archbishops under a pope). In the fragile positioning of the fourth-century Egyptian Church to its others—within the Christian communion, in the face of alternative churches of Egypt led by heresiarchs (the subject of tableau four), vis-à-vis the State (the Roman Empire) with its persecutions or endorsements of the Alexandrian Church—the activities of opposition become more dangerous. If Flaubert encapsulates these theological, political, ideological, and philosophical counter-currents in the 'temptations' of his Antoine, he also exploits the already alternative position of St Anthony the Great regarding the Church of Alexandria. St Anthony eschewed both membership and leadership of it to remain outside institutions and established religion the whole of his lifetime, despite being born and dying a Coptic Christian. His commitment and spiritual leadership as anchorite and true believer of this Church were without question, however. It was on this wisdom, zeal, and inner knowledge that Athanasius called when the Church faced serious rival claims to its authority in matters of faith, conduct, leadership, and doctrine. Although there were several heresiarchs such as Valentinus and Montanus vying for supremacy, the most notable and dangerous was Arius. The Arian heresy named after him was the major reason why the Church held its first Council in AD 325 at Nicaea.[5] Anthony the Great was not present (because outside the Church), but Athanasius consulted him regarding right understanding of the full divinity and humanity of Jesus Christ within the Trinity. The Church's first doctrinal statement, the Nicene Creed, was the result. It was designed to counter heresy (similar beliefs held by alternative, rival, churches), and to end internal controversy (factions led by powerful Christian bishops). However, its 'final' position on the three persons and oneness of the Trinity, their substances and relations, was far from the last word on these matters, or on the overall authority of the Church and Bishop of Alexandria. After the life and times of St Anthony, which Athanasius recorded for further theological ends as the *Vita Antonii* (as mentioned briefly in the Introduction), further councils were called to resolve theological matters again related to the divinity/humanity of Christ and the substances and relations of the persons in the Trinity. Two such issues and their councils have retrospective-prospective significance for the topics treated in the *Tentation*. The first was the claim of the deposed patriarch of Constantinople, Nestorius (b. c. AD 381–6, d. 451 in the Thebaid in Egypt where Flaubert specifically situates his Antoine), that 'distinct divine and human persons are to be attributed to Christ' (*OED*). The theological implications and ramifications of this heresy concerned not only the substance and place of the Son vis-à-vis the Father within the Trinity, but also the nature of the Incarnation (whether Jesus was of the same or of different substance from God). For Nestorius Jesus was not God, for he scandalously remarked that 'God is not a baby two or three months old'.[6] This meant that the term 'Theotokos' ('God-bearer') could not then be applied to the Virgin Mary. At the Council of Ephesus in AD 431—Ephesus held the Virgin Mary in particular regard as the Mother of God—Cyril, Bishop of Alexandria, excommunicated Nestorius and upheld (Nicene) orthodoxy. This endorsed the union of divine and human natures in Christ. As Chadwick puts it, these 'constitute a single entity (*hypostasis*), so that one may ascribe the supernatural miracles of the Godhead to the manhood and the natural weaknesses of the manhood to the Godhead [and say] that God was born at Bethlehem or that the impassible and eternal word suffered and died' (*EC*, 195–6). However, the understanding of this union of divine and human natures of Christ (the nub of 'heretical' positions to it) became the bone of contention that began to split Christendom itself into Eastern Orthodox and Western Christianity. At a second Council of Ephesus in 449, Monophysite doctrine was again on the line (*EC*, 200–5). Like the Eutychian heresy, it considered that the person of the incarnate Jesus had only one divine nature. Pope Leo asserted the permanent distinction of the two natures (divine and human) of the incarnate Jesus. It was not until the Council of Chalcedon (AD 451) that a definition was found to resolve the question. Christ was perfectly God and man and consubstantial with the Father (in his Godhead) and with human beings in his manhood, but this unity was 'made known *in* two natures without confusion' (*EC*, 204).[7] Egypt and Palestine were very hostile to the 'two natures'; Constantinople and Rome violently opposed 'one' nature.

The schism caused by the Monophysites concerning their differences from the Constantinopolitan refinements of the Nicene Creed then widened further thanks to several factors. The lack of a common language, the claims of the Pope for ultimate jurisdiction, and marriage of priests (only monks, not priests, are celibate in Orthodoxy) led to controversy over the *Filioque*, that is whether the Holy Spirit proceeds from the Father and from the Son (Roman Catholicism), or from the Father only (Eastern Orthodoxy). Probably introduced in Spain and ratified at the third Council of Toledo in 589, the *Filioque* was interpolated into the Creed as a safeguard against Arianism. From Catholic Spain usage spread to France and Germany to be openly welcomed by Charlemagne.[8] The bitter battle for 'purist' stances on this as on all other matters of 'right' doctrine caused the Great Schism of East and West, the resulting two natures of a Church of one substance, Christianity. Anthony of Egypt would therefore have recognized the Alexandrian Church in its medieval (and nineteenth-century) guise since 'it continued to live in a Patristic atmosphere, using the ideas and language of the Greek Fathers of the fourth century', and of course the 'original' Nicene Creed (that is without the *Filioque*). He would not have recognized (in all senses of the term) the Western Church, where the tradition of the Fathers was replaced by Scholasticism, 'that great synthesis of philosophy and theology worked out in the twelfth and thirteenth centuries' (*W*, 62). 'Alexandrian' heresies and Alexandria's vibrant philosophical schools in the fourth century may now appear less irrelevant in the light of Antoine's intensive meetings with 'Western Christian' as well as Eastern 'others', as the fourth chapter will remap. As for the Holy Spirit as third person of the Trinity deriving from the Father, this 'Comforter' for St Anthony the Great in Athanasius' *Vita Antonii* was no doctrinal or philosophical idea. He was instead the practical giver of spiritual gifts for use in the Body of Christ (the 'Church').[9] The saint's ministry as thaumaturge, the spiritual healer of body and mind, was renowned for its manifestation of these gifts. St Anthony not only overcame spiritual powers (his temptations), he also exorcized those possessed by demons, manifested discernment of spirits, wisdom (his spiritual council to Athanasius), revelation, and prophecy (to those who came to him in the desert). The medieval St Anthony, and the Antonines of Saint-Antoine l'Abbaye in the Dauphiné, with their healing ministry to those with 'St Anthony's Fire' (ergotism), develop the thaumaturgy of St Anthony the Great.[10] Flaubert's Antoine, however, is never seen undertaking any miracle or spiritual healing, but only resisting temptations of the religious mind in every tableau. Nevertheless the spirit rather than the letter of church law remains Antoine's stance regarding all Establishment religions.

Like Anthony the Great before him, Antoine in tableau four also observes but stands outside institutionalized church practices concerning the Eucharist or major festivals, of which many have been major points of doctrinal difference between Eastern Orthodoxy and Western Christianity. Easter as fixed or movable feast, the metamorphosis of communion wine into the blood of Christ as real (transubstantiation) or symbolic, uses of leavened or unleavened bread, who should receive bread and wine at the Eucharist, are examples. However, both Eastern and Western Churches saw in Anthony's exercising of spiritual gifts the hallmarks of sanctity, and thus recognized him as saint through official church canonization. His superlative eremitism and foundational role in monasticism also won him the title of Anthony 'the Great' in both main branches of the Christian Church. It is this epitome of sainthood, the St Anthony of repute in Athanasius' *Vita* or hagiographic monastic traditions, on which Flaubert relies in the mind of his readers to disorient and reorient them. Although several key episodes from well-known sources authenticate the known future of Anthony's status in Flaubert's Antoine (as the ending also provocatively intimates), it is Antoine's 'un-muscular' humanity, difficult solitariness as saint-to-be, and struggle against intensely seductive rival world views that the reader must suddenly square with prior hagiographical expectation. This gap leaves room for Flaubert to pay especial attention to the one attribute of St Anthony the Great that goes without notice, his appellation as St Anthony *of Egypt*. As Chapter 1 will explore in more detail, tableau one overtly serves the ends of foregrounding this specific geopolitical and historical context for its vital importance on several levels for the remainder of the text. We therefore 'tour' Egypt with Antoine, both the desert in the area of Lower Egypt in which he has spent most of his daily life and the Alexandria of his times. With blind Didymus, we are given insights into its economic and social history and topographical significance, observe its temple ruins from older Egyptian civilizations or occupying empires to 'see' the cyclical fall of other gods. Antoine's retrospection also opens up Alexandria's live theological and philosophical debates. Concomitantly with such consistency of point of view, Antoine's position is also strategic. He remains constantly the *insider* of (Christian) Egyptian-ness.[11] Because of this altogether familiar Egyptian 'air' he breathes, his lived eremitical experience (home, the religious everyday) is a given, and therefore needs no explicit elucidation, whereas 'foreignness' to this is what preoccupies Antoine (and the *Tentation*) throughout. Nevertheless, Antoine's constant and concertedly Egyptian perspectives shine light on the new or imported institutions, powers, religions, and ideas of his epoch. In the development of the counterpoint tactics used by Montesquieu in his *Lettres persanes* (1721), these newcomers prove not so much 'strange' (other), but strangely similar to counterparts in nineteenth-century France.

Reader disorientation (a tactic Flaubert also employs from the outset in *Salammbô*) is thus the all-important starting point for the *Tentation*. Getting inside Antoine's Orient, his 'Egyptian-ness', is the means by which reader reorientation takes place. We have to see what Antoine sees, his hallucinations, visions, and nightmares, and how he makes sense of them. Egyptian-ness is therefore not simply a backdrop for Antoine or something in itself, but a static locus and changing value holding the various time frames of the *Tentation* firmly together. Anthony of Egypt as Antoine's precursor and model therefore stands as shorthand for the intermeshing of person and place in micro-macrocosmic dimensions and time frames that the *Tentation* fully exploits. What constitute the elements of Egyptian-ness that are the water for Flaubert's strange fish Antoine?[12]

Les Coptes sont les chrétiens d'Égypte. Leur nom, issu de l'arabe *Qibt*, n'est rien d'autre qu'une abbréviation du grec *Aiguptios*, 'Égyptien', lui-même dérivé de *Hikuptâh*, nom religieux de l'ancienne capitale du pays, Memphis. Dans un même héritage, les Coptes allient à un christianisme original et bien acculturé

un peu de la mémoire des pharaons, beaucoup d'apports de l'Égypte hellénis-
tique et byzantine, et le dynamisme d'une arabité à l'épanouissement de laquelle
ils ont largement contribué.[13]

The seeming tautology of person and place is revealed here in the
etymology and retranslation of the 'Copt' as the quintessential Egyptian,
but one sharing the longer history of ancient Pharaonic culture, Hel-
lenist and then Roman invasion of Egypt (from AD 30). This history
was not primarily economic, but predominantly religious: the ancient
Greek historian Herodotus qualified Egyptians of the fifth century BC
as more religious than any other race since their belief system informed
all aspects of cultural organization. Two salient features distinguished
ancient Egyptian religion of the Pharaohs from other Eastern religions.
Although the Egyptian system adopted polytheistic elements, it had a
unifying god, the great god Amon of Thebes, identified with Re the sun
god. The second main belief was that death was not the end or the entry
into a lesser state, but the more optimistic metamorphosis into something divine. The building of the Pyramids and the Egyptians' highly
developed skill of embalming epitomized such observance and practice.
Egypt's rich religious heritage thus provided an immediately fertile soil
for the new religion of Christianity, where Jesus (and his resurrection)
was instantly comparable with Osiris. The Coptic Church then retrospectively adopted Old Testament Egypt for itself. The story of Joseph
or Moses' initiation into the wisdom of the Egyptians prefigured its
welcome to Jesus and the Holy Family when they sought refuge from
the persecution of Herod the Great.[14] For the Coptic Christian Church,
this same experience of persecution constituted its founding moment
and defining history. St Mark allegedly preached the new religion in
Alexandria around AD 43–8 and was probably lynched there at Easter
(AD 62 or 68) by worshippers of the god Serapis. There were many
martyrs for the Christian faith under the subsequent persecutions of the
Roman Emperors Decius, Diocletian, and Galerius. Their reigns frame
the life and times of St Anthony the Great. Martyrdom and persecution
thus become essentially religious forms and expressions of resistance to
mark out a belief against its rivals. Vicious use of persecution by both
the 'Christian' and 'pagan' Church alike is the double bind Flaubert's
Antoine (like his model) faces. When the Roman Emperor Constantine
famously converted to Christianity in AD 313, he made it the state

religion not just of a nation but an empire for the first time.[15] But Christianity then became the destroyer and persecutor of those polytheistic religions which had previously persecuted it. Although Constantine's marriage of earthly and heavenly powers has been heralded as a founding moment of Western Christendom, an emperor involved and interfering in matters of Church and State was almost more problematic for the authority and government of both institutions. Constantine, not Athanasius, called the first Council of Nicaea, for example.

The early Christian Church in Alexandria did not emerge solely from conversions of pagan emperors or worshippers of Egypt's other gods such as Serapis. Members of the already thriving Jewish community (which had suffered persecution under Trajan in AD 115–17) also converted. Arguably, all the developments of the early Christian Church were in fact Jewish. The Jews of Alexandria had translated the Bible into Greek (the Septuagint). Their allegorical method of biblical interpretation established by the Jewish Philo of Alexandria (*c.* 30 BC– *c.* AD 40) was what the Christian Church adopted, and a community of Jewish ascetics had already begun to live in semi-desert communities in ways that Paul the hermit and St Anthony develop in their own forms of monasticism. In Alexandria, the rapid establishment and institutionalization of the new Christian Church and Christian catechetical school (established by Demetrios, AD 189–232, Bishop of Alexandria) were helped directly by the long heritage of the schools of Jewish exegesis and Greek Neoplatonism as oppositional, but also symbiotically developing, philosophies. Part II will investigate the importance of these schools as academies and seats of learning in more detail. For Part I, the many rival philosophical and Gnostic ideas emanating from counterparts in other schools and spearheading the writing of important theological treatises by famous leaders and teachers in the Christian catechetical school (such as Athenegore, Pantene, Clement, Origen, and Denys) together form the ideological setting for the *Tentation*. The 'primitive' Church was therefore neither unlettered, nor in a separatist ghetto from the melting pot of rival claims to truth. The 'Egyptian' temptations of Antoine's religious mind all derive directly from this historical context and history of ideas, especially in tableaux three to five.

While Greek was the language of learning in Alexandria, the Christian school also translated the Bible and other works of apologetics into the demotic and other vernaculars. The Orthodox Church (Greek and Russian) would subsequently take up this language policy as its Christianizing mission to other lands, unlike the Church of Rome with its insistence on the use of Latin as the sole liturgical tongue. From the third century AD, the active production of Coptic literature, mostly of religious import, was largely thanks to the development of an adapted Greek alphabet to denote the spoken Egyptian language that had evolved from the time of the Pharaohs. It would be the discovery of the Rosetta Stone, with its hieroglyphs, demotic, and Greek translations, and the place of *Coptic* as the code-breaker, that would enable Champollion to read and translate the ancient Egyptian hieroglyphs. It is possible that Anthony of Egypt read and wrote Coptic, although tradition also has him unlettered and taught directly by the Holy Spirit. Whether one wishes to judge as anachronistic or faithful Flaubert's representation of Antoine the reader-interpreter of Scripture in tableau one, the point is surely this. As fourth-century Christian Copt, he is quintessentially a mediator, like the script of the Rosetta Stone between the belief systems of ancient Egypt and nineteenth-century Muslim Egypt colonized by France. That Antoine may also be mediating controversial theological issues in nineteenth-century France by retrospective-prospective analogy in the *Tentation* now requires a brief examination.

RELIGION IN THE FRANCE OF FLAUBERT

As unlikely protagonist but also canonized saint to be, Antoine's challenge to religious authority and authorities therefore includes nineteenth-century French Catholicism as part of a longer history of religious conflicts and persecutions past and future.[16] Tableau five will indeed remap this recurrent pattern of the overthrow of empires and gods. The French Revolution's bid to destroy Catholic Christianity with its cult of saints and Gregorian calendar (to match the ending of absolutist monarchy and divine right) was nothing new. Julian the Apostate (AD 361–3) had sought likewise to destroy the early Church established by Constantine, and restore paganism. He failed, as did revolutionary France with its replacement institutions in the form of the Directory, the Cult of Reason with its goddess erected on the Place de la Bastille, and the Revolutionary Calendar. None stood even a tiny test of time.[17] Like the early Alexandrian Church after Julian, nineteenth-century French

Catholicism was re-established as state religion, theological institution, and doctrinal authority through the power of an emperor, in this instance, the anti-Catholic Napoleon I. When he signed the Concordat with the Pope in 1801, this triumph for the Roman Catholic Church (and its Calendar) was however a mixed blessing, but in ways strikingly parallel to Constantine's institutionalization of the Christian Church as the state religion in St Anthony's time. Doctrinal conflicts were not resolved but fuelled, both within the Church and with its Christian and non-Christian others in fourth-century Egypt as in nineteenth-century France. The so-called 'heresies' of the fourth tableau of the *Tentation* then surely reflect and project these by implication. The *Tentation*'s exploration of the questionable 'triumph' of the Church thus remaps in other worlds the watershed event of the Concordat (rather than the Revolution[18]). Three main overlapping arenas need brief mention and expansion in the sections below. First, the Concordat indirectly also instigated the (re)establishment of France's other Christian Churches. Perhaps more important for the context of tableau four, it also spearheaded the emergence of a specifically French 'New Christianity', the 'church' of the Saint-Simonians. Second, it affected the huge upsurge in grass-roots French Catholicism and popular religious belief as opposed to the practice of institutionalized faith. Third, it encapsulated Napoleon's authority and priorities in matters earthly and spiritual: his vision for a new 'Holy Roman' French Empire would expand south into the (Muslim) Middle East (Egypt), and north via Protestant Germany and England as far as Orthodox Russia in an economic-scientific but not religious crusade.

Histories of religion of nineteenth-century France focus mainly on the post-revolutionary re-establishment of the Roman Catholic Church as official religion.[19] Its conservative and liberal wings are then framed in opposition to post-Enlightenment anti-clerical and anti-religious movements, including socialism and positivism.[20] Napoleon's signing of the Concordat in 1801 thus epitomizes the misalliance of church and state powers. Historians cite gendered education and curriculum policies for an industrializing nation, or the demarcation of male and female spheres, which the 1804 Code Civil enshrined in property law and rights, to demonstrate the Concordat's innate conflict of interests for both parties. Its uneasy entente marks the main reason why anti-religious, ideological, and political movements and counter-movements gathered momentum and power as the century unfolded.[21] The *Tentation*'s centrally 'religious' focus however challenges such over-neat polarizations or 'religious' history of nineteenth-century France as allegedly a 'secular' state. The Revolution's aim of separating matters spiritual from earthly will not occur until 1905.[22] Appendix 2 provides a chronology of events and dates pertinent to nineteenth-century French 'religious' history that find parallel discussion in the *Tentation*. Greater or lesser separation of the State and Catholic Church across the turbulent and changing politics of nineteenth-century France is framed in this appendix by the legal history of the right to divorce for men and women, or its repeal, across the period. My reason is to underline the effectiveness I am arguing for this book as a whole, the remapping of one dimension of culture when it is seen more clearly through a parallel other. After the time of St Anthony, divorce of people or institutional powers ever reflects the schism that would separate the Church of Alexandria (Eastern Orthodoxy) from Western Catholicism.

As Chapter 4 will therefore discover, the *Tentation* richly challenges the view that nineteenth-century France was a dualistic ideological world with reactionary Roman Catholicism on one side and much more enlightened free thinkers outside the Church on the other, who might have had some deist or comparative religious leanings. Both these polarized 'camps' were already a set of rival factions and subgroups, all bent on a remarkably similar search for truth. Regarding French Roman Catholicism, long-standing inner factionalisms continued unabated into the nineteenth century. Ultramontanists (literally 'beyond the mountains') wanted Rome to have more jurisdiction and power to intervene in matters affecting the 'true' faith concerning the new philosophies and religious groups of the age. They saw the Pope and Rome as holding final authority for any national Roman Catholic Church. On the contrary, the Gallicans sought more power and authority for the French Catholic Church independent of Rome, so that a less shackled France might pursue modernizing foreign and economic interests and compete with rivals such as Germany and England. Latin or vernacular preaching and teaching was a further core debate for both groups, one that would have ramifications for the wider secularizing university and education reforms that Napoleon and Guizot instigated, and that Jules Ferry would later enshrine. In counterbalance, the Fidéistes privileged faith and religious/spiritual knowledge, and claimed to exclude the role of reason. Meanwhile notable 'Catholic' apologists, writers, and thinkers such as Chateaubriand, Joseph de Maistre, or Lammenais, attempted to find a middle path between religion and philosophy (following the example of medieval Scholasticism and the adoption of Aristotelian thinking into theology).[23] The Catholic Church's history of internal division, controlled to encompass 'purists' of various hues, was not new. The Jansenists in the seventeenth century for example had already challenged its dogmas by their belief that only a tiny predetermined elect could become Christians able to lead an austere moral life. Such groups find their fourth-century models in the 'heresies' of tableau four. What was new, thanks to the Revolution, was the dissolution of the Church in all its various brotherhoods (Jesuits, Trappists, Chartreux, Benedictines, Dominicans, Antonines). Their full reinstatement to various educative and pastoral roles in the 1840s interestingly occurred long after official recognition of rival Reformed Churches and Judaism in France (in 1802 and 1808 respectively). The impact in France of Jewish, Russian Orthodox, and Lutheran communities on the Catholic Church and theology is largely unwritten in histories of the French Catholic Church of the period.[24] The *Tentation*'s inclusion of Jewish, Gnostic, as well as Christian and Neoplatonic sects in its melting pot of 'churches' and dogmas in the fourth tableau of the *Tentation* paints an altogether more rounded picture tantamount to the strongly religious climate of nineteenth-century France. Moreover, the direct interaction of fourth-century Alexandrian 'churches' with non-Christian Alexandrian schools (as examined briefly above) also finds parallels in the impact of Judaism and the Confession of Augsburg on education and scientific endeavour in nineteenth-century France. Again critical appraisals of France's Catholic or determinedly secular education policies in the nineteenth century sideline consideration of these others.[25] Georges Cuvier, for example, known more famously as the father of palaeontology and comparative anatomy in France, was unusually also the official in charge of the Mission of Protestant Churches of France. Established in 1822, it distributed funds for the training of ministers and the founding of schools. Cuvier used this and his other key scientific positions to promote science in the secondary educational curriculum for Catholic and Protestant schools alike, and before Jules Ferry. Tableau seven will return to some of the peculiar visualizations of Cuvier's science curriculum in another guise. It is also worth recalling that nineteenth-century

historians of 'mysticism' in France such as Erdan explicitly labelled
Protestantism a 'heresy' alongside Martinism, animal magnetism, table
turning, Isis cults, and Freemasonry.[26] In its first half, the *Tentation*
overtly remaps such labelling and the richer 'Church' of nineteenth-
century France by analogy with the religious melting pot of third-
and fourth-century Alexandria and through the judgements of Antoine.
We will discover in its second half how Flaubert's protagonist overtly
lives 'La France mistique [*sic*]' through his 'visions' or 'hallucinations'
as not only religious but also scientific.[27] The authenticity and contents of such visions, and who adjudicates the true from the false, will
prove problems in the history of religion and the history of science of
nineteenth-century France.

The lifespan of the many powerful cults and Gnostic churches
founded by charismatic leaders in opposition to the early Christian
Church in Alexandria rarely lasted beyond the lifetime of their leaders.
This pattern resurfaces not only in the Directory's Cult of Reason,
but also in the subsequent bids by new cult leaders in nineteenth-
century France to replace outworn religious ideas, rites, and irrelevant
practice. Comte and positivism are obvious examples. More pertinent
with respect to the anchoritic thaumaturgy of Anthony the Great,
however, were the Saint-Simonians. Responding to the aloof luxury
and authority of the Church of Rome and its self-seeking bishops and
priests, they sought to establish a social, utopian religion to address
the huge problems of poverty, lack of basic education, prostitution,
and unemployment of the 1830s that the official Roman Catholic
Church largely chose to ignore.[28] Their leader, the charismatic Prosper
Enfantin, founded a philanstery ('monastery') in Menilmontant in 1832
to promote the new brotherhood. A religion of progress, confined to
a community of men who had left their families, this venture was
bound to fail.[29] However, because in its inspiration it was a well-
organized counter-cultural movement with many adherents among the
educated[30]—many of its leaders including Enfantin were trained engineers at the newly established École Polytechnique—it redirected its
utopian communitarian mission in a second bid (this time including
women) to found a new religious Saint-Simonian community in Egypt
in 1833. They believed that when the Great Mother was identified
there as mate for their leader le Père Enfantin, the new vision for
humanity and community could then be birthed. A second belief was

that the land could be made fertile (through the building of irrigation systems), and that a canal could be cut through the Isthmus of Suez. If this 'New Jerusalem' foundered because of arguments about leadership, Saint-Simonian 'doctrine', and the mismatch between utopian ideas and practical living (such as the sharing of women and women's rights), the harsh reality of the desert climate was an overriding factor. When cholera and other illnesses struck, the Saint-Simonians returned to France definitively. However Enfantin and other Saint-Simonians were among the most powerful lobbyists and fund-raisers for the Suez Canal—Enfantin created the 'Société d'Études pour le Canal de Suez' in 1846—and its eventual realization by de Lesseps.[31] Arguably the Egyptian community also failed by being a derivative, socio-politically inspired copy of community life lived by a spiritual 'rule', such as that instigated by one of the founding anchorites, St Pachomius of Egypt (286–346).[32] One point is certain. Charismatic leadership is only one part of the successful founding of any 'Church'; inspired believers are equally necessary for the continuation of any cult, sect, or major church, and in large numbers rather than via intellectual or separatist groups. Nearby to Menilmontant, Montmartre would see the erection of the Sacré Cœur (begun in June 1875 but not consecrated until 1919), as an act of atonement and jubilee after the Commune and defeat in the Franco-Prussian War. Popular Catholic fervour was clearly no minority expression of faith.

In spite of the Revolution and probably because of its sanctions, popular 'mystical' religious fervour in nineteenth-century France was stronger than in the pre-revolutionary period.[33] For the uneducated (and obviously non-intellectual), poorest classes in both the city and the country, specifically 'Catholic' religious expression was fuelled by a number of recurring miraculous events spanning the 1830s to 1870s. Most centred on sightings of the Virgin Mary. In 1830 Catherine Labouré had a visitation to her humble room at 140 rue du Bac in Paris by the Virgin who sat in her chair and talked to her about the state of devotion in France. A special medal was struck of the Virgin Catherine saw, 'a woman clothed with the sun with the moon under her feet and a crown of twelve stars on her head' of Revelation 12: 1.[34] Only when the cholera epidemic of 1832 hit France including Paris did believers snap up these 'miraculous medals', to seek the Virgin's intercession for protection against the disease. Another mystical sighting of the Virgin Mary by Maximin Giraud and Mélanie Calvat occurred at La Salette in 1846. In 1858 the uneducated Bernadette Soubirous had her first of several visitations from the Virgin in Lourdes. These 'trance appointments' were witnessed by growing crowds of believers and sceptics alike who flocked to Lourdes to see for themselves. The Virgin appeared again in Pontmain in 1871 to five peasant children. Both La Salette and Lourdes rapidly became pilgrimage sites, and the Roman Catholic Church had to adjudicate whether these miraculous visitations were authentic or hoaxes:

What became unusual about Lourdes was the Church's swift approval of the Marian visions and the extraordinary development of the shrine over the final quarter of the nineteenth century. After initially trying to ignore, even discount, Bernadette's visions and the crowds who flocked to see her, the local bishop proclaimed the apparitions to be authentic in 1862. Some ten years later the Augustinian Fathers of the Assumption, a Paris-based religious order, made Lourdes the site of their national pilgrimage. With the help of the railway and the Catholic popular press, the Assumptionists transformed Lourdes into a site of mass pilgrimage, bringing hundreds of thousands of devout Catholics to the shrine each year.[35]

Only these apparitions of the Virgin in France among the proliferation of sightings of her were recognized as authentic by the Catholic Church. Bernadette's ecstatic visions therefore serve as a contemporary phenomenon and 'reality check' for the many 'visions' or 'temptations' which visit Flaubert's Antoine, which modern critics have read as figments of an overwrought imagination, hallucinations, or diagnosed in psychoanalytic terms as sexual repressions or drives,[36] but never as 'real' events of the period. What Flaubert thus introduces through his reworking of the figure of St Anthony into his Antoine is a carefully grafted amalgam of legendary, miraculous, tendentious, and strangely 'modern-day' miracle visitations, beliefs, visions, or incredible mindscapes that no avowedly rationalistic person would countenance. Outside Antoine's mind, the reader must ultimately decide how to adjudicate between authentic and inauthentic manifestations, that is take up the position of 'papal', agnostic, atheist, or scientific sanction.

Debates at the time in the Catholic and anti-clerical press concerning the reality of Bernadette's visions hinged around several factors. Her peasant, illiterate background and her young female (and hence hysterical) propensities epitomized popular credulity of the times, evident in the huge crowds she attracted, and the healings that allegedly took place during the visitations. Worse still, these events illustrated how Catholic dogma had grafted in vestiges of pagan beliefs and local superstitions such as belief in relics or places with 'magical' properties. All of these Flaubert might readily have swept up in his final version of the *Tentation* as a mock-medieval satire whereby his Antoine could lampoon these very similar nineteenth-century occurrences, popular and regional mindsets, and the folly of the Catholic Church in perpetuating such outmoded ideas by authenticating them.[37] Instead, Flaubert very clearly rejects every vestige of the medieval Anthony as used in the storyline of popular street theatre and puppet shows,[38] and in the iconography of the Antonines as thaumaturgical and hospitaller order. Surely this is why the famous pig most importantly goes from the final version of the *Tentation* much to the consternation of critics? Only then can Flaubert underscore the 'modern' medievalist beliefs of rationalistic and positivist nineteenth-century France on the one hand, and the ongoing religious and scientific problem on the other of authenticating relics and old bones. With delicious irony, Flaubert's revivified, fictional Antoine 're-embodies' the debate reported in regional and national French presses in the 1850s (when Flaubert was revising his *Tentation*) concerning the relics of St Anthony the Great himself, which required the direct adjudication of the Roman Catholic Church and the Confédération des Rites.

Although St Anthony in the *Vita Antonii* expressly asked his two disciples not to look for his body so that it could not then be venerated, his bones were 'found', transported to the Church of St John the Baptist in Alexandria in AD 529, and then moved to St Sophia in Constantinople in AD 670 because of the invading Muslim Saracens.[39] The bones remained there until they were translated to La Motte Saint Didier (renamed Saint-Antoine l'Abbaye) in the Dauphiné in the eleventh century due to the visions of its liege lord, Guillaume of Chateauneuf de l'Albenc, and his disobedient son Jocelyn who died before a basilica could be built to house their reliquary. The Benedictines of nearby Montmajour completed the task, and the Antonine order was established mainly thanks to a serious plague in 1089 (like the 1832 cholera epidemic) which ravaged the region but enhanced the reputation of this hospitaller order. A long-running and fantastic rivalry raged from the thirteenth century between Saint-Antoine l'Abbaye and the nearby Benedictine Saint-Julien in Arles over who had the real bones of St Anthony, since they were a major source of revenue from pilgrimages and alms, until the Revolution destroyed both religious foundations and their most precious reliquaries, but not the bones.

It was shortly after the Concordat that religion and scientific method intervened. In 1802 the 'Commission d'Examen' officially itemized the bones and reliquaries belonging to the Église Saint-Julien at Arles, and noted whether the glass and seals for each were cracked or intact.[40] A further inspection by the Commission in 1838 was more scientific in that it checked the reliquaries against documentary evidence about St Anthony's bones dating from before the Revolution. Once more, the Église Saint-Julien relics were declared authentic. Doubt lay only in the mind of the incumbent of the Église Saint-Julien, Abbé Montagard, who had previously moved St Anthony's bones into one of the vaults of the church and destroyed all the supporting evidence. The matter was undisturbed until one Abbé Louis Toussaint Dassy started rumours in 1844 that the real bones of St Anthony were in the Dauphiné, not Arles. Two publications fuelled what could then be called a battle of the bones. In 1855 Dassy published *Le Trésor de l'église abbatiale de Saint-Antoine en Dauphiné ou la vérité sur les reliques du patriarche des cénobitiques.* In 1856 Joseph Séguin's *Dissertation d'Arles, contre les pères de Saint-Antoine en Viennois* was published posthumously by his descendants. The regional and national press entered on both sides of the debate, which grew so acrimonious that the Confédération des Rites was called upon in 1859 to make a final judgement. It confirmed that the Église Saint-Julien were the keepers of the authentic bones. A new reliquary complete with glass was then commissioned from the Maison Nicolas-Rosier in Lyon and sent to Arles on 15 January 1860. The reliquary containing the 'bones' of St Anthony is however still on display today in Saint-Antoine l'Abbaye. St Anthony's bones have therefore reappeared at strategic moments in French and church history, for example in the run up to the Crusades against the Muslim 'Infidel', in internecine strife between various Roman Catholic religious orders in the late Middle Ages, in nineteenth-century France. These appearances are no more or less spectacular or fantastical than other miraculous Marian sightings and apparitions occurring in various places in mid-nineteenth-century France in which the Roman Catholic Church and other 'authorities' had directly to intervene. Flaubert's *Tentation* is thus asking its late nineteenth-century and modern readers to suspend both belief and disbelief, since real events of strictly religious significance are precisely those of the fictional text.

So when is a relic a hoax or authentic? When is a miracle of healing a miracle or a medically explicable phenomenon since Lourdes requires the test of medical experts? Who defines genuine and proper from counterfeit and improper ideas, relics, appearances, healings, revelations, or books? While Roman Catholicism as the official religion in nineteenth-century France had its governance of education increasingly trimmed back as the century unfolded, it intervened actively in affairs of public morality, especially where it saw the safeguarding of the faithful and Truth from the dangers of false ideas or alternative religions. Consequently, where philosophy and science largely reclassed their activities as secular domains outside the aegis of Catholicism and its Church, the Church blacklisted secular ideas through regular encyclicals and the regular addition of heretical books to its codex. If counter-authorities in the ascendant inevitably challenge absolutist power and official Authority (secular/political or spiritual), the latter's stand becomes almost the more important since without such resistance, opposition would be meaningless. What was true for Athanasius and the Alexandrian Church facing numerous heresies and internal schism is equally so for Pope Pius IX and Roman Catholicism in the mid-nineteenth century defending its position in the teeth of so many rival claims to truth and authority. The Church's pronouncements on which of its great adherents should be canonized, and on whether visitations or bones were genuine, are not then purely internal, or strictly religious matters, but a test of church and papal authority itself to adjudicate on their public implications alongside the authorities of reason and science. The many encyclicals that mark the reign of Pius IX demonstrate this concern, as also his resolve to pronounce on doctrinal matters that had been rumbling for centuries because their significance was now manifest in lived reality. In the long papacy of Pius IX, two doctrinal matters stand out, and very clearly recall Athanasius' authority as Bishop of Alexandria representing the Church universal to spell out the theology of Jesus as fully man and fully God.

The question of the Incarnation and person of Jesus was back on the table not only with Renan's 'scandalous' *Vie de Jésus* in 1863 (which will be discussed in Chapter 3); also back was the question of the 'divine' nature of Mary as 'Theotokos'. While the Assumption of the Virgin Mary, her bodily translation into heaven, had long been recognized (15 August is still a public holiday to celebrate this in modern secular France[41]), it was her 'spiritual' birth that now concerned the Catholic Church in its understanding of Jesus' conception by divine insemination and birth by a Virgin. Albeit incredible or a contravention of the laws of biology for non-believers, the story also lacked divine logic for the Roman Catholic Church, unless the Mother of God similarly was born immaculate, and so free from the impurities that Eve brought to humanity in the Fall. In 1854, Pope Pius IX resolved the issue of the Virgin Mary's sinless womb in her defining role as 'Theotokos' by enshrining the Immaculate Conception into her own birth.[42] In our brief outline of early church history (and schism) above, Pius IX could not more clearly (or paradoxically) be endorsing the spiritual position of his Eastern Church other, Monophysite understanding of the *one* spiritual substance of Christ as begotten not made, pure although born 'of the flesh'. The Marian apparitions and sightings, like their authentication before and after this new addition to 'Nicene' doctrine, are therefore no isolated or popular religious phenomena, but centrally connected to Church self-affirmation through authoritative dogma and theology about the person of the Virgin herself and with the Trinity.

Central tenets and their institutionalization may first appear fabulous yet they are vital to the life or death of an ideology, Church, or scientific theory. Although the Immaculate Conception had a longer tradition in both Eastern and Western Christendom, its enshrining by Pius IX as Roman Catholic dogma (which the Eastern Orthodox Church continues not to recognize) led logically to the second major ratification of inherent belief. The early Church, on which the life and times of St Anthony the Great is a fourth-century window, saw itself as built on the work of Christ, his apostles, and the prophets wherein the Church Fathers were the direct disciples of the apostolic church planting of Paul, James, Mark for the Church in Egypt, and of course Peter for Rome. Pius IX understood the nature of his papacy as a direct lineage of this transmission of Truth, and papacy as itself the supreme arbiter of it, whether secular or theological (such as the doctrine of the Immaculate Conception). In 1864, Pius' *Syllabus Errorum* placed on a codex the books and ideologies deemed inimical to Roman Catholic theology and teaching. As its name suggest, the *Syllabus Errorum* makes the distinction between error and truth rather than complete untruth, and papal ability to adjudicate between them. However, for his role to have final authority, Pius IX then needed to enshrine papal infallibility as dogma, which he did at the first Vatican Council in 1870. Popes then, like the Blessed Virgin, transcend the human lot—propensity to err and to error—because of their holy headship or 'immaculate conception' of the papal mind. Surely the significance of Vatican I and the first Council of Nicaea are too similar not to be comparable? Moreover, it is Antoine, like St Anthony the Great before him, who is the most suitable judge of the wisdom of church folly by being among the Established Church's most revered insider-outsiders.

'Egyptian' critical perspectives on the Church of Rome, then, constitute Flaubert's deliberate choice of St Anthony the Great as exemplary model for his nineteenth-century Antoine faced with so many similar counter-*theological* as well as counter-philosophical ideas of religious inspiration. Antoine follows to the letter the anchoritic and quintessentially religious nonconformism of Anthony the Great outside the Established Church (but not in an alternative, anti-catholic philanstery like the Saint-Simonian community). The certain (because future perfect), iconic saintliness of his Antoine must then be taken as read, a move critics have failed to see as essential to Flaubert's critique because they have been caught up in the non-debate of Flaubert's own beliefs or lack of them.[43] The powerful reason for this given is that Antoine strictly speaking cannot then be judged 'anti-Catholic', only deeply un-Catholic in his stances, since the Roman Catholic Church had yet to be established from the perspective of fourth-century Alexandria. By exploiting just this perspective on nineteenth-century France, Flaubert can then highlight what is preposterous about its tenets of faith and dogma. How 'orthodox' these are can then only be judged paradoxically by the definitions and lights of coexisting 'heresy', the motor of all the temptations. Antoine is thus no passive palimpsest or *tabula rasa* on which more enlightened syncretistic religious ideas will be written in the *Tentation*. Like the Rosetta Stone, this informed Coptic seer will negotiate and interpret the many monstrous imaginings, theological and non-theological, of his age and that of nineteenth-century France.

THE EGYPT OF NINETEENTH-CENTURY FRANCE

If the disorientation-reorientation that allows the reader to judge
nineteenth-century Catholic France pivots in the *Tentation* precisely on
Antoine as *Coptic* intermediary and seer, his position cannot explain
the all-important connection between the times of St Anthony of Egypt
and modern *Muslim* Egypt of post-revolutionary France. Flaubert's own
journey to Egypt and the Middle East in 1849–50, and biographical
reference to it in his *Correspondance,* do not suffice either, although he
was impressed enough with his meeting with the Coptic Patriarch in
Cairo to record the event in a letter to his mother.[44] Napoleon's mission
to conquer Egypt in 1798, and France's occupation of it until 1801 (and
the Concordat), immediately links the two Egyptian worlds inextricably.
Even the best critics on Flaubert's 'orientalism' have surprisingly failed
to comment on, let alone analyse, this parallel historical situation with
regard to the *Tentation*.[45] For example, the Mameluke governors of this
Egyptian Protectorate under the Turkish Sultan and the Sublime Porte
in Constantinople that Napoleon encountered in 1798 look very little
different in their despotism from Constantine's autocratic rule of Egypt
as Roman Emperor in the fourth century. Napoleon's short-lived defeat
of the Mamelukes and military 'coalition' government (the Divan) was
however no less authoritarian than theirs regarding militaristic, civil,
colonialist, and expansionist objectives. The Mamelukes wanted to
extend and modernize Egypt as a major trading economy: Napoleon
wanted it likewise for France's industrializing and expansionist agendas
as foothold and trading hub for Far Eastern markets. We will be returning to these power structures and their parallelism in Chapter 2. Yet if
Napoleon's model for Empire was as 'Roman' as Constantine's at this
pivotal moment in post-revolutionary and pre-first Empire France, his
mission was not to (re-)Christianize Egypt. On the contrary, he strove
from the outset of his French occupation to win over the Mamelukes
and sheiks by emphasizing his pro-Muslim sympathies as leader from an
enlightened country that had dethroned their mutual arch-enemy, the
Pope. His intentions therefore did not interfere with Islamic teaching
or religious expression.[46] Nonetheless, his mission was to civilize this
backward, 'medieval' state,[47] and in a manner that only the more clearly
delineates the paradoxes of the new (Republican) yet still hierarchical
(monarchist) orders of French international politics. What Napoleon

envisaged for the political liberation of Egypt was the promotion of its *ancient* cultural capital and Pharaonic legacy of superiority in the sciences and the arts repatriated to it by France through their successors, Enlightenment sciences and technologies of progress.[48] A chronology of major dates and events of this mission is found in Appendix 3.[49] The key point to note is that 167 'savants' (chemists, natural scientists, mathematicians, engineers, experts in Middle Eastern languages) were recruited by the Commission of the Sciences and the Arts (itself created only in late 1797) to accompany Napoleon's occupying forces bound for Alexandria in 1798. Napoleon could thus justify blatant military expansionism and French colonialism by promoting enlightened scientific endeavours such as archaeology at the same time. His departure for France in 1800 cut short this idealism and raw conquest, leading to the retreat of French military and scientific invaders back to Cairo and British defeat of General Menou in 1801.

For the French in France and native Egyptians after 1801, Napoleon's campaign in Egypt was a watershed event. Appendix 4 provides a chronology of major dates and events interlocking the modernizing progress of both nations.[50] For Egypt, its fragile history of development as a nation state (it had only in 1767 proclaimed independence from Ottoman rule under Ali Bey) would paradoxically be set on a firm footing after 1805. As a Mameluke (an order of former white Egyptian slaves who were known for their military prowess, despotism, and autocracy), Bey continued the Mamelukes' traditional roles held since the thirteenth century, as Egypt's administrators within the Ottoman Empire. In 1786, however, an Ottoman expeditionary force landed at Alexandria and defeated the Mamelukes, but their leaders, Mourad Bey and Ibrahim Bey, took control of Egypt in 1791 by signing an agreement with the Ottoman Sultan to pay a yearly tax. Their defeat by Napoleon led to a similar set of power-sharing agreements. France recognized the re-establishment of the authority of the Ottoman Sultan Mahmud II in Egypt, ratified by the treaty of Paris on 25 June 1802. However, the Sultan made Mohammed Ali (1769–1849) the official Pasha of Egypt. Like Napoleon in France, Mohammed Ali had modernizing designs, to combine military campaigns with infrastructural, socio-economic, and intellectual reforms. While strongly nationalistic—Egypt as a nation state derives from his rule—the Pasha recognized the necessity of alliances with Britain and France for the furthering of Egypt's strategic economic position as a properly nineteenth-century capital of the Middle East, as well as gateway to Africa and Far Eastern trade. The Pasha's sons Ismail and Ibrahim continued to extend Egyptian territories (into the Sudan, 1820—Ismail was assassinated—and Syria 1828). By 1840 the British sought to reduce French control of the Mediterranean and so required Mohammed Ali to withdraw from Syria and other lands taken since becoming Pasha. Under the convention of London (1840), Egypt was once more to become a province of the Ottoman Empire with lands extending only to its former borders of 1805. In exchange, Mohammed Ali who would rule until 1848 gained the title of Viceroy for his descendants from the Sultan (Abdul Mdejid). Continuing the Pharaonic tradition of Egyptian despotic rule—he had 400 Mamelukes massacred in the citadel of Cairo in 1811—Mohammed Ali ensured Egypt's 'European' future as a Mediterranean power. He also saw the inauguration of the Mahmoudieh Canal in February 1821. Built by Egyptian peasant (fellah) labour, it was the first waterway in Egypt to link Alexandria with the western tributary of the Nile. His younger brother Saïd succeeded him in 1854 (after the death of his son Ibrahim and nephew Abbas) and continued his work of modernizing Egypt's economic infrastructure. In November 1854 Saïd granted the concession for the Suez Canal to Ferdinand de Lesseps; and thanks to the British, the first railway linking Alexandria and Cairo was built and opened in 1857, with the Cairo–Suez railway completed in 1859, not least to facilitate the work of cutting through the Isthmus of Suez. If Saïd's 42 per cent share in the Suez Canal Company (founded in 1858 and in which the French had a 52 per cent share) effectively brought his successor Ismail's (Ibrahim's son) state into debt, the Suez Canal was inaugurated in 1869 in the presence of the Empress Eugénie and Napoleon III. To try to prevent national financial collapse, Ismail sold Egypt's share in the company to Britain, but bankruptcy was declared in 1876, returning financial control to France and Britain. Only two years after Flaubert's death, the occupation of Egypt by the British (15 July 1882) left the country nominally part of the Ottoman Empire but in effect controlled by Sir Evelyn Baring as British Consul, and a pawn in the bigger, century-long economic game between France and Britain for control of trade routes east and south. In 1899 the Sudan would be returned by the French to Britain; in 1904 (with the Entente Cordiale), England was given free rein in Egypt in exchange for France taking full control of Morocco.[51]

Clearly the political climate of nineteenth-century France, its shuttling between empires and republics, its autocratic emperors, Napoleon I and III, is integrally linked to but also mirrored in the rule of Mohammed Ali and his successors. The *Tentation* will explore such principalities and powers in its second tableau by comparative analogy.

For France, colonial expansion meant more than intense military and economic rivalry with Britain for overseas markets and products. Of greater strategic importance was France's inferior position to the supremacy of Britain or Germany in the nineteenth-century industrial, scientific, and cultural wars, of which many were played out on Egyptian soil. The work of the 167 'savants' between 1798 and 1801, chosen to undertake science primarily based in the field in Egypt rather than in ivory towers, was foundational for France becoming a worthy rival to British dominance in Egyptian archaeological discovery.[52] Although the discipline of Egyptology did not exist until the 1820s, active development of its branches—archaeology, knowledge of ancient languages and deciphering of hieroglyphics, comparative religious study—like the work of plundering Egyptian artefacts to inaugurate national collections in museums in Paris and London, led to its inception. One of its main French instigators was Dominique Vivant Denon (1747–1825), who was among the 167 'savants' on Bonaparte's Egyptian expedition.[53] Thanks to his early training in Boucher's atelier and work as an engraver, Denon made many drawings of the antiquities he visited in both Lower and Upper Egypt. He also amassed a huge collection of artefacts before he returned with Napoleon to France in August 1799. He then published the two-volume *Voyage dans la Basse et la Haute Égypte* in 1802 (a foundational source for all future study of Eygptian antiquities, it was translated into English and German shortly after its French publication) before the first volume of the monumental record of the expedition, *La Description de l'Égypte,* appeared in 1810 dealing with 'Antiquités'.[54] From 1802 onwards, however, Denon was more than occupied with a bigger project, as General Director of Museums. During the first Empire, he organized the 'Musée Napoléon', which would become the Louvre, a wing of which facing the Seine is named after him and is situated behind the modern pyramid entrance.

If Denon visited Rosetta, the famous stone was discovered on 19 July 1799 by a French officer, Pierre François Xavier Bouchard, and it was quickly brought for examination to Napoleon's newly founded 'Institut d'Égypte' in Cairo, the home and hub of the savants' work. As 'enigma machine'—a plurilingual translation of the same text in ancient Egyptian hieroglyphs, demotic, and Greek—its significance beyond the immediate deciphering of its text was that it provided the key to reading other hieroglyphs. Various important steps were taken by the Frenchman Silvestre de Sacy and Johann David Akerblad, a Swede (that the demotic expressed foreign proper names by alphabetic signs), and Thomas Young in England (that groups of hieroglyphs corresponded to Greek words; and he sensed they were also phonetic). Working along similar lines to Young, Jean-François Champollion finally deciphered the Rosetta Stone in 1822. As mentioned above, the discovery that Coptic was very similar to the demotic text on the Rosetta Stone was no small part of the cracking of the code. This 'victory' over the English however also guaranteed France a serious place within the study and translation of ancient languages and comparative religions, fields which English and German experts largely dominated.[55] Champollion would then visit Egypt to apply his knowledge of Coptic, Ethiopian, Sanskrit, Chaldean, Persian, and ancient Egyptian hieroglyphics before being nominated a member of the Académie d'Inscriptions in Paris. In 1831 he was appointed to the chair of history and Egyptian archaeology at the Collège de France, a year before his early death of apoplexy. If Egyptology was now securely founded in France's academies, Egyptomania would await its spectacular expression in the Exposition Universelle of 1867,[56] where a reconstruction of Pharaonic tombs was organized under the supervision of Auguste Mariette. Ismail Pasha was the invited guest of honour at the inauguration ceremony. Mariette, who had discovered the entrance to the Serapeum in Memphis, was asked by Ismail to found and then direct the Egyptian Museum in Cairo 1858–80.

Part II of this study will examine the further significance of the museums of Paris and their Alexandrian (and Cairene) models in the dialogue about knowledge that the *Tentation* so explicitly remaps across all of its tableaux, but especially in tableaux five to seven. For the onward purposes of studying the *Tentation* as fictional remapping of religion and science in nineteenth-century France, suffice it to say that the seemingly static Egypt of St Anthony the Great has now proved a prism, the better to reflect larger interconnecting dialogues about ecclesiastical and imperial power, authority, domination and expansionist 'geographies' of knowledge. All coalesce in the ancient Egypt of fourth-century Alexandria as mirror for nineteenth-century France understood by means of its Egyptian campaigns. Let us now set out with Flaubert's Antoine on the *Tentation*'s disorienting mission to explore the fictional remapping of France's expedition to Egypt. Antoine's hallucinatory visions may then prove less of a phantasmagoria and more the work of creative and scientific genius.[57]

1

Description of Egypt

Il avait publié la *Tentation de saint Antoine*, troisième manière: long dialogue à la fois lyrique et savant qui, disait-il, 'devait être si rapide qu'il produirait l'effet de vision'.[1]

Rapidity of action would be the last phrase to come to mind to sum up the first tableau, or the *Tentation* as a whole. Endless description seems more to the point and a reason for the first chapter heading. It is in fact the transliteration of the title of the monumental, encyclopedic work on ancient and modern Egypt that resulted from Napoleon's Expédition.[2] In similar vein, a vortex of impossibly erudite and interminable referents disguised as 'temptations' seems rather closer to the mark than any 'effet de vision'. Their 'dialogue' with Antoine appears more of a relentless harangue than an encounter between equals. Description of Egypt from Antoine's point of view, vision, and knowledge, however, is the quintessential work (and hence action) of this seemingly static tableau in order to unify time, manner, and place, and to set the scene for the drama of conflicting powers and ideologies that fills the unfolding text. Part I has outlined the case for the *Tentation*'s three disorienting geographies—concentrated in ancient, fourth-, and nineteenth-century Egypt—and strikingly comparative religious histories—fourth-century Egyptian and nineteenth-century French Christianity and their others—folded into one another. For the inner and outer spaces and time frames of the text (as its surfaces and deeps) to inter-reflect as well as represent both 'the timelessness of icons and manuscript illuminations' and identifiable milieux of fourth-century Egypt mentioned in Part I, the first tableau is pivotal as map for the text's geographies, hagiographies, and semiologies. Antoine is the beholder we need to follow in all three if we are to make any sense with him of his 'vision' of nineteenth-century France. Critical failure to pay proper attention to the many facets of this opening tableau has meant that its keys to reading ensuing tableaux may also have been missed. Remapping tableau one from Antoine's perspectives will thus begin to shed light on the baffling plethora that has made the fantastic library of the *Tentation* so offputting to newcomer and specialist alike.[3]

GEOGRAPHIES

The 'medieval' Egypt that late eighteenth- and early nineteenth-century European and French travellers such as Volney (1757–1820[4]) discovered and documented on their first encounters, commencing mainly at Alexandria, included reference to the ruinous state of this country of Pharaonic and Roman antiquities, the desert landscape with its palette of mineral colours, the mêlée of peoples, languages, customs, goods, and animals visible and audible in the thronging markets and streets of Alexandria and Cairo. Noises, smells, colours all signified the exotic and alienating features of this Egypt which was both changeless and constantly changing with each new ruler-despot or set of internal strife and factionalism religious and national. In preparation for his own visit to Egypt and the Middle East with Maxime Du Camp in 1849–51, Flaubert had certainly read Volney as a key reference work although it is not listed in the bibliography for the *Tentation*.[5] To avoid anachronism, however, and at the same time graft contemporary experience of travel including his own into the timelessness of the Egypt of St Anthony the Great, Flaubert situates his Antoine from the outset in the seemingly stylized Egypt of Herodotus or Strabo, particularized to fit the context of Athanasius' hagiographical account of the *Vita Antonii*.[6] This desert region of Lower Egypt was where Anthony spend most of his life as the 'father of monasticism' and which Flaubert encapsulates in the incipit of the *Tentation*: 'C'est dans la Thébaïde[I], au haut d'une montagne, sur une plate-forme arrondie en demi-lune, et qu'enferment de grosses pierres' (*Tent*, 51).[7]

Gothot-Mersch first note instantly flags Flaubert's 'error' in situating his saint in the 'Thébaïde'—St Anthony did indeed spend the early, but not latter part of his life there prior to the Arian controversy— to 'symbolize' Antoine's eremitic desert dwelling. Athanasius' Anthony retreated from the Thebaid to Pispir near Memphis (a major site for the cult of Isis), where he established a monastic settlement. At the end of his life (the stage we are to imagine for Antoine), Anthony withdrew to Mount Colzum ('au haut d'une montagne') above the shores of the Red Sea (near the modern Suez), his cave becoming the site of the Coptic monastery of St Anthony. The mistake is that of the literal-minded critic not Flaubert. He was too well-read and informed, and too alert to authenticating detail everywhere in the *Tentation*, to have made such a deliberate 'error'. As with so many others in the *Tentation*, this detail which is a proper name allows the layered strata of significance to unfold later in the work and find a connective and analogical 'logic'. In this case the choice of milieu resonates with the longer history and importance of Thebes in ancient Egypt, and for the nineteenth-century archaeologist or Egyptologist. It was a locus of stratified temples to Amon, the Egyptian god of the sun (a Jupiter figure in the Egyptian pantheon), built and rebuilt by ancient Egyptian, Greek, and Roman rulers to their gods who will parade in this order in tableau five. Persons and places also interconnect in counterpoint since the pagan god Amon also resonates with the name of Antoine's disciple Ammon and of course the love-interest of the work, *Ammon*aria.[8]

Although the geography of Alexandria and the *Tentation* is more fully wrought in the dream sequence of the second tableau (as will be discussed in Chapter 2), Flaubert's opening décor therefore presents a rich amalgam of 'truth' and 'error', fact and fiction, artistic licence and 'photographic' accuracy in an allegedly topographical setting, homing in from the general to the particular (region, mountain top, semi-circular plateau surrounded by stones, Antoine's hut). However, the reader must also look out from the close-up on the few objects in the darkness of Antoine's 'cellule' to the wide-angle vistas only a mountain top (or a seer) can provide. What one is then physically enabled to 'envision' as if in the place of Antoine himself is further determined by the state of the light: 'le soleil s'abaisse' (*Tent*, 51). The monstrous hallucinations that come to Antoine in the half-light (within the space and light of the demi-lune),[9] or the bright sunlight (such as the face of Christ in the sun at the end), are then at once figments of his imagination *and* accounts of the reality of desert experience. Together they form the 'effet de vision' that the reader must piece together throughout the *Tentation* and the quandary of whether to dare to read *literally* in this work, as well as 'symbolically' as Gothot-Mersch chooses to do, to 'explain' the 'errors' or 'incongruence' of the narrative.

If we read the second and third paragraphs of the opening *mise en scène* as exercise in how to read the signs in front of us, literal and figurative meanings are completely enmeshed so that the real and imaginary/symbolic can readily change places. Description of what can be glimpsed 'inside' the 'cabane'—the 'cruche', 'pain noir', 'un gros livre', 'deux ou trois nattes', 'une corbeille'—names objects as things and yet signs or symbols depending on the reader's inclination. The hut is at once a 'Church' with an altar and Eucharistic elements set out upon it, and a reflection of the simplicity of Anthony's daily eremitic life, making rush mats and baskets to enable him to buy the bread. Outside the hut the cross and the 'vieux palmier' similarly mirror one another, but separate sign and natural phenomenon at the same time as they also mark out the precarious nature of 'Christianity' perched on this old religious landscape. Such economic and minimalist stage setting is thus Beckettian *avant la lettre* in its multiple interpretations,[10] but distinctly frames Flaubert's Antoine as future father of monasticism having overcome not only the outer desert, but, more importantly, overcoming the inner desert as well.[11] Antoine is therefore no novice hermit, plagued in the outer desert with blatant temptations of the flesh such as the seven deadly sins (Pride, Covetousness, Lust, Envy, Gluttony, Anger, and Sloth). As altogether medieval concepts their parts are drastically reduced in the 1874 text. In the inner desert, however, their temptation is more subtly invasive via the clamouring desires of the human carnal mind, especially the religious mind exercised and long practised in asceticism, solitude, poverty, life of prayer, and contemplation. This inner desert (and the intensity of the space of Antoine's mind to which the reader is a party) will be where Antoine is tested by onslaughts of deceptively familiar doctrines and ideas for the remainder of the text. In parallel, Antoine's practical basket making directly reflects his inner spiritual work: the separating of grain from chaff in the winnowing basket symbolizes the act of discernment and prayer.

If critics have overly looked into the *Tentation* in terms of its genesis and sources for their own sake, they have not looked out and down from it sufficiently, as the third paragraph of the *mise en scène* actively suggests should be a reading strategy. Concentric circles of vision open out and down from this high vantage point even if the ring of stones presents an immediate visual block, but also 'viewfinder'.[12] Where such views from a height will be later magnified by the Devil taking Antoine on the flight into space in tableau six, the immediate vista below the palm tree is of the Nile which 'semble faire un lac au bas de la falaise' (*Tent*, 51). Semblance and reality (and seeing as believing) will be questioned at every juncture of the ensuing text, but always within bounds of the *credible*. Realistic description and mirage are one and not the same in this instance.[13] Rippling water is a common illusion in the clear air and light of the desert sand, and sand aplenty lies beyond the ridge, 'immenses ondulations parallèles d'un blond cendré s'étirent les unes derrière les autres' (*Tent*, 51). Indeed, it was Monge who explained how mirages work at the second lecture of Napoleon's Institut d'Égypte in Cairo on 28 August 1798. Caused by the heating of the sand, the layer of air immediately above becomes rarefied and acts as a double-refracting mirror so that any real palms or villages on the horizon 'appear' close by, while the lakes of water are but an upside-down image of the edges of sky shimmering because of the vibrations of the light.[14] Further still is the chain of the Libyan mountains, also wall-like. The setting sun makes the purpling clouds look like a giant mane in the blue dome of the sky. Colours—'blond cendré', 'couleur de craie', 'violettes', 'teinte gris perle', 'pourpre', 'voûte bleue'—become a brown in the fading light, the blues a 'pâleur nacrée'; everything on the ground *appears* as hard as bronze, but suspended in the air is such a fine powdery gold that it 'se confond avec la vibration de la lumière' (*Tent*, 51–2). Here we have poetic attention to the natural world that merges physical and metaphysical description with the wonders of modern science and technology. Thomas has for example noted that the 'blond cendré' bespeaks the ash of steam engines and railways that have just become part of the French landscape.[15] Antoine's 'vision' is also their future: railways will appear in reality in the landscape of Egypt from 1851 thanks to the modernizing far-sightedness of Mohammed Ali and his successors. Thus the jewels and metals, colours and shimmering forms, are lyrical and 'erudite' in the sense of being religiously and scientifically informed, and will recur and metamorphose in various guises throughout the remainder of the text. The descriptions of wall and floor mosaics or flora and fauna in tableau four for example reuse all these component parts in new composite variations on seemingly different but actually similar themes.

Thus the *Tentation* everywhere plots the (in)credible through merging and shifting viewpoints and screens, and by analogy and refracting contrast. Just as 'miraculous' appearances in the manner of Antoine's visions have been discovered to have a real historical base in the many sightings of the Virgin throughout France from 1830 to 1870, so Antoine's 'religious' visions may have hugely future 'reality' as illustrated in the discoveries of nineteenth-century science.[16] Before the future can be mapped onto the present of the text, Antoine must first survey for the reader the interleaved geographies of his mind and of Egypt. This includes the past regions of his outer and inner desert experience, all modelled on his great precursor, simply recalled and capitalized under the title 'l'Ermite' (*Tent*, 51).

HAGIOGRAPHIES

The main purpose of the first tableau is to provide the reader with Antoine's spiritual credentials and curriculum vitae from his own mouth, but derived in his own version directly from Athanasius' hagiography exemplifying the *vita* form itself, the *Vita Antonii*. Critics have not noticed the unusual nature of Antoine's soliloquy (and therefore its importance): he will not pronounce again, or speak with any of the interlocutors who invade his space, in the ensuing tableaux of the *Tentation* at such length. Antoine's monologue reconstruction of episodes from his past therefore acts mainly as signposting for the 'temptations' to be visited upon him later (based principally on a past already lived, but come back to 'haunt' him in monstrously subverted form). But the angle of vision on his 'exemplary' past (of hagiography that will also be his future) is importantly the frame of his imperfect humanity in the present (incomplete saintliness), his 'grand soupir' (*Tent*, 52).

One of the problems already encountered with the description of real and figurative geographies above and Flaubert's highly economic, schematic, universalizing, yet detailed and specific choice of words is finding a reliable filter to read them appropriately and less erroneously. Clearly because the *Tentation* is not a parody or satire of the *Vita* or its religious remits,[17] a first premiss for reading Flaubert's Antoine, however differently he is recast, is that he remains largely faithful to the original St Anthony and the *Vita Antonii*. Without adherence to major 'lignes de force' of the character, namely his legendary, exemplary, saintly (but not biblical) status as thaumaturge and victorious adversary against theological and spiritual deception, Flaubert would lose the critical impact of variation on a known and recognizable figure, and the critical force this book is suggesting is the *raison d'être* of the whole. Failure to account for these 'lignes de force' has meant that even the best critics and editors of the text such as Gothot-Mersch make simple category mistakes. Her note to this 'soupir' serves as a clear example. Borrowing from the received critical wisdom Gothot-Mersch sees this as *ennui*, that is an integral part of 'l'absence totale d'enthouiasme dans l'ascèse' (*Tent*, note 3). An altogether Romantic sentiment, Baudelairian *ennui* might be foremost in the mind of a nineteenth-century or modern literary scholar. While this contemporary mental and poetic state is certainly a part of Antoine's characterization, it is also anachronistic without due recognition of its altogether spiritual form, acedia or accidie.[18] This is spiritual sloth, apathy, sadness, and indifference, a further sin of the flesh that aspiring anchorites needed to combat. For the faithful, this sin discouraged them from their religious work and the related sadness it brought would lead to feelings of dissatisfaction, discontent, and thus unhappiness with their present lot. By his first words, Flaubert's Antoine describes his spiritual temperature (acedia), and situation of dryness befitting experience of the 'inner' desert, and hence contrasting rectitude and resilience when compared with the seemingly easier, more victorious, past that he starts to recount. The whole first section discusses his past prayer life, his trips to fetch water while singing hymns, his basket and mat weaving, and his intercessions. All of this constitutes his *diligence*, the virtue which directly counteracts acedia as its opposite deadly sin. The zeal and attention to detail necessary for diligent work is captured in the humorous 'Ensuite je m'amusais à ranger tout dans ma cabane' (*Tent*, 52) since we have already had the inventory of his possessions. Antoine is therefore no hermit aspiring to the overcoming of acedia even if Hilarion in the third tableau squarely places Antoine's character under this besetting deadly sin: 'Voilà que tu retombes dans ton péché d'habitude, la paresse' (*Tent*, 92), in order to throw it back at his master as spiritual laziness to rethink articles of faith and conduct. It is the more invidiously *spiritual* guises of the seven deadly sins that Flaubert returns to the 1874 text, even if their popular 'medieval' forms have largely disappeared.[19] Flaubert's huge underscoring of Antoine's acedia-diligence in spiritual overcoming from the outset of the text thus sets up intertextual faithfulness to St Anthony the Great as model on the one hand and, on the other, provides the creative psychological and narratological determinants of the *Tentation*. Antoine's *stance* of withstanding/return to prayer allows the increasing magnitude of the temptations in unfolding tableaux to become visible, ending literally and metaphorically with the most monstrous in tableau seven. The bathetic 'happy end' (narrow victory), Antoine's vision of the face of Christ, is then 'true' to Athanasius' version and biblical precedents as it is also hugely ironic (as critics prefer to note).[20] We will be arguing in Chapter 7 that its irony lies elsewhere than as deflationary of Christianity, since Antoine ends the text as a modern ecstatic, a 'precursor' of St Theresa, and successor of the great biblical visionaries such as Daniel and St John the Divine.

Antoine's opening sigh is not therefore as aspirant, but as 'exhalant', offering a pneumatic/spiritual response to his situation in human and eternal time.[21] His 'dark night of the soul' is thus encapsulated in this moment of intense spiritual dryness (the inner and outer desert are one), which is always the place of spiritual attack, but then new *revelation*. But Flaubert further underscores this spiritual psychology by emphasizing Antoine's condition as 'misérable'. While the 'misérables' (the poor in spirit) of the beatitudes are assured that they will see God, this detail further authenticates not only Antoine's spiritual but also ethnic identities. Copts were renowned as 'misérables', as reported by many travellers and eighteenth-century 'ethnographers' such as Joseph Michaud (1767–1839).[22] The original Anthony of Egypt was also of wealthy, Coptic, origin and both his parents were Christians.[23] Antoine is now ready to tell us of his life in his own, hagiographical, words.

Athanasius' *Vita Antonii* would have been unknown to French readers without Greek or Latin (both of which Flaubert could attempt), although they would have been familiar with vernacular, medieval, hagiographies of which Voragine's *Légende dorée* is the most obvious.[24] Flaubert plundered Voragine for his version of St Julien l'Hospitalier, and the story of St Anthony entitled 'Saint Antoine, Ermite' (chapter 21), may be the intertext for that capitalized job description above. Voragine's severely abridged version of Athanasius' model focuses on Anthony's early training in the Egyptian tombs in the overcoming of devils, his working of miracles, his sayings and visions, the most important of which was the rise of Arianism and its persecution of Christians. Anthony's spiritual interventions on this and throughout his saintly life are narrated in a rather matter-of-fact manner since his exemplary life is precisely that. It is the most colourful passage from Voragine's Anthony that Flaubert most clearly embroiders in Antoine's soliloquy, his early experience in coenobitic life in the 'tombeau d'un Pharaon'. Compare the following section from the first of the six sections in Voragine's version with Flaubert's distillation:

Aussitôt Antoine vendit tous ses biens, en donna le produit aux pauvres, et alla se faire ermite au désert. Il eut à y soutenir des tentations innombrables de la part des démons. Un jour qu'il avait vaincu par sa foi le démon de la luxure, le diable lui apparut sous la forme d'un enfant noir, et, se prosternant devant lui, se reconnut vaincu. Une autre fois, comme il était dans une tombe d'Égypte, la foule des démons le maltraita si affreusement qu'un de ses compagnons le crut mort et l'emporta sur ses épaules: mais . . . il se releva et demanda à l'homme qui l'avait apporté de le rapporter à l'endroit où il l'avait trouvé. Et comme il y gisait, accablé de la douleur que lui causaient ses blessures, les démons reparurent, sous diverses formes d'animaux féroces, et se remirent à le déchirer avec leurs dents, leurs cornes, et leurs griffes. Alors, soudain, une lumière merveilleuse remplit le caveau, et mit en fuite tous les démons; et Antoine se trouva aussitôt guéri. Et alors, comprenant que c'était Jésus qui venait à son secours, le saint lui dit: 'Où étais-tu tout à l'heure, bon Jésus . . . ?' Et le Seigneur lui répondit: 'Antoine, j'étais là, mais j'attendais de voir ton combat; et maintenant que tu as lutté avec courage, je répandrai ta gloire dans le monde entier!' Et telle était la ferveur du saint, que lorsque l'empereur Maximien mettait à mort les chrétiens, il suivait les martyrs jusqu'au lieu de leur supplice, espérant être supplicié avec eux; et il s'affligeait fort de voir que le martyre lui était refusé.   (*LD*, 87–8)[25]

D'abord, j'ai choisi pour demeure le tombeau d'un Pharaon. Mais un enchantement circule dans ces palais souterrains, où les ténèbres ont l'air épaissies par l'ancienne fumée des aromates. Du fond des sarcophages j'ai entendu s'élever une voix dolente qui m'appelait; ou bien, je voyais vivre, tout à coup, les choses abominables peintes sur les murs; et j'ai fui jusqu'au bord de la mer Rouge dans une citadelle en ruines. Là, j'avais pour compagnie des scorpions se traînant parmi les pierres, et au-dessus de ma tête, continuellement des aigles, qui tournoyaient sur le ciel bleu. La nuit, j'étais déchiré par des griffes, mordu par des becs, frôlé par des ailes molles; et d'épouvantables démons, hurlant dans mes oreilles, me renversaient par terre. Une fois même des gens d'une caravane qui s'en allait vers Alexandrie m'ont secouru, puis emmené avec eux. (*Tent*, 53)

Gone are any 'comfortable' words in Flaubert's version that prove Christ's presence encouraging Anthony all the while to overcome. The textual, dramatic, and perhaps also Romantic irony is that Flaubert's Antoine will have to wait for this 'reward' for his perseverance against the demons and battles with temptation and Satan until the last, anti-climactic line of the text. However, more realistic and non-fantastical modes of narration are embroidered into the new version. While in keeping with Voragine's matter-of-factness (which will contrast with Philostratus' endlessly miraculous *vita* of Apollonius in tableau four), the imaginative elaborations are at once 'biblical' and 'scientific'. The 'choses abominables peintes sur les murs' (which will be further exploited in tableau five) evoke the prophet Elijah's experience of being shown the abominations and crawling things on the walls of the temple by 'a figure like that of a man' (Ezekiel 8: 2, 9–10).[26] At the same time, Flaubert is making direct reference to the archaeological discoveries by Champollion of the hieroglyphics in the tombs of the Valley of the Kings. Emphasis on the fauna of the region also sets in place what will prove a running thread in the analogical narratives of ensuing tableaux leading inextricably to the strange creatures of tableau seven. The demon birds also provide the narrative link with Antoine's specu-lations (*Tent*, 55 and following) of what he might have done with his life had other directions been taken. His seemingly irrelevant account of Ammon going to Rome while he stayed at home, speculation on his greater effect had he become either a teacher-philosopher or taken religious orders, puts in place two episodes from the life of his modern alter ego to which we will return in Part II.

Throughout Antoine's retelling of his curriculum vitae, what has gone from Voragine is the miraculous, apocryphal, or apophthegmatic con-tent. Flaubert's Antoine makes himself out to be a rather 'un-muscular' Christian, one who does not appear to have accomplished anything that would mark him out as extraordinary (let alone a saint) in any way. His account seems merely a 'textbook' copy of the key components or episodes which constitute a *vita*—the formulaic account of early child-hood and education, call to a religious vocation, rejection of parents and the world, oppositions (secular and spiritual) and their victorious overcoming, mature period of activity and wisdom (including visions, miracles, and bodily translations to other parts of the globe), declining years, and final glorious death—and those lessons which determined the genre of which Voragine's is the imitation.[27] Similarly Anthony's involvement with church and state politics (consultations by Athanasius regarding Arian heresy or by Constantine regarding the nation state), or more personal disappointments—not to be among the martyrs, the loss of Hilarion his disciple—are made out to be incidentals in Flaubert's version.[28] If Antoine's soliloquy about his past can then be fitted into one long breath, the struggles to overcome even greater onslaughts in the ensuing text will 'prove' his spiritual stature only the more. Antoine's severely downplayed recapitulation of his past also prevents him committing the sin of pride or claiming (anachronistically) some particularity for an individual self.[29]

  Antoine's humble account therefore relies on others having told a different story of exemplary, even supernatural, life for him, including rapture or flights in the spirit.[30] The paradox is that the less Antoine gives the reader to particularize or aggrandize himself, the more he will do precisely that in contrast to the two-dimensional 'hero' stereotypes such as Apollonius to come. Thus his greatest actions and overcoming *of the past* are confined to a list, as if in one breath:

C'est par mon ordre qu'on a bâti cette foule de retraites saintes, pleines des moines portant des cilices sous leurs peaux de chèvres, et nombreux à pouvoir faire une armée! J'ai guéri de loin des malades; j'ai chassé des démons; j'ai passé le fleuve au milieu des crocodiles; l'empereur Constantin m'a écrit trois lettres; Balacius [*sic*], qui avait craché sur les miennes, a été déchiré par ses chevaux; le peuple d'Alexandrie, quand j'ai reparu, se battait pour me voir, et Athanase m'a reconduit sur la route. Mais aussi quelles œuvres! Voilà plus de trente ans que je suis dans le désert à gémir toujours! J'ai porté sur mes reins quatre-vingts livres de bronze comme Eusèbe, j'ai exposé mon corps à la piqûre des insectes comme Macaire, je suis resté cinquante-trois nuits sans fermer l'œil comme Pacôme; et ceux qu'on décapite, qu'on tenaille ou qu'on brûle ont moins de vertu, peut-être, puisque ma vie est un continuel martyre!   (*Tent*, 60–1)[31]

Flaubert not only exploits Voragine's St Anthony here: for example Bal-lachius, an Egyptian leader and Arian, is specifically mentioned in the last section. He also expands (and downplays) St Anthony's (and hence Antoine's) prowess and exemplariness as anchorite, healer, and miracle worker by direct comparison with other saintly contemporaries (Macar-ius, Eusebius, Pachomius) as also told in Voragine's *Légende dorée*.[32] What the reader is to witness are Antoine's present spiritual onslaughts, the attacks on his human carnal mind and lived theology. Antoine's confrontation and combat then allows pointed critical comment by analogy on similar nineteenth-century French authorities, principalities, and powers.

Flaubert is however also drawing from the most modern version of the *Vita Antonii* for the many exploits that are now pluralized in the above passage. In 1858, a less expurgated French translation of Athanasius' text was available for the first time, the *Vie de saint Antoine par saint Athanase* by the Abbé Auguste-François Maunoury. Despite appearing on Flaubert's bibliography for the *Tentation*, it has never been the subject of critical comment. Maunoury was a prolific scholar and popularizer of Greek and Latin texts often for younger readers. As the preface to his *Vie de saint Antoine* overtly states, it was for this young audience (the target age is 7 upwards) that he relates the story for its imaginative and moral appeal, but with the theological longueurs of the original (such as the Arian heresy debates) deliberately excised. Maunoury puts in a nutshell the status and significance of Anthony almost over and above his renown as the 'father of monasticism' for his readers thus:

Saint Antoine est un des hommes les plus admirables que le christianisme ait produits. Destiné par la Providence à créer la vie monastique, il l'a tout d'un coup élevée par ses conseils et par ses exemples à une hauteur qu'elle n'a point dépassée dans les âges suivants. Il se retire au fond d'un désert et les peuples l'y suivent, attirés par sa sainteté. Des villes se fondent autour de sa cellule. On s'entretient de lui, non-seulement dans toute l'Égypte, sa patrie, mais dans l'Asie, à Constantinople, à Rome, en Espagne et dans les Gaules. Ce moine sans lettres fait l'étonnement d'un siècle fécond en grands hommes. Les docteurs invoquent son autorité sur les plus hautes questions de la théologie; les païens le vénèrent; les hérétiques le redoutent. Saint Athanase l'appelle pour confondre les ariens.... Le grand Constantin, maître du monde, lui envoie des ambassadeurs, reçoit ses conseils avec respect.... La vie, les combats et les miracles de saint Antoine nous ont été racontés par un témoin qui a longtemps vécu avec lui, par un des plus fermes génies dont l'Église s'honore, par saint Athanase.[33]

It will be against this blueprint (*Tent*, 60–1 above is arguably a calque of it) that Antoine will be configured as central protagonist situated from the outset at the point in his life where Maunoury's sketch ends, that is still undergoing the onslaughts of spiritual attacks on his mind and faith in a fourth-century AD Egypt, but as a mature veteran of ideological, theological, and spiritual battles. Asia, Constantinople, Rome, and 'Gaul' will indeed invade his 'cell' in Flaubert's version as subsequent chapters will elucidate. However, a few of the most graphic, vivid, and imaginative scenes in Maunoury's version (describing Antoine's attacks from and overcoming of demons in many guises especially in his early initiation into his eremitical and thaumaturgical vocation for example) are retained or deployed overtly by Flaubert. This is because they belong strictly to the formative, rather than the mature, part of Anthony's career, and are consequently misplaced in the final *Tentation*. They have in fact already been overtly reworked by Flaubert into revisions of his *Légende de saint Julien l'Hospitalier*.[34]

Flaubert's mosaic of unextraordinary sources is then the 'scientific' authentication for what seem the most incredible or fantastical elements in Antoine's past life and experience as they issue from his own mouth in this opening scene. The even more fantastical patchwork of experiences to come (based on 'real' sources or events) will map onto nineteenth-century French realities. If Flaubert had originally lacked the 'plan' for the *Tentation*, and psychological depths for his main protagonist, both are vitally here in Antoine's soliloquy which introduces the reader to all the key players to come. Not least of these are the heresiarchs and the Gymnosophist (*Tent*, 53) in readiness for tableau four, or Hilarion and the intellectual and spiritual melting pots of Alexandria (*Tent*, 54) in readiness for tableaux three to five, and then five to seven, of the *Tentation* respectively. Only retrospective reading of these shorthands (or Antoine's principle of naming only certain people or events of the past, the better to elucidate the present and the future) allows their fuller comparative significance to emerge. Flaubert can then take huge liberties with his own (anti-)hagiography of Antoine, as he will do with St Julien and Hérodias in the *Trois Contes*, to introduce 'purely' fictional elements or characters as foils for the more 'serious' contents. Two figures apart from Ammon at the end of Antoine's soliloquy exemplify this gross unfaithfulness to any source, Ammonaria, and Didymus the Blind who, as Gothot-Mersch punctiliously notes, is an anachronism. In actual fact so too is Ammonaria. Because both figures are blatantly *additions*, both have several strategic and connective functions for Flaubert's remapping of nineteenth-century France through their framing of thoroughly legendary fourth-century Egyptian religious historicity.

Ammonaria was a virgin and martyr in Alexandria in AD 250.[35]
Little is known about her, especially perhaps because she has failed to
find a designated place with the many other virgin martyrs (including the 11,000 virgins) that intersperse the tales of male saints in
Voragine's *Légende dorée*.[36] Catholic dictionaries of saints however
ascribe to 12 December Saints Ammonaria, Mercuria, Dionysa, and
another even more shadowy Ammonaria, all martyred together in
Alexandria during the persecutions of Christians in the reign of the
Emperor Decius. The first Ammonaria endured all manner of hideous
tortures for her faith, but failed to recant. Eventually the judge was so
humiliated by Ammonaria's steadfastness and refusal to submit that he
ordered her beheading by the sword. Flaubert's Ammonaria is everywhere an at least double figure as *virgin*-martyr/temptress-*inspiration*,
as her clothing and the responses of other *men* to her everywhere
illustrate. The first reference to her is in Antoine's earliest memories of
his necessary departure from his home and affluent family to respond to
his call to eremitism, poverty, and celibacy. As cattle herd, Ammonaria's
youth ('cette enfant'), unfettered movement and freedom ('Elle a couru
après moi. Les anneaux de ses pieds brillaient dans la poussière'), and
almost boyish attire ('sa tunique ouverte sur les hanches flottait au vent',
all *Tent*, 52) are underscored. It is the 'vieil ascète' leading Antoine
away who yells abuse at her as 'temptress' to his pupil's resolve, who
speaks for the moralizing reader's interpretation of Ammonaria's place as
the 'love-interest' in a work.[37] Ammonaria reappears again in Antoine's
reminiscences, this time when he has become the 'father' of other hermit
followers to connect with his 'soif du martyre' (*Tent*, 54). This takes
him to Alexandria in his desire to become one himself at the time
of intense persecution (under Decius) and in front of the Temple to
Serapis (the significance of which will be developed in the second and
later tableaux), where he witnesses the violent whipping of a naked
woman who may have been Ammonaria. She then comes to his mind
again when he returns to reminiscences of his early life at the beginning
of the seventh tableau (*Tent*, 217) when he speculates whether she
would ever have left his dying mother, and then on her lithe body
and long hair as she undresses for bed. These reflections of the virgin-
martyr/inspiration-temptress are then the direct link to the apparitions
of the Vieille and her younger accomplice whom Antoine mistakes for
Ammonaria but who is quickly seen to be more of a Queen of Sheba

figure. Ammonaria's young body and her resolve remain locked together throughout the text in the horror of this period of the history of the early Church, where the pursuit of martyrdom even became a sect in its own right.[38] Flaubert will make much of the excesses of all religions in what ensues. Ammonaria is therefore a harbinger of spiritual excesses— religious persecution, martyrdom, eremitism, zealotry, and misplaced sexual prurience-abstinence—and a figure of perdurance which brings Antoine to the final scenes of the text. As female double her name heralds the many ambiguous doublings that will occur concerning various male figures with Christian/anti-Christian significance. One such is the male version of her name, Am(m)on, both an early Christian martyr and an Egyptian god with the status and equivalent function of Jupiter.

Didymus is mentioned only twice, here and in tableau seven. His function is not merely as a 'bon vieillard'. Renowned as blind from the age of 4 onwards he was one of the most learned men of his age in matters doctrinal and intellectual, although Flaubert is quite specific in naming only the former 'aucun ne l'égalait dans la connaissance des Écritures' (*Tent*, 53). If Didymus is inserted here as the first master (of Antoine) in a study of master–disciple relationships—Antoine's own with Hilarion is a major motor for divergence and dissensions that allow the heretical aspects of the text to emerge, the master–disciple relationship of Apollonius and Damis will be a turning point in the work[39]—Didymus has a much more significant place as a shorthand for Antoine's own stand and stance in the third, fourth, and final tableaux. Flaubert allows his Antoine to lead the blind Didymus around major landmarks of Alexandria, so that the reader may 'see' all signifiers of the indomitable power of Egypt as trading nation and hence as importer of ideas and religions from every known, exotic, and far-flung corner of the globe summed up in the phrase 'des Cimmériens vêtus de peaux d'ours, et des Gymnosophistes du Gange frottés de bouse de vache'. In this melting pot, antagonism and factionalism is the obvious effect of multicultural influx, from the Jews who refuse to pay taxes to 'des séditieux qui voulaient chasser les Romains', leading in a second breath to the 'hérétiques, des sectateurs de Manès, de Valentin, de Basilide, d'Arius—tous vous accaparant pour discuter et vous convaincre' (*Tent*, 53). Flaubert will construct the fourth tableau around this sentence as key to the mapping of (nineteenth-century) heresies.[40] On the arm of

Didymus, Antoine is already seen as the overcomer of them all, but especially Arianism, since Didymus was one of the principal opponents of this heresy and much respected by Athanasius for his Trinitarianism (that is the unity of the Trinity as *treis hypostaseis, mia ousia* at the heart of Roman Catholic doctrine).[41] Because Didymus was a follower of Origen, who was later anathematized for his heretical teachings, his important writings (for example against the Manicheans and on the Holy Spirit) were considered heretical and hence were not collected into medieval treatises. Flaubert may have accessed some references to Didymus' extant works as they come down through Tillmont (volume x) and Migne (volume xxxix). However, Didymus' position in Alexandria strategically encapsulates the theological and philosophical debates which Antoine and Hilarion will pursue in tableau three. Didymus was the head of the famous Catechetical School of Alexandria for more than fifty years and was a major teacher of Scripture (Jerome and Rufinus were his pupils), but had an equal reputation in grammar, rhetoric, geometry, and arithmetic. In short, he was the polymathic head of one of the world's primary academies.[42] Didymus is therefore the embodiment of knowledge (religious and secular) of this period, all branches of which Flaubert will exploit and interweave as the forms and ideas which will manifest themselves in Antoine's mind. We will return to how he is a prefiguration of important nineteenth-century men of religious 'science' in Part II.

SEMIOLOGIES

The *legendary* Anthony has therefore become a factual retelling in Antoine's mouth, to bring the reader to the 'present' of narration and history through the geography of Alexandria and its environs (*Tent*, 56). Fourth-century daily life in the city Alexandria looks much the same as from time immemorial (and for French nineteenth-century travellers), presented as an idyll of almost utopian harmony. As Gothot-Mersch has noted (*Tent*, 293), this passage owes much to Strabo. Merchants go boating from Canopus on holidays, drinking to the sound of tambourines. The countryside beyond the city seems at peace, but in a relation of master to peasant. Nineteenth-century readers would, however, have been richly aware of the very negative associations of

Canopus, and it seems significant that this place name is the only one which particularizes this passage. Antoine's final speculation on whether he might not better have become a soldier than an anchorite makes the connection. At the Battle of Canopus (end of March 1801), the French were roundly defeated by the Anglo-Ottoman army. Denon's *Voyage dans la Basse et la Haute Égypte pendant les campagnes du général Bonaparte* (1802) would chronicle the massacre and the dead bodies strewn on the beaches. His *Voyage* also chronicles his visit to the ancient ruins of Canopus, particularly the temple of Isis, known as a place of 'volupté' and of miraculous healings. Denon's work is not in the bibliography for the *Tentation*. It is however remakable how closely his *Voyage* at this juncture reverberates with the *Tentation* (and Flaubert's own experience of Egypt), by providing a seamless transition from ancient Canopus to the jackals to Antoine lying on the ground on his side before moving to the final section of tableau one (the 'Bible'-reading scene):

Le sol n'a rien conservé de l'antique volupté canopite;... cette ville, jadis si délicieuse, et qui n'offre plus qu'un aspect triste et sauvage. Il est vrai que le canal dont parle Strabon, qui communiquoit d'Alexandrie à Éleusine, ce qui par un embranchement arrivoit à Canope, et apportoit la fraîcheur, a disparu de telle sorte qu'on ne peut en distinguer la trace, ni même concevoir la possibilité de son existence.... Enfin cette ville, qui rassembloit toutes les délices, où affluoient tous les voluptueux, n'est plus maintenant qu'un désert que traversent quelques chacals et des Bédouins: je n'y trouvai point des derniers; mais je vis un chacal, que j'eusse pris pour un chien, si je n'avois eu le temps d'examiner très distinctement son nez pointu et ses oreilles dressées, sa queue plus longue, traînante, et garnie de poil comme celle du renard.... [J]e repris la route d'Aboukir.... Je me mis en route par une nuit obscure... mais à trois heures du matin j'arrivai à Rosette, et j'allai me reposer voluptueusement, je ne dirai pas dans mon lit, je n'en avois pas vu depuis mon départ de France, mais dans une chambre fraîche, sur une natte propre.[43]

Wild monster beasts, Eleusinian mysteries, 'voluptés', Isis all lie ahead for Flaubert's Antoine. In the immediacy of the text and the breaking of any illusion of idyll,

Dans l'obscurité blanchâtre de la nuit, apparaissent çà et là des museaux pointus, avec des oreilles toutes droites et des yeux brillants. Antoine marche vers eux. Des graviers déroulent, les bêtes s'enfuient. C'était un troupeau de chacals.

Un seul est resté, et qui se tient sur deux pattes, le corps en demi-cercle et la tête oblique, dans une pose pleine de défiance.   (*Tent*, 56)

The figurative, allusive, and literal all coalesce here to entwine and unfold the three levels of reading that the *Tentation* will constantly engage, notwithstanding the layering of these in time and space. Are these monsters demons in disguise, intertexts from Denon, or 'simply' jackals? How should we read these signs with Antoine? And even if the 'C'était un troupeau de chacals' unequivocally determines that literal meaning is the correct level on which to read, why does one creature stand in 'human' defiance on two legs? Is this prefigurative of a lineage of creatures to come?

It is exegesis, then, that is the final lesson in reading the *Tentation* that tableau one teaches, the theme perfectly meshed with content, Antoine's study of the 'gros livre' in the (saving) shadow of the two arms of the cross. Only the most obvious of the five Bible quotations given, the third and fifth, have elicited critical mention because they obviously provide proleptic signposts to the main set pieces in tableau two, the story of Nebuchadnezzar and the Queen of Sheba.[44] However, these five seemingly unrelated and bizarre fragments from different books of the Bible need to be examined further since this is the only part of the *Tentation* where Antoine demonstrates the lessons he has learned from his Bible teacher, Didymus, and by inference where he reveals his own *via contemplativa* and understanding of Scripture. While all five introduce severally a number of scenes to come, more importantly they impart advice between the lines to the reader on how Antoine's responses to the temptations in later tableaux should also be read.

The deeper connections between these disparate Bible texts are carefully constructed, although the apparent sense is of some rather ignorant person randomly opening the book at various points as if it might tell their fortune.[45] Antoine's state of mind is also carefully noted: the first reading depends on his deliberately chosen starting point, the Acts of the Apostles, although Antoine has no specific passage in mind. Peter's vision of the tablecloth covered with animals of every clean and unclean kind for a devout Jew includes reference to the divine voice commanding Peter to get up and eat. Antoine's almost flippant response is the unfinished 'tandis que moi...' because of his continuous fast, but the command to eat all foods most obviously heralds the feast of Nebuchadnezzar in tableau two, and also the theme of prohibitions (divine and secular). A more 'random' opening of the 'gros livre' the third time finds Antoine's commentary on this king bowing down to Daniel, although the specific connections with the well-known feast and its aftermath are not made. It is the reader who is left to provide the appropriate contexts or hold in question unresolved pieces of the text. The debates about the kinds of animals depicted in this divine vision to Peter will for example find other meanings in the final tableau of the monsters, as too will the fact that Nebuchadnezzar (and Antoine) are reduced to moving 'à quatre pattes'. Moreover, this sole New Testament reading reframes the mirage in the initial geographies of the tableau to alert the reader to another mode of 'real' visual experience, visions. This particular vision and the horror of Peter's response offer a paradigm by which to validate experiences Antoine is about to have (and will have had since his spiritual credentials are to be taken as *read*).

But the idea of prohibitions and their reversal that can be interpreted behind the story of the divine tablecloth directly links by some lateral thinking to the second, much less familiar Bible passage, which Antoine arrives at by the combination of the now rustling wind in the pages and his momentary glance heavenwards. Either a comic introduction of 'chance' or a representation of the movement of the Holy Spirit as the wind of the Word, Antoine next reads from the Book of Esther (the only book in the Bible to be named after a Jewish queen). The horror of the Jews' massacring of their enemies (Esther 9: 5) is glossed at much greater length by Antoine thus demonstrating his knowledge of the *contexts* of what seems a totally inhuman extermination of enemies because they are enemies. Early church history after Anthony's death will prove a repetition: the Christian persecution of the pagans and Neoplatonists includes Hypatia their most famous woman philosopher. Excess and huge numbers link the two readings quite explicitly: orgies of consumption and frenzied killing of enemy others ultimately define spectacularly degrading characteristics of the human spiritual animal. The immediate context of the Battle of Canopus brings a chillingly contemporary, and French, spin to this second reading. It also prepares for the thematic agendas of Antoine's later behaviour (self-flagellation) and 'hallucinations', especially tableau four with its many idolaters, fanatical self-immolators, and martyrs for 'true' or false religions.[46]

The fourth Scripture (2 Kings 20: 13a) matches the second for its unfamiliarity, and how Antoine arrives upon it; his laughter at imagining Nebuchadnezzar on all fours causes his hand to disturb the leaves of the text. Antoine does not expound on the context or outcome of Hezekiah's action (God punishes his disobedience), but gives his imagination fuller play on the excessive amounts of treasures in the king's storehouses and the nature of demonstrating kingly power by showing it off. Hezekiah's act was one of folly (is there a thinly veiled reference to the overreaching misuse of wealth by Louis XVI?), but it leads in Antoine's exegetical mind—'il feuillette vivement' (returning the wind in the 'feuilles' of the previous reading to conscious human act)—to a counter-example, 1 Kings 10, where Solomon (representing the pinnacle of known human kingly power and knowledge, and wisest anointed ruler of the children of Israel) displays all his wealth and knowledge before the visiting Queen of Sheba (representing all the power, wealth, and knowledge of the East). Antoine's all-important gloss on the final reading will be analysed in more detail in Chapter 2. The reading lessons to learn for the *Tentation* are then that its (inter)texts and tableaux should be read individually (in their own contexts), collectively for their perspectives on analogous histories or themes and their variations, and with a strong eye for chronology and geography. While shuttling by analogy forwards and backwards between ancient and modern forms of similar events in the history of civilization(s) and the Old and New Testaments, Antoine is in fact reading the Scriptures *in reverse chronological order.* This vital point will pertain to the overall remapping that the whole *Tentation* undertakes as we will discover in Chapters 5 and 7. This reading of Scripture backwards from New to Old Testaments, like Antoine's curriculum vitae (incomplete 'hagiography'), also looking backwards in time to come forwards to the present of narration (which is in the reader's past), is particularly significant. The Old Testament is not so much a prefiguration of the New as its foundation *en abyme.* Implicit too in this whole interconnected set of exegeses is the idea of the Fall, and towards superstition, as Chapter 5 will elucidate.

Antoine, moreover, concludes his readings at a pivotal moment in Old Testament church history—just after Solomon's building of the

Temple, a zenith prior to his 'adulteries' with the other gods of the East thanks to his many wives—of which the establishment of the Christian Church in the teeth of these established religions is a further New Testament echo. The papacy of Pius IX offers a further direct, nineteenth-century French parallel and contrast,[47] clearly illuminated by Antoine's *retrospective* reflections on his own life of poverty and self-abnegation as against the pomp and circumstance of the 'Pères de Nicée'. Whereas Voragine's version based on Athanasius presents the Arian crisis as a prophecy given to Anthony,[48] Flaubert removes any overtly prophetic, visionary insights from his own character by his remarkable cameo of Antoine *recalling* and *judging* the events as if he was an eyewitness and protagonist at the Council of Nicaea, called by Constantine in 325:[49]

Les Pères de Nicée, en robes de pourpre, se tenaient comme des mages, sur des trônes, le long du mur; et on les a régalés dans un banquet, en les comblant d'honneurs, surtout Paphnuce, parce qu'il est borgne et boiteux depuis la persécution de Doclétien! L'Empereur lui a baisé plusieurs fois son œil crevé; quelle sottise! Du reste, le Concile avait des membres si infâmes! Un évêque de Scythie, Théophile; un autre de Perse, Jean; un gardeur de bestiaux, Spiridion! Alexandre était trop vieux. Athanase aurait dû montrer plus de douceur aux Ariens, pour en obtenir des concessions!...Ah! Que ne puis-je les faire exiler tous par l'Empereur, ou plutôt les battre, les écraser, les voir souffrir! Je souffre bien, moi! (*Tent*, 61–2)

How wickedly Flaubert remaps modern 'Conciles' and their confraternities ('[ils] se tenaient comme des mages') since Vatican I called by Pius IX during the rule of Napoleon III has taken place in 1870 shortly before Flaubert finishes the final *Tentation*. These 'mages' will also be transformed otherwise in tableau two and in tableaux six and seven. Power will rarely be the glory in the *Tentation*.

Antoine's lessons on exegesis in tableau one implicitly inform the reader about the mesh of theme to content, but also both to context(s) in the *Tentation* to come. As a patchwork of pieces about greater wholes, the lessons emulate the *Stromata* of Clement of Alexandria (*c*.150–*c*.215) in form and aim ('stroma' means a coverlet, bedspread, or sack in which to put bedclothes[50]). This was to challenge solely symbolic or allegorical readings of Scripture, and the rich tradition of scriptural interpretation as instigated by the Jewish exegete Philo of Alexandria, who had translated the Hebrew Bible into Greek (the Septuagint). As Georges Minois puts it,

Alors que jusqu'là, l'exégèse chrétienne était restée de type judaïque palestinien, c'est-à-dire recherchait dans les textes les sens prophétique, apocalyptique et typologique, Clément distingue cinq manières d'interpréter l'Écriture: il faut y distinguer le sens historique, le sens doctrinal et théologique, le sens prophétique, le sens philosophique, le sens mystique. La détermination du sens mystique, qui se fera par la méthode allégorique philonienne, devra utiliser toutes les richesses de la culture grecque, et en particulier les connaissances scientifiques. Celles-ci, appliquées au donné de la révélation scripturaire, permettront, par une démonstration logique et certaine, de parvenir à l'évidence, à la vérité unique, à la connaissance absolue, à la gnose. Clément prône la collaboration entre la science humaine et la révélation divine pour atteindre la vérité.... Non seulement il doit y avoir lecture parallèle du livre de la nature et du livre inspiré, mais le déchiffrement du premier doit aider à la compréhension du second, qui reste essentiel.[51]

Origen would be Clement's pupil, and hence connect with the life and times of St Anthony. The *Stromata* are seen as watershed works alongside those of Origen and St Ireneus in bringing intellectual (rational) understanding to Scripture in the fullest sense and to distinguish 'proper' exegesis from traditions seeking hidden meanings in names and numbers.[52] Clement's *The Instructor* (the *Paedogogus*) is mentioned in Flaubert's bibliography for the *Tentation*. The *Stromata* are a similarly baggy monster of subjects covered in the *Tentation*. Exegesis of Scripture for its historical implications is resoundingly on the agenda among exegetes in nineteenth-century France, such as Renan, as the third chapter will explore.

Out of these seemingly disconnected but connected points of fact, it seems clear that attention to detail and the bigger pictures lie at the heart of reading the *Tentation*. Literal, allegorical, figurative, comparative, analogical, and reverse chronological modes of interpretation will be used in the chapters to follow as we remap nineteenth-century French ideas through the 'temptations' of Flaubert's Antoine. The fun of the text can then be sought out to displace the overwhelming erudition. Flaubert's balancing act is to make Antoine true to what would have been known in his fourth-century contexts, in order to prevent him becoming an anachronism for his nineteenth-century ones, yet as visionary viewer of them, their best commentator. Reading guided by Antoine at several levels at once is thus *de rigueur*. Following Clement of Alexandria the *Tentation*'s first chapter has begun literally with the Book of (a) Life, and will end with the Book of Nature, to come full circle to where it began, in descriptions of the geographical and historical land of Egypt.

2

Principalities and Powers

The unities of time and place set up in tableau one shade seamlessly (by the dwindling half-light) at its end into the action of tableau two. Antoine's physical perception of the arriving shadows, the extinguishing of his torch, and his ensuing mental blackout as the images whirl vertiginously around him cut through all the time frames of waking consciousness (past, present, conditional, future) and take the reader into worlds beyond it—dream and nightmare, vision and apparition, hallucination and delirium, hearing 'voices'—although not into the Freudian unconscious.[1] These much-considered phenomena by Romantics such as Coleridge and Baudelaire experimenting with alcohol- and drug-induced mental states were under extensive physiological and psychological scrutiny by nineteenth-century French philosopher-scientists such as Esquirol, Garnier, and Maury.[2] Medicine was also examining the physiological and mental symptoms of epilepsy and syphilis.[3] Yet it is not on these netherworlds of medical science that Flaubert's critics of this tableau have focused (although intriguingly Flaubert uses the medical term 'cataleptique' (*Tent*, 70) as vital connector to 'Alexandria').[4] No critical examination has been mounted either on how this scene parodies Underworlds such as Virgil's Hades, Dante's Hell, Egyptian Places of the Dead through its descriptions of mazelike cities, thanks to Antoine's specific reference just before attempting to seize his knife ('Si j'étais mort pendant ce temps-là, c'était l'enfer! l'enfer irrévocable' (*Tent*, 69)). Critics have also failed to comment on Flaubert's Devil presiding, unnoticed, over its whole in a Gothic caricature of himself as giant, Dracula, or vampire.[5] Instead, through reading mainly from Freudian psychoanalytic or genetic critical perspectives critics have been most fascinated by the powerful brew of debauchery (Nebuchadnezzar's feast, his eating grass like a cow), animal drives, and sexual temptation (the Queen of Sheba's seduction).[6] Whatever their approach, most critics of the 1874 *Tentation* then concur with Taine shortly after its publication that the Queen of Sheba set piece is particularly magnetic, not least aesthetically, as the high note in an otherwise monotonous and dull work.[7]

But has critical familiarity with these two lyrical characters, which allegedly titillate or entertain the reader's fantasies, bred critical contempt for the rest of this thoroughly 'purple' tableau?[8] The 'Nebuchadnezzar' scene constitutes only a tiny, concluding, section of the first half of a tableau comprising the longest, and most systematically 'oriental' and 'exotic', descriptions of the *Tentation* as a whole. Flaubert has also set up some very clearly biblical references to Nebuchadnezzar and the Queen of Sheba through Antoine's exegeses on them directly and *by analogy* with other readings in the first tableau. Critical comparison of Nebuchadnezzar or Sheba with these biblical others has never been undertaken. And has critical bedazzlement with Sheba blinded critics to the blunt 'message' at the outset of the second tableau in Antoine's first 'dream' sequence, that exotic transports in dreams can paradoxically land the dreamer in a world of everyday reality? Picking up on tableau one's particularized reference to and descriptions of Canopus, Antoine dreams he is on a boat to join the revelry at the temple of Serapis there, also joining other *dreamers of dreams* induced by this god. All he can then dream within his dream, however, is 'qu'il est un solitaire d'Égypte' (*Tent*, 65). If Antoine is only brought back to his own present reality in space and time by dream work disorienting and reorienting the very familiar, do the larger than life, biblical figures of resplendent and superlative Eastern power in this tableau fantastically describe not exotic oriental Old Testament worlds, but nineteenth-century France and its landscapes of God and (M)ammon?

TURNING THE TABLES: 'NEBUCHADNEZZAR'S' FEAST

Ugly reality, that the jackals have stolen his little remaining food, brings Antoine back to earth with a bump, but his fury triggers the monstrous tablecloth (as parody of Peter's vision from his first reading, and Tantalus in Hades) covered with all kinds of meats and anthropomorphized sweetmeats, many of which are unknown to him, but recognizable as prepared confections, 'hachis', 'gelées', 'ragoûts', and 'mousses' (*Tent,* 66–7).[9] These logical connections between tableaux one and two are also underpinned by continuities with key episodes from sections two and three of Voragine's hagiography of the legendary St Anthony, namely the giant Devil and the trove of gold:

> [II] Étant venu dans une autre partie du désert, il y trouva un grand disque d'argent... 'Satan, c'est encore un de tes tours! Mais tu ne parviendras pas à ébranler ma volonté.' Et comme il disait cela, le disque s'évanouit en fumée. Il trouva ensuite une énorme masse d'or; mais il l'évita comme le feu, et s'enfuit sur une montagne où il resta vingt ans, éclatant de miracles.... [III] Saint Antoine raconte qu'il a vu, un jour, certain diable de haute taille qui, osant se faire passer pour la Providence divine, lui dit: 'Que veux-tu, Antoine, afin que je te le donne?' Mais le saint, s'armant de sa foi, lui cracha au visage... et aussitôt le diable s'évanouit. Une autre fois le diable lui apparut dans un corps d'une taille si haute que sa tête semblait toucher le ciel.... il s'avoua qu'il était Satan. (*LD,* 88–9)[10]

But the climax, the plate with the single loaf which multiplies, and an overt reference to Jesus' miracle of feeding the 5,000 ('C'est un miracle, alors, le même que fit le Seigneur'[11]), returns Antoine to realization of its counterfeiter. The Devil is not merely tempting Antoine, but doing so in a manner similar to the Temptation of Christ in the Wilderness, of which the first temptation was to turn the stones into bread. Flaubert's 'Imitation of Christ' here is both completely in keeping with the spirit of Athanasius' *Vita Antonii,* and its letter (the episode of the *profane* not sacred cup to follow), and the wider comparative religious implications of this scene (to herald the episode of Apollonius and Damis in tableau four). Antoine's covetous desire and its curbing to wallow in the gold coins turns into his further desire to have revenge on the 'flesh' (and thus again enact the second Bible passage from Esther of tableau one[12]), his attempt to take up the 'real' knife inside his 'cabane'. His 'catalepsy' at this point, like his initial dream, transports him in a lengthy digression around worldly Alexandria ('Il se croit à Alexandrie' (*Tent,* 70)) rather like his 'real' perambulations with Didymus in tableau one. As transition to the excesses of Nebuchadnezzar's feast, this digression has evoked critical ire for its forced device of translation via the giant mirror of the 'Phare d'Alexandrie' to Constantinople. Surely, in eliding the two meanings of 'cataleptic', Flaubert ironically prepares such effects in Antoine? As 'observer', he first experiences a seizure or trance which suspends consciousness and sensation, but transports him, and second, in the philosophical sense of the word, Antoine opens his comprehension or apprehension of these richly material geographies. And surely the 'mirror' effect has already been set up in microcosm, the cup full of gold coins bearing the heads of Egyptian and Persian potentates (*Tent*, 69)?[13]

Like the Bible passages of tableau one, the point to be made is that this giant mirror of the Alexandria lighthouse reflects *backwards* to the time of the greatest Babylonian ruler, Nebuchadnezzar, as well as forwards, to Constantine's (ab)uses in the present of Antoine's story of the new state religion of Christianity for secular power-mongering ends, and to the nineteenth-century France of Napoleon I and III. Consequently, this episode is extremely telling as remapping of despotic power as a constant in the history of civilizations and their rulers from Old Testament to New Testament times and unabated in the nineteenth century, in the Ottoman Empire, Alexandria, and France (see Appendices 3 and 4). The description allegedly of ancient Alexandria (until the lighthouse mirror) derived from Strabo[14] is both authentic and carefully analogous with Haussmann's Paris, but with more detail than simply its boulevards and general architecture as critics have noted.[15] The 'suite ininterrompue de constructions royales: le palais des Ptolémés, le Muséum...le Soma qui contient le tombeau d'Alexandre' and 'l'autre extrémité de la ville...un faubourg des fabriques de verre, de parfums et de papyrus' (*Tent*, 71) looks strangely like the Louvre, now including its Muséum Napoléon as founded by Denon, and an industrializing Paris with its factories and ateliers to the north and west. More specifically, the 'pylônes égyptiens [qui] dominent des temples grecs', the 'obélisques apparaissent comme des lances' (*Tent*, 70), bring to mind Paris's new 'Egyptian' buildings and monuments. On 25 October 1836 the Luxor obelisk, gift of Mohammed Ali, was erected in the Place de la Concorde in Paris after being transported by special boat under the supervision of Champollion. Thanks too to the vigorous encouragement instigated under Napoleon I of the activities of masonic lodges under a specifically French 'Grand Orient' (to break with and rival British supremacy in this domain), many masonic temples in Paris were constructed in Egyptian style.[16] The largest Egyptian reconstruction of all, however, was in the north-east corner of the Champs de Mars, the

'Parc Égyptien' built for the Exposition Universelle of 1867 and inaugurated by Ismail Bey. Auguste Mariette (Ismail's director of the Muséum d'Égypte in Cairo), had specific jurisdiction over the project and the various Egyptian exhibits it contained, including how to 'decipher' the ancient history from the monuments and exhibits as explained in his *Exposition Universelle de 1867: aperçu de l'histoire ancienne d'Égypte pour l'intelligence des monuments exposés dans le temple du parc égyptien*. For the curious, but less well-informed, visitor, Charles Edmond's guide to the exhibition drew richly from Mariette's publication, but made the three integrated sections of the *parc* a voyage of discovery of Egypt, past, medieval, and present. The introductory 'coup d'œil général' of the Exhibition puts this in a nutshell:

Dans le TEMPLE, qui est une restauration scrupuleuse de celui de Philé, l'Égypte antique a ramené devant notre esprit les plus lointains souvenirs du monde. Dans le palais ensuite, qui est lui-même un type de ce qu'on appelle dans le pays un SELAMLIK, nous avons fait . . . connaissance avec la civilisation arabe de l'Égypte. Enfin la cour, avec ses établis d'ouvriers-marchands, construite, du reste, elle-même sur un modèle en usage, sur le modèle d'un OKEL . . . , nous a montré l'Égypte engagée dans la voie nouvelle.[17]

Near the 'Okel' or 'caravanserail' (an *auberge-magasin*-bazaar-atelier-market in one, where visitors could see local produce and partake of refreshments) were stables where different breeds of camel and donkeys were on display. Not so very far away was another new Bazaar, where the public was also able to purchase goods from the East. Paris's first department store, the Bon Marché, opened in 1865.[18] This modern 'circus' and temple to Mammon did not literally throw Christians to the lions, but challenged the values of traditional Catholic piety by presenting the glitter of the material world as more fascinating than the life of the hereafter. Edmond's catalogue of the various exhibits in the Egyptian temples similarly focuses on consumer choice of an ideological kind. In describing Egypt's gods to make them comprehensible for devout and nominal Catholics, his use of comparison and stress on religious parallelism challenges Catholicism and Christianity as the one true faith. One entry serves as an illustration:

Les prêtres égyptiens enseignaient un Dieu unique, incréé, immortel, auteur du ciel et de la terre, qui s'est engendré lui-même et perpétuellement s'engendre encore lui-même. C'est à peu près notre *nature* érigée en divinité, conçue comme l'universelle force, comme la toute-puissance éternelle, créatrice et conservatrice, comme l'ensemble enfin de toutes les influences du monde sur l'homme et de nous-même sur le monde.... Il se manifeste aux hommes beaucoup plus comme le Jéhovah des Juifs, dans le monde extérieur, que dans le for intérieur, comme le Père, que Jésus sentait si intimement. Il ne manque pourtant pas d'être allié de près à la première personne de la Trinité chrétienne.[19]

If Flaubert will everywhere exploit this comparative religious, explanatory, critical method especially in tableaux four and five, he does so directly in Antoine's 'Alexandrian' transportation specifically to Constantinople:[20] Antoine 'arrive devant la façade du palais, décoré par un groupe en cire qui représente l'empereur Constantin terrassant un dragon' (*Tent*, 73).[21]

Every aspect of the Constantinople-'Nebuchadnezzar' scene is thus richly prepared by the Alexandria–Paris comparative topographies. The merchant ships crowded together in a bay in the shape of the crescent moon (like the Alexandrian corniche) underscore the huge trading power and economic wealth (Mammon) of this 'ville neuve'.[22] In the time of Anthony the Great, the city of Constantinople was indeed only recently founded, as pinnacle of Constantine's empire building project in 324, the year before the Council of Nicaea. The civic mosaics offering the Emperor conquered cities on platters (*Tent*, 73) are also redolent of Constantinople's particular development of mosaics for the rich decoration of Christian churches, where the Virgin Mary was depicted on a throne receiving from Constantine his dedication of the city to her.[23]

The layering of significance is everywhere at least doubled and refracted through the person of Flaubert's Antoine. His orgy of revenge on 'luxe' and 'volupté' on a personal scale (*Tent*, 72) is now magnified on an imperial scale by Constantine, potentate personified by his throne with two crouching lions at its foot.[24] The latter's revenge and mirth regarding recent events in his work of 'civilization' is more sinister (note Flaubert's use of 'on'): 'Dans les villes d'Antioche, d'Éphèse et d'Alexandrie, on a saccagé les temples et fait avec les statues des dieux, des pots et des marmites' (*Tent,* 73–4). Napoleon I's Expédition d'Égypte had also sacked the many temples for artefacts to transport to Paris.[25] Moreover, Constantine (like Napoleon I and III), is now only paying lip-service to the state religion of Christianity/Roman

Catholicism for expansionist ends. Internal ecclesiastical controversies can all better be controlled through brokered deals with the episcopate (Constantine instigated Nicaea) (*Tent*, 74), as Napoleon I would so skilfully achieve in the Concordat (1801) and his coronation by the Pope in 1805. The women are now behind the windows of the church (and harem), architectural symbolism of their 'domestic' place under the Code Napoléon of 1804. The new religious signs are on public display in the middle of the Circus which mirrors that of Imperial Rome. Constantine's statue has been erected to underscore his godlike status but also syncretistic position atop the 'petit temple de Mercure' (*Tent*, 74).

Antoine's gloating pleasure at the comically menial tasks of the Pères de Nicée, whom he had singled out in tableau one for their doctrinal improprieties—all are 'stable boys' in the lowliest service of the new Pope/Potentate mucking out, grooming manes, and polishing hooves[26]—might again reinforce the peculiar religious psychology of his 'holy' revenge as modern version of the Jews' massacre of their persecutors in the quotation that Antoine has read from Esther.[27] This comic scene is however the means whereby Flaubert links Antoine's earlier revelling in the gold with his own reduced status to come on all fours, in order to serve the comparative ends of the whole of the remaining tableau. The metamorphoses of potentates into beasts, and specifically asses (some of whom can talk), are not only the preserve of biblical figures such as Nebuchadnezzar, but the stuff of Greek transformation stories concerning kings (Midas, King of Phrygia), and lesser mortals and their offences against specifically *Egyptian* gods and goddesses (who return in tableau five). The specific comparative religious intertext here is Apuleius' *Golden Ass*, a work written in *c*.AD 150 as a paean to the Egyptian goddess Isis, an initiate of whose cult was Apuleius himself.[28] His character Lucius is punished for his inordinate curiosity about the dark arts as practised by his host's wife Pamphilë, who can turn herself into an owl and back into a woman with the help of an antidote administered by her slave Fotis, who has become Lucius' lover. Fotis procures both sight of Pamphilë's transformation and a pot of the magic unguent for Lucius, but the plan backfires horribly when he smears himself with the wrong ointment which makes an ass of him. Flaubert does not exploit the rambunctious situation comedies that befall Lucius as ass in his 'Nebuchadnezzar'. Instead, this 'pagan' magic and miracle intertext sets up a composite story at once with the Book of Daniel and with similarly fantastical transformation tales to come, including not only those of Apollonius in tableau four, but also the mythical metamorphoses that tableaux five and seven will remap. Indeed as Graves notes in his introduction, 'Even St. Augustine writes doubtfully: "Apuleius either reported or invented his transformation into asinal shape"; and Lactantius in his *Divine Institutes* is distressed that the miracles of Apuleius, like those of the gymnosophist Apollonius of Tyana, are quoted by anti-Christian controversialists as more wonderful than those of Jesus Christ' (*GA*, 13). The issue of the miracles of Jesus as unique will be raised by Hilarion in the third tableau.

The eventual retelling of the story of Nebuchadnezzar from the Book of Daniel in tableau two is further prepared in Antoine's vision through his ascendancy as 'un des grands de la Cour, confident de l'Empereur, premier ministre!' which immediately leads to Constantine placing 'son diadème sur le front' (*Tent*, 75). This is no obscure reference, but one encapsulated in the third reading of tableau one. Antoine here finds himself in a comparable position with Constantine to Daniel with Nebuchadnezzar *after* Daniel had described, and then interpreted, Nebuchadnezzar's *dream* about the giant composite statue being four great kingdoms. Daniel's interpretation caused Nebuchadnezzar to recognize Daniel's God as the true God, just as later Constantine would be converted in a 'vision'.[29] Antoine's elevation to the heights of courtly favour now readies him to join with the experiences of both 'pagan' and biblical precursors in the scenes to come, their metamorphosis of power into degradation, glory into humiliation, and most of all inordinate curiosity into asinine brutishness.

Chapter 1 noted how Flaubert erased the miraculous, prophetic, and visionary aspects of the *Vita Antonii* in tableau one from Antoine's curriculum vitae to underscore his humanity. Flaubert's reworking of the various wonders and dreams, the 'purple' passages from the Book of Daniel known to readers, similarly debunks by focusing on earthly pomp hiding very human folly. Eastern potentates and despots offending the gods by overweening power and excessive wealth (material possessions and exotic pleasures of the table) have in their debaucheries required satiety in more sacrilegious tastes such as making 'pots et marmites' of temple artefacts (Constantine) or drinking 'dans les vases sacrés' before breaking them (*Tent*, 76).[30] What no critic of this passage has however noticed, or investigated, is that Nebuchadnezzar in the Book of Daniel does not drink from the sacred cups. It is his son Belshazzar who gives 'a great banquet for a thousand of his nobles' (not rows of priests as in Flaubert's version[31]) with much wine flowing, and who orders the cups to be brought from the royal treasury where his father Nebuchadnezzar had deposited them. Belshazzar's act of profanation leads to the appearance of the unknown hand writing 'Mene, Mene, Tekel, Parsin' on the wall, and to Daniel's interpretation of the writing (in Daniel 5). In Daniel 6 Belshazzar's successor, Darius the Mede, issues the edict that all are to bow down and worship him as a god. Daniel's failure to obey lands him in the lions' den, with the familiar miraculous outcome. Although Daniel 5–6 offers clear links to themes Flaubert's *Tentation* has already set up—Christians thrown to lions under the persecutions of Decius and Diocletian, the writing on the wall temptingly parallels Champollion's recent deciphering of the Rosetta Stone—Flaubert chooses instead to 're-purple' these passages by omitting all miraculous events, the better to underscore and rehistoricize their 'fantastical' reality: successions of Eastern potentates (including Constantine) have all succumbed to setting themselves up as gods. Flaubert names Belshazzar simply 'Le Roi'. It is juxtaposition of this paragraph and the following one where Antoine 'lit, de loin sur son front, toutes ses pensées' and becomes 'Nebuchadnezzar' (*Tent*, 76) that has caused the two to be elided. Antoine then experiences Excess in its superlative forms thanks to this composite scene, including all its 'bassesses', epitomized in becoming a brute beast on all fours on the table, which 'beugle comme un taureau'.[32] By being physically on all fours, and cut with a stone, Antoine returns to the reality of his 'cabane'.

Flaubert is too careful to have made a careless error in his reading of Daniel. What he has done here is to compose a mosaic of Eastern rulers of vaunting power who have all been dethroned by overextension of their humanity in their bid to become like gods. Nebuchadnezzar and Belshazzar the Babylonians, Darius the Mede, and Nero the Roman by implication (*Tent*, 75), have all lost their kingdoms as well as reason.[33] Some like Nebuchadnezzar and Nero have even gone 'mad'. Therein lies the link to the fourth reading of tableau one, from 2 Kings 20, the story of Hezekiah showing all his many possessions to the Babylonians (who will under Nebuchadnezzar strip Jerusalem of all its possessions, but *after* he too has repented of his arrogance in his own power and near fatal illness, and after his lifetime).[34] By choosing not to invoke any divine interventions into this kingly encapsulation of the rise and then Decline and Fall of Empire,[35] Flaubert is quite specifically examining Constantine's legacy as endless return of the same, and by implication judging that of Napoleon I and III. Napoleon I's defeats crowned by Waterloo and exile mark his overstretching of imperial power and bid to forge a new, secularized, Holy Roman Empire through his challenge to the Vatican State. In spite of the 'victory' of the Suez Canal and expansion into Algeria and Morocco, Napoleon III at the time of writing the final version of the *Tentation* will have been trounced by Germany in the Franco-Prussian War. 'Restitution' and returning to 'right' mind were encapsulated in Catholic backlash and fervour, marked by the sanctioning of the building of Sacré Cœur as 'penance'. How more pseudo-Byzantine could the choice of architecture for this basilica in Montmartre be, with the mosaic image of Christ (as Pancreator) on the main dome?

In the *Tentation*, the overruling of earthly potentates by God's ultimate intervention and justice in Daniel and 2 Kings is never shown, only ironically debunked in the 'saintly' person of Antoine. He is stopped 'at the right moment' by the cut from the stone under his hand from travelling any further into the world of false power and glory, ecclesiastical as well as political. But his transportation to 'Constantinople' and experience of 'Nebuchadnezzar/Constantine's' feast (redolent of the reform banquets described in *L'Éducation sentimentale*) reveal a larger comparative lesson in the anatomy of powers and principalities. There is indeed nothing new under the sun, even if the labels change and Antoine's 'dreams', invoked by his opening dream *en abyme* of journeying to dream at the temple of Serapis, only recount other worlds which are strikingly like his own. The reference to Serapis (like Canopus in Chapter 1) is a very clear shorthand for the composite effects everywhere exploited in this 'Nebuchadnezzar' section. The Alexandria of Christianity and Serapis evokes the time of Constantine, but also that of the ancient Egyptian Ptolemy Soter, the first Greek Pharaoh. This astute ruler took advantage of harnessing Egypt's principal gods, especially Osiris-Apis (the god of the *Underworld*), to the new Greek imports (gods of Hades) to extend his power and hide the necessary persecutions of those gods and men formerly in the highest places. In a dream (like Nebuchadnezzar), he saw a vision of a huge composite statue, which became the composite god Serapis. St Mark would be lynched by the worshippers of Serapis for preaching the new religion in Alexandria in AD 62 or 68. Tableau two, through biblical referents, only the more clearly comments on composite 'pagan' or 'Christian' principalities and their powers of persecution, past, present, and future, in preparation for the levelling of 'comparative religions' in tableau five.

GIFTS AND KNOWLEDGE: THE 'QUEEN OF SHEBA'

The Bible reading about Hezekiah showing the Babylonian envoys his wealth is also the hidden middle term linking Flaubert's version of 'Nebuchadnezzar' to the grand finale of tableau two, the arrival of the Queen of Sheba. In 1 Kings 10: 4, when given a grand tour of Solomon's wealth, 'the food on his table, the seating of his officials, the attending servants in their robes, his cupbearers, and the burnt offerings he made at the temple of the Lord, she was overwhelmed'.[36] This is however in apposition to seeing 'all the wisdom of Solomon and the palace he had built'. In the first tableau, Antoine read the first verse from 1 Kings 10: '*La Reine de Saba, connaissant la gloire de Solomon, vint le tenter, en lui proposant des énigmes*' (*Tent*, 59).[37] His gloss is not about sexual temptation at all, but a speculation on the verb 'tenter' (to test as well as to tempt), which he connects (as exegete) to the Temptation of Christ by the devil in the Wilderness (where there is also no sexual temptation). If read from the optic of tableau one, Antoine has the Arian controversy already behind him, together with visitations from bishops such as Athanasius, and the world ruler of the period, Constantine, seeking his wisdom. As the future father of monasticism (and adversary of rival religious dogmas and philosophical creeds as tableau four will amply demonstrate) he then adds:

Mais Jésus a triomphé parce qu'il était Dieu, et Salamon grâce peut-être à sa science de magicien. Elle est sublime cette science-là! Car le monde,—ainsi qu'un philosophe me l'a expliqué,—forme un ensemble dont toutes les parties influent les unes sur les autres, comme les organes d'un seul corps. Il s'agit de connaître les amours et les repulsions naturelles des choses, puis de les mettre en jeu?... On pourrait donc modifier ce qui paraît être l'ordre immuable? (*Tent*, 59)

It is quite clear that Antoine is emphasizing the testing by the Queen of Sheba primarily of Solomon's *wisdom* and *knowledge* (which turn out to be even greater than she had been led to believe, and indeed greater than her own). If this 'science' offers insights into laws of the universe as 'amours et répulsions', thereby to set up the whole lascivious seduction (Sheba) versus absolute repulsion (Antoine), such linking seems extremely contrived on Flaubert's part, and a strange return to the 'medieval' concepts of the seven deadly sins that the final version of the *Tentation* had otherwise largely erased, for example the daughters of 'Luxure' (Adultère, Fornication, Immondicité) in the 1849 *Tentation*.[38] Chapter 6 will examine the relevance and necessary connections of Antoine's 'interpretation' and exegesis here, which needs must be mediated by Babylonian and modern 'mages' and 'magiciens', since this is the 'Babylon' tableau *par excellence*, modern and ancient. The enigma remains the reader's to combine Sheba's overtly sexual testing of Antoine here with his earlier biblical glosses.

For Gothot-Mersch, genetic study of the key scenarios and *brouillons* for the 1874 text leaves absolutely no doubt about the seductive intent and content of the Queen of Sheba scene (which Neiland further interprets as also a seduction of the reader):

(*Luxure*) la reine de Saba—moins insister sur le luxe, la faire plus lubrique. + |elle lui donnera tous les genres de la volupté| – 'mais je me moque de ses Richesses', dit Antoine—alors elle insiste sur les trésors de sa personne. elle sait des secrets de volupté.
Il s'en délivre.[39]

'Volupté' for Gothot-Mersch neatly covers the gamut of sexual and intellectual 'voluptés' the Queen of Sheba can offer Antoine, symbolized in the little box (the 'trésors de sa personne') she tempts Antoine to possess.[40] Neiland uses the same evidence, but prefaces it with a later, complementary folio to clinch the reworking of Fornication and Immondicité in the 1874 Queen of Sheba:

Formes ignobles & cependant qui excitent. Donc ce n'est pas la chair en soi qui excite mais *un certain esprit qui est en elle.*—& souvent cette force est d'autant plus gde violente que la *Laideur* est plus gde.—charme de la Prostituée parce qu'elle est prostituée,—s'enfoncer dans l'Être. l'animalité c'est s'enfoncer| plus avant dans la Nature dans l'Être|.[41]

The last two elements above seem to link with, and further emphasize, the bestial degradations of Antoine on all fours on 'Nebuchadnezzar's' table. Indeed, at the end of the *Tentation* Antoine will famously survey 'l'animalité', to envisage its states as 'Être la matière!' All this weight of genetic critical evidence cannot however explain Flaubert's blatant departures from the biblical Queen of Sheba, yet Antoine's contradictory glosses of her 'biblical' roles, unless there is more to 'Sheba' than meets the eye, just as there was more to 'Nebuchadnezzar' as composite figure. Given Flaubert's consummate play with biblical intertexts for the 'Nebuchadnezzar' section of the tableau, and that Antoine's longest exegesis is of the fifth, final, and climactic 'Queen of Sheba' reference in tableau one, a 'biblical' rereading of this section will show the *Tentation's* potentially more sacrilegious critiques of Catholic pomp and power than any reading of an 'anti-religious' Flaubert can muster from the genetic evidence.[42] As Tournier will later envisage for his *Gaspard, Melchior et Balthazar,* taking a leaf from Flaubert's books, stories of wise men from the East bringing gifts of gold, frankincense, and myrrh can be revised by the words of the donkey or a fourth king for deeply critical ends.[43] Flaubert has already paved the way by transforming 'Sheba' into a singular, female, Eastern 'mage', complete with her 'boîte' as gift of her potent 'esprit qui est en elle' to Solomon, the Old Testament King of the Jews and overtly the precursor of Constantine in his founding of a palace and a temple to the glory of God.

Tableau two stands out from all the others as having the lengthiest descriptions to contextualize the ensuing temptation figures. It was Taine who praised Flaubert's coup in his descriptions of the Queen of Sheba's costume,[44] and the luxurious and mysterious spices, cloth, and jewels she shows Antoine (*Tent*, 80), a voluptuous expansion of the verse following Antoine's quotation from 1 Kings 10: 2: 'Arriving at Jerusalem with a very large caravan—with camels carrying spices, large quantities of gold, and precious stones—she came to Solomon and talked with him about all she had had on her mind.' Since Flaubert's descriptions have attracted critics such as Taine for their splendid authenticity, did Flaubert embroider one or several sources for Sheba's costume and the emporium of exotica which are her possessions and baggage?

Even before she is properly visible or discloses her name, this superlative queen is 'une femme si splendidement vêtue qu'elle envoie des rayons autour d'elle' (*Tent*, 78). This dazzling light is not reflective like the giant mirror of the lighthouse of Alexandria that transported Antoine to Constantinople-Babylon, but blindingly dazzling, making her person rival (sacrilegiously) the all-important final image of the *Tentation*, the face of Christ in the aureole of the sun. It is only when she has descended from her litter that the many details of her magnificent attire can be enumerated, its gold brocade, trimmed at regular intervals with precious stones (pearls, jades, sapphires), its tightly cinched bodice in richly embroidered colours depicting the twelve signs of the zodiac. Her symbolic high heels—one shoe with silver stars and a crescent moon, the other with golden droplets and a sun in the middle—imply that the cosmos is on her feet. Her costume indeed mirrors her later words to Antoine: 'Je ne suis pas une femme, je suis un monde' (*Tent*, 84), such that possession of even a tiny part of her body beneath her clothing will invoke more overwhelming feelings than the conquest of an (earthly) empire (*Tent*, 85). The whole seduction pivots round Sheba's possessions (note the framing 'J'ai' which starts each lengthy enumeration of her wealth of costly luxuries) as honey pot to lure Antoine to possess her in her spider-like seduction to possess him. The resplendent clothing and her form to be revealed beneath are however a mirage that disappears at Antoine's repulsion of her with the sign of the cross at the end of the scene. This is no ordinary queen-courtesan or harlot. Costume, retinue, Flaubert's scenarios emphasizing luxury and lasciviousness, all derive from a further 'Babylonian' figure of equivalent female mythical magnitude to Nebuchadnezzar, the Great Prostitute in Revelation 17 and 18:

One of the seven angels . . . said to me, 'Come, I will show you the punishment of the great prostitute, who sits on many waters. With her the kings of the earth committed adultery and the inhabitants of the earth were intoxicated with the wine of her adulteries.'

Then the angel carried me away in the Spirit into a desert. There I saw a woman . . . dressed in purple and scarlet . . . glittering with gold, precious stones and pearls. She held a golden cup in her hand, filled with abominable things and the filth of her adulteries. This title was written on her forehead:

> 'Mystery
> Babylon the Great
> The Mother of Prostitutes
> And of the abominations of the earth.'

I saw that the woman was drunk with the blood of the saints, the blood of those who bore testimony to Jesus.... After this I saw another angel ... and the earth was illuminated by his splendour. With a mighty voice he shouted: 'Fallen! Fallen is Babylon the Great! She has become a home for demons and a haunt for every evil spirit, a haunt for every unclean and detestable bird. For all the nations have drunk the maddening wine of her adulteries. The kings of the earth committed adultery with her, and the merchants of the earth grew rich from her excessive luxuries.' ... The merchants of the earth will weep and mourn over her because no-one buys their cargoes ... of gold, silver, precious stones and pearls; fine linen, purple, silk and scarlet cloth; every sort of citron wood, and articles of every kind made of ivory, costly wood, bronze, iron and marble; cargoes of cinnamon and spice, of incense, myrrh and frankincense, of wine and olive oil, of fine flour and wheat; cattle and sheep; horses and carriages; and bodies and souls of men.

Flaubert has transformed the 'Queen of Sheba' into the Great Prostitute (note the capital P in the second scenario quoted above, which neither Gothot-Mersch nor Neiland has observed), as superlative Queen of Queens and spirit of *possession* (of every kind of carnal, material, exotic, and spiritual seduction). She is indeed a 'world', representing everything that is contrary to that of the saints, and from time immemorial since an angel explains the *mystery* of her representation to John in Revelation. 17: 18, 'The woman you saw is the great city that rules over the kings of the earth.' Constantinople of Antoine's times was indeed claiming to be just this city, rivalling Alexandria and of course Rome, and to be greater than the city of Solomon. But like 'Babylon the Great', Sheba is greater than any kingdom of the world that a king, even Nebuchadnezzar, Solomon, Constantine, or Napoleon III, could build in Paris or *represent*. Consequently, 'Sheba' is then the queenly embodiment (as Salammbô is of Tanit in *Salammbô*) of all the greatest goddesses of the East, of Babylon, Egypt, and Phrygia, Ishtar, Isis, Cybele, and Diane of Ephesus.[45] They will all parade in tableau five.

Other details can now be explained more readily, and not as the pure inventions of Flaubert. First, the mythical, phoenix-like Simorg-Anka is an Eastern version of this 'detestable bird' of Revelation, a prefiguration of the many other composite beasts that will parade in the final tableau. Second a monkey lifts Sheba's skirts to make visible her bare legs.[46] A further biblical intertext from Isaiah 47, however, provides Flaubert with his 'petit détail qui fait *vrai*', the inspiration for that astrological bodice, the cosmological shoes, and secret knowledge as magic and sorcery:

Go down, sit in the dust, Virgin Daughter of Babylon: sit on the ground without a throne . . . Lift up your skirts, bare your legs, and wade through the streams. Your nakedness will be exposed and your shame uncovered. . . . Sit in silence, go into darkness, Daughter of the Babylonians; no more will you be called queen of kingdoms . . . You said, 'I will continue for ever—the eternal queen!' . . . Now then, listen, you wanton creature, lounging in your security and saying to yourself, 'I am, and therefore there is none besides me' . . . in spite of your many sorceries and all your potent spells. . . . Your wisdom and knowledge mislead you when you say to yourself, 'I am, and there is none besides me.' Disaster will come upon you, and you will not know how to conjure it away. . . . Keep on, then, with your magic spells and with your many sorceries, which you have laboured at since childhood. . . . Let your astrologers come forward, those stargazers who make predictions month by month, let them save you from what is coming upon you. Surely they are like stubble . . .

The missing connections Gothot-Mersch was looking for between Flaubert's Queen of Sheba and magic powers are amply provided by these texts from Isaiah and Revelation read though one another. Antoine's renunciation of the Great Prostitute (his sign of the cross) is then completely in keeping with the warnings in Proverbs (the Wisdom of Solomon) to beware the snares of the glittering adulteress. Flaubert's 'Queen of Sheba' is then tempting both Antoine and the reader with enigmas of arrant power cross-dressed in seductive female form. Her sin of pride (there being none beside her) allows Flaubert to conclude his tableau on the topic of overweening potentates, male and female, who vaunt themselves as gods and goddesses, but who all without exception fall with their empires. More than skilfully preparing tableau five, 'Sheba' as 'Queen' of the 'World' also causes readers to recall its 'Prince', the Devil, lurking over tableau two, but who will emerge fully in tableau six to take Antoine on his ride into space (the cosmos). Like his transport to Constantinople, Antoine's transport there (in literal and figurative senses) will be of the order of St John the Divine in Revelation, including its terror and 'catatonia'. More immediately in the *Tentation* the 'Queen of Sheba' as female 'Mage' also heralds Hilarion in tableau three and Simon the Magician and Apollonius in tableau four, since their religion of the East is 'Babylonian' as too are the Eleusinian mysteries.

The description of the Queen of Sheba's dress, perhaps especially the zodiac bodice and the 'cosmic' shoes, has particularly nineteenth-century French resonance, however. The zodiac discovered at Dendera was one of the major artefacts that the Expédition d'Égypte brought back to France and marks significant advances in French Egyptology. It was illustrated and described by Denon in the *Description d'Égypte* and Champollion would complete his decoding of ancient Egyptian hieroglyphs at Dendera and other temples dedicated to Isis. In the context of nineteenth-century French religion, Flaubert's Queen of Sheba has even more sacrilegious pertinence, especially since Antoine has earlier wanted to roll in the many gold coins that spilled from the 'magic' cup (*Tent*, 69). Her initial image in a blaze of light describes her as 'clothed with the sun with the moon under her feet'. This was the vision of the Virgin in 1830 that Catherine Labouré had struck as the 'Miraculous Medal' and whom historians of the period connect with the Woman in the Apocalypse (Rev. 12).[47] Flaubert falls short of giving his Sheba 'a crown of twelve stars on her head'; these become the twelve signs of the zodiac on her breast. His other variations likewise just fail to tip his intertextual reworking into contradiction with the Babylonian Virgin/Whore above. Although blue as the colour of the Virgin is everywhere apparent in Flaubert's Sheba—her high chignon with spiralling gold chains is powdered blue as are the cushions she reclines upon—she remains an Eastern goddess even though the cut of her dress is strikingly similar to the rich medieval costuming of the Virgin as Queen of Heaven in iconography and as described by the children at Pontmain who sighted her in 1871.[48]

In the first version of the *Tentation*, the Virgin-Mother was described like a Venus, to underscore the comparative religious and symbolic aspects of her character.[49] Flaubert has not, as critics constantly state, removed this figure from his final version, but more artfully conflated images of the Virgin as recorded in contemporary sightings of her in France with the Whore of Babylon in his Queen of Sheba. What makes his intertextual travesty the more sacrilegious is that it then becomes a direct critique of the Marian cults that spread through France from 1830 onwards as a result of these apparitions. More importantly for this tableau which pivots on Constantine as the Emperor/Statesman of the Church, Flaubert's critique is also of their ratification by Pius IX. Most notable is the appearance of the Virgin at Lourdes in 1858, the shining lady 'more gleaming than gold' appearing to the 14-year-old and illiterate Bernadette Soubirous eighteen times in a grotto nearby. Like Antoine at the start of tableau two, Bernadette would go *into a trance*, watched by the crowds. On one occasion she scraped the ground at the place where there was a hidden spring. On another (like Antoine) she ate grass as instructed to do by the apparition as a penance. The church authorities told Bernadette to ask the Lady her name, which was duly supplied at the sixteenth appearance: 'I am the Immaculate Conception', which Bernadette claimed she had never heard of before.[50] Pope Pius IX had however just proclaimed the Immaculate Conception as Roman Catholic dogma in 1854. Ernest Renan perhaps best sums up the Virgin Mary phenomenon in the introduction to his *Vie de Jésus*:

La première tâche de l'historien est de bien dessiner le milieu où se passe le fait qu'il raconte. Or l'histoire des origines religieuses nous transporte dans un monde de femmes, d'enfants, de têtes ardentes ou égarées. Placez ces faits dans un milieu d'esprits positifs, ils sont absurdes, inintelligibles, et voilà pourquoi les pays lourdement raisonnables comme l'Angleterre sont dans l'impossibilité d'y rien comprendre.... Toutes les tentatives religieuses que nous connaissons clairement présentent un mélange inouï de sublime et de bizarre. Lisez ces procès verbaux du saint-simonisme primitif, publiés avec une admirable candeur par les adeptes survivants. A côté de rôles repoussants, de déclamations insipides, quel charme, quelle sincérité, dès que l'homme ou la femme du peuple entre en scène, apporte la naïve confession d'une âme qui s'ouvre sous le premier doux rayon qui l'a frappée! Il y a plus d'un exemple de belles choses durables qui se sont fondées sur de singuliers enfantillages.... La dévotion de La Salette est un des grands événements de notre siècle.[51]

Zola would also write a novel about Lourdes as the new site of God and Mammon.

To remake a 'Virgin Mary' in travestied form as both Queen of Heaven/Great Prostitute of Babylon appearing to his Antoine after a period of fasting would have appealed hugely to Flaubert's sense of the 'grotesque rire' (with which his Queen of Sheba exits). His 'Isis' in tableau five then bears a striking resemblance to a 'Virgin lactans'. Antoine is however no simple peasant bedazzled by the appearance of a golden lady, but an anchorite of long practice and authority. The two main episodes of the second tableau, like its particular and figurative cityscapes which frame the whole, are also a reworking of the second temptation of Jesus, where Satan tries to make Jesus bow down to him in exchange for all the kingdoms of the world (over which he has dominion). In tableau six, the counterweight to tableau two, the Devil will try again to make Antoine do just this. Antoine (like Jesus) here eschews the temptations of the powers and principalities by making the sign of the cross. In Old Testament terms, Antoine rebuts 'Sheba' as Joseph had to deal with the sexual intentions of Potiphar's wife.

There is one small section of the text which bridges the composite 'King' (Nebuchadnezzar) and 'Queen' (Sheba) figures which has again proved troubling to specialist critics of the *Tentation*, Antoine's mortification of his flesh by harsh self-flagellations.[52] The highly composite figures of this tableau and careful choreography of several intertexts of both biblical and non-biblical inspiration surely require a compositional response to this part of the text. By analogy in Antoine's mind, he is entering into a shared suffering with Christian martyrs flayed by their emperor-persecutors (*Tent*, 77), which only brings Ammonaria again to his mind. The question whether she is a virgin martyr (see Chapter 1) or whore (prefiguring the 'Sheba' figure about to arrive),[53] saint or temptress, has been resolved by critics by assigning her a role as temptress/repentant whore in disguise.[54] The Magdalene, both whore and repentant Christian in one, has fascinated the imagination of Christian iconographers down the centuries.[55] The excesses of abstinence (sustenance and sexuality) and gluttony/lust are surely also being weighed up in this tableau as the equally appalling faces of 'religious' excess in preparation for their sect-defining practices in the various heresies to parade before Antoine in tableau four. His alikeness to them is therefore being prepared for this later scene to underscore the painful similarity between religious observances, 'Eastern' or 'Christian', but the spiritual differences between them. Ammonaria thus serves as no less of a mirror than that of Alexandria, but in counterbalancing female form to 'Sheba' in this scene. As Muse/angel she arrives to inspire Antoine to remain steadfast, even if he can never achieve her place as virgin martyr. She will appear again in counterfeit at the crucial juncture of tableau seven.

Composite reading by analogy is the lesson that Antoine sets in place in this second tableau, as illustration of his radically anti-establishment 'biblical' modes of exegesis as set out in tableau one. Flaubert's mosaic of intertexts drawn from the Bible proves intensely 'modern' in its emphasis on reading more for analogy with contemporary history and less for layers of symbolism. Antoine has now encountered in his contemporary Alexandria and its new equivalent Constantinople all the kingdoms of the Old Testament earth (and seen the hollowness of their 'splendours') by connecting all the Bible readings of tableau one, where the display of all the greatest civilizations prior to the Roman Empire has now found its remapping and crystallization in 'Nebuchadnezzar' (Babylon, Constantinople, Persia, Egypt of the Ptolemys) and 'Sheba' as the spirit of the possession of the earth. In all the glittering and purple splendour of its principalities and powers, the underbelly of 'civilization', has also been revealed—rampant greed, power, seduction, and destruction of enemies. By direct analogy, the belated empires of Napoleon I and III only show their feet of clay.

The more dangerous compromise that Antoine has thus narrowly avoided is episcopal affiliation with powers of the world, which set themselves up as omniscient gods with 'divine right'. Revelation has come through lifting the skirts on the grandeur of pseudo-gods to show their all-too-human power. Their debasements at the table or under their glittering appearances now prepare Antoine for his third temptation (like Christ) in the wilderness, a claim to spiritual exception outside his mortal coil. Antoine has now perused the apostles, the prophets and the kings of Scripture, its greatest apocalyptic visionaries (the visions of Daniel in the Old Testament and of John the Divine in the New Testament). He now has to meet the Tempter in the guise of his master disciple, Hilarion, whose arguments may prove just as seductive as Sheba's charms.[56] Having dealt with earthly pride, Antoine must now face spiritual pride and how it connects him inevitably to the Fall.

3

The Master Disciple

Where the second tableau allowed Flaubert to assail and almost over-whelm his Antoine with the superlative earthly splendour of legendary kings and apocalyptic queens taking on the status of gods, the third tableau appears to turn its back on bedazzling visionary experience (or hallucinatory nightmare), lush description, and exotic transportation to return to the mundane, homespun world of Antoine's inner reflections.[1] Antoine's solitary state is short-lived, however, since it is immediately invaded by 'un enfant sur le seuil de sa cabane', whom Antoine connects to the entourage that has just departed as 'quelqu'un des serviteurs de la Reine' (*Tent*, 86). From manuscript evidence, Gothot-Mersch notes Flaubert's concern both to link Hilarion's entry with the preceding episode of the Queen, and to make him the expositor of various points of Christian dogma, which in turn herald the heresies in tableau four. Hilarion therefore takes over the role that Science played in the first version of the *Tentation*.[2] In the only article dedicated to the figure of Hilarion, Lily Ann Lilley further points out his distinction as the major new character in Flaubert's final version of the *Tentation*, and as the means by which method and order are brought to the mad plethora of forms and ideas about to be unleashed.[3] For Lilley, Hilarion's role as focalizer of ideas challenging religious dogma is summed up in the question he asks Antoine at the end of tableau three (*Tent*, 96): 'Désires-tu connaître la hiérarchie des Anges, la vertu des Nombres, la raison des germes et des métamorphoses?', the three parts of which her arti-cle elaborates. While my own contribution to understanding Hilarion went some way to recuperating his historical basis as the disciple of St Anthony the Great, and to showing Flaubert's exploitation of him as challenge to master–disciple relations in preparation for the Apollonius and Damis set piece which concludes tableau four, no investigation of the Hilarion–Science–Devil metamorphosis at the heart of the dynamic movements of the *Tentation* was mounted.[4] It is this larger dynamic that this chapter now investigates.

The key to unlocking various temporal and semantic strata in tableau three is indeed Hilarion, but first and foremost as figure of interlinking *substitutions* (a *pars pro toto*), all issuing from his historical antecedent, so as to foreshadow Science/the Devil. By making Hilarion function as the quintessential go-between in the *Tentation*, whether as 'serviteur de la Reine', disciple double of his more eminent master/father of monasticism, or harbinger of ideas being formulated within what was a nascent discipline in the fourth century AD, New Testament theology, Flaubert may then also employ Hilarion's fourth-century personas to unlock figures in nineteenth-century French science such as Geoffroy *Saint-Hilaire* as Starr has so cogently argued.[5] As linkman between religion and science, theology and philosophy, Hilarion's parts will prove almost seamless with those of the Devil in tableau six.[6] Yet how Hilarion's roles (Gothot-Mersch) or his provocative question (Lilley) fit together with his various metamorphoses (so that the Devil appears to be a further transformation of him) have never been pressed further by these or other specialist critics. His at least double agency and deceptive likenesses will prove intrinsically important to the 'big' tableaux (four and five) ahead.

Tableau three is then no interlude scene heralding them in. Its contents and form are clearly and carefully matched. Unlike tableau one (Antoine's unfolding soliloquy) and tableau two (luxuriant, interleaved descriptions of earthly fleshpots of power and 'luxure'), or the plethora of conflicting belief systems to come (tableaux four and five), the third tableau is utterly sparse in terms of descriptions, objects, and characters, just as it is also sparing with Antoine's words. Its contrastive force— with things of the self (tableau one), the world (tableau two), or religion(s) (tableau four)—is however its singular power. Close-up focus on the workings and defences of Antoine's carnal and saintly 'esprit' (as mind and spirit) is drawn out by a single, well-attuned, newcomer other standing in a lunar spotlight (*Tent*, 86). As in tableau six (which is marginally the shortest of the work, but not the most intense by dint of its necessarily more exorbitant subject matter of the flight into space), Antoine the un-saintly saint is placed into an intimate dialogue with an assailant who is here a powerful *human* equal, and into the position of interlocutor/respondent and then defender of the faith. By exploiting at the same time the forms of the Socratic dialogue and a legal defence, assertions about central matters of Christian belief, faith, and dogma come under close scrutiny and fire for the first time in the *Tentation, before* the so-called tableau of the heresies.[7] If the dialogue between Antoine and Hilarion seems preparatory of the theological issues to come, and of the counterpoint master–disciple relationship of Apollonius and Damis (who seems merely to echo his master's words to end tableau four[8]), tableau three is also a dialogue scene of the utmost structural importance to the *Tentation*. The intense and intimate debate between Antoine and Hilarion is a personification of the debate between Faith and Reason which is further magnified (literally) in tableau six. These seemingly irreconcilable terms and positions by the very nature of their first premisses will however prove neither as clear-cut nor as neatly polarized. On closer inspection of Flaubert's Hilarion through histor-ical, fourth-century optics (and nineteenth-century ones in Part II), his prerogatives as Antoine's master disciple will turn out to show his desire to be the greatest, like the disciples of Jesus before him.[9]

DE-LIONIZING THE *VITA*

When the historical Hilarion (*c.*291–371) is so little known—the *Légende dorée* for example has no entry for him—why and how does Flaubert invest in him? Should he then be read as an almost imaginary or legendary figure, or are fact and imagination in play? One certainty is made clear in tableau one, Hilarion's status as Antoine's beloved *disciple*. As next-generation successor to Anthony as paradigmatic figure, he has had every reason to be overlooked as derivative, just as Jerome's *Vita Hilarionis* is often criticized as being a copy of Athanasius' *Vita Antonii*.[10] The fictional Hilarion's substitutive nature(s) paradoxically then allow Flaubert much more creative freedom in the *Tentation*, since he could not deviate far from his sources for the more famous St Anthony. The issue is not the status or contents of Hilarion's *Vita*, but its already legendary writer St Jerome, another direct disciple of Athanasius/Anthony. Probably best known for the famous healing of the lion's paw, this part of Jerome's post-conversion story also takes the 'lion's share' in Voragine's *Légende dorée*. By reworking only the pre-conversion part, Flaubert de-lionizes Jerome and his *vitae* literally and metaphorically; through his own Hilarion he questions the nature of intellectual conversions. Where Voragine designated Anthony the capitalized 'Ermite', Jerome is simply labelled 'Docteur', thanks to his training and intellectual life prior to conversion. These are highly redolent of Hilarion's:

Dès sa jeunesse il vint à Rome, et s'y instruisit pleinement dans les lettres grecques, latines et hébraïques. Il eut pour professeur de grammaire Donat, et pour professeur de rhétorique l'orateur Victorin: ce qui ne l'empêchait pas d'étudier avec ardeur les Saintes Écritures. Mais un jour...la simplicité du langage dans les livres des Prophètes l'offusqua si fort qu'il ne voulut plus lire que Cicéron et Platon. Or, vers le milieu du Carême, il fut pris d'une fièvre subite qui faillit le tuer. Et comme déjà l'on préparait ses funérailles, soudain il se vit conduit devant le tribunal de Dieu. Interrogé sur sa condition, il répondit qu'il était chrétien. Mais le juge: 'tu mens, tu n'est pas chrétien, mais cicéronien!'   (*LD*, 553)

Like all conversion stories, renunciation of the wiles of the world (in this case study of profane books) and ardent devotion to the things of God save Jerome, who becomes a desert father in the region around Bethlehem. The questioning inversion of these values for sainthood (sacred/profane) in Hilarion is what provides the fundamentals for Flaubert's character as 'Ciceronian' in speech and philosophical knowledge of theology and the Scriptures. The *Tentation*'s contemporary context, as Part I elucidated, is the various encyclicals of Pope Pius IX and his *Syllabus Errorum* actively targeting 'profane' knowledge and books. Hilarion's substitutions are all precisely to do with *versions* of truth, and with questioning how some truths are upheld over others. As Antoine's master disciple, the fictional Hilarion's spin on his theological subjects thus questions the apologetics inherent in Athanasius' and then Jerome's 'authoritative' *vita*e, and consequently Voragine's and those of later, including nineteenth-century French, exponents to come.

So if Flaubert substitutes Jerome's pre-conversion *vita* for Hilarion's, to provide his character's ironically 'non-Christian' intellectual credentials (signalled in his 'rouleau') and 'source' for his knowledge on the wide range of matters encapsulated by the tableaux over which he presides (three to five), this does not explain his incongruent, monk-like emergence specifically from Sheba's entourage. Substitution is again the link since the manner in which the unmasked, composite, 'Queen of Sheba' departs finds replication in the character of Hilarion. Her mocking laughter, the 'hocquets' and 'ricanement' with which tableau two ended, are embodied in Hilarion's name—in Greek it means 'cheerful'—and the laughter and hilarity that Antoine and he also share (in tableau five), which turns into mockery of the saint.[11] Lateral comparisons are then several. Unlike Anthony's Coptic parentage or Solomon's direct lineage from the house of David, Hilarion's biographers such as Jerome note his 'pagan' parentage and heritage. He is as 'foreign' in blood and religion as Sheba vis-à-vis Solomon/St Anthony. More important still is the biblical Sheba's extensive Eastern wisdom as her predominant characteristic (in the tradition of magi, whether astronomers or magicians), and hence the motive for her journey to meet with and talk to Solomon about all the things on her *mind*. Hilarion similarly shares a prodigious wisdom summed up by the only significantly individualizing descriptive detail given about him, his 'tête prodigieusement grosse' (*Tent*, 86).[12] Illustration of its mental capacities in terms of the clarity, analytic enquiry, authority, and devastating logic of his arguments and questions is the agenda of tableau three.[13] The huge contents of this super-brain, mirrored in the ever-increasing size of Hilarion's form in tableau three from dwarf to giant, will spill out in tableaux four and five. But this 'monde' in (male) intellectual terms matches and replaces the much-quoted Queen of Sheba's 'je ne suis pas une femme, je suis un monde' (*Tent*, 84). How such knowledge was obtained is explained by a further detail from the historical Hilarion's 'pagan' heritage, his education and prowess in the Alexandrian schools (probably the Greek because of his pagan birth, rather than either the Jewish or the Christian establishments) prior to his conversion and subsequent spiritual apprenticeship under St Anthony.[14] If 'Sheba' as acme of the Eastern other (and Whore of Babylon) prefaces the gods, beliefs, and knowledge systems of the East to come (including 'mages') in *female* guise, Hilarion continues in male Scholastic (Neoplatonic and Ciceronian) key the multifaceted theme of where Western knowledge (*Scientia*), wisdom, and rhetoric find their sources. As epitome of Greek, Roman, and Mediterranean learning behind the polytheistic world of the gods of tableau five, Hilarion is then Sheba's 'Western' substitute and comparator in ways which Chapter 5 will explore further. As product of the most renowned 'Academies' and 'Institutes' of his time in Alexandria—its schools represented the pinnacle of Greek/Roman, Egyptian, Persian, and Jewish education and learning in astronomy, mathematics, medicine, the arts of textual exegesis and rhetoric, philosophy, and law for the training of priests, philosophers, teachers, and the learned in every field—Hilarion's education also mirrors its thoroughly modern, nineteenth-century French parallel, as we will discover in Part II. Finally, and perhaps most intrinsic to the effect this tableau has on the reader, Hilarion forces out another level of the overwhelming and terrifying intimacy of the Queen of Sheba figure in tableau two, not this time in terms of an erotic or sexual seduction, but of a no less intense spiritual one.[15] Tableau three, if it does nothing else, speaks of the deep trust (the baring of the soul) of the elder–disciple of the faith, its intense, unequivocal, and unquestioned basis in love which goes beyond even the finest intellectual mentor-master–pupil relationship. What is at stake in this tableau is this ideal of highest mutual respect and male friendship in body, mind, and spirit (the historical Hilarion's emulation of all parts of Anthony's lifestyle and legacy[16]), but in the form of its shadow, the concomitant horror of the fictional Hilarion's manifest spiritual, doctrinal, and intellectual *betrayal* of Antoine's spiritual directorship as the *Tentation* progresses. It was precisely such horror for the Church that the heretical defection to Montanism of its leader Origen represented. Hilarion's directorship of the heretical 'esprit(s)' of the age that will next appear to Antoine thus constitutes Flaubert's most radical deployment of, yet departure from, the historical Hilarion, so as to reveal the 'historical' problem of disciples who betray the (one true) 'Church' in fourth- and nineteenth-century contexts.

Antoine's spiritual son, the 'enfant' Hilarion as verifiable disciple of St Anthony, therefore puts the *elder* (spiritual director)–disciple authority relationship under extreme attack by (almost) inverting its balances of power as master disciple leading his master. Whereas the sixth tableau's mirror-image dialogue between Antoine and the Devil as supernatural educator is obviously between unequals, the terrible *similarities* of position and levels of human knowledge and experience (temporal, theological, intellectual) between Antoine and Hilarion are everywhere underscored, not least in the physical description given at the outset about the new antagonist: 'petit comme un nain, et pourtant trapu comme un Cabire, contourné, d'aspect *misérable*. Des cheveux blancs couvrent sa tête prodigieusement grosse; et il grelotte sous une méchante tunique, tout en gardant un rouleau de papyrus' (*Tent*, 86).[17] This is in effect almost a copy of the physical description of Antoine of tableau one, 'misérable', ragged, a white-haired ascetic, with his 'Écritures' as his only possession. As monster in the mirror, Antoine's nemesis in this 'Jekyll and Hyde' tableau sets out to threaten all the bases and hallmarks of Athanasius' Anthony as father of monasticism. Perhaps only because Anthony's iconic place in both the Eastern Orthodox and Catholic traditions is known—as elder or spiritual father respectively[18]—can Flaubert exert such intense pressure on his saint from this juncture of the text until Hilarion's 'departures', the first provisionally after only the first third of tableau four, the second by his 'replacement' by the Devil as his spiritual opposite number at the end of tableau five. It is not without dramatic irony that Flaubert can authenticate these 'contrived' dictates of plot in the historicity of Jerome's *Vita Hilarionis*. Hilarion returned to Egypt (in AD 356) to see his former master prior to setting out in what would be the last fifteen years of his life on his Mediterranean mission.

For readers familiar with the *Vita Hilarionis*, however, Flaubert follows exactly the same procedures as his recasting of St Anthony as Antoine. The mould of the exemplary *vita* is emptied of all the miracles and fantastical episodes that particularize individual paragons, to highlight remarkably similar experiences and hence question whether they are repetitions, parallels, or variations on a theme.[19] If Flaubert's enormous artistic licence is everywhere apparent in his reworking of Hilarion and Antoine in this scene, he is arguably only taking a leaf from the books of earlier hagiographers who composed 'un art consommé de la greffe et de la jointure' for their own propagandist purposes (*StJ*, 10). Their versions then contrast markedly with two-dimensional, too superhuman, *vitae* (such as Philostratus' *Apollonius*) or too clichéd supernatural figures such as Flaubert's Devil. In Deleuzian terms it is perhaps only the Devil as simulacrum who can then fittingly take over from Hilarion as copy.[20] For the powerful substitutions of tableau three to work their terrible logic, some theological copy from hagiography is still required.

Flaubert's Hilarion is not only the younger, inverse mirror image of Antoine (and Jerome), but a figure of further *saintly* substitutes ('jointures'), to match the composites ('greffes') of 'Nebuchadnezzar' or the 'Queen of Sheba'. Two will now be explored, to leave a non-theological third for later discussion in Chapter 5. The first (like the third) depends on similar versions of Hilarion's name, but also abundantly replicates parts of the historical Hilarion's story (not least as a vigorous opponent of Arian heresy, and Hilarion's removal of the monster serpent of Epidaurus). Significantly for a remapping of nineteenth-century France in the *Tentation*, this figure, the *French*-born St Hilary of Poitiers (*c*.315–*c*.365), had pagan parents like Hilarion, and was in fact made a Doctor of the Church by Pope Pius IX in 1851 at the Synod of Bordeaux.[21] Hilary's account can be found in the *Légende dorée* and opens with striking features redolent of Flaubert's Hilarion which I have emphasized in the following quotation:

Hilaire, évêque de Poitiers, originaire de l'Aquitaine, *brilla parmi les hommes comme l'étoile de Lucifer parmi les astres* ... il s'était mis ... tout en restant laïc, à mener une vie d'un moine: si bien que, *en raison de sa vie et de sa science,* il fut élu évêque. Et il défendit contre les hérétiques, non seulement son diocèse, mais la France entière, ce qui ne l'empêcha pas d'être un jour exilé, en compagnie du bienheureux Eusèbe, évêque de Verceil, l'empereur ayant écouté l'avis de deux autres évêques qui avaient été corrompus par l'hérésie d'Arius, ainsi d'ailleurs que l'empereur lui-même. Et lorsque cette hérésie se fut propagée partout, l'empereur ayant permis à tous les évêques de se réunir pour discuter la vérité de la foi, saint Hilaire se rendit à la réunion; mais lesdits évêques obtinrent de l'empereur l'ordre, pour lui, de retourner aussitôt à Poitiers. Et comme, durant son retour, il était descendu dans l'île de Gallibaria, qui était toute pleine de serpents, aucun de ces animaux n'osa l'approcher; et lui, il planta au milieu de l'île un poteau, et défendit aux serpents de le dépasser, de telle sorte que la moitié de l'île fut pour eux non comme une terre, mais comme une mer.

(*LD*, 79)[22]

Follower *au pied de la lettre* in Anthony's footsteps as defender of orthodoxy against Arian heretical positions among elevated clergy, St Hilary's roles have earned him the title of the 'Athanasius of the West'. First an orator, Hilary became a Christian through study (like Hilarion in the Alexandrian schools) which led him to the convictions that

man is in the world for the practice of the moral virtues which must be rewarded hereafter, that there is only one God, the eternal and creative first cause, and that the Word of God who became incarnate in Jesus Christ is likewise eternal and of one substance with the Father.... He was praised by Augustine and Jerome as the 'illustrious teacher of the churches'... The influence of Origen is strong in his writings.[23]

These included *De Synodis* or *De Fide Orientalium*, an epistle addressed in 358 to the semi-Arian bishops in Gaul, Germany, and Britain, expounding Hilary's pro-Nicene views, and the *De Trinitate Libri* xii, composed in 359 and 360. For the first time, a successful attempt was made to express in Latin the theological subtleties elaborated in the original Greek. Hilary also intervened directly against Arian bishops by his attendance at various synods and councils. He secured the successful excommunication of Saturnius, the Arian Bishop of Arles, and his two supporters and was exiled for four years after failing to counter Arian predominance at the Synod of Bitterae (Béziers) in 356. At the Council of Seleucia in 359, Hilary joined the Egyptian Athanasians against the Arians, and in 364 he impeached the Arian Bishop of Milan, Auxentius. If none of these latter details colours Flaubert's Hilarion because anachronistic, Hilary operates nevertheless as a mediating, mirror figure on two counts.[24] The first is to raise a crucial issue of this tableau, whether the role of the true saint as successor of the apostles is more properly inside the Church or outside it (as anchorite). The second is to effect the substitution between the historical, Palestinian, Hilarion and his nineteenth-century *French* replication as a refracting mirror of names, *Saint-Hilaire*. This is the move that Peter Starr makes, but only through the homophonic, rather than historically overlapping, let alone theological, similarities of the name.[25]

IMITATIONS OF THE LIFE OF CHRIST

A St Hilarion or Saint-Hilaire substitute, Flaubert's Hilarion epitomizes the theological counter-attack. Where the splendidly composite figures of earthly temptations to power, Nebuchadnezzar and Sheba of tableau two, appealed to Antoine's senses to seduce his humanity, Hilarion's more invidious continuity with Anthony's historical disciple pertains not to material, but spiritual being, and thence to the theological core of Antoine's very existence (and self-definition). In preparation for his replacement by the Devil, Hilarion everywhere displays his 'science' of the *mise en question* in the *Tentation* by replicating the Devil's mode of temptation of Christ in the wilderness, encapsulated in the question: 'Did God say?' The Devil took Jesus to the holy city and had him stand on the highest point of the temple in order to challenge him to throw himself off and be saved by angels so as to overstep his human and divine natures as the Son of God.[26] Hilarion now throws Antoine before the model of ecclesiastical leadership of Alexandria, Athanasius, who was the mastermind of the knottiest points of the Nicene Creed, the 'substance' of Jesus as second person of the Trinity. By everywhere casting Athanasius down—his questionable authority as bishop, his far from Christian character traits and shaky church politics, his even shakier theology about Christ by allegedly naming him 'l'homme du Seigneur' at the Council of Nicaea let alone his limited intellectual understanding of 'le Verbe' (*Tent*, 89–90)—Flaubert's Hilarion docs not cast doubt by pointing only to the weight of such evidence against a saint (centring on his all-too-human errors of judgement). Rather, as privileged insider to Antoine's faith and eldership, he appeals to Antoine's indubitable spirituality by tempting his teacher to step from his central, humble ascetic role *outside* church hierarchy for a higher place inside it, Athanasius' (and so to fall to spiritual pride): 'Si l'on t'avait mis à sa place, c'eût été un grand bonheur pour tes frères comme pour toi. Cette vie à l'écart des autres est mauvaise' (*Tent*, 90). When Antoine (imitating Jesus) rebuts this temptation to hold spiritual authority in the world, because his life of the spirit (and withdrawal from the world) is alone valuable, Hilarion (in line with the insider authority of his historical persona as founder of monasteries) further appeals to exemplary spiritual models in the history of the Church to formulate two further arguments to draw Antoine to deny his spiritual vocation as (future) father of monasticism. By the question, 'Est-ce que Jesus, était triste?' (*Tent*, 90), and evoking a Jesus who never cut himself off from life, Hilarion challenges Antoine's withdrawal from the world to learn discernment and only then to open the doors of his cell as a 'mépris du monde'. He turns the knife further by arguing that Antoine's acts of holy suffering (we witnessed his flagellations in tableau two) are in any case only a poor imitation of the 'purest' forms of denial of the world as practised by the (heretical) Montanists (not by Christians, he implies). Hilarion's naming of this group here not only provides a cue for figures of extreme forms of spiritual practice in the next tableau such as the Circoncellions. From Antoine's own discerning response, 'Mais c'est la vérité de la doctrine qui fait le martyre! (*Tent*, 91), Hilarion parries 'vérité' with 'erreur' and 'disordres', since acts of martyrdom stem from multiple motives which he sums up as a 'vertige'. Hilarion clinches this round by listing Church Fathers who chose martyrdom (Denys, Cyprian, and Gregory) and those who condemned it (Peter of

Alexandria and the Council of Elvira). Such contradiction among 'the authorities' cannot be truth for Hilarion, who will not take dogma as the answer to such ecclesiastical dispute either. However Antoine defends his position of faith and conduct in the remainder of the tableau, Hilarion has a further *spiritual* precedent ready as next line of unassailable attack. His mental and verbal prowess, like his outward form as persona of the copy, quintessentially pivots on substitution, the science of slipping an alternative, contrary, or problematic (heretical) thought or fact into accepted authority or arguments about 'truth' to pull the rug from under it at every juncture. Further key examples in tableau three illustrative of Hilarion's *theological* acumen as against Antoine's defence of faith concern the status of the revealed 'truth' and authority of Scripture—he points to the many irreconcilable contradictions of detail in the Gospels—or more seriously, the theological non-sequiturs of Christ's ministry, where the limits of his human and divine powers seem to be drawn differently in the various Gospel accounts, as in the story of the woman with the flow of blood, for example (*Tent*, 94–5).

Hilarion's adoption of Hilary's oratorical 'sciences', together with his stand against spiritual leaders in doctrinal error in a specifically French heritage as next-generation disciple of Anthony, immediately offers Flaubert the richest possible analogy with arguably *the* most controversial nineteenth-century French commentator on matters theological, Ernest Renan. As the chair of Jewish studies after a crisis in faith which occurred after he had taken the tonsure and entered the Catholic priesthood, Renan was a leading authority on the Hebrew Bible and history of the early Church. It was his *vita*, the *Vie de Jésus* (1863) and a French imitation of Strauss's *Leben Jesu*, which rocked the Catholic establishment (both its Ultramontanist and liberal wings) as well as the Protestant Churches, and even evoked the ire of Deists.[27] Flaubert read Renan's *Vie de Jésus* prior to writing the final version of the *Tentation* where it is Hilarion who is the most significant new addition. Why Flaubert critics including Seznec have never made this connection between Hilarion and Renan, or seen the huge relevance of Renan's *Vie de Jésus* for the debates in tableau three let alone four or five, can be explained by failure to acknowledge Flaubert's extensive interest in theological enquiry.[28] Instead, Flaubert's utter abhorrence of blindly accepted church dogma has been sufficient critical excuse to close all further investigation of religious questions as they are remapped in Flaubert's *œuvre*. Closer inspection of Renan's nineteenth-century *Vie de Jésus* provides ample evidence of Flaubert's indebtedness to it for Hilarion's arguments in tableau three, both for their contents and form. As prefiguration of Renan, Hilarion's stance as trenchant critic and insider theologian (rather than apologist) then makes it hard to agree with critics' assessments of Flaubert's religious stance behind the *Tentation* as 'syncretistic' or even anti-clerical.[29] Use of the *Vie de Jésus* in the bigger picture of this tableau offers a much more nuanced reading of Flaubert's own 'theology'.

One of the most striking features of Hilarion's words is his huge authoritativeness (which Antoine endorses) issuing from a stance of intimate knowledge of Scripture, theology, and philosophical method of enquiring doubt, questioning scepticism, and ability to press hard on contradictions in the established facts.[30] This is precisely Renan's stance and his method of conveying his 'science' in an informed and logical style. Since he is no longer a priest and hence apologist, but a historian and critical commentator on religious texts, he sets out his stall very clearly in the introduction to the *Vie de Jésus*:

Le travail de critique a été l'œuvre des théologiens libéraux. Mais il est une chose qu'un théologien ne saurait jamais être, je veux dire historien. L'histoire est essentiellement désintéressée. L'historien n'a qu'un souci, l'art et la vérité (deux choses inséparables, l'art gardant le secret des lois les plus intimes du vrai). Le théologien a un intérêt, c'est son dogme. Réduisez ce dogme autant que vous voudrez; il est encore pour l'artiste et le critique d'un poids insupportable....

Moi, je suis un critique profane; je crois qu'aucun récit surnaturel n'est vrai à la lettre; je pense que sur cent récits surnaturels il y en a quatre-vingts qui sont nés de toutes pièces de l'imagination populaire.... La première tâche de l'historien est de bien dessiner le milieu où se passe le fait qu'il raconte. Or l'histoire des origines religieuses nous transporte dans un monde de femmes, d'enfants, de têtes ardentes ou égarées. (*VJ*, 11 and 19 respectively, italics in the original)

Renan is clearly labelling himself a 'critique profane' here (like the early Jerome), and blatantly separates the synthesizing efforts of Clement of Alexandria (in the *Stromata*) from 'new', more scientific (philosophical and historical) modes of exegesis. Compare his method of interpretation to Hilarion's arguments in the second half of tableau three:

On dit: 'Ma conviction est faite, pourquoi discuter?' et on méprise les docteurs, les philosophes, la tradition, et jusqu'au texte de la Loi qu'on ignore.... Nous n'avons de mérite que par notre soif du Vrai. La Religion seule n'explique pas tout; et la solution des problèmes que tu méconnais peut la rendre plus inattaquable et plus haute. Donc il faut, pour son salut, communiquer avec ses frères—où bien l'Eglise, l'assemblée des fidèles, ne serait qu'un mot,—et écouter toutes les raisons, ne dédaigner rien, ni personne. Le sorcier Balaam, le père Eschyle, et la sibylle de Cumes avaient annoncé le Sauveur. Denys l'Alexandrin reçut du Ciel l'ordre de lire tous les livres. Saint Clément nous ordonne la culture des lettres grecques. Hermas a été converti par l'illusion d'une femme qu'il avait aimée. (*Tent*, 92–3)

It seems no accident whatever that Hilarion unrolls his 'rouleau' here after this barrage of arguments that have as their target Antoine's spiritual authority and his carnal mind. A further stance of mockery—Hilarion pretends to become the unknowing disciple once more—it is also the unrolling of his argument and method à la Renan. From this point on, Hilarion's topics all come directly from the issues covered in the *Vie de Jésus*, although it is very probable that the earlier question, 'Est-ce que Jésus était triste?' is a sly reference to Renan's discussions of Galilee as 'souriante'.[31] Hilarion's very different, 'modern' (that is 'Greek' and sophist) reading of texts is then set in opposition to that already witnessed by Antoine's interpretation of his 'Écritures' in tableau one.

The biggest giveaway that 'Hilarion' is a substitute player for Renan's *Vie de Jésus* turns however on extensive discussion of miracles (*Tent*, 93), since these are Renan's biggest bone of contention, on which depend his whole doctrinal view of who Jesus was. Compare Hilarion's significant set of questions undermining the question itself with Renan's introduction:

La parole de Dieu, n'est-ce pas, nous est confirmée par les miracles?...Qu'est-ce donc qu'un miracle? Un événement qui nous semble en dehors de la nature. Mais connaissons-nous toute sa puissance? et de ce qu'une chose ordinairement ne nous étonne pas, s'ensuit-il que nous la comprenions? (*Tent*, 93)

Les miracles sont de ces choses qui n'arrivent jamais: les gens crédules seuls croient en voir; on n'en peut citer un seul qui se soit passé devant des témoins capables de le constater; aucune intervention particulière de la Divinité, ni dans la confection d'un livre, ni dans quelque événement que ce soit, n'a été prouvée. Par cela seul qu'on admet le surnaturel, on est en dehors de la science, on admet une explication qui n'a rien de scientifique, une explication dont se passent l'astronome, le physicien, le chimiste, le géologue, le physiologiste, dont l'historien doit aussi se passer. Nous

repoussons le surnaturel par la même raison qui nous fait repousser l'existence des
centaures et des hippogriffes: cette raison qu'on n'en a jamais vu.

(*VJ*, 9, italics in the original)

If Antoine does indeed 'see' mythological creatures such as unicorns in
the final tableau of the *Tentation,* as Chapter 7 will discuss, this passage
takes up Renan's earlier elucidation of how his method as historian
can neither countenance the supernatural (including miracles), nor the
Bible as revealed authority, and provides the 'link' to the ensuing topics
that Hilarion raises, 'literal' reading of Scripture, the discrepancies of
(i) detail (*Tent,* 94) and more crucially (ii) theology about the divinity
and/or humanity of Jesus (*Tent,* 95) as given in the different accounts of
the Synoptic Gospels and the Gospel of John:

Quant aux réfutations de mon livre . . . qui ont été faites par des théologiens ortho-
doxes, soit catholiques, soit protestants, croyant au surnaturel et au caractère sacré des
livres de l'Ancien et du Nouveau Testament, elles impliquent toutes un malentendu
fondamental. Si le miracle a quelque réalité, mon livre n'est qu'un tissu d'erreurs.
Si les Évangiles sont des livres inspirés, vrais par conséquent à la lettre depuis le
commencement jusqu'à la fin, j'ai eu tort de ne pas me contenter de mettre bout
à bout les morceaux découpés des quatre textes, comme font les harmonistes, sauf
à construire ainsi l'ensemble le plus redondant, le plus contradictoire. Que si, au
contraire, le miracle est une chose inadmissible, j'ai eu raison d'envisager les livres qui
contiennent des récits miraculeux comme des histoires mêlées de fictions, comme des
légendes pleines d'inexactitudes, d'erreurs, de partis systématiques. Si les Évangiles
sont des livres comme d'autres, j'ai eu raison de les traiter de la même manière
que l'helléniste, l'arabisant et l'indianiste traitent les documents légendaires qu'ils
étudient. La critique ne connaît pas de textes infaillibles; son premier principe est
d'admettre dans le texte qu'elle étudie la possibilité d'une erreur. Loin d'être accusé
de scepticisme, je dois être rangé parmi les critiques modérés, puisque, au lieu de
rejeter en bloc des documents affaiblis par tant d'alliage j'essaye d'en tirer quelque
chose d'historique par de délicates approximations.

(*VJ*, 8, italics in the original)

Renan's *Vie de Jésus* erases the supernatural in favour of a Jesus as
exemplary 'charmeur', who offered a sublime and distinctive message
for the crowds (the Sermon on the Mount).[32] Logically, Renan's historical account accepts that Jesus was a verifiable person and leader of
a movement that infuriated the Orthodox Jewish authorities, but then

stops with the Crucifixion, explaining the Resurrection as the ardour of the women and his disciples wanting to believe the empty tomb. Renan therefore puts Jesus in an inferior place to God in the Trinity, not on the side of divinity but of humanity, albeit of superior kind.[33] Jesus is then a created being in and with nature (so as mortal can only die, not rise again). In the fourth century AD and since, there is a name for de-emphasizing the divinity of Jesus: Arianism.

Because Hilarion's most subversive invasions of Antoine's accepted beliefs are relentless barrages of argument couched as questions, Flaubert's character however stops short of Renan's assertions and hence his heretical position. Yet in his battle for Antoine's mind, Hilarion's 'Greek' and essentially Neoplatonic stance—his desire for abstraction is 'Platonic', yet his stand on evidence is 'Aristotelian'—reveals the schools in which he was initially trained as those which still define his 'theology'. His insistence on terminology, for example 'le Verbe' (rather than 'Christ' or 'Jesus'), shows him as a seeker after pure thought, the Idea and the Ideal.[34] The Roman Catholic Church's truck with Greek philosophy, particularly the influence of Aquinas in the Middle Ages, is perhaps most vociferously questioned by the *Tentation* here. Logically, Hilarion's positions will become the voice of Scholasticism in the medieval sense. Antoine is, however, no philosophical *naïf* or rabid antagonist to reason in tableau three. Near its end he patiently says to Hilarion, 'Il faudrait beaucoup de temps pour te répondre!' (*Tent*, 95). Although it is to Antoine's 'pensée', his spiritual curiosity about knowledge and systems (whether 'anges', 'nombres', or 'germes'), that Hilarion can appeal at the end of this tableau, Antoine's free will at the same time permits enquiry but not any encroachment on his beliefs, faith, or stand on doctrine, or vocation as *contemplative* desert father outside the institutional structure of the Church.

Hilarion's 'pure' reason as against Antoine's 'pure' faith is thus at the heart of the similarities and absolute differences of this tableau, which only discernment of the spirit of both, as well as of their age, can settle regarding either 'purity'. Hilarion's persuasive *mise en question* reveals his 'Devil's advocacy' precisely because it rests fully upon the 'science' (*scientia*) of his natural man. His is not merely the quest for knowledge and for truth in philosophical mode, but also in the sense of nineteenth-century science (opposed to 'faith' or 'religion'). Again it is the Renan of *La Vie de Jésus* which provides the key to these substitutions.

La science seule est pure; car la science n'a rien de pratique; elle ne touche pas les hommes; la propagande ne la regarde pas. Son devoir est de prouver, non de persuader ni de convertir.... Seule la science cherche la vérité pure. Seule elle donne les bonnes raisons de la vérité et porte une critique sévère dans l'emploi des moyens de conviction. Voilà sans doute pourquoi jusqu'ici elle a été sans influence sur le peuple.

(*VJ*, 23, italics in the original)

Hilarion's science in the nineteenth-century sense will be made manifest in tableau five, but all his parts can now be fully accounted for within his single persona and this scene (in response to Lilley) as some negative, altogether human trinity (Antoine as holy father, Hilarion as 'holy' son and unholy spirit) counterfeiting the one in which Antoine believes. Throughout the tableau, Antoine has refused Hilarion's argument as temptation to what would be tantamount to apostasy but this is because his open-mindedness—he frequently asks questions of Hilarion—stems from his steadfast and firm position of faith: Antoine's clear and constant use of 'non' and 'au contraire' for example quietly affirms his 'orthodoxy'. Moreover, in response to Hilarion's discussion of Athanasius, Antoine's utterance of 'Calomnie!', 'c'est un blasphème!' (*Tent*, 89) clearly signals a strongly held doctrinal position from which to judge such matters.[35] Again by refusing to spell out what Antoine believes, Flaubert may safeguard his saint as not deviating from the 'Faith' (and hence his saintly status), but also leave the reader (whether committed Catholic, agnostic, deist, or atheist) to interpret the nature of what this doctrinal stance is. At the end of the tableau, Antoine's openness to what comes to his *mind* is unchanged ('Oui! oui! ma *pensée* se débat pour sortir de sa prison' (*Tent*, 96, emphasis added)), as too his ability to discern lie from truth, or more importantly overlapping and deceptively similar truths, along the way. Readers should take note that only open-mindedness to one's 'semblable' and 'frère' brings informed demolition of intellectual arrogance and prejudice.

Antoine's monologue (tableau one) has now become a dialogue, not
with the world and the 'flesh' (tableau two), but with his treacherously
similar disciple in the faith. Only through dialogue can the mutual
differences in position behind the words of individual speakers be drawn
out (discerned). Antoine's 'orthodoxy' (faith) like Hilarion's questioning
(reason) are thus the necessary synergy of the *Tentation* that permits the
reader to judge the whirling plethora of similar 'religions' and 'sciences'
in fourth-century Alexandria as also representative of those circulating
in nineteenth-century France, or indeed today. Without the strong voice
of 'orthodoxy' and its close alternative positions, whether adding to
or taking away from central tenets, how can one formulate, know,
or defend one's own beliefs? However 'Hilarion' (like the historical
Hilarion, St Hilary, or Renan) changes the shape of theological arguments by substitution (the motor for the two tableaux to come through
metamorphoses of similar 'germes' of religious ideas): the moral that
is tacitly unfolding is that all reasonable belief systems demonstrably
'die' (like the gods of tableau five) if they do not have 'believers' and
'questioners'. Flaubert will return to the logic of this cultural pattern
through Antoine's final 'response' to Hilarion at the end of tableau
five, and to the Devil at the end of tableau six which causes both to
'disappear'.

Faith and Reason are thus not oppositional but appositional in the
Tentation, like Antoine and Hilarion (and this book's structure into the
two parts of 'religion' and 'science'). Consequently, Flaubert balances
the positive and negative logic of substitutions (imitation and mockery)
in his double agent, Hilarion, by borrowing historically authentic elements about him from Jerome's *Vita Hilarionis* to turn them to critical
advantage. More clearly than critics such as Gothot-Mersch, Lilley, or
Starr have elucidated, we have uncovered the most logical proofs for
Hilarion as the vital linkman between the beliefs of the East (issuing
from the 'Queen of Sheba' in tableau two) and those of the West
(Greek, Neoplatonic as explored in tableaux five to seven in various
guises) *both* centred upon the so-called 'heresies' of tableau four literally
and figuratively in the text. As philosopher of (comparative) religion
including Christianity like Renan, rather than as (iterative) defender
of Antoine's orthodoxy, Hilarion is then ideally placed to introduce
and comment upon 'orthodoxy's' various alternative sects, cults, and

religions of third- and fourth-century Alexandria in tableau four, and the 'pagan' 'gods' that Christianity deposed in tableau five. By stopping short of Renan's Arianism, but steering Hilarion strongly towards systems and orders grounded in the material, Flaubert has in him another nineteenth-century French 'scientist' substitute, Geoffroy Saint-Hilaire, whose *œuvre* can only be put in place once Hilarion's further work in tableaux four and five, and the Devil's in tableau six, have been accomplished.

Hilarion therefore sums up what is new about the 1874 *Tentation,* and how it remaps its earlier versions and religious ideas in play in nineteenth-century France. For readers unknowing of such intertextual 'doubles' (genetic, historical, the play on Hilarion's saintly names), Hilarion's superlative oratory is paramount as key to understanding the *Tentation* as text about religious science. As supreme orator, Hilarion everywhere plays the part of devil's advocate (literally and metaphorically). In his relentless questioning of how any credal position comes to assert (and uphold) its final authority, Hilarion's bid for rational articulation of belief—his theo-logical roles in tableaux four and five to come—strikes at the heart of the central problem facing the early Church, like any major belief system. Authority and truth cannot rely on revealed knowledge, but need to be given clear articulation. The life and times of Anthony the Great epitomize the need of the Christian Church at the Council of Nicaea to set out its creed (credo) by which to judge error, or worse heresy, *within* its ranks and to institute a system of arbitration and authority to uphold and judge this one 'pure' faith in the light of its many rivals. French nineteenth-century science we will discover will also come to the same places. This is the reason why religion matters to Flaubert's articulation of his age.

But it is not Hilarion's questioning of tenets of faith that constitutes Flaubert's censure of contemporary religious 'Orthodoxy' and its authorities, but Antoine's monosyllabic rebuttals of authoritatively articulated, but tendentious, doxa. What more sublime critique of the vaunting omni*science* of nineteenth-century Roman Catholicism specifically enshrined in the new dogma of *papal* infallibility can there be than in Antoine's lived negations of institutionalized religion and establishment authorities? Because we are however unlikely to side with this sublime prophet in the wilderness (Antoine) but follow the appeal of the clever doubter (Hilarion), Flaubert then draws his readers through him into the fourth tableau by veiled adoption of the questions underlying Renan's *Vie de Jésus*, and concerning the key mysteries of the Trinity and the Incarnation that make Christianity a distinctive Church vis-à-vis either rival Eastern or Western Neoplatonic beliefs. Who was Jesus? How did Jesus the Son of God fit within the Trinity and what was his relation to its two persons, God the Father and the Holy Spirit? Was Jesus then fully God and fully incarnate in human form? Or was he a demigod who gave up his divine attributes to descend to human experience, or a superhuman being who, although embodied in a human, did not taste mortality because he was divine and hence could work miracles as part of his innate being? In more 'Neoplatonist' and indeed Eastern religious terms, was Jesus a hypostasis or an essence, a pure spirit, a demiurge, an eon, or an archon? Was he higher or lower than the angels, part of 'la hiérarchie des Anges, la vertu des Nombres, la raison des germes et des metamorphoses?', to recall Hilarion's summation of what Antoine might desire to know about? We may in reply recite the Apostles' Creed since this is Antoine's overt response to counter-ideologies in tableau five. Or we may try to understand his tacit (Eastern) Orthodox theological explanations since Anthony the Great counselled Athanasius about these mysteries.[36] Here is Timothy Ware's modern Orthodox explanation, so that we can launch into the 'Jesus debates' of the fourth tableau with both Antoine and Hilarion:

The main work of the Council of Nicaea in 325 was the condemnation of Arianism. Arius, a priest in Alexandria, maintained that the Son was inferior to the Father, and, in drawing a dividing line between God and creation, he placed the Son among created things: a superior creature, it is true, but a creature none the less. His motive, no doubt, was to protect the uniqueness and the transcendence of God, but the effect of his teaching, in making Christ less than God, was to render impossible our human deification. Only if Christ is truly God, the council answered, can He unite us to God, for none but God Himself can open to humans the way of union. Christ is 'one in essence' (*homoousios*) with the Father. He is no demigod or superior creature, but God in the same sense that the Father is God: 'true God from true God,' the council proclaimed in the Creed which it drew up, 'begotten not made, *one in essence* with the Father'.... It was the supreme achievement of St Athanasius of Alexandria to draw out the full implications of the key word in the Nicene Creed: *homoousios*, one in essence or substance, consubstantial. Complementary to his work was that of the three Cappodocian Fathers, Saints Gregory of Nazianzus...(?329–?90), Basil the Great (?330–79), and his younger brother Gregory of Nyssa (died 394). While Athanasius emphasized the unity of God— Father and Son are one essence (*ousia*)—the Cappodocians stressed God's threeness: Father, Son, and Holy Spirit are three persons (*hypostasis*). Preserving a delicate balance between the threeness and the oneness of God, they gave full meaning to the classical summary of Trinitarian doctrine, *three persons in one essence*. Never before or since has the Church possessed four theologians of such stature within a single generation.   (*W*, 22–3)

4

Statements of Faith(s)

Alongside Antoine, Hilarion also leads the reader into the *Tentation*'s pivotal set piece in various subsections, the enormous 'basilique' context for the fourth and longest tableau. Its incomprehensibility issuing from the plethora of clamouring voices gathered there has not surprisingly elicited mainly negative response from readers and critics, so that the final version of the *Tentation* (like the first) has been written off as 'raté'.[1] The paucity of specialist critical study of this centrepiece tableau also speaks volumes. The only Flaubert scholars to have pronounced upon it have been bookish experts of the erudite and arcane such as Seznec and Bowman.[2] Their work has only been endorsed by recent genetic critics such as Séginger for this tableau's comparative religious contents, to further underline Flaubert's syncretism.[3] While anglophone critics such as Orr and Pasco have addressed the theological questions raised by tableau four to support a much less 'anti-Christian' reading of the *Tentation* as a whole,[4] the tableau's problematic contents and structure have remained unexamined. Yet the reader's same guide Hilarion has already taunted Antoine about his sloth and closing his mind: 'Voilà que tu tombes dans ton péché d'habitude, la paresse. L'ignorance est l'écume de l'orgueil. On dit: "Ma conviction est faite, pourquoi discuter?" ' (*Tent*, 92). Antoine has however taken the step through curiosity of allowing himself to be led where he might not otherwise have chosen to go, whereas Flaubert's readers, especially his critics, have refused to break with their 'habitudes' when it comes to tackling the *Tentation*'s overtly religious, and indeed sacrilegious matter. Arguably, then, Antoine represents the radical 'free thinker' of tableau four, *confronting* all the many rival religious positions and doctrines to his own most dearly held beliefs as the only way to test their validity *and* the standpoint of his own faith. As Valentine Cunningham puts it:

And the history of the Christian Church consists in large measure of conflict between *haereses*, the various choosers and their groups. . . . All reading involves choices about meaning. So all reading is *haeresis* neutrally, unpejoratively regarded. *Haeresis* is the degree zero of interpretation . . . the best reading is heretical in its negative meaning, that interpretation of texts is furthered by *haeresis*, by *haeretikoi*.[5]

It is Antoine 'the believer', not Hilarion 'the questioner' (agent provocateur), who therefore paradoxically provides the model for any serious commentator of this scene: she or he needs both the will to test previous, fixed belief and accepted critical dogma thereby to discover both weak spots and personal prejudice, and the daring to engage with subjects that may be strongly antipathetic to personal belief systems since greater understanding may come through the process. If Jean Seznec's work on this tableau of the 'heresies' therefore remains an unchallenged 'authority', it is thanks to his critically heretical reading after Cunningham's definition.[6] Any new reading of tableau four must handsomely acknowledge Seznec, but not take his work as fixed or the final word (critical dogma). Because heretical reading of Seznec (and Bowman) on this central tableau of the *Tentation* is long overdue, what follows will also attempt to read it heretically, with the open, critical mind of Flaubert's Antoine. Precisely because his model St Anthony the Great never joined 'the Church', he could remain its most useful commentator and above all its critic. Tableau four will prove not only the religious 'clé de la voûte' of the whole work, but the turning point for its vertiginous remainder. Not least this is because Antoine stays its course (including its cataleptic moments), whereas the reader's much more intellectually attractive and 'modern' commentator Hilarion mysteriously disappears after barely the first third of the tableau. Surprisingly critics have not questioned why, even though Hilarion's acerbic comments essentially enrich the comparative religious dimensions of tableau five (and tableau three) where he is present throughout.[7]

Tableau three was very much a one-to-one theological dialogue between seeming *spiritual* equals to allow their huge differences to emerge. In that tableau four literally runs on from the third, this principle of difference and similarity in religious and doctrinal matters is also expanded, to match Hilarion's literally increasing size and authority. This time, however, the tenets of the many faith positions and articulations of belief are not tacit, but explicit, personified by their master founders/guru upholders, or expressed *en groupe* by disciple/converts. The elder–disciple relation that structured tableau three is thus refracted kaleidoscopically in tableau four, to close as I have argued elsewhere on the Apollonius–Damis/master–disciple relationship as a negating variation on a theme.[8] Where Hilarion took up a range of (heretical) counter-positions in tableau three for Antoine's comment in dialogue, tableau four is the multiple of Hilarion-like assertions and challenges (substitutions of his substitution), but with Antoine as almost silent, observer-commentator of these harangues, unequal and singular to their overwhelming number and voice. The conflict and rivalries of conviction in tableau three that similar beliefs necessarily provoke inside and outside a 'faith' find magnification by individual group voices in tableau four, and on a bigger scale of difference—from angry and fanatical dogmatism to sectarianism and persecution—with its concomitant outcome of direct opposition, *in extremis* in excommunication or martyrdom of 'heretics'. It was precisely such doctrinal difference that the early Church sought to resolve by means of its great councils and the formulation of its Nicene Creed.[9] Interestingly it is not in tableau four, its most obvious position, that Antoine recites it, but tableau five.

Seznec's work on the sources of tableau four, especially Beausobre and Matter, has amply demonstrated Flaubert's creative rule of using intertextual authorities throughout the *Tentation*, but does not ponder the reasons for this beyond an aesthetic love of 'real' detail. Yet what is crystallized in the words of the protagonists in tableau four is strategic, as the discussion below will demonstrate. Verification of these words through discovery of (further) sources only adds to weightier erudition. What is needed for the bigger remapping of the text is heretical reading that assists readers in how to respond to the seemingly unending parade of hectoring 'hérésies'. The honest reader glazes over because of boredom and hence inattention, or because ignorance and incomprehension (or too much erudition à la Seznec) causes uncertainty as to how to understand the maelstrom of obviously 'important' figures clamouring to be heard. What this chapter proposes to explore is not other intertextual detail for itself (although some new intertexts will be added to make some inroads into the huge bibliography that specialists have never analysed). On the contrary, and as a 'basilique' forerunner to Proust's conception of his *A la recherche* as 'cathédrale', the focus is squarely on trying to *follow* the rationale for Flaubert's choices (*haeresis*) in terms of quirky detail—why did particular elements among their perfectly possible alternatives attract his attention given the breadth of his reading specifically for this tableau?—and in terms of the order of appearance of the *haeretikoi* that were finally chosen.[10] For newcomers and specialists alike, one must also dare to ask what the overarching structure of the tableau is as a whole that might explain its purpose. In this tall order for a new heretical reading, I merely return in different form and different priority to the unanswered questions that Seznec grappled with and offered some solutions for, namely (and chronologically in his study): 'l'intérêt profond de l'épisode et sa véritable portée' (15); the 'mystery' source in two volumes mentioned in Flaubert's letter of 9 September 1856 to Bouilhet which Seznec considers a rereading of Beausobre, rather than a new work (17); the classification problem of the Gymnosophist 'parmi les hérétiques' (32), which Seznec resolved by a source within a known source, an article by the Abbé Mignot in the same volume as an article by the Abbé Foucher (33); and Flaubert's prime place among his rival contemporaries such as Taine and Huysmans as surely expressing in his *Tentation* ' "l'idéal" de . . . leur vision du monde religieux aux premiers siècles de notre ère?' (46 and final remark). Furthermore I will enlist Seznec's method of taking Flaubert's bibliography for the *Tentation* with the utmost seriousness (meaning having read the works cited[11]), and of lateral bibliographical detective work therein (which Seznec amply demonstrates in his separate chapter on Apollonius of Tyana, where texts other than Chassang's which appeared too late in 1862 for the second version of the *Tentation* had to have been consulted). My heretical departures from Seznec are not so much that I see the Apollonius episode as integral to the fourth tableau and its logical conclusion, but that tableau four as a whole, if read with open rather than closed ears, is about more than the 'monde religieux aux premiers siècles de notre ère'.

The opening sentence of this chapter contained vital countermeasures for tackling inattention and incomprehension and suggested the procedure for heretical rereading of this tableau for all its vertiginous detail as if it was the 'St Anthony' triptych by Hieronymus Bosch. The first is the *frame* that every critic has missed because it is so obvious, the 'basilique' scene setting as the way of looking at the tableau's bigger picture. Second, Antoine's position throughout is its constant reference point as curious observer-commentator-respondent to what is before his eyes (and ours). Reconsideration of these constants then clarifies what the function of tableau four is in understanding the *Tentation* as a whole, not least its artistic remapping of the geographies of religious expression as intrinsic to their histories.

THE UNIVERSAL 'CHURCH'

By contrast again to the paucity of description and concentration on only two, similarly matched protagonists in tableau three, tableau four is a shocking array of descriptions and figures, images and sensations bombarding the imagination. The opening description, which appears only to set the scene, is surely also suggestive as *enlightenment* of what is to follow. Unlike the pale moonbeam which lit Hilarion in black and white in tableau three, the whole and then individual parts of the crowd before us are lit in glorious technicolour like a huge magic lantern show:

> La *lumière* se projette du fond, merveilleuse comme serait un *soleil multicolore*. Elle *éclaire* les têtes innombrables de la foule qui emplit la nef et *reflue* entre les colonnes, vers les bas-côtés,—où l'on *distingue* dans les compartiments de bois, des autels, des lits, des chaînettes de petites pierres bleues, et des *constellations peintes* sur les murs.   (*Tent*, 97, emphasis added)

Seznec's extremely valuable work elsewhere in the forgotten corners of Flaubert criticism offers a 'real' source for this description and its effects, Flaubert's visit to the Crystal Palace exhibition in London in 1851 and his detailed notes on the Indian and other artefacts he saw there.[12] As 'mother' of all Great Exhibitions in Europe, we are similarly party to a 'Great Exhibition' of the East in what follows in this tableau as preface to tableau five, a huge 'cabinet de curiosités', not in terms of bizarre and exotic artefacts, but living, glittering exotica of customs, rites, and beliefs, all with their common, extraordinary 'magical' religious force and refractions in various guises: 'Leurs yeux fulgurent extraordinaire-ment. Ils ont l'air de bourreaux ou l'air d'eunuques' (*Tent*, 97). Both categories bespeak the fanaticism of bodily comportments in the name of religion(s) in the scenes to come.

But this is no Crystal Palace or Temple to Progress, neither is it a church. Flaubert quite expressly calls it a 'basilique', although this vital detail has escaped critical notice. Its multicoloured light effect, including the painted constellations on the walls, can only be sparkling mosaics, marbles, and richly enamelled gilt work more familiar in mosques than (Catholic) churches, and lit by a central dome.[13] This is no mosque either, since Muhammad has yet to enter the stage of religious history. Rather, the clue has already been given in the second tableau, Antoine's transportation to Constantinople and his visit to the palace of Constantine (which *prefaced* the set pieces of the Eastern monarchs, Nebuchadnezzar and the Queen of Sheba). We are now next door, in the basilica which Constantine built to make his city the spiritual, as well as political, capital of Roman Christendom, and to distinguish it from pagan and polytheistic Rome. It seems no accident that the whole tableau has its setting in the famous Basilica of St *Sophia*, since what follows is an array of rival Eastern mystery and wisdom cults. As he did for the palace in tableau two, Flaubert again makes extensive use of Jules Labarte's *Le Palais impériale de Constantinople et ses abords, Sainte-Sophie, le forum Augustéon et l'Hippodrome tels qu'ils existaient au dixième siècle*, to furnish specific descriptions of St Sophia church.[14] Its immense size, the mosaics and multicoloured marbles, the innumerable columns and side chapels divided from the main nave are all described in this source. By moving east from 'Alexandria' to Constantinople once more, reconnection is made with all of the 'wisdom' of tableau two, of the land of Sheba (its magi, magicians, Sabean cults) and Babylonian and Persian religions (figured by Nebuchadnezzar and Xerxes as oppositional Old Testament rulers all framed in Antoine's Scripture readings in tableau one). Where Alexandria's ports in tableau two were described in a similar 'coup d'œil', the overview of this worldly city as cultural melting pot of trade then breaking into interior ports and quarters (*Tent*, 70), the 'nef' and alcoves likewise circumscribed by this basilica as 'City of God' contain all the ingredients of religious rite and practice.[15] Constantinople is no less a melting pot of travellers from the extent of the Roman Empire, 'du pays des Germains, de la Thrace et des Gaules, de la Scythie et des Indes', from climes frozen and sun-baked (*Tent*, 97). All have their distinctive markers (hats or observances), but importantly they are 'voyageurs', that is pilgrims, motivated by spiritual rather than economic ends.

Before the main protagonists are spotlighted for particular scrutiny in this 'celestial city', the initial effect for the observer is nevertheless one of careful order within the disorder created by the huge variety of the crowd. From this initial bird's-eye view, the colonnaded open partitions and side chambers clearly separate, segregate, and classify the whole into recognizable parts and subsequent reconfigurations. This is the pattern for understanding the seeming chaos of the ensuing tableau, which is more organized than it first appears. Initial but false recognition is then the further structural warning given to the reader who decides to stick close to Antoine's shoulder. That all the diverse figures recognize Hilarion should, in the light of tableau three, suggest that he is in some way substitutive of them all, and that therefore Antoine's unchanging sameness may distinguish their manifold similarities, differences, and inter-reflections. The same is true of the changing and seemingly opposing décors of tableau four (like their subsections), since all are linked by various shimmering (and deceptive) light–shadow effects and 'mirrorings', often by means of the amulets or images the protagonists wear around their necks or are holding. In the first third of the text (strategically all within Saint Sophia) for example

Les colonnes se balancent comme des troncs d'arbres, les amulettes aux cous des Hérésiarques entrecroisent des lignes de feux, les constellations dans les chapelles s'agitent, et les murs reculent sous le va-et-vient de la foule, dont chaque tête est un flot qui saute et rugit. (*Tent*, 113)

MARCELLINA

Autrefois, j'étais diaconesse à Rome dans une petite église, où je faisais voir aux fidèles les images en argent de saint Paul, d'Homère, de Pythagore et de Jésus Christ.

Je n'ai gardé que la sienne.

Elle entrouvre son manteau. (*Tent*, 118)

The 'real' of their various 'miroitements' from the initial mosaics quoted above will recall for the careful reader the seemingly forced transition in tableau two by means of the mirror of the giant lighthouse between Alexandria and Constantinople, and the mirage effects at the very outset of the *Tentation*, the scene of which (the Nile like a serpent) this one again becomes when Antoine is enclosed by the giant snake of the Ophites, and is thence returned to his 'cabane' (*Tent*, 122). This moonlit Nile then refracts Antoine back to a prison containing Christians to be thrown to the lions,[16] the 'colonnes' of the basilica (like the flickering light in the Ophites' upper room with its strange 'fût de colonne'

(*Tent*, 119)) now its 'barres', and Marcellina's 'mirror' (above) making it
'Rome'. When the horror of the lions' advance on their human prey (like
the Ophite snake) causes Antoine to close his eyes, and to open them
on a 'plaine aride et mamelonneuse', the white shapes in the darkness
and what glitters again sharpens the new focus: 'Des yeux brillent dans
la fente des longs voiles' (*Tent*, 127). This sub-scene of the Patrician
women under persecution visiting the tombs of their martyred relatives
then closes with 'flambeaux'; 'Le ciel commence à blanchir' and a seeming cut, before 'Le soleil brille' launches the scene of the Gymnosophist,
which critics have always considered out of place in this tableau of the
'heresies'. It is beautifully reflected, however, by correspondences (as
Baudelaire's famous poem with its 'vivants piliers') with the quotation
above about the heresiarchs' amulets and the glittering eyes ('fulgurants')
of the opening, like those of the patrician women:

Antoine voit nettement à travers des bambous d'une forêt de colonnes, d'un gris
bleuâtre. Ce sont des troncs d'arbres provenant d'un seul tronc. . . . l'ensemble
de toutes ces lignes horizontales et perpendiculaires, indéfiniment multipliées,
ressemblerait à une charpente monstrueuse, si elles n'avaient une petite figue
de place en place. . . . Sous les rameaux les plus bas, se montrent çà et là les
cornes d'un bubal, ou les yeux brillants d'une antilope . . . Aux quatre coins de
son bûcher flambent quatre feus. Le soleil est juste en face.   (*Tent*, 129–30)[17]

It will be the burning torch which will consume the dried stick of
the Gymnosophist, comically ending his 'scene' on his final word,
'l'Anéantissement' (*Tent*, 132), but like tableau two and the arrival of
the Queen of Sheba, it acts as the logical connector for the new, and
final visitors under the spotlight of the tableau, Simon the Magician
and Apollonius and Damis.

 Thus the dazzling, multicolour 'son et lumière' of the opening is a
unity of recognitions of the broadest church (the 'basilique') as a series
of inter-reflecting mosaics. If the various changing décors of this scene
operate a whirling effect of the spaces, places, and 'vertiges' of earlier
tableaux, tableau four is more than just a beautiful spiral pattern (like
that of the python in its midst).[18] This structure is richly suggestive
of, if not eternal return, then the re-emergence of the similar albeit in
some variant guise. Heresies, in a nutshell, are such endlessly generative
re-versions of pivotal elements of the 'one true faith', emerging in their
time and season with the theological movements of the 'official' Church,

but requiring its credal position and doctrines to have been firmly established against which 'heresy' can be judged.[19] The Council of Nicaea to formulate the Creed had only just accomplished its work. With an Antoine post Nicaea—his visit to 'Constantine' in tableau two was important preparation—Flaubert has hence matched form to content in tableau four, with huge economy of inter-reflection. We are left, however, with very uncomfortable dizziness, since 'heresy', like Hilarion, has expanded enormously—the Indian Gymnosophist-Brahman midpoint, for example, belongs to another eastern religious system altogether— and it has only narrowly failed to overwhelm Antoine in its coils, rather like the Ophite snake. Seznec, aware of precisely the category mistake the Gymnosophist implies, seemed to toy with the idea that another classification of this tableau of the 'heresies' might then be necessary, but rejected it, not least because of the clear 'heresies' subheading in Flaubert's bibliography.[20] The obvious question behind Seznec's solution for the Gymnosophist remains unaddressed: is tableau four really that of the *heresies*? If not, how should it then better be classified? And has Seznec missed an even bigger question, namely what makes one doctrine alongside many compelling, even similar, contenders the 'one' and 'true', thereby consigning the false others as 'heresies'?[21]

The Gymnosophist is not the only representative of a different Eastern religious system in the middle of tableau four. It ends with the Pythagorean Apollonius, who was believed to be the disciple of Simon the Magician. Moreover, the whole sequence of 'heresiarchs' opens with Mani, founder of Manicheism, a separate Gnostic *sect* rather than a heresy.[22] The main heresy vexing Athanasius, Bishop of Alexandria, at the time of St Anthony the Great, and which triggered the need for the Nicene Creed, was Arianism. In tableau four, Arius interestingly is made to wait until the *second* part of the first main décor, its first speaker after the description of 'reflecting amulets' above. Surely any 'tableau of the heresies' based seriously on the *Vita Antonii* (as the *Tentation* has proved in tableau one) ought rather to have begun with Arius, and ensured that none of its protagonists exceeded the religious geography of Alexandrian Christianity of the third and fourth centuries? If any more evidence were needed that Seznec's designation is seriously flawed, the 'heresies' section of Flaubert's bibliography contains works that any informed reader let alone specialist in matters theological would have classified as more relevant under other headings, and pulled into it several works that are listed elsewhere.[23] On all these points, this cannot be called 'the tableau of the heresies', although Christian heresies make up a vital element of its many parts.

Explanation of the place in the whole tableau of the Gymnosophist, as too its opening and closing figures, can immediately be resolved by its spatio-temporal context, which gathers under the one roof, a basilica called St *Sophia*, all the rival Eastern wisdom religions, mystery cults, and emergent Christian heresies which were the teeming brew in the Alexandria in the lifetime of St Anthony. The (Indian) Gymno*sophist* is then clearly connected to, but also properly situated outside, this Middle Eastern 'Church' (as *body* of believers), as is the singular Apollonius the Pythagorean who is thus a necessary link to the 'gods' in tableau five.[24] Flaubert therefore strictly and carefully uses the frame word 'basilique' to cover only the variant belief systems to early Christianity from Mani to the Ophites. From the Ophites to the end of the tableau, we are not in 'Constantinople', but back in 'Egypt' (Antoine's 'cabane', via 'Rome' and 'India'). The tableau would then appear to have the form of a double lens or helix. Should its participants then be divided into two intersecting groupings, sorting its Christian heresies from other Eastern religions and sects sharing similar but different ideas?[25] Or should this dualistic structure be discounted for a unifying one? After all the Gymno*sophist* is hidden by 'des troncs d'arbres provenant d'un seul tronc'and his doctrine is of 'le Grand Tout'.[26] Would this 'doctrine' unify all the figures as belonging to the period of the early Church at the time of its persecution by Rome and then establishment by Constantine, or is some further overarching classification (other than 'heresies') needed? Is an answer to this larger structural and semantic problem to be found in Flaubert's (in)famous bibliography?

One text squarely in the 'hérésies' subsection does indeed offer an authority for the main order of appearance of the many figures in the tableau, the Abbé Pluquet's *Mémoires pour servir à l'histoire des égarements de l'esprit humaine par rapport à la religion chrétienne, ou dictionnaire des hérésies, des erreurs et des schismes*, a work in two volumes.[27] If the keywords in Pluquet's appositional title are suggestive of the classificatory problems just raised, one short and one rather longer quotation from the first volume should make the case. The first, on the origins of philosophy, states that the 'Collèges de Prêtres devinrent donc des assemblées de philosophes qui cherchèrent comment et par quel méchanisme tout s'opérait dans la nature'(*DH*, 52).[28] 'Mages chaldéens', 'Prêtres égyptiens', 'Philosophes indiens' are all then given as examples in that order. The second is found in chapter 6, entitled 'Des Hérésies & des Sectes qui s'élevèrent pendant le second siècle':

Ainsi, les philosophes orientaux qui adoptèrent le christianisme et qui n'y trouvèrent point l'éclaircissement d'une infinité de questions que *la curiosité humaine* forme sur l'origine du mal, sur la production du monde, etc. se reprirent... vers leurs anciens principes, qui devinrent comme un supplément aux dogmes du christianisme.... C'est ainsi que le système des émanations des Chaldéens, la croyance des génies, la doctrine des deux principes, s'unirent en partie aux dogmes du christianisme, et servirent à expliquer l'histoire de la création... et formèrent les systèmes théologiques de Saturnin, de Basilide, de Carpocrate, d'Euphrate, de Valentin, de Cerdon, de Marcion, d'Hermogène, d'Hermias, de Bardesanes, d'Apelle, de Tatien, de Sévère, d'Héracleion, des Sethiens, des Caïnites, des Ophites. Presque tous admettaient une intelligence suprême et des génies dont ils augmentaient ou diminuaient le nombre, et qu'ils faisaient agir au gré de leur imagination. On vit donc les dogmes de la philosophie orientale, pythagoricienne, platonicienne, stoïcienne, les principes de la cabale, les pratiques de la magie, employés, non-seulement pour expliquer les miracles et les dogmes du christianisme, mais encore pour se rendre les génies propices et pour s'élever à la perfection. Ici, ce sont des talismans... là, ce sont *des nombres* qu'on porte: les uns pour se détacher de la terre et s'élever au ciel, s'interdisent tous les plaisirs; les autres les regardent comme une contribution qu'il faut payer aux *anges créateurs*... ceux-ci marchent nus comme Adam et Ève dans l'état d'innocence; ceux-là condamnent comme un crime, l'usage des alimens propres à exciter les passions.

Tous prétendaient pratiquer ce que Jésus-Christ était venu enseigner aux hommes... tous, sans exception, reconnaissaient donc les miracles de Jésus-Christ et tous avaient fait quelque changement dans leurs systèmes, pour les expliquer.... Quelques-uns de ces chefs formèrent des sociétés assez étendues; telle fut la secte des Basilidiens, des Valentiniens, des Marconites.... Un ambitieux s'éleva parmi eux, prétendit que leur doctrine était plus parfaite que celle de Jésus-Christ, s'annonça comme le réformateur de la religion que Jésus-Christ avait enseignée; il prétendit que dans l'Évangile, Jésus-Christ promettait d'envoyer le Saint-Esprit pour enseigner une religion plus parfaite que la sienne; il annonça qu'il était le Saint-Esprit, ou le prophète par la bouche duquel le Saint-Esprit faisait connaître aux hommes cette religion plus parfaite; il eut les extases, se fit des disciples qui se prétendirent inspirés, et formèrent une secte très-étendue, qui se divisa bientôt en différentes branches qui ne différaient que par quelques pratiques ridicules.

Un des dogmes de cette secte, était qu'on ne pouvoit éviter le martyre; ainsi beaucoup de Montanistes souffrirent la mort dans la persécution et cependant la secte se perpétua jusqu'au cinquième siècle.... La plupart des hérésies des deux premiers siècles étaient un alliage de philosophie avec les dogmes du christianisme. (*DH*, 136–8, emphasis added)

Not only is the main order of the heresiarchs in tableau four accounted for in this 'structural' intertext, but so too are the introductory links to it from tableau three, Antoine's 'Curiosité humaine' and Hilarion's tempting 'Désires-tu connaître la hiérarchie des *Anges*, la vertu des *Nombres* . . . ?' (*Tent*, 96, emphasis added). On these bones Flaubert uses other sources (such as Matter and Beausobre), as the 'flesh' to furnish individual details, and intersperses Pluquet's lists with Church Fathers who veered towards, or defected to, one or other of these heresies such as Origen to Montanism. Pluquet's two-volume work does not, however, name Mani specifically (there are only nameless 'Chaldéens'). If this figure is a key to introducing the heresies proper, and the overall structure by which Simon the Magician and Apollonius are neatly linked, none of these figures is mentioned in Pluquet. Most vitally of all, Hilarion's third place to tempt Antoine's curiosity, 'la raison des germes et des métamorphoses' embodied as the Gymnosophist's transmigrations of souls, does not have its source in Pluquet either, even though this two-volume work may qualify it better than Beausobre as Seznec's 'mystery' resource in Flaubert's letter to Bouilhet. Moreover, the Gymnosophist is too vital in his dramatic representation of 'métamorphoses' to leave him to the fate of Seznec's obscure source within another obscure source, or merely as another kind of sage or even sophist. Pluquet takes the heresies structure in tableau four a long way, but not far enough to retain 'doctrinal error' ('égarements') as the keyword for the whole tableau. Is some closer observational work from Antoine's viewpoints, and beyond the initial glitter of the individual players, the better way to proceed?

When it comes to the final version of the tableau itself, the word 'hérésies' is not in fact used; only its cognates are mentioned, 'hérétiques' (once) and 'Hérésiarques' (twice in the régie), at strategic junctures in the specifically 'basilique' scenes, although there is a final instance in Antoine's mouth just before Simon arrives which will be treated below. The first usage is the word 'hérétiques', as one element of an extraordinary list of cognate invectives in the mouth of the anonymous 'homme', who then turns out to be Tertullian:[29]

Ah! imposteurs, brigands, simoniaques, hérétiques et démons! la vermine des écoles, la lie de l'enfer! Celui-là, Marcion, c'est un matelot de Sinope excommunié pour inceste; on a banni Carpocras comme magicien; Aetius a volé sa concubine, Nicolas prostitué sa femme; et Manès, qui se fait appeler le Bouddha et qui se nomme Cubricus, fut écorché vif avec une pointe de roseau, si bien que sa peau tannée se balance aux portes de Ctésiphon!... Brisez les images! voilez les vierges! Priez, jeûnez, pleurez, mortifiez-vous! Pas de philosophie! pas de livres! après Jésus, la science est inutile! (*Tent*, 107)

The term 'Hérésiarques' is used twice at the end of the 'basilique' section to underscore its singular personifications and inter-reflections as a group. In its first usage, the amulet quotation above, the heresiarchs are set in opposition to the nameless crowd of singing Christians:

Cependant,—du fond même de la clameur, une chanson s'élève avec des éclats de rire, où le nom de Jésus revient.

Ce sont les gens de la plèbe, tous en frappant dans leurs mains pour marquer la cadence. Au milieu d'eux est

ARIUS

en costume de diacre. (*Tent*, 113–14)

Shortly afterwards, all the heresiarchs form a circle around Antoine (to prefigure the Orphite snake, or in the form of a 'magic' circle), becoming the *choric* 'Nous avons des martyrs plus martyrs que les tiens, des prières plus difficiles, des élans d'amour supérieurs, des extases aussi longues' (*Tent*, 116). This is in response to Antoine's words of address to them (in terms which again do not include 'heresiarch', yet echo in quite different tone those of Tertullian above): 'Docteurs, magiciens, évêques, et diacres, hommes et fântomes, arrière! arrière! Vous êtes tous des mensonges' (*Tent*, 116). Recalling Hilarion's claims to authority in tableau two, the final act of the heresiarchs as nameable group (closing with Mani) is to brandish their respective 'rouleaux',[30] to lay claim individually to the 'final' authority of their particular doctrinal texts. Antoine escapes to encounter the 'Ébionites' in a dark corner as the final religious group (Jewish) to be met before being dragged to the Ophites' upper chamber (by Hilarion?). Mani's place at the beginning of the tableau and among the heresiarchs brandishing their

'Évangiles' is then a clue, providing we look at *Antoine's* categorizations and not the fanatical Tertullian's. Antoine classifies his interlocutors not according to (Nicene) Credal credentials, but as different kinds of cultic teacher-leaders (although they are also fallible men, phantoms then lies[31]). There is one implied, overarching, generic label that links them all, 'Gnostic'. These serious seekers and teachers of *gnosis* (wisdom) are like Antoine himself making *revealed knowledge* claims (whether philosophical, 'scientific', religious, or intellectual). Jacques Matter's *Histoire critique du gnosticisme et de son influence sur les sectes religieuses et philosophiques des six premiers siècles de l'ère chrétienne* is therefore as important for its overarching title as it is to the detail of tableau four, and it is centrally in the 'heresies' subsection of Flaubert's bibliography.[32] St *Sophia* as context for the whole tableau has now revealed its supremely Gnostic content, and Antoine's (and Hilarion's) place within it. It was Antoine's desire and curiosity to *know* as a way to expand his own 'gnose' that got him here in the first place, dictates his onward meetings with the Ophites (arguably the quintessential Gnostics[33]), and then with their related representatives of other Eastern mystery religions, the Gymnosophist, Simon the Magician, and finally Apollonius the Eleusinian and Pythagorean. As the long quotation from Pluquet above indicated, two conflicting and complementary religio-metaphysical-philosophical systems from Persia/India and Greece-Rome converge in 'Alexandrian' guise. But what distinguishes Antoine (and allows him to hold to his own experiential version of truth and belief despite the seemingly overlapping claims of his rivals) is his simple faith. This keeps him (literally and metaphorically in the tableau) from entanglement in complex systems and hierarchies of initiation, and provides his un-bookish discernment of the clamouring figures as 'mensonges' and 'fantômes' (that is untrue and unreal). Christianity is no less revealed as a religion and set of beliefs, but it relies not on monistic, dualistic, or arcane metaphysical systems and complicated hierarchies of forms (emanations, eons, etc.) or elect elites, but on simple faith in mysteries of the *Trinity* as told in the Gospels and apostolic texts and accessible to any. Antoine's common sense (that of the people) is therefore the touchstone for the dazzling theological and religious 'éblouissement' that is the plethora of tableau four. If we have in the word 'Gnosis' answered the riddle of its overall structure, context, and form, it is only with Antoine that we may start to understand what is being shown behind its dazzle.

ANGLES ON VISION

If clamour and religious cacophony sum up this tableau, Antoine is unusually silent within it. When he does make an observation, it is therefore a marker of his un-containable expression, to countermand the voice(s) in question. His reactions are visceral as much as 'intellectual', his most varied of ripostes occurring at the outset *after* Mani's various pronouncements—'[il] se mit à rire: "Ah! ah! quelle absurde imagination!" ' (*Tent*, 99); 'Je ne connais rien . . . qui nous empêche . . . de le croire' (*Tent*, 100), and finally, 'Ah! l'abomination!' (*Tent*, 101)— setting a pattern for the remainder of the tableau, of (i) incredulity (at the words of Saturnin, Valentine, Simon the Magician), (ii) horror and revulsion (the Priscillianists), and (iii) initial attraction, then utter repulsion (Tertullian, Apollonius). His apparently more ameliorated, 'intellectual', response to the heresiarchs (quoted above) nonetheless contains in its middle 'arrière! arrière!', a very firm rejection. It will be this mode of response that Antoine most uses with Simon and Apollonius, the latter's amazing feats of spiritual athletics being an increasingly unwanted diatribe (because unstoppable), and an almost laughable annoyance.

Antoine's longest speech of the tableau occurs after the conflagration of the Gymnsophist in the only moment of the scene where he is alone at his 'cabane' (perhaps recalling the start of tableau three). In his confusion over what is real and unreal around him, Antoine is however completely lucid in his summation of what has passed before him concerning the banality of (i) the Gymnosophist—'Cette mort est commune parmi les sages indiens. . . . Quelle haine de la vie il faut avoir!' (*Tent*, 132)—(ii) martyrs of all stripes (their most extreme, the Montanists, are not named), and (iii) the Gnostic figures preceding them (each leader ultimately as anonymous as the next) as

la foule des hérésiarques . . . Quels cris! quels yeux! Mais pourquoi tant de débordements de la chair et *d'égarements de l'esprit*?

C'est vers Dieu qu'ils prétendent se diriger par toutes ces voies! De quel droit les maudire, moi qui trébuche dans la mienne? Quand ils ont disparu, j'allais peut-être en apprendre davantage. Cela tourbillonnait trop vite; je n'avais pas le temps de répondre. A présent, c'est comme s'il avait *dans mon intelligence* plus d'espace et plus de lumière. Je suis tranquille. (*Tent*, 133, emphasis added)

If Flaubert seems to use the word 'hérésiarques' in the manner that Seznec described the fourth tableau as that of the '*hérésies*', the vital distinction is contained in Flaubert's exact use of the first part of the Abbé Pluquet's title: *Mémoires pour servir à l'histoire des **égarements de l'esprit** humaine par rapport à la religion chrétienne*'. Heresy (false doctrine) is not the most dangerous subject of this tableau, but rather those magnetic proponents who first pedal such ideas. By analogy (the hidden touchstone term), the Christ of Christianity and his claims are everywhere being scrutinized as if through the world view of the early (rival) *haeretekoi* (leaders of their respective 'churches') of the second and third centuries AD. Flaubert is here *reversing* the usual order of orthodox priority (working from Christianity to its others). By working from its contemporary others the claims of Christianity are under scrutiny. The stories of Simon and Apollonius *after* this juncture directly serve this end, but thereby only show their comparative shortcomings. These miracle workers have only one 'disciple', claim divine credentials as gods in human guise (like Jesus), but like the Gymnosophist leave no 'church' behind them, and hence remain *outside* the 'basilique' part of the structure.[34] By direct inference, but without heavy theology, Antoine knows and shows exactly where he stands on matters of doctrine and faith, perhaps even more so after the Gymnosophist section, since he recognizes Christianity's greater Church and enlightenment *intellectually*. The final third of the tableau seems to build on this broader space— the 'tourbillonnements' are past tense—so that Antoine's other spiritual qualities can be reflected for us in the fantastical acts of his 'magical' interlocutors as counterfeits to his 'real'.

The overarching 'lumière' of St Sophia of the first half of the tableau, the self-immolation of the Gymnosophist by fire in its middle, logically move it to conclude with two 'charismatic', post-Old Testament 'Mages', so as to unpack the work of the supernatural (miracles, healings, exorcisms, flights in the 'spirit', predictions, prophecies) through human adepts. The first is Simon, readily identifiable by readers from the Acts of the Apostles, who sought to buy the Holy Spirit from the disciples. Against the exorbitant truth claims of his fictional remake, 'Je suis Jupiter, Apollon, le Christ, le Paraclet, la grande puissance de Dieu, incarnée en la personne de Simon!' (*Tent*, 137), Antoine's calm rejection with the facts constitutes his most demolishing speech of the tableau (*Tent*, 137–8). Antoine's curiosity (*gnose*), however, allows his antagonist a second wind, to boast of his magic acts. In the most wonderfully theatrical thunder and lightning (recognized by Simon as an act of God!), Simon's attempt to 'baptize' Antoine with fire in his version of the tongues of flame appearing on the heads of the believers at Pentecost (Acts 2: 2–4) is, along with Ennoia and himself, extinguished by Antoine's prayer-like, but comically practical, cry: 'Ah si j'avais de l'eau bénite!' (*Tent*, 139). In this very 'Catholic' antidote, why is Antoine's prayer answered, and why is there a cold, thick, and fetid fog left behind Simon, dispersed only by a sudden gust of wind? The stage (like the basilica) again bespeaks the person within it. Antoine's humble spirituality, but also spiritual gifts from the Holy Spirit (as manifested in the forms of the storm and gust of wind), are clearly implied here, especially the gifts of knowledge and discernment of spirits, which St Anthony the Great had in abundance. He could often smell the (unclean) spirit in another, hence the fetid smell left in the fog behind Simon. Through use of his spiritual gifts in his measured responses to adversaries, Antoine thus demonstrates his own discipleship, that he has indeed learnt well (unlike Hilarion, Priscilla and Maximilla, Ennoia, or Damis) from his master Didymus the Blind. The 'anachronism' of Antoine on Didymus' arm in tableau one now reveals its purpose. Post Nicaea, the doctrinal debates among bishops (like the battle of the 'rouleaux' in tableau four) continued to rage about the persons of the Trinity and their substance. Where Athanasius provided key formulations for its Christology, it was Didymus who followed in his *De Spiritu Sancto* with a theology of its pneumatology.[35] Significantly with regard to the *Tentation*, it was at the Council of Constantinople in 381 that the Church formulated the role and provenance of the Holy Spirit: 'We believe in the Holy Spirit, the Lord, the Giver of Life, who proceeds from the Father. With the Father and the Son he is worshipped and glorified. He has spoken through the Prophets.'

The longest (and most tedious) part of tableau four, where Antoine's own patience (like the reader's) is sorely tested, concerns Apollonius of Tyana. His lengthy life story (in glorious technicolour) is one fabulous and boastful litany of wonders and miracles. Seznec (1949) has devoted a whole chapter to showing how Flaubert culled and carefully reconstructed this episode from Philostratus, but he does not explain the purpose of this attention to detail or its significance for this section of the tableau. With Hilarion the commentator (substitute of Renan) and discounter of miracles being absent, Antoine's reactions and discernment must then be the reader's. What makes Apollonius' acts paradoxically the more unbelievable is that they are so instantly comparable to those of the *earlier* Christ and his disciples the apostles. The familiarity of Apollonius' (belated) acts renders them derivative. In the light of our discussion of tableau three and Flaubert's careful non-portrayal of Antoine's healings or other miracles, the extensive enumeration of those of Simon and then Apollonius is not so much a syncretistic or comparative religious set of analogues. Rather, the counterfeit and the real are everywhere the question amid this whole tableau of the *spirits* of this age of things quintessentially spiritual: Sophia, 'Esprits', 'Minerve', 'le Saint-Esprit', 'Le Paraclet' are all mentioned specifically. Antoine is only able to dislodge the powerful spirits of Simon and the invasive Apollonius because of his (well-known) experience of discerning and combating spirits and demons in innumerable guises. His return to the cross and prayer is his positive stand against all unholy spirits.

The final words of Apollonius to Damis are however significant for they bring the whole tableau full circle: 'Par-dessus toutes les formes, plus loin que la terre, au-delà des cieux, réside le monde des Idées, tout plein du Verbe! D'un bond, nous franchirons l'autre espace; et tu saisiras dans son infinité l'Éternel, l'Absolu, L'Être!' (*Tent*, 159). They offer a Pythagorean form of non-material Being confounded with a philosophical, Platonic, form of 'God' redolent of the Neoplatonic schools of Alexandria (as revived by Plotinus during the period), and a cosmology in three worlds and spaces ('formes', 'Idées' ('Verbe' but not Christ), 'l'Éternel' (but not God)) as a Greek version of Manicheism with which the tableau began. If Apollonius rises from the earthly sphere to the heavenly beyond, this only re-enacts the movement from Mani's 'globe' to his cosmological system issuing from an impassible God. Antoine's final combat in tableau four with the unholy spirit empowering Simon the Magician and the Jesus-like Apollonius in appearance comes squarely back to the question of God, and the much bigger 'theological' challenge that this tableau is presenting, not least from Antoine's own admissions that so many other doctrines and 'ways' are believable: Who(se) is the true God? Return to Mani's first response to this question allows the ensuing order, and hence meaning, of the sections of tableau four to emerge.

Significantly, Mani is given the most detailed contextual description of all the sectarian leaders of tableau four. On his golden throne, he is 'beau comme un archange, immobile comme une statue, portait une robe indienne, des escarboucles dans ses cheveux nattés, à sa main gauche un livre d'images peintes, et sous sa droite un globe. Les images représentaient les créatures qui sommeillaient dans le chaos' (*Tent*, 98). Also prefiguring the Gymnosophist in terms of his Indian provenance and immobility, it will be his 'rouleau', and his cosmology, that distinguish his doctrines from the Gymnosophist's 'Grand Tout' (belief in transmigration and 'l'Anéantissement'), or Apollonius' 'l'Éternel, l'Absolu, L'Être'. Mani explains that 'Au sommet du ciel le plus haut se tient la Divinité impassable: en dessous, face à face, sont le Fils de Dieu et le Prince des ténèbres;... Il n'y a qu'une seule âme—universellement répandue, comme l'eau d'un fleuve divisé en plusieurs bras' (*Tent*, 99). In a nutshell, *a Gnostic version of the Trinity* opens a tableau which orders its doctrinal advocates and *heretikoi* around variant arguments about the three persons of the Holy Trinity and their relationship. The section where Hilarion is present—Mani, Saturnin, Cerdon, Marcion, Bardesane, Valentine, the Herniens, the Priscillianists, Basilides, the Elkhesites—is a running discussion about orders of creation from a 'God' as ineffable, evil, an 'angel', a god in delirium, etc., from whom a series of emanations (including some version of a 'Jesus' figure or a 'spirit' figure) form hierarchies of spirits and then forms of matter. Nowhere does the (triune) God the 'Father' appear in this or any following 'trinity', of which Apollonius' arguably forms the last. The second part of Mani's doctrine, how the 'divine spark' enclosed in man's body can be liberated, allows the full dualism of his doctrine to be revealed, while spearheading the soteriological practices that define the factional *groups* who take the stage after Hilarion's departure from tableau four. Mani's doctrine of salvation is again completely counter to a Gospel of *grace*, since it is by works (of abstinence or indulgence in specific acts) and initiations that the elect adherent advances, and according to predetermined stages.[36] Although Montanus (like Mani[37]) also claims to be the 'Paraclet', it is the extremism of his cult of abstinences and martyrdom (already mentioned by Hilarion in tableau three) that brings this section to a close. Even the seemingly less 'fatherly' God of the Old Testament did not press the people of Israel to the point of self-sacrifice (or as the Gymnosophist will show to self-immolation), or make individual election a criterion for salvation.[38]

The reason why Arius then opens the *second* movement of the tableau is because of his perfect logic in Flaubert's ordering of it as a tableau on the Trinity.[39] Arius heads up those heresiarchs disputing its second person, but focused on the nature and substance of their versions of either a Jesus or a 'Christ'. Specified as a 'diacre', Arius also impels other major church leaders into the debate which nowhere states the perfect divinity and humanity of the Jesus Christ of the Nicene Creed and Christianity.[40] Much of the doctrinal argument was compounded in the early Church (including the Gnostic Churches) by the fourth Gospel of John, with its well-known opening, 'In the Beginning was the Word'. This issue concerning Jesus as 'le Verbe' was extensively discussed by Renan in his *Vie de Jésus*, sifting evidence for a historical Jesus as we explored briefly in Chapter 3. It is precisely this question about the authority of the Synoptic and other Gospels that then underpins the second part of this section of the tableau, the various heresiarchs each waving his doctrinal 'rouleau'. While Mani's 'prophécie de Barcouf' may seem incongruous as the concluding text since it is not an 'Évangile', Flaubert's knowledge of Gnostic documents reaches beyond even the rich source of Matter's *Histoire du Gnosticisme*. In the multiple *Encyclopédie théologique* published by the Abbé Migne formed of different 'dictionnaires', the *Dictionnaire des apocryphes* (referenced in Flaubert's bibliography but under 'Christianisme (exigèse)') included the recently translated *Pistis Sophia*, deemed one of the most important Gnostic texts, and discovered long before the now famous Nag Hammadi Dead Sea Scrolls.[41] Although by its very title the *Pistis Sophia* would have fitted superbly into the St Sophia frame of this section of the tableau, Flaubert never uses the obvious, because it may be too specific or appear too 'modern'. A reading of the *Pistis Sophia*, however, has the same effect that Apollonius' iterative narrative will have on Antoine, for it reveals a dizzying series of emanations and eons (like those uttered by Flaubert's Mani *and* Valentine in Iranian *and* Egyptian guises), endless attacks by the almost equally powerful devil and his legions on, and endless repentances by, Sophia, the thirteenth eon attempting to regain access into the Pleroma.[42] This 'face à face', like Mani's between 'le Fils de Dieu et le Prince des ténèbres', is then translated by the Ophites to allow the Manichean aspects of the Gnostic anti-Trinity to be revealed. The

Ophites' serpent (the devil) is the 'good' 'God' of their cosmological orders whose knowledge and truth (Science) brings 'salvation'. The Christian understanding of God-created free will for man, like man's original disobedience as his choice rather than something determined, is also absent, except in the person of Antoine. His implicit, unverbalized stand on the Trinity as formulated by the Nicene Creed is the touchstone for what makes all the other doctrines 'heretical', that is their untenable differences over one God in three persons, and the Incarnation of Christ as fully God and fully human. Flaubert is therefore supremely catholic in this tableau by nowhere stating Catholicism (except perhaps Antoine's comical cry for some holy water!) or orthodox theology except by default. With hindsight, Antoine's reactions to Mani's first utterances that framed the tableau perfectly sum up all of the alternative doctrines (and trinities) of tableau four, as well as their peddlers: 'quelle absurde imagination!' (*Tent*, 99).

REMAPPING THE HOLY IN THE LAND OF NEW RELIGIONS

For the nineteenth-century French unbeliever or nominal Catholic, let alone the modern reader, incomprehension concerning tableau four would derive as much from complexities and mysteries of inter-reflecting Gnostic belief systems as from shaky knowledge of official theology or Catholic dogmas. What can be certain is that Antoine, however unorthodox Flaubert's representation makes him, must remain true to his faith and saintly persona as a Church Father outside its institutional forms. In this tableau Antoine proves an active discerner of the many clamouring spirits of his age. Unlike the claims of all the other heresiarchs, Antoine's discernment does not lie in his own authority or special powers. Consequently he makes Flaubert's best possible critic of Pope Pius IX as new heresiarch of a Church of the Immaculate Conception and the infallibility of popes. The representational message of tableau four might then best be summed up in the admonishing words that are repeated in the Book of Revelation (2–3) concerning the seven churches (and their errors including entertaining the Nicolaitians who feature in the *first* section of tableau four): 'He who has an ear, let him hear what the Spirit is saying to the Churches.' Antoine's *observations* are his 'ear' testing the spirits and churches of his age behind what is visible and seemingly similar to allegedly Christian tenets. Flaubert is then no Catholic apologist.[43] By presenting the most theological tableau of the *Temptation* in the most un-theological (heretical) of forms, Flaubert only repeats his love of paradoxical creative practices demonstrated elsewhere in his œuvre. But Flaubert's creative choices (*haereses*) in tableau four have proved no 'syncretism' either. Not only has the ordering of heresiarch mouthpieces, the structure and context of tableau four, shown a coherent and logical *curiosity* (Antoine's) about his faith *vis-à-vis* its others, these are the best optics for what is distinctive about his own faith. The many anti-trinities only better show (but do not tell—the Creed is not recited until the next tableau) the 'mysteries' of the Trinity. Such a heretical creative method on Flaubert's part underscores the greater (comparative) religious importance of the tableau for the *Tentation* as a whole, and far beyond the bookish source criticism of Seznec on the one hand, or academic comparative religion of Creuzer-Guigniaut on the other, since tableau four is as 'comparatively religious' as tableau five. The latter's survey of *other* world religions rivalling Christianity can now be seen to be very strongly prefaced by the multicolour lenses of fourth-century, 'Coptic', church history as the best commentator on its nineteenth-century heritage(s).[44] Why Flaubert went to such extraordinary lengths to paint so accurately the history of the early Christian Church through the smoke (the Gymnosophist) and mirrors (Mani, Apollonius) of its similar, Eastern, adversaries and their 'unholy trinities' is not some nostalgic attempt to reconstruct an 'ideal' moment in the burgeoning early Christian Church around St Anthony. Rather, the maelstrom of glittering belief systems in the big Eastern marketplace has a peculiarly energizing, if almost overwhelming, effect upon Antoine, as well as stirring his better judgements. What might the point therefore be?

It would be easy to read tableau four as an open debate examining truths, since Truth is unobtainable to humans although religions, sects, heresies, and schism are based on such a claim. Antoine's seemingly naive and simplistic summing up of all the heresiarchs—'Vous êtes tous des mensonges', that is, not the truth—also seems the same conclusion by a different route that Bouvard and Pécuchet discover when they run up against the wonderfully inconsistent and utterly unreliable 'authorities' they read on all manner of encyclopedic topics. But Antoine's summation also shows no small authority to judge such truth claims, and Flaubert's art everywhere, if it avoids concluding, always allows strongly critical judgements to be made. Rather than setting Truth against truths in a false binary (this is the motor of fanaticism and the excessive practices everywhere lambasted in the *Tentation*), tableau four has proved everywhere to be an operation of *Gnosis* to encompass *all* revealed beliefs. Only some, personified in Antoine, stand up to greater scrutiny, challenge, and history than others. Is it too absurd an imagination to ask whether Flaubert is using Antoine to observe post-Revolution 'Enlightenment' France, one no less peopled with 'Gnostic' heresiarchs, conflicting forms of 'gnose', new doctrines, systems, and 'churches'? Flaubert's (in)famous bibliography for the *Tentation* is richly endowed with works by contemporary French 'Gnostics', dressed up as comparativists of religion, philosophy, history, as well as experts on such esoteric matters as the devil and the soul.[45] Although direct one-to-one analogy would not be Flaubert's style, two examples of comparative analogies between 'heresiarchs' or doctrines of Antoine's 'period' and those of nineteenth-century France seem striking, but critics have never made the connection. The most obvious, because matching the longest and most 'fantastical' *vita* of Apollonius of Tyana in its journeying and miracle working, is the colourful life of Anton Franz Mesmer (1734–1815).[46] In the manner of all beliefs that stem from their proponent, mesmerism is now considered a form of hypnotism, whereas at the time it was propounded and practised by its 'heresiarch', it was the power and energy of animal magnetism, the 'fluid' of the macro- and microcosm, that could produce healings when the 'laying on of hands' focused these resources. There is a long article on Mesmer in the two-volume *Dictionnaire des sciences occultes et des idées superstitieuses* published by the Abbé Migne.[47] The second also comes from this 'un-Holy Spirit' section of tableau four as a further proponent of 'absurde imagination' of Flaubert's own time, mirroring the person of Simon the Magician. Eliphas Lévy was a charismatic proponent of Kabbalah, and the hidden symbolism of Gnostic 'knowledge' as a way to reach supreme Knowledge (a science of the universe). Martinists were his disciples: Balzac, Gauguin, Hugo, Alexandre Dumas, and others counted among his friends; Flora Tristan adopted his ideas into her politics.[48] 'Illuminés' of many stripes thus vied for the space that Catholic factionalism between its Ultramontanist or Gallican wings left wide open, the place of ideas and systems that might better speak to the current age and herald one striving for Perfection and Progress. Whether these Illuminati and Eclectics were leaders of 'secular religions',[49] or 'traditions orphiques',[50] their 'Gnostic' roots and search for supreme knowledge (science) bring their fictional representatives in tableau four very much closer to home. Gnosis is the natural ally of Science or its chief antagonist. This is why Antoine (Gnosis) and Hilarion (Science) must meet up once more to view belief systems outside Egypt's borders which had made their homes within it, not least in the Alexandrian schools. Hilarion's now vastly increased size denotes his ascension in authority and oxymoronic form encapsulated in the first description of him as 'trapu comme un Cabire' (*Tent*, 86). 'Le culte des *Cabires* célèbre donc: "la continuité ininterrompue de la vie même telle qu'elle se manifeste par une suite d'ascensions de ce qui est le plus profond à ce qui est le plus élevé." Il pourrait y avoir là une source des métempsychoses.'[51] Antoine will remain our Egyptian observer (as Copt) of the same phenomena, but as the descent of the gods. Let us now visit their Alexandrian schools to understand some further parallels between the scientific ideas of their times as a way of remapping those of nineteenth-century France, not least through its explorations of Egypt.

PART II

SCIENCES OF THE GODS: GODS OF THE SCIENCES

The Egypt and Alexandria of the religious life and times of St Anthony the Great and Flaubert's nineteenth-century France have now proved rather similar as regards their empire-building, sovereign control of the affairs of Church and State, and of dissenting, heretical voices challenging these authorities. Faith (religion) and Reason (science) embodied in Antoine and Hilarion have also proved not to be two irreconcilable antagonists, but necessary provocations of what is significant in their non-identical twin on their shared journey of the knowable. This vital dialogue with similar others was what inspired Clement of Alexandria to incorporate Greek and Jewish philosophical understanding into his theological reflection in the *Stromata* and into his comparative exegetical method: theology and philosophy both deal in 'myth and metaphysics' to evaluate what we can know.[1] For Clement, empirical and revealed knowledge were of equal weight, even if he was also seeking to redress the balance in the favour of the former because of Philo's emphasis on symbolic meanings in the interpretation of texts. Thus far, this book has also erred on the side of reading Flaubert's *Tentation* at its most literal by attending to its clearly demarcated contexts (geographical and historical), precise naming of things (the dream trip to Canopus and the temple of Serapis for example) and the face value of Antoine's words (his commentaries and biblical exegesis). This led very quickly, however, to seeing their equally figurative import as signposts to the analogous topographies of France's nineteenth-century civilization and culture. By prizing the *Tentation* out of genetic or source critical erudition, focus on what any reader can observe has turned the seemingly meaningless or eclectic descriptions of the 'orient' (Chapter 2), or 'heresies' (Chapter 4) into critical remapping of very similar underlying frames of reference. Gnostic and 'Greek' ways of categorizing knowledge constitute the essential structures behind ancient and modern principalities and their powers. Through Hilarion's emergence from 'Sheba's' train, the acme of Eastern earthly, spiritual, and cultural power and knowledge was been brought to 'Egypt', whilst Hilarion's Western, 'Greek', mind formed there (in the powerful arguments of Stoics, Aristotelians, and Pythagoreans) has further assailed Antoine's seemingly unschooled defence of faith forged in experience, not establishment dicta (religious or scientific). Tableau five is a response to East and West, the death of all their gods, and to Hilarion's bid through his vaunting knowledge to become a god himself.

Antoine's visionary and veritably Gnostic bent as searcher for truth,[2] however, is what has enabled him (and the reader) to review the ever-increasing metaphorical and literal enormity of knowledge. In large part its power, horror, and authority is directly due to Hilarion's expanding physical size to match his encyclopedic lead and analytical weight. The 'horrors' of Gnosticism (tableau four) as umbrella term for the excesses of religious practice and imagination will only be magnified by the gods' dramatically excessive forms of demise along with the previous might of their former civilizations in tableau five. The greater familiarity of its mythologies of Egypt, Greece, and Rome for an enlightened nineteenth-century and modern audience then makes the final two tableaux anticlimactic at best, in part also because they lack Hilarion's acerbic comparative religious commentaries. At worst, tableaux six and seven degenerate into hyperbolically monstrous anachronisms; the Devil's ride into the 'macrocosm' is only surpassed by the preposterous 'ark' with all the hybrid and fantastical monsters of the 'medieval' human imagination or manuscript illumination. Seznec's authoritative work on these monsters (tableau seven), the Indian and other gods (tableau five), and non-pronouncement on tableau six has therefore dictated how the final part of the 1874 *Tentation* is read, even among more recent French genetic critics.[3] Challenge to Seznec has been mounted only by more foolhardy

Anglophone critics—Carmody on Indian gods, Starr and more recently Cuthbert on the monsters.[4] Tableau six remains the critical black hole.

But several lessons on how to reread the *Tentation* have now emerged from the two intrinsically connected angles of vision established in Part I. The first is the 'bird's-eye' view that frames and then determines the order and structure of otherwise incomprehensible parts. Second-order narratives (and parallel histories) depend on and emerge from comparison and contrast regarding details in spatial contiguity, and inter-reflecting themes and topoi. Temporal reflection on the present (fourth-century Alexandria, nineteenth-century France) can only be recounted because the text's subjects consistently undertake comparative (Proustian) narrative searches into past time, whether Antoine's curriculum vitae, church history from New to Old Testament, or the history of Egyptian civilization from modern to ancient. Spatio-temporal disorientation and reorientation were then grounded in the second angle of vision, Antoine's *Egyptian* mind's-eye view throughout, with its curious, informed discernments but unspoken first premisses because they were of a pedestrian homeliness. His conservative, passive stability (return to his humble 'cabane' at the end of each major scene) then also contrasted with Hilarion's effulgence and sceptical lines of new questioning, with his demonstrably fickle commitment to one credo or 'master'; he emerged from 'Sheba's' train, goes missing in tableau four, before deserting Antoine just before the latter's fantastical flight into space.

The forging of deeper parallels through carefully stage-managed spatio-temporal shuttling, or the turning of seeming opposites embodied in Antoine and Hilarion into similarities, in fact constitutes the main dynamic of the *Tentation* and hence our remapping of it. Consequently in the overall, seven-part structure of the work we can expect the topics in the first three tableaux to find their distorting mirror image in tableaux five to seven, turning upon the fourth tableau of the Gnostics (Eastern and Western). Hilarion's vital presence in the central zone, tableaux three to five, matches his substitutive practices (and persona) as expert in the nineteenth-century science of comparative religion. Logically, he must then effect the turn of the text to the religion of comparative science. Chapter 5 will investigate how this is achieved in his other non-religious personas, and why Flaubert then removes Hilarion's more glittering distraction of surfaces to ensure that Antoine's remains the only optic for the reader in tableaux six and seven (to match tableaux one and two). As the culminating two tableaux are the least religious of the *Tentation*, why is the reader lumbered with an unsaintly saint to view their subject matter? Or are these tableaux somehow connected to tableau five and Hilarion's revelation of himself as the Promethean reach of human *scientia*? Is that singular tree hiding the Gymnosophist in the middle scene of tableau four (*Tent*, 129–30), and hence the pivot of the whole *Tentation*, a comparative religious allusion to the Tree of Knowledge in Genesis, the unvoiced myth of creation and destruction inferred by comparison with the alternative myths of tableau five, and Antoine's ironic return at the very end of the *Tentation* to the beginnings of life? And when he has shown consistent mortification of his flesh as sign that sinful man is part of his Trinitarian theology, why does Antoine not classify knowledge (gnosis or science) as a sin? Is Antoine's natural supernaturalism paradoxically Flaubert's best vehicle to reveal knowledge of the cosmos (tableau six) and the microcosmos (tableau seven) in visionary guise?

Syncretistic, relativist, or comparative mythological readings of the *Tentation* to date do not add up to explaining its fifth let alone final tableaux or finale, and provide no answers to the above questions. They also cannot explain why the Devil, who has no Greek or Roman analogues, plays such a big part in tableau six. Is he precisely the paradox of the *invraisemblable* whereby Flaubert may defamiliarize the scientific 'verities' of his contemporary France and show the spirit of his age? If there is no longer belief in God, where does that then leave the Devil? Is the ending of the *Tentation* then not so much pan*theistic* as pan-*creational*? To answer some of these questions and argue for the dialogic premises of this book as a remapping of religion through science and vice versa, Part II has the daunting job of reconfiguring the same religious landscapes of Part I for science. Moreover it needs to answer why the *Tentation* literally and figuratively grows more fantastical and monstrous through the final three chapters to its climax, to show how this 'scientific' half brings out the true colours of the 1874 *Tentation*. Ultimately this reprise aims to argue for Flaubert's remapping within it as a truly scientific religious masterpiece. At the same time, we need to set up how tableaux five to seven match the fourth- and nineteenth-century parallelisms of Part I (and *religious* subjects of tableaux one to four) in their 'scientific' subject matter and times.

Mirroring the three sections of Part I, we therefore need to return first to the metaphysical melting pot of fourth-century Alexandria, to find out about its Greek (not Jewish or Christian) schools and their sciences of 'reason', philosophy, mathematics, and astronomy. Their ready comparison with the 'schools' of Paris and their scientists in the new Republic of nineteenth-century France will then draw out some of the deeper parallels between the two main historical time frames everywhere in critical tension in the *Tentation*. Are Hilarion and the Devil then vehicles of non-religious standpoints on the same big unanswered questions about life, the world, and the universe that the first part proposed in religious terms? For science, what is the meaning of life and where does it begin? What does it mean to be human in the order of material things? Is the human being an animal, a 'god', or something in between? And if nineteenth-century French science strains the limits of *vraisemblance* of Antoine's fourth-century AD *spiritual* world view, how can his Coptic Egypt find its necessary recentring in the Egypt of nineteenth-century France?

THE ALEXANDRIAN SCHOOLS

One of Flaubert's principal sources for his accurate portrayal of Hilarion's schooling and fourth-century science as paradigmatic of the Greek Alexandrian schools was Vacherot's three-volume *Histoire critique de l'école d'Alexandrie* of 1846, which is listed under 'Christianisme (exégèse)' in the (in)famous bibliography for the *Tentation*. While much of the contents of volume i (book 2, chapters 1–3) is culled for tableau four to provide numerous details in its various sections, and volume ii for the structure of Neoplatonic and polytheistic understandings of 'cosmic' gods for tableau five, the history of the legacy of the Alexandrian schools (volume iii) appears largely absent because beyond the time of St Anthony.[5] The preface to Vacherot's Neoplatonic apology provides the programme for the whole, not least the historical value of the philosophy of Alexandria to determine truth and error in the philosophies of the nineteenth century. Historically, however,

[l]'école d'Alexandrie, ou le Musée, ne doit point être confondue avec l'école philosophique qui porte le même nom. Le Musée ... comprenait toutes les sciences connues et tous les exercices de la pensée, philosophie, mathématiques,

physique, médecine, philologie, littérature. Toutes les écoles grecques y coexis-
taient... C'était, en un mot, une véritable Institut et non une école.... Le seul
caractère commun aux écoles qui composaient cette grande société littéraire et
scientifique, c'est qu'elles avaient toutes apporté et conservaient religieusement
l'esprit grec au milieu d'une ville orientale.... L'école d'Alexandrie commence
donc vers 193 et finit vers 529. (*HCEA*, i, pp. ii–v).

Although not listed in Flaubert's bibliography, it would have been
unusual if he had not also consulted the two other major histories
of the Alexandrian schools published at the same time as Vacherot's,
especially given that the *Histoire de l'école d'Alexandrie comparée aux
principales écoles contemporaines* (1844) was written by Matter, whose
work on Gnosticism Flaubert had already used extensively, and given
that Vacherot signals the publication of another excellent work on his
subject in the preface to his belated third volume, Jules Simon's two-
volume *Histoire de l'école d'Alexandrie* of 1844–5.[6] The preface to the
first volume of Simon's work sums up the importance of the École
d'Alexandrie as pinnacle of learning of the period:

En philosophie, l'école d'Alexandrie est tout à la fois la première école éclec-
tique, la première école mystique et la première école panthéiste... L'école
d'Alexandrie est une école de puissante métaphysique qui couronne toute la
philosophie de l'antiquité. Elle répond par le mysticisme aux théories des
anciens sur la connaissance, et par le panthéisme à leurs spéculations sur la
nature de l'absolu. A l'époque où Ammonius Saccas et Plotin fondent leur école,
la recherche de l'absolu est le problème capital.... Dieu fut placé au-dessus des
sens et de la raison à des hauteurs tellement inaccessibles, qu'il fallut absorber
le monde en lui, pour n'en pas faire, comme les Stoïciens, un Dieu inutile, ou,
comme les Éléates, un Dieu solitaire.[7]

While an extensive study of Simon as a major intertext for the 1874
Tentation lies outside this book, hugely intriguing reverberations strike
the attentive reader, not least Simon's study of Apollonius of Tyana in
chapter 2 of the first volume, entitled 'philosophes et polygraphes du
premier et du deuxième siècle. Éclectisme', which was published *before*
Chassang's work on Philostratus appeared in 1862.[8] Contextualized in
Simon's history of Alexandrian eclecticism (the term which Bowman
considers to be the best overall configurative label for the *Tentation* as a
whole) is the following:

Pythagore... parti de l'Asie mineure pour aller briller dans la Grande-Grèce... était comme l'écho de la sagesse de l'Orient... Apollonius de Tyane, que la tradition nous représente comme visitant tour à tour les mages et les gymnosophistes, est évidemment un pythagoricien; Apulée, initié à tous les mystères... avec sa science cosmopolite, est avant tout un disciple de Platon.[9]

In this potted lineage lies the essential structure for the major sections of tableau four of the *Tentation* (in reverse order and building on tableau two as well as signalling master–disciple relationships) and, more importantly, evidence for Flaubert's reading to resolve the logic of the Gymnosophist in Seznec's elaboration of the 'heresies' and the mystery two-part volume to which Flaubert refers in his letter to Bouilhet. More vital to tableau six, however, is that many of Simon's detailed discussions of Plotinus' speculations on God proffer the lines of argument that Flaubert's Devil in tableau six uses in his demolition of Antoine's God.[10]

Neither Vacherot nor Simon, however, explicitly mentions the science of this Alexandrian Muséum in terms that we might readily recognize or apply to the final tableaux of the *Tentation*. The scientific topics treated in tableaux five to seven are abundantly clear on the contrary in the preface to Matter's second volume of his *Histoire de l'école d'Alexandrie comparée aux principales écoles contemporaines*:

en rivalisant à la fois avec les sanctuaires de l'Égypte et les académies de la Grèce, le musée devint la première et la plus célèbre des institutions de l'antiquité.... Je distingue ses travaux en six groupes: 1° *sciences naturelles ou physiques*; 2° *études médicales*; 3° *mathématiques, astronomie et géographie*; 4° *histoire*; 5° *philologie et littérature*; 6° *religion, philosophie morale et politique*... il est évident que ce ne sont pas les lettres, que ce sont, au contraire, les sciences qui dominent dans le monde grec que représente l'école d'Alexandrie. Ce qui caractérise le travail intellectuel de la race hellénique avant Alexandre, c'est la création poétique et la création philosophique. Ce qui le distingue après cette époque, c'est d'abord l'observation, tant celle de l'homme et de la nature que celle des nations.... Enfin le génie de l'observation et de la critique triompha nécessairement dans ce monde de syncrétisme que fit Alexandre.[11]

The nature of these sciences is then unpacked in separate chapters, the first devoted to 'sciences naturelles ou physiques' and constituting the main work of Aristotle on zoology, botany, mineralogy, and physiology as a vast heritage of science. After him, Theophrastus contributed enormously to botanical knowledge, not least his discovery of the sexes of plants. The latter's disciple Strato took forward much of Aristotle's work in zoology with his 'dissertations sur la *Nature humaine*, la *Génération des animaux*, la *Mixis*, la *Nourriture et* la *Croissance*, les *Animaux fabuleux*, ou sur les animaux dont l'existence est mise en doute' (*École* 2, 10). Matter notes the fine line between progress in zoology, for example science as we know it, and its being mired in 'ces récits de choses merveilleuses'. He returns at the end of the volume to the weird and wonderful variations of (barbarian) and monstrous humankind in travelogues and ethnographical enquiry of the period, 'ces hommes à tête de chien . . . , ces pygmées dont les plus grands avaient deux coudées de haut et auxquels leur chevelure servait de vêtement . . . ces hommes au corps couverts de plumes et vivant au parfum des fleurs . . . les *Areimaspes* à un seul œil . . . ces hommes aux pieds d'une aune de long' (*École* 2, 285–6). Mineralogy also is less to do with chemical analysis than with the magic properties of certain stones (*École* 2, 12). Tableau seven will return to all of these in different guise.

A second main chapter considers 'physique—chimie—optique—acoustique—métérologie'. Although the same problems with 'le merveilleux' pertain to physics, the Greek Alexandrian schools demonstrate particular strengths in (Euclidean) mathematics and astronomy. Matter's *Histoire* then focuses on the importance of lunar and solar calendars and zodiacs (inherited from the Babylonians) as part of the eclectic 'symbolisme céleste' developed from Asia, Egypt, and Greece. Knowledge of the regular movements of the stars, as well as the ability to predict planetary influence, had astrological and economic significance. Prediction of the seasons, and hence the best time to plant or harvest, was vital to agricultural and cultural success. Although the Chinese are thought to have first invented calendars, Babylonian priest-astronomers, as did later their ancient Egyptian counterparts, developed calendars and zodiacs. Moreover, accurate prediction of the annual flood of the Nile, and hence irrigation of crops, was essential to its agrarian might. Flaubert will revisit this event in tableau five and the zodiacs of Isis,[12] just as Napoleon and a party of his savants would also participate in it in 1798. The zodiac calendar at Dendera was also among the most major discoveries in French Egyptology and became famous as one of the major plates of the *Description d'Égypte*. Zodiacs and star gazing then provide the cue for the key scientific figure of the second century AD:

Le plus savant des astronomes d'Alexandrie est Claude Ptolémée.... Né à
Ptolémaïs d'Hermias, ville de la Thébaïde, si l'on en croit un auteur du moyen-
âge.... il réunit en un seul corps de doctrine le savoir astronomique du monde
grec, enrichi de ce que son instruction propre et ses appareils lui permettaient
d'y ajouter.... un homme qui prétendait recueillir tout ce qui se trouvait de bon
chez ses prédécesseurs et qui avait la double ambition d'être exact et d'ajouter
à ce qu'il résumait, a dû s'appliquer à un langage concis et à un choix sévère
[mais] il est verbeux et superstitieux. En effet, il est le seul astronome éminent de
l'École d'Alexandrie qu'on accoure d'avoir consacré un écrit spécial aux rêveries
de l'astrologie. (*École* 2, 228–31)[13]

If we have in this short résumé of Matter the historically verifiable science of St Anthony's life and times that enables Flaubert to explore the
zoological, mathematical, ethnographical, and astronomical advances
of nineteenth-century France in tableaux five to seven, we also have
alternative, and almost more essentially 'Greek', sources to challenge
Seznec's 'classical' appraisal of tableau seven of the 'monsters' and their
'medieval' provenance. The fabulous nature of all these sciences will
prove the pudding in Chapter 7 to reveal the monsters of nineteenth-
century French science. Those undertaking study of them were very
aware of these 'Greek' sources.

Matter's two-volume work is not of course immune to his own
nineteenth-century prejudices and failures of understanding concerning
the spirit of the age of second-century Alexandria, epitomized in his
assessment of the importance of Ptolemy's 'science' of astronomy as
astrology in another guise. There was no distinction between the arts
or sciences of astronomy and astrology in Ptolemy's time or in the 'Old
Testament' Babylonian worlds of Nebuchadnezzar, Sheba, and Daniel
(conveyed to Antoine in tableau two). The *scientific* importance of
the Babylonians, ancient, and second-century AD Egyptians will prove
pivotal in tableau five to preface Antoine's space flight in tableau six.
Among the first astronomers were the priests of Babylon; tablets dating
from around 550 BC record their astronomical observations. Claudius
Ptolemaeus was not only 'the most learned astronomer', but also the
most important *Egyptian* scientist of the second century AD, the lone
representative in Appendix 1. His book on planetary theory, known
as the *Almagest*,[14] could be described as possibly a first encyclopedia of ancient science, since it collected centuries of Babylonian and
ancient Greek (including Aristotle's) observations of the planets and

their motions, the aim of which was to prove that the earth was the centre of the universe. It is in the *Almagest* that Ptolemy's 'system of the world' is found, his intricate, mathematical, mapping of circles within circles as a method of calculating the motions of planets.[15] Ptolemy's other works show the range of fourth-century Alexandrian 'science' for they include a work of *astrology*, the *Planispherium* (the attempt to map the heavens onto the plane of the equator), the *Geography* (the attempt to map places by latitude and longitude coordinates since maps were notoriously difficult to copy), and the *Optics* (studies of colour, refraction, and reflection). The Ptolemaic system of the world would survive over 1,500 years until Copernicus dethroned it with his heliocentric system, which historians of astronomy note was a revision of the Greek Aristarchus' unpopular proposal in the second century BC. The Greek Alexandrian schools as model 'institutes' of the sciences would also survive for over a millennium in nineteenth-century French form.

THE MUSÉUM NATIONAL

In tableau one, Antoine and his master Didymus toured major landmarks on the topographical and intellectual-spiritual maps of Alexandria as hothouse of known learning, rival ideas, and belief structures. Included on the itinerary are the Muséum, the Serapeum, the Library, and the École d'Alexandrie, all seats of *scientific* knowledge to prepare the second half of the *Tentation* and its monstrous worlds of science appearing like their religious counterparts in the 'temptations' of tableaux five to seven. Post-revolutionary and nineteenth-century French founding of museums in former palaces (such as the Louvre) could not have had more directly Egyptian inspiration since the word 'Muséum' originates from the palace of the Muses in ancient Alexandria. Indeed the status of this ancient foundation inspired the renaming in 1793 of the pre-revolutionary Jardin du Roi as the Muséum National d'Histoire Naturelle in the Jardin des Plantes.[16] The private collections of kings (including their Bibliothèque Royale) already prefaced by Antoine's Bible excerpts in tableau one were thus commandeered by the Directory specifically for the civilizing, scientific missions of the new Republic to modernize and expand its territories, intellectual and geographical. From the very outset the Jardin des Plantes was envisaged as a scientific research institute but, unlike the École d'Alexandrie of Ptolemy, it was also to be a *public* organ to educate and disseminate research in science. The male professoriat and their scientific research and publication in mathematics, natural sciences, botany, physics, chemistry, and astronomy continued to be the prerogative of a tiny elite. However, the remit for each chair was to extend the Muséum's collections so that the very forefront of work in a field could go on display in the public galleries and cabinets. Each chair holder was therefore required to disseminate the importance of discoveries in his particular scientific fields by means of publication, public lectures, and annual series of free, but more specialist, science courses. *Aides-naturalistes* were trained under him and then sent to posts in the French provinces and colonies, with oversight over regional collections, or (scientific) curriculum provision in educational establishments in the départements they served. The aim was to make the Muséum France's premier national museum to compete internationally on an equal footing with the world-class collections of its previously superior rivals (such as England and Germany). If the propagation and acclimatization of non-European species of plants in the Jardin des Plantes or animals in the Ménagerie showcased living specimens alongside those preserved in the Muséum's cabinets and galleries, the juxtaposition of the living with the dead also allowed natural scientists to study in particular the similarities and differences between fossil remains and living species (vegetable and animal). The general public could then also view these many marvels and wonders in the cabinets of the galleries of comparative anatomy and the Ménagerie, or in the Jardin's open-air plantings and giant glasshouses. These public exhibits of science (such as mummified animals, fossil monsters, and preserved specimens displaying normal or 'abnormal' forms in bell jars) were thus as fabulous and stimulating for the imagination as the many wonders on display in fairground freak shows.

Although bearded women, dwarfs, Siamese twins, and other monstrous human specimens were the staple of fairground shows from medieval to nineteenth-century France, there was one new phenomenon, Sarah Baartman the 'Vénus Hottentot', who was publicly exhibited in London and Paris for her 'wondrous' sexual parts which were concealed by an apron. Science was not exempt from complicity in 'studying' human 'freaks'. Georges Cuvier examined her (when alive) and dissected her (when dead), and she was part of the public natural history collections of the Muséum (and then the Musée de l'Homme until 1974) until she was repatriated to her native South Africa and Cape Town on 6 May 2002.[17] Animal monsters, particularly hybrid forms of creature, were almost more popular to draw fairground publics. Best known in the 1820s and 1830s in France was the 'Feejee mermaid', exhibited by P. T. Barnum in Europe and America, and uncovered as a clever graft (and therefore a hoax) by William Clift.[18] If Mr Salgado's basilisk (a creature who will return in tableau seven) was being promoted in London not Paris in the same period, France experienced 'biblical' plagues of frogs, which seemed to appear miraculously from nothing after heavy rain. Again scientists were not exempt from belief in these phenomena: one M. Maudry, curator of the natural history museum of Poitiers, attested to seeing two falls of frogs in 1809 and 1822 (B, 260–1). Very closely allied to these curious beliefs about showers of frogs was the much more ancient idea, documented by Aristotle, Ovid, and other authorities of spontaneous generation. 'One of the most remarkable fallacies in the annals of spontaneous generation was the widespread credence that a class of so-called *zoophytes*, spontaneously generated hybrids between animals and plants, existed' (B, 201). We will return in Chapter 7 to the 'spontaneous generation' from matter that is Antoine's 'epiphany' in the famous 'Être la matière' passage which closes on the miraculous appearance of the face of Christ. Institutional authority, both religious and scientific, requires similar mechanisms and ultimate adjudicators to tell the charlatan from the genuine scientist, hoax mermaid (like fake relic) from real specimen, and monster from myth or fossil remains. Popular belief shows itself equally drawn to the fabulous and fantastical things of the supernatural and the unnatural.

Where Part I considered the importance of ultimate church authority and its work in councils to determine its creed, science was not exempt from the same hierarchies and authorities to regulate and authenticate its activities. Much of the old hierarchization of scientific authority and governance, method, and publication as practised in the École d'Alexandrie in Ptolemy's time is reflected in the structures of the Muséum. Specialist experts (chairs) oversaw and pronounced on new work in their own and related fields and headed exhaustive collaborative publications. Cuvier's monumental *Histoire naturelle des poissons* (1828–48) would be a case in point. Where travellers' tall tales and eyewitness reports of strange creatures and peoples of the known world had interlaced the 'science' of the Greek Alexandrian schools (*École 2*, 285–6),[19] the Muséum also depended on their modern equivalent, networks of explorer travellers (often with serious amateur scientific expertise[20]) sending specimens of all kinds. Classification, dissection, study, mounting, and publication were all the domain of expert scientists trained at the Muséum. While they attempted to make the definitive break between empirical fact and fabulous myth, the science and method of empirical observation could not rule out 'doctrinal' error or fable altogether since no pure or objective science exists. In parallel with the role, authority, and work of the bishops of the early Christian Church and its councils such as Nicaea to resolve matters of creed, major differences of scientific opinion and authority continued to stimulate, provoke, and also split the community of the Muséum. Rivalries and factionalism, powerful patronage systems ranged against brilliant outsiders, shape religious and scientific communities with equal force and similar results; schism occurs more frequently than pruning of dead wood to permit new growth or diplomatic correction of error (heresy).

Chief among the brilliant outsiders of relevance to the *Tentation* who made their scientific careers at the Muséum and the Institut from the crucial beginnings of Republican science and its patronage systems were the Normandy-born mathematician and astronomer Pierre-Simon Laplace (1749–1827), and the Montbéliardais Georges Cuvier (1769–1832), who was, unusually for this still broadly 'Catholic' seat of science, a lifelong Lutheran. Because of his creed he had spent the Revolution in exile in Normandy (as tutor to the son of the Duc d'Héricy who also knew Laplace), studying indigenous molluscs, fish, and other marine invertebrates. Both men went on to dominate their fields with positive and then negative repercussions when younger disciples with rival ideas found contradictory evidence to the facts established by their master-experts. Laplace for all his brilliance in geometry, probability theory, and understanding of the motions of planets would remain a staunch supporter of the erroneous, corpuscular theory of light, which Fresnel would overturn with his theory of waves in 1821. For all of Cuvier's undisputed pre-eminence in the fields of comparative anatomy, ichthyology, and as the father of palaeontology, his mind closed to anything except his fixed classifications of all animals into four 'règnes', with no missing link conjoining any of them, led to the famous 'querelle des analogues' with Geoffroy Saint-Hilaire, his former collaborator and promoter, and which rocked the Muséum and the European scientific establishment when it came to a head in 1830. Chapters 6 and 7 will return to both of these figures in more detail.

Early stages of an institution's life often prove the most fascinating, since this period often coincides with greatest experimentation. While there was an unusual continuity and organizational seamlessness thanks to the same personnel (in Fourcroy, A.-L. de Jussieu, and the former 'Jardinier du Roi', André Thouin) between the *ancien régime*'s Jardin du Roi and the Jardin des Plantes of the first Republic, its 'Republican' statutes guaranteed its ongoing development (and stagnation) through the first Empire and into subsequent regimes of nineteenth-century France. Some of its initial figures were more radical about its public and civic missions. Cuvier took the educative remits of the Muséum extremely seriously, especially promotion of science on the secondary-school curriculum (for boys) and in his public lectures, which included numerous women who were otherwise barred from access to science. He is perhaps best known for his lectures which conjured up complete animals, which no human had ever seen because they were extinct species, from a single fossil tooth or bone. His calling up of the dead derived from his intimate knowledge of comparative anatomy, especially regarding the functions of parts of the body in relation to one another. The teeth or musculature of carnivores could not be mistaken for those of herbivores for example.

No less of a believer in the supreme magic of science to efface all previous superstition was the young chair in mechanics, Napoleon Bonaparte. When Talleyrand sent him on the mission to conquer Egypt for France in 1798, Napoleon's Expédition included 167 savants in all branches of science (very much mapped onto Matter's discipline divisions of the École d'Alexandrie above). Laplace and Cuvier were both approached to be among this number. Both refused. Expert nineteenth-century French science for them could mean only the serious work within the Muséum and its collections. As in Part I, it is however Napoleon's Expédition that allows us to make that essential missing link between the *scientific* world of St Anthony the Great and the Paris of nineteenth-century France. This was before the History of the École d'Alexandrie was set by the Academy in Paris as a research dissertation subject in 1818, or the History of Gnosticism in 1826 for which Jacques Matter would win the prize with his *Histoire critique du Gnosticisme*.[21]

ANCIENTS, ANTIQUITIES, AND ARCHAEOLOGIES OF KNOWLEDGE

If knowledge of the ancients (Babylonian, Egyptian, and Greek) is at its zenith in the Greek, Jewish, and Christian schools of Alexandria in the third and fourth centuries where the *Tentation* is set, the modern legacy of 'Greek' and Latin knowledge, especially in the sciences of nineteenth-century France, is therefore under close comparative scrutiny and evaluation. Since Antoine's visions and temptations have taken him back from his paradigmatic present to the greater past of ancient Egypt and Babylon in tableau two, we can expect similar retrospective vistas in the second half of the text to include prospective fantastical worlds such as those of the sciences of nineteenth-century France. To effect this coup of time travel and play with authority and fable, fact and fantasy, Flaubert seems carefully to have laid down strata of knowledge which Antoine 'views' as sites of the history of civilizations such as the Thebaid, the ancient tombs of Heliopolis, or the temple of Serapis. Foucaultian 'archaeologies of knowledge' are thus reflected also by analogy in the 'antiquities' that Antoine surveys on his Alexandrian itinerary,[22] since the science of Egyptology in France is substantively developed through Napoleon's Expédition and the collections brought back to France to be housed in the Louvre.

Napoleon may not have been fully aware of this longer Egyptian tradition of the 'monuments' to ancient learning which the Alexandrian schools of Anthony's time amply attest as 'Academies' and 'Institutes' for the sciences and the arts of their day. Napoleon's vision for his Institut d'Égypte in Cairo, however, strangely retranslates the Alexandrian Muséum via Paris's Muséum National, but as a new hybrid version of the recently created Institut National de Paris of 1795. Napoleon's replanting of French science in Cairene soil epitomized his mission to convert Egypt not to Christianity, but to the modernity of French science and technology. He probably also envisaged it as a hothouse of scientific innovation to be repatriated to France. Geoffroy Saint-Hilaire probably best personifies this end in his extensive documenting of his new discoveries and ideas in correspondence with Cuvier and Lacépède throughout his stay, and in his extensive collections which were transported back to Paris to augment and develop the collections at the Muséum National.[23]

Napoleon's Institut d'Égypte took over four adjacent palaces in the Nasrieh district of Cairo to house the many savants accompanying his military campaign, including Geoffroy Saint-Hilaire. These buildings contained the library, Berthollet's 'cabinet de chimie' reconstructed lock, stock, and barrel from the École Polytechnique in Paris, and other laboratories and their equipment, all shipped from Toulon to Alexandria and then transported overland. Academic seminars for the French members of the Institute were held regularly in the main room of what had been Hassan Kachef's harem and were inaugurated shortly after the Institut was set up. The first number of the Institut's scientific review, the *Décade égyptienne*, was published in October 1798 on the Institut's printing press (also shipped from France). Soon physics and chemistry laboratories were in operation, and, to house the specimens of antiquities and natural history (alive and dead) that were rapidly being amassed, a 'cabinet d'histoire naturelle', a small archaeological museum, and a menagerie were created. To all intents and purposes, this was a mini Jardin des Plantes 'acclimatized' to Cairo. While Egyptians had no part in these ventures, they were employed in the various workshops set up in the district to make instruments for mapping, for hydro-geological surveys, or other operations undertaken by the expedition. All fitted into the triple mission that Napoleon envisaged for the Institut: it was to study Egypt encyclopedically, proselytize 'Enlightenment' science vigorously to the un-enlightened' Egyptians dominated by 'medieval' Islamic learning based on the Koran, and respond to the practical needs of the occupation's governors.[24] By its membership, mainly leaders in their fields among the savants, it fostered interdisciplinary responses to problems and necessary collaborations when specific expertise was not available. For the interdisciplinary-minded, of which the young Étienne Geoffroy Saint-Hilaire was one and the first president, Monge, another, the Institut provided a rare opportunity to pursue various research interests at once. Jomard commented, 'On se flattait alors de jeter les fondations d'une nouvelle école d'Alexandrie.'[25] We will be returning to the significance of Geoffroy Saint-Hilaire's pioneering interdisciplinary work in Chapter 7.

The Institut also invited notable figures from the Muslim elite of Cairo to attend lectures given by Institut members on various discoveries, translated into Arabic, and witness chemical experiments (usually chosen for their maximum visual impact). Similar propaganda events were mounted to impress the larger populace on public holidays, the most notable being the demonstration of a new marvel, the red, white, and blue Montgolfier balloon launched on the first anniversary of the French occupation from one of the main squares in Cairo. Egyptian grandees observing the wonders of French science inside the Institute challenged the wisdom of Geoffroy Saint-Hilaire expounding for so long on one of the myriad of indigenous fish when the Koran specifically delimited the number of species of swimming creatures as those of the air and land.[26] The Egyptian public was equally unimpressed when the uncertain lift-off of the Montgolfier brought it swiftly back to terra firma. Famously and much cited by critics of Napoleon's Expédition,[27] the events were documented with a large dose of cynicism and pouring of cold water on the French pretensions by the Egyptian al-Jabarti.[28] His assessment of the technical and organizational superiority of French science in terms of its equipment, shared community, and breadth of learning is a precious testimony from an informed outsider.[29]

If the science of the second part of the *Tentation* depends almost more on comparative anatomies of knowledge than was the case for the comparative religious focus of Part I, the essentially curious but static observations of Antoine remain key to the success of Flaubert's transformations of fourth- and nineteenth-century scientific investigation into one another. Like al-Jabarti, Antoine's indigenous Egyptian Gnosis permits the text to explore in more depth (and by contrast its familiar others) 'Western', 'Mediterranean', polytheistic, and richly humanistic aspects of Egypt's civilizations, buried deep in ancient Egypt but also found on its more recent Graeco-Roman surface. It seems no accident that so much of tableau five therefore showcases metamorphoses of gods (already prefigured by Nebuchadnezzar's reduction and transformation from 'god' to herbivore), whether their degeneration and demise or their subsequent new manifestations through cultural hybridization. Pantheism and anthropomorphisms in myriad guises take over seamlessly from the monotheisms and deisms of Part I since all belong to the monstrous human imagination. To match the questionable certitudes of faith and credence in Part I, Part II now challenges scientific infallibility (objectivity), and the definitive powers of empirical method to adjudicate between the counterfeit and the real, part or whole, paradigm shift or delusion. If the gods of tableau five metamorphose into a Devil (tableau six) and monsters (tableau seven), it will be monsters that will prove the true test of nineteenth-century transformations in the natural sciences, not least Lamarck's theory of 'transformisme'. And as the famous Muséum of Alexandria turns into the post-revolutionary Jardin des Plantes, so this new Garden of Eden needs must examine its secular myths of science as progress plucked directly from its tree of knowledge.

In the thinkers of the Enlightenment who shaped the prevailing idea of progress, a Christian narrative of sin and redemption was joined with a Greek philosophy of liberation through knowledge. In Plato, this was an explicitly mystical philosophy, closely akin to those developed in India around the same time. For Hindus and Buddhists, history is a recurring dream; salvation is found in an awakening from time. In the secular faiths of the Enlightenment, this mystical gnosis becomes scientific knowledge; the aim is no longer wisdom, but control of the natural world. The message of all progressive creeds is that human emancipation comes from the growth of human power.... Fortunately, the Earth is larger and more enduring than anything produced by the human mind.[30]

John Gray's words to introduce his scathing critique of myths of modern progress, not least nineteenth-century positivism, neatly sum up the major themes and ideas that Part II of our study contends that the *Tentation* is exploring through the fantastic of the fictional ground of fourth-century Alexandria. Its newest religion on the block, Christianity, represented a vibrant, intellectually challenging threat to the predominant Neoplatonism of the Greek schools and Pythagorean mathematics since some of the finest minds (including Didymus the Blind) were both theologians and mathematicians of the first order. It was not the Trinity in itself that contributed most to this vibrant turmoil of ideas, although this new triune God stimulated dualistic systems (whether Platonic in the divide between Idea(l) and base matter, or Manichean in the equipotent conflict of good and evil), as well as naturalisms' god(s) in nature with no specific philosophy except preordained fate (pantheism, Brahmanism, polytheism) to find sharper definitions for their own tenets and beliefs. Not unsurprisingly, the three 'hypostases' of Athanasius' Creed rapidly found new expression in the threefold attributes of the Neoplatonic deity, as immutable, first cause, and intelligence,[31] just as Clement, Tertullian, and Origen had revamped Greek Platonism for their own theological ends. 'Peculiar' in the Trinity was the person of Jesus as perfectly God and perfectly human, which bridged the impossible gap between the spiritual and material worlds, but as redemptive for both individuals and the world from the original sin of the first Adam (and Eve). Any Greek, Jewish, or Gnostic explanations of good and evil, or the Adamic divine spark of Jewish Kabbalah or Manichean eons repairing ancient enmities between opposing forces, had no philosophy or system to match this new moral religion that affected the uneducated and uninitiated and caused them to convert in such numbers.

To combat the rival ideology, the 'Greek philosophy of liberation through knowledge' quoted above had then to be peddled even more actively in the Greek schools in the face of this 'Christian narrative of sin and redemption', but more specifically to rethink the order and origin of things, natural and supernatural. If one of the underlying principles of this new religion was selection of man as alone different from the rest of creation (to work with God in its husbandry), Gray is quite clear in calling this 'Exceptionalism' 'Christianity's unhappiest myth', since therein lies human power for destruction as well as construction. In its heretical and secular manifestations such as liberal humanism, human exceptionalism as rational animal has determined belief in progress and civilization; man's perfectibility of himself and of creation is achievable through his own science.[32] Some of the major nineteenth-century French scientific discoveries, achievements, and new technological developments can be found in Appendix 5.[33] Hilarion in his Greek science in so many ways embodies this nineteenth-century utopianism. In positivism and the cults of progress of nineteenth-century France we see the most direct inheritors of Greek liberation of knowledge and a secularized creed of redemption as equally rooted in a fifth-century heresy that lies just outside the *Tentation* (like Nestorianism), but which is suggested by it, Pelagianism. If Nestorius questioned the incarnate God Jesus (and his mother's divine or human womb), Pelagius questioned original sin and its hereditary transmission (and hence Jesus' divine and human mission): 'According to Pelagius, we sin by a voluntary imitation of Adam's transgression, corrupted indeed by external environment and by successive wrong choices that weaken the will's resolution, but never by a fault inherent in the "nature" with which we were born into the world.'[34] We may be more familiar with Jean-Jacques Rousseau's version of these beliefs in his *Émile*, which the fictional Victor and Victorine in Flaubert's *Bouvard et Pécuchet* so comically disprove. Pelagius had a running battle with Augustine concerning the generation of sin by sexuality. Surely these interconnected themes lie behind Flaubert's seemingly gratuitous disclosures of Antoine's self-flagellation (his cognizance of his fallen humanity and interest in generation). The very structure of a text about 'Temptations' (of all aspects of Antoine's humanity in body, mind, and spirit, in imitation of Christ), eludes the most obvious generation of sin arising from sexual thoughts ('Sheba', 'Ammonaria') with (sexual) generations of monstrous creatures as more interesting than cerebral phantasmagoria. The antediluvian aspects of St Anthony's beliefs (in the Fall, the tree of the knowledge of good and evil) then contrast starkly with Science's freedoms from Christianity epitomized in Hilarion's Greek Alexandrian schooling or naturalism's undifferentiated positioning of man (and gods) in the same laws of birth and death and the life cycles of history and civilization (the Gymnosophist, Buddha, but of course also Darwin). Is Antoine's literal and symbolic prostration that spurs the 'être la matière' passage the most pristine moment that secular humanity can reach? Are the new wonders of nineteenth-century science the sign of its progress out of the dark ages of religion, or its renaissance of forgetting this past in the archaeology of its knowledge?

5

A *Comédie (sur)humaine*

After the exhausting disorientation of Antoine's confrontation with Gnosis in all its Eastern religious and abstract forms in tableau four as a remapping of the many schools of knowledge and wisdom in Alexandria in the fourth century AD, the fifth tableau appears to return to more familiar ground for educated nineteenth-century French readers of the *Tentation*. Not only would schooling in Greek and Latin classics have been part of their secondary-school curriculum (if they were boys), the pantheon of Egyptian gods would have had equal cultural currency thanks to major displays (such as the Exposition Universelle of 1867) of over half a century of French Egyptology in the aftermath of Napoleon's Expédition. Educated women writers such as Louise Colet or George Sand also exploited classical and other mythology in their poetry and fiction. Although not its primary aim, Seznec's identification of the many mythological intertexts Flaubert drew from Creuzer and the classics for the details of the 'gods' in the 1849 *Tentation* therefore also pinpoints the mythological resource bases familiar to well-educated nineteenth-century French readers:[1] Plutarch, Theocritus, Ovid, Apuleius, Pliny, Catullus, Suetonius sit alongside immense interest in comparative religion spearheaded by more specialist compendia by Guigniaut, or studies on specific non-Western religions and mythologies such as Burnouf.[2] Apart from Carmody, Seznec's work on the gods and their orders in the first *Tentation* has not been challenged or applied to the final version, even among critics post-Seznec well versed in the classics.[3] The problem of the 'voice of God', and why it should return to conclude tableau five's troupe of gods with largely material and anthropomorphic forms has also not been tackled.[4] Thus the importance of nineteenth-century study of world mythologies and comparative religion as established by Seznec with reference to Guigniaut has been used by recent critics of the *Tentation* to support a relativist reading of this tableau, and thence a reading of the finale as 'pantheistic' and syncretistic.[5] As well as failing Antoine's innate status as saint, tableau five is where Antoine recites the Nicene Creed even if this is 'the stupidest of responses' as Starr contests.[6] Moreover, the epiphany which brings the text to its climax when Antoine is confronted with raw matter needs to fit with more than some 'comparatively religious' overall logic, even if it is read with heavy irony. This set piece is clearly framed by natural history and informed by a 'scientific' vision of nature rather than by religious (Christian or comparative) contexts, to show the saint's fundamentally unchanged belief system (including a view of creation) embodied in Antoine's undramatic return to the work of prayer and contemplation as his last act in the text.

If the last three tableaux are then a remapping of the history of *scientific* ideas of nineteenth-century France through the religious eyes of a fourth-century saint, tableau five clearly sits in a strategic position as the operator of this transformational turn from Gnosis to Science with or without Hilarion. The alienated reader of tableau four also needs to be brought back to more familiar ground for good reason. And this reason is to defamiliarize familiar mythologies, especially the heritage of Greece and Rome, for science and not just comparative religious ends. If Egypt has a central role to play here, so too does Hilarion as he transforms his functions of tableau three into those of tableau five by the 'magic' of his name and the major topics he coordinates. Given that these concern questions of life and death and encompass gods and civilizations as much as the life cycle of lesser mortals, his own necessary departure (like his arrival) also reveals its logic. Why is this not a final, pyrotechnic or nihilistic end (like the Gymnosophist) but as the huge 'angel' of Science?

Matching the fearful, cataleptic disorientations of the East in tableau four, defamiliarization of the 'Greek' West in tableau five will prove a theatre of alienation techniques for specific purposes to be worked out in subsequent tableaux. As partly a measure of light(er) relief for the reader, these techniques include the ludicrous and laughable to set the tone for tableau five as a fantastical series of metamorphoses of disintegrating gods, broken idols, and comically unnatural or earthy forms such as the scatological Crepitus. Remarkably little critical attention has been paid to the farcical but also dark humour of tableau five, let alone to the grotesque deities whose numerous body parts and monstrous couplings defy any but mythological belief.[7] If light relief or the comical have not been critical watchwords for the *Tentation*, why does Flaubert then stretch reader credulity almost to the limits through the grimly farcical at this late stage in his preposterous text? Could this scene be Flaubert's (mocking) answer to Balzac's 'Comédie humaine' with a 'comédie (sur)humaine' which is also sur(naturelle)?

REMODELLING NATURE'S GODS

In contrast to the broad church setting in tableau four of abstract ideas and mystery religions of the East, tableau five opens specifically within 'real', 'contemporary' Egyptian contexts and settings. Antoine's initial reconnection of the previous scene to the figures of the second tableau is not some forced, 'biblical' flag to prepare the 'voice of God' dying away at the tableau's end, but a reorientation of the powers of the East to their very similar Western counterparts. The geographical mediating point between the two is Egypt, but *ancient* rather then modern (fourth century or nineteenth century), a religious and 'scientific' civilization and culture of unequalled importance prior to the rise of the great Babylonian, Persian, Greek, or Roman empires on which France's own is belatedly sited. If St Anthony the Great spent a vital initiatory phase living in the ancient tombs, Flaubert's Antoine now elaborates this part of his curriculum vitae (mentioned in tableau one) to describe what he has seen on their walls, and specifically the tombs of Heliopolis. This ancient site was originally where Atum (god of the rising and setting sun on the earth's horizon) was worshipped before this god was subsumed (transformed) as the solar deity Re, or Horus of the two horizons. As falcon-headed man and god of the sky (overarching sun and moon), Horus was allegedly the son of Osiris and Isis. Horus' phoenix-like return from the dead is among the main themes that Hilarion will pursue. Prior to the establishment of the Alexandrian schools at the end of the fourth century BC, Heliopolis was also an important centre of cultivation, notably grain growing on the fertile Nile alluvium (the 'breadbasket' of ancient Egypt), and the most famous ancient seat of learning in philosophy and astronomy. Fourth-century AD Christianity will see the destruction of remaining 'pagan' temples to Horus, Isis, or imported gods (before Julian the Apostate briefly reinstates polytheism after the death of Anthony the Great). In the history of nineteenth-century Egyptology, the well-preserved hieroglyphics of the Heliopolis site further enabled Champollion to extend his knowledge of deciphering ancient Egyptian papyri and their pictograms. So while it appears that Antoine is describing 'monstrous' animals (demons in disguise in Athanasius' version) to comply with the *vraisemblance* of his early Christian experience (note the use of the past tenses), his description is also (and ironically) 'scientific'. It is as if Antoine were reading the script from the Expédition d'Égypte about the principal half-human/half-animal gods of Egypt, or looking at the images of Pharaonic gods with their inscrutable painted eyes:

Quand j'habitais le temple d'Héliopolis, j'ai souvent considéré tout ce qu'il y a sur les murailles: vautours portant des sceptres, crocodiles pinçant des lyres, figures d'hommes avec des corps de serpent, femmes à tête de vache prosternées devant des dieux ithyphalliques; et leurs formes surnaturelles m'entraînaient vers d'autres mondes. J'aurais voulu savoir ce que regardent ces yeux tranquilles.

Pour que de la matière ait tant de pouvoir, il faut qu'elle contienne un esprit. L'âme des Dieux est attachée à ses images...

Ceux qui ont la beauté des apparences peuvent séduire. Mais les autres... qui sont abjects ou terribles, comment y croire?...

Et il voit passer à ras du sol des feuilles, des pierres, des coquilles, des branches d'arbres, de vagues représentations d'animaux, puis des espèces de nains hytropiques; ce sont des Dieux. Il éclate de rire.   (*Tent*, 160–1)

This opening passage to tableau five must surely be the clue and cue for reading the final (in)famous 'être la matière' epiphany, since the themes, imagery, vocabulary, and tense structure around that vital 'j'aurais voulu' are its mirror image. Antoine's hilarity (a rare occurrence in the *Tentation*) at this first parade then neatly summons Hilarion, who, we recall, initially came to Antoine on the back of the mocking laughter of the Queen of Sheba. The main 'parade of the gods' then opens from this naturalistic ensemble of the vegetable, mineral, animal, monstrous, and supernatural 'gods' as a huge joke about the strange things that humans believe in and worship. Antoine's shared laughter with Hilarion—comedy only works *in communitas* and with distance from the butt of the joke—by implication states his position regarding religions with idols (paganism, polytheism, Hinduism, Buddhism). As Christian inheritor of Jewish taboos on representing God in any form,[8] Antoine eschews worship of humanoid or animal gods, natural forces, or planets understood as gods. Hilarion will further blur over-neat categories (animism, anthropomorphism) by laughing mockery of comparative religious glosses on the ludicrous forms passing before Antoine's and our eyes:

Alors défilent devant eux, des idoles de toutes les nations et de tous les âges, en bois, en métal, en granit, en plumes, en peaux cousues.

Les plus vieilles, antérieures au Déluge, disparaissent sous des goémons qui pendent comme des crinières. Quelques-unes, trop longues pour leur base, craquent dans leurs jointures et se cassent les reins en marchant. D'autres laissent couler du sable par les trous de leurs ventres. (*Tent*, 161)

Nineteenth-century archaeology will have in fact discovered such gods of Egypt now toppled from their commanding positions and lying in fragmented pieces at Heliopolis, for example, sand trickling from real holes in their stomachs as Maxime Du Camp's photographic record of his mission to Egypt accompanied by Flaubert amply attests.[9] Simi-larly, discovery of mummies of the Pharaohs and their temple animals (crocodiles, ibises, vultures) will reveal bodies preserved beneath their 'peaux cousues'. Our laughter with Antoine and Hilarion from the urbane rationality of the modern scientific imagination is precisely where (and how) Flaubert can then operate the all-important inversion of the ludicrous as the deadly serious, and the farcical as the most intensely 'real' and scientific of this tableau. The laughable 'old gods' will prove everywhere to be about modern idols which will presumably fall from their perches also, since this is the order of things.

Although open-ended and seemingly slight, Antoine's commentary quoted above has similar weight to his Bible exegeses in tableau one as key to remapping the ideas to come. With incredible economy, what Antoine pinpoints is the rationale of the human religious spirit. The power perceived in matter (Nature) by humans caused them from time immemorial to worship, and thereby to attempt to control, greater forces beyond their understanding dressed as a pantheon of gods. 'L'âme des Dieux est attachée à ses images' neatly but ambiguously covers the whole range of human idolatries, monstrous representations, and graven images in both Eastern and Western religions, Indian, Baby-lonian, Egyptian, Graeco-Roman, and among the Druids and Gauls. Only through the logic of human desire to harness the powers of these gods, whether by official orders of worship or the more clandestine dark arts of magic and sorcery, can bowing down to the 'abjects ou terribles' as well as to benign, beautiful gods be explained. This tiny phrase again subsumes worship as placation, of those terrifying and un-representational forces such as the thunderous 'voice of God' of Moses and the Old Testament, or the dreadful Moloch (*Tent*, 162, and note 85). At the same time, Antoine's gloss also focuses on mythological time behind even antiquity in precisely vague terms—'Les plus vieilles, antérieures au Déluge'—as the starting point for the transformations of 'gods', and the civilizations established around them that are the visible substance of the tableau. This detail will prove pivotal for tableau seven.

Un-suppressible laughter at gods which are sheep and half-animal rapidly discloses the 'powers of horror' when idols and gods 'se rap-prochent du type humain' (also implying Christ), and where religious rite and human sacrifice become a quintessential force of 'civilization'.[10] Antoine's response to deities such as Moloch is exactly the same as his reaction to the many systems of Gnosticism, the single word, 'Horreur!' (*Tent*, 162). Such tacit reconnection with the previous tableau releases the comparative religious anti-*apologium* of Christianity by default in the remainder of the tableau, skilfully put in the mouth of Hilar-ion. Seemingly very *different* alternative 'gods' who initially also lack 'form'—Buddha, Oannès, the Babylonian sky gods (as planets)—then generate a pantheon of deities or demigods who have shape, form, and specific characteristics (like the Gnostic Eons). Unlike Christianity, however, all the 'gods' pertain to mythological time before ancient history, and have more interesting and varied shape, transformations, and numbers of body parts than the God of Moses as ultimately but a 'voix'. Where Hilarion was a mocking double of a Renan of the *Vie de Jésus* in tableau three to spearhead the 'Arian' and other heresies of tableau four surrounding the person of Christ, he repeats the process by upholding biblical perspectives in the teeth of other world religions, their principal gods and 'creation' stories. His script is not Creuzer-Guigniaut, however, since the order of the parade of gods neither follows its geographical exploration east, nor concentrates on a par-ticular pantheon before moving comparatively to another. Tableau five starts with Buddha and India, moves to Egypt with Oannès, travels to Babylon (land of the magi, Nebuchadnezzar, and neighbour to Sheba), re-traverses the territory of the gods of Persia (and Manicheism), before returning to the Mediterranean from Ephesus to Egypt, and thereby to its imported gods from Greece and Rome. Focus on gods of the cosmos (in various pantheons) give way to goddesses of nature (Diana of Ephesus, Cybele, Isis), which in turn yield to more anthropomorphic deities (the gods of Egypt morph into the gods of Greece who segue into those of Rome) endowed with 'human' virtues and vices, and powers over generation and destruction. The 'household' gods of Rome (the Manes and Lares) and the 'Rabelaisian' Crepitus bring an anticlimactic grand finale (and scatological humour) to this parade of the death of the gods in all shapes and sizes.[11] Ironically, the silencing of wind in another form, the invisible 'voix de Dieu', marks out absence of the supernatural in this twilight of the gods.

The repeated death of gods as principal subject of tableau five nonetheless reveals a striking contradiction in terms since to be a god in the first place implies immortality. Like earthly potentates, empires, and all forms in the natural world, however, the law of death makes way for the law of new birth for gods also, whether the end is violent (persecution, cataclysm, invasion by another power, rapid killing) or a gradual decline (ageing, illness, decay, slow ebbing of vitality). By way of humour as quintessentially human response to the surety of mortality of all things, Flaubert presents both kinds of end allotted to the various gods in this 'comédie surnaturelle'. Oannès jumps into the Nile and is gone in a flash (*Tent*, 171); the pantheons of Indian deities encompassing Brahman, Buddhist, and Hindu gods disappear in black comic forms (in a continuous present) of self-immolation:

Alors un *vertige* prend les Dieux. Ils chancellent, tombent en *convulsions*, et vomissent leurs existences. Leurs couronnes éclatent, leurs étendards s'envolent. Ils arrachent leurs attributs, leurs sexes, lancent par dessus l'épaule les coupes où ils buvent l'immortalité, s'étranglent avec leurs serpents, *s'évanouissent* en fumée. (*Tent*, 170, emphasis added)

and Diana of Ephesus is comically depersonified as she undergoes nature's natural processes:

Qu'ai-je donc… moi l'incorruptible, voilà qu'une *défaillance* me prend!

Ses fleurs se fanent. Ses fruits trop mûrs se détachent. Les lions, les taureaux penchent leur cou; les cerfs bavent épuisés; les abeilles, en bourdonnant, meurent par terre.

Elle presse, l'une après l'autre, ses mamelles. Toutes sont vides! Mais sous un effort désespéré sa gaine éclate. Elle la saisit par le bas, comme le pan d'une robe, y jette ses animaux, ses floraisons,—puis rentre dans l'obscurité.

(*Tent*, 176, emphasis added)

The first movement of the tableau closes with the words 'Tout s'évanouit' (*Tent*, 182) to allow humour to turn to tears, and for the Egyptian deities of death (as rebirth) to reground Antoine in his native context which then turns into the Greek Mount Olympus, whose familiar gods are one by one disempowered, overpowered, or made impotent. Minerva, 'frappée au front, tombe par terre à la renverse' (*Tent*, 192); Hercules 'est écrasé sous les décombres' (*Tent*, 193); Neptune 's'*évanouit* dans l'azur' (*Tent*, 193, emphasis added). By the time the various gods of Rome arrive, readers (like Antoine) are fatigued by the endless panoply of lesser and lesser gods. Boredom is itself a contributory factor in the death of gods, for without worshippers they slowly but surely die, replaced by newer deities who have stolen their attributes and followers. The more terrible the gods, the more final is their overthrow. The fatiguing parades however show the same patterns of the limited human imagination to invent truly new gods from the rubble and broken pieces of older deities, a key point to which the concluding remarks for this tableau will return. Something significant, though, is at stake. Instead of going back to the birth of religions in mythic time (and every tableau in the *Tentation* has progressed retrospectively to this point), the parade's chronological sequence moves *forwards* to the conflicting pantheons of the (fourth-century AD) 'present' (and their ruins) under Constantine. What is the reason for the new reversal of order towards the future, and what is the point of this exaggerated and almost bowdlerized version of comparative religious exposition? Has Hilarion been given a fourth-century and nineteenth-century role that underpins the science of this tableau to match his mouthing of Renan's 'scientific' version of a historical Jesus in tableau three?

The clue to resolving these questions and to finding some missing link between them resides with Hilarion's 'master' Antoine in his opening gloss to tableau five, what I described as 'the rationale of the human religious spirit'. The bid to control greater forces by setting them up as gods is of course homologous with the rationale for the human scientific spirit, the bid to manipulate nature and hence become like the gods.

The 'power' that links both religion and science, but at the same time detaches humans from the powers of the gods or Nature, is magic. Heliopolis, Antoine's tomb of the Pharaohs, is also the city dedicated to the first of ancient Egypt's sciences, alchemy (from which metallurgy and modern chemistry derive). It is not without enormous irony that Napoleon attempted to blind Muslim dignitaries with the marvels of French nineteenth-century science epitomized by Berthollet's chemistry experiments at the Institut d'Égypte in Cairo, and as 'revenge' for the visit of bogus fortune tellers. Napoleon's private secretary, Louis Antoine Fauvelet de Bourrienne, recorded the reactions of the Muslim guests with interesting use of comparative analogy:

[Bonaparte] neglected no opportunity of showing off to the Egyptians the superiority of France in Arts and Sciences . . . Some days after the visit of the pretended fortune-teller he wished, if I may so express myself, to oppose conjuror to conjuror. . . . The General expected to be much amused at their astonishment; but the miracles of the transformation of liquids, electrical commotions, and galvanism, did not elicit from them any symptom of surprise. . . . When they were ended, the sheik El Bekri desired the interpreter to tell M. Berthollet that it was all very fine; 'but', said he, 'ask him whether he can make me be in Morocco and here at one and the same moment'. M. Berthollet replied in the negative . . . 'Oh, then', said the sheik, 'he is not half a sorcerer.'[12]

Magic is then the taboo double of both religion and science. In the Old Testament, sorcerers and magicians are anathema; in the New Testament, the dark arts of Simon Magus, like the practices of the Great Prostitute of Revelation, are utterly condemned. The strategic place of magic in the theological discussions of tableau four (its last third embodied in Apollonius) and tableau two (the longer 'Queen of Sheba' section) can now be rediscovered as having a 'scientific' import. In fourth-century Alexandria, the ongoing practice of magic—horoscopes, chiromancy (which was also allegedly birthed in Thebes in ancient Egyptian times), amulets, and charms—as well as development of demonological systems within the Neoplatonic schools which threatened 'serious' work in science, philosophy, and religion, caused writers such as Origen to outlaw it. Indeed Constantine saw magic as so closely bound up with pagan and polytheistic worship (which he sought completely to eradicate) that he passed two laws in 319 with the severest penalties for any who practised 'l'art divinatoire et l'aruspicine privée'.[13] Although not in the overt time strata of the *Tentation*, the medieval and Renaissance Church took a similar line against necromancers and alchemists who were often both major figures in the sciences and professing believers in Christianity. Sir Isaac Newton is another famous case in point. Moreover in nineteenth-century France, the great mythographer 'scientists' of comparative religion, Guigniaut, Baudry, and Maury, include in their ranks a 'scientific' historian of magic. In place of Renan's *Vie de Jésus* in the mouth of Hilarion to argue comparative New Testament religion, Flaubert inserts Maury's *La Magie et l'astrologie dans l'antiquité et au moyen âge: étude sur les superstitions païennes qui se sont perpétuées jusqu'à nos jours* as counterpoint to Old Testament (comparative) religions and their *sciences* in tableau five.[14] Antoine's gloss in tableau one of the 'Queen of Sheba' biblical intertext (*Tent*, 59) now makes perfect sense: Solomon's sublime science is his 'science de magicien'.[15] It is time that Maury's intertext was put on the critical map for Flaubert's *Tentation*,[16] not only to enhance our rereading of it, but also as a way to rediscover the science–religion debates central to the works of other nineteenth-century novelists, poets, and historians such as Michelet (of *La Sorcière* of 1862). For tableau five, Maury's *Magie* works innumerable 'tours' in the overall logic of Hilarion's tripartite role (tableaux three to five). It also provides us with some answers to the intrinsic logic of tableau five as springboard for tableaux six and seven, and Hilarion's replacement as Science by the Devil.

No intertext, as Seznec's magisterial source work for the *Tentation* amply demonstrates, is ever a decoding machine with direct equivalences. However Maury's *Magie* (like the Rosetta Stone's three versions of its text) is a code-breaking work for tableau five and its ramifications for the remaining tableaux on three levels. The first is structural and provides a clear answer to why Flaubert orders his 'gods' as he does, where the 'voix de Dieu' comes from, and why it culminates the parade. The second level pertains to the many densely allusive details which Flaubert replicates from Maury throughout tableau five. The third is configurative of the ideological stances and critiques that the *Tentation* reworks in the fictional dialogue of this tableau. Maury's introductory paragraph sums these up:

Les sciences physiques n'étaient à l'origine qu'un amas de superstitions et de procédés empiriques qui constituaient ce que nous appelons la magie.... Cette science avait pour but d'enchaîner à l'homme les forces de la nature et de mettre en notre pouvoir l'œuvre de Dieu. (*Magie*, 1)

Maury's history of the science of magic is in two parts. The first maps the civilized world from its earliest 'peuples sauvages' and cultic practices based on fetishism (chapter 1) through a major second chapter ('la magie et l'astrologie des Chaldéens, des Perses et des Égyptiens') introducing astrology as central to magic, religion, and science. The following three chapters now look very déjà vu from the viewpoint of tableau five in the *Tentation*: chapter 3 tackles magic and astrology for the Greeks, chapter 4 investigates magic in Rome and the Roman Empire, and chapter 5, 'La Magie dans l'école néoplatonicienne', neatly brings us to the Alexandria of the life and times of St Anthony.[17] The next chapter then discusses Christianity's crusade against magic and astrology rooted in Old Testament laws against it (Genesis, Leviticus, 1 Kings), finding in the Old Testament Satan (of Job) 'l'Ahriman juif' (*Magie*, 97), and concluding with Constantine's outlawing of public and private magic practices. Chapter 7 focuses on medieval Christendom's reconfiguration of pagan gods and heroes in the form of the Virgin and the saints.[18] It ends with a direct connection between Rome and the superstitions of France:

En France, les fées, les *Fata* ou *Fatales* de l'antiquité, confondues avec les druidesses, dont le souvenir ne s'était pas totalement effacé, les génies ou *Lares* familiers, devenus les luitons ou lutins, des follets, des esprits servants, les anciens druides et les bardes transformés en enchanteurs... (*Magie*, 188)

The fitting place of the 'Archi-galle' as a Gallic cousin german of Cybele cults (*Tent*, 178) can now be explained. The final two chapters of part I discuss 'la magie orientale' (including Buddhist inheritance from Shivaism, and disciples of Sakya-Mouni drawing their demonology from Brahmanism) and 'magie et astrologie depuis la Renaissance jusqu'à nos jours'. The second part then translates the configurations of power inherent in magic and astrology into nineteenth-century terms to qualify the opening statement that, 'Si la magie eût exclusivement reposé sur la crédulité et le mensonge, son règne n'aurait pas été de si longue durée, et l'avènement des sciences y eût mis certainement fin' (*Magie*, 225). Physiological and psychic phenomena (treated extensively from psychological and medical scientific angles elsewhere in Maury's work[19]) such as dream, hallucination, hypnotism, somnambulism, catalepsy, and the hearing and seeing of supernatural beings are all highlighted in a first chapter. A second maps a history of fear of demon possession (Christian and Hindu, among the fourth-century Messalian sect and among the desert fathers). Chapter 3, with its subtitle of 'les mystiques rapprochés des sorciers', enlarges on the role of the imagination with regard to visions and apparitions. Maury notes and quotes a 'curious' passage in St Basil which is surely the absolute giveaway that *La Magie* is Flaubert's compositional and expository source for tableau five:

Que sera-ce donc, écrit-il, que la voix du Seigneur? Faut-il entendre aussi par là une percussion imprimée à l'air par des organes vocaux, un ébranlement de l'atmosphère qui vient apporter le type des idées jusqu'à l'oreille de celui à qui la parole s'adresse? N'est-il pas au contraire bien plus vraisemblable que ce n'est ni l'un ni l'autre, et que la voix de Dieu est quelque chose de tout particulier, un je ne sais quoi, une image vive, une vision claire et sensible qui s'imprime dans l'esprit des hommes auxquels Dieu veut communiquer sa pensée; une vision qui doit présenter quelque analogie avec celles qui s'impriment dans notre imagination lorsque nous avons un songe en dormant? Personne n'ignore en effet qu'il n'y a réellement aucune percussion, aucun ébranlement de l'air, lorsqu'en rêve nous croyons entendre certains bruits, certaines paroles qui ne sont assurément pas apportées d'une manière physique à notre oreille et que nous percevons seulement dans notre esprit, où elles viennent s'imprimer. C'est à peu près de la même manière qu'il faut admettre que la voix de Dieu se fait entendre dans l'âme des prophètes. (*Magie*, 339–40)

The disembodied 'voix de Dieu' in the *Tentation* is also as beautifully double-edged as in this quotation, for it ironically tests the very 'reality' of all of Antoine's 'visions', 'temptations', 'hallucinations', or 'imaginations' that make up the contents of this and every tableau. Are the visions real because he is a saint and therefore a party to the voice of God like the prophets of old? Are the visions false, the work of demons as experienced by ascetics in all the world religions? Or in the frame of nineteenth-century psychology as part of the medical sciences, are such phenomena 'ordinary' functions of the subconscious which can be scientifically stimulated and controlled (Maury's final chapter examines the use of narcotics)? Like Renan, Maury concludes with the rational, scientific view of his subject and, like Renan, discounts miracles (such as stigmata): 'L'esprit scientifique est précisément l'opposé de cette disposition au merveilleux entretenue par l'ignorance des lois physiologiques'

(*Magie*, 445). Unlike Renan, however, Maury's final remarks discount the miraculous by replacing it with science's greater wonders: 'Aucun miracle, aucun prodige n'égale assurément en grandeur le spectacle des lois générales de la création; aucune apparition, aucune vision ne prouve, plus que la révélation de l'univers, l'existence de l'Être infini qui engendre, entretient et résume toutes choses' (*Magie*, 446).

If Antoine will indeed view these 'lois générales' in tableaux six and seven, his epiphany at the end of the *Tentation* now has Maury's conclusion as its (scientific) precedent. In tableau five the mortality of the gods, when examined as a class, demonstrates a remarkably similar (and human) morphology. The emphasis added in the quotations from the *Tentation* above now reveals the nineteenth-century 'scientific' gloss on the various ends of the gods in Flaubert's remodelling of them to the letter and spirit of Maury's *Magie*. Their 'vertiges', 'défaillances', and 'épanouissements' are not supernatural, but rather natural and physiological phenomena. The gods are now dead not just to Christianity in the fourth century, but also to science in the nineteenth, which can explain them in psychological instead of comparative religious guise.

Yet it is not only thanks to the structure and topics of Maury's *Magie* that tableau five becomes such a virtuoso comedy of transformations turning the supernatural into the natural in scientific imitation of mythology's (and Ovid's) metamorphoses. Many of the authenticating details of the tableau are also taken directly from it. Only two of the most strategic will be examined for the purpose of answering the hard questions posed above, since space does not permit an in-depth study after the manner of Seznec's *Les Sources de l'épisode des dieux*. The details Flaubert reworks all come from chapters in the first part of Maury's text, and determine the logic of tableau five with its subsequent others.

In chapter 2, 'La Magie et l'astrologie des Chaldéens, des Perses et des Égyptiens', there is a description of the famous tower of Babel, 'monument consacré aux sept planètes', Babylonian temples (like that at ancient Heliopolis) serving the dual purpose of being 'véritables observatoires' (*Magie*, 23):

Une longue suite d'observations mirent les Chaldéens en possession d'une astronomie théologique reposant sur une théorie plus ou moins chimérique de l'influence des corps célestes appliquée aux événements et aux individus. Cette science, appelée par les Grecs *astrologie* ou *apotèlesmatique*, fut, dans l'antiquité le titre de gloire des Chaldéens.   (*Magie*, 23–4)[20]

Flaubert reworks this description by whisking Antoine to just such a ziggurat observatory, so that Hilarion can explain Babylonian renown in astronomy (and astrology) in general, and exact observation in particular:

Des sept planètes, deux sont bienfaisants, deux mauvaises, trois ambiguës; tout dépend, dans le monde, de ses feux éternels. D'après leur position et leur mouvement on peut tirer des présages;—et tu foules l'endroit le plus respectable de la terre. Pythagore et Zoroastre s'y sont rencontrés. Voilà douze mille ans que ces hommes observant le ciel, pour mieux connaître les Dieux.

ANTOINE
Les astres ne sont pas Dieux.

HILARION
Oui! disent-ils; car les choses passent autour de nous; le ciel, comme l'éternité, reste immuable!

ANTOINE
Il a un maître, pourtant.

HILARION montrant la colonne:
Celui-là, Bélus, le premier rayon, le Soleil, le Mâle!
—L'Autre, qu'il féconde, est sous lui!   (*Tent*, 172–3)

The proper names here, their rather confused connections or significance, are taken directly from this chapter in Maury. If the priests of Babylon formed colleges (for religion and science like the magi of Persia),

[l]es Perses honoraient comme leur grand prophète Zoroastre, *Zarathoustra* ou *Zerduscht*. ... Zoroastre devient donc ... pour Grèce et pour Rome l'inventeur de la magie, le patron des mages persans confondus avec les Chaldéens de Babylone.   (*Magie*, 34–5)

La connaissance des phénomènes célestes faisait en Égypte, comme en Chaldée, partie intégrante de la théologie. Les Égyptiens avaient des collèges de prêtres spécifiquement attachés à l'étude des astres, et où Pythagore, Platon, Eudoxe, avaient été s'instruire [*sic*] ... On trouve encore aujourd'hui la preuve de cette vieille science sacerdotale dans les zodiaques sculptés au plafond de quelques temples, et dans des inscriptions hiéroglyphiques mentionnant des phénomènes célestes.   (*Magie*, 43–4)

Entre ces planètes, Saturne, ou comme les Assyriens paraissent l'avoir appelé, *Bel l'ancien* ... astre le plus élevé ... le révélateur. (*Magie*, 27)

Not only are magic and astrology linked to religion and the science of astronomy, Flaubert also manages through Hilarion's rewording of Maury to transform one set of high priests of magic and science into another, to elide the worship of stars with the exact science or astronomy on the one hand and comparative religion on the other. Many of the planets in our solar system are indeed named after 'gods' whose attractions or repulsions were thought to describe eclipses or other astral patterns. Flaubert thus borrows from Maury's translation of the Babylonian *Planispherium* into 'Greek/Latin' and classification of their stars (gods) into three male and two female, '*Bel* (Jupiter) *Merodach* (Mars) *Nebo* (Mercure) *Sin* (Lune) *Mylitta* ou *Baalthis* (Vénus)' (*Magie*, 27), to reconnect the cosmic, generative (sexual), and 'scientific' aspects of the 'gods'.

Flaubert's most wicked humour, dressed up in Hilarion's final two explanations, will not however become fully apparent until the next tableau. *Belus* as Saturn is indeed the seventh star, the furthest known to astronomers in the solar system until the nineteenth century, and proved revelatory for the discovery of Neptune and Pluto.[21] For the purposes of the logic of tableau five, Maury's intertext makes very clear that Hilarion's mocking of theogonies and theosophy (or the nineteenth-century 'science' of comparative religion in other words[22]) is the magic conjuring trick that turns cosmogony and astrology into cosmology and astronomy. Hilarion's discussion of 'magi' thus reconnects him to the source of his own appearance at the end of tableau two in the train of the 'Queen of Sheba', and re-emergence from tableau four's ending on Apollonius as Pythagorean. Like the magus herald of the macrocosmic visions of the heavens in tableau six, the logic of tableau five for chapter 6 is now established. Why Hilarion must cede his place to the Devil will be addressed below.

Naming is a clue to the most important interleaving of time frames in the *Tentation* as the above quotations exemplify. Flaubert's most bizarre terminologies (as the final tableau of the 'monsters' will also demonstrate) are also his most researched. A second set of details from Maury for tableau five, this time for the 'familiar' and most domesticated gods of the Romans, the Lares (and their popularization throughout the

Roman Empire in Gaul as 'lutrins'), helps to unpack the contemporary 'scientific' significance of what seems a rather pointless list of minor gods with too many accoutrements:

Et il lui montre, sous des cyprès et des rosiers, Une autre Femme – vêtue de gaze. Elle sourit, ayant autour d'elle des pioches, des brancards, des tentures noires, tous les ustensiles des funérailles. Ses diamants brillent de loin sous les toiles d'araignées. Les Larves comme des squelettes montrent leurs os entre les branches, et les Lémures, qui sont des fantômes, étendent leurs ailes de chauve-souris.... Les Dieux rustiques[131] s'en éloignent en pleurant, Sartor, Sarrator, Vervactor, Collina, Vallona, Hostilinus,—tous couverts de petits manteaux à capuchon, et chacun portant, soit un hoyau, une fourche, une claie, un épieu.

HILARION
C'est leur âme qui faisait prospérer la villa...

LES LARES DOMESTIQUES
... vêtus de peaux de chien...
Qu'ils étaient doux les repas de famille... Dans la tendresse pour les morts, toutes les discordes s'apaisaient; et on s'embrassait en buvant aux gloires du passé et aux espérances de l'avenir.

Mais les aïeux de cire peinte, enfermés derrière nous, se couvrent lentement de moisissure. Les races nouvelles, pour nous punir de leurs déceptions, nous ont brisé la mâchoire; sous la dent des rats nos corps de bois s'émiettent.

(*Tent*, 201–3)

If Gothot-Merch's note 131 refers to manuscript evidence that Flaubert sought Maury's expertise for this part of the *Tentation* through the intermediary of Frédéric Baudry, Maury's *La Magie* has never previously been identified as the source. In chapter 4 ('Magie à Rome et dans l'Empire romain') there is the following:

La conjuration des *lémures* ou fantômes, envoyés par les morts, le culte des mânes et des lares étaient associés à diverses pratiques d'un caractère tout magique. La déesse Mana-Geneta, à laquelle, comme à Hécate, on sacrifiait des chiens, avait beaucoup d'analogie avec cette divinité des nuits... Pour détourner les mauvais génies, les larves ou spectres, on recourait à des sacrifices expiatoires accompagnés d'exorcismes. (*Magie*, 70)

In all civilizations and religions with extensive rituals for the dead (Egypt, Rome) the soul's intermediate and intermediary status (rather than its transmigration or metempsychosis into other life forms as in the East) is a source of fear:

Les démons ayant été, dans l'origine, pour les Grecs les âmes des morts assimilées à des divinités, ainsi qu'on le voit par Hésiode, ce nom s'appliqua bientôt aux divinités intermédiaires entre Dieu et l'homme, reconnues par presque tous les philosophes grecs...Ils [les démons] furent confondus avec les mânes, les lares, les génies latins.

(*Magie*, 87, in chapter 5, 'La Magie dans l'école néoplatonicienne')

Again Flaubert's wicked sense of humour is at work in the relevance of these comparative religious 'facts' as strikingly pertinent to nineteenth-century scientific 'cults' of the dead with all their necessary tools. Instead of burying preserved bodies, palaeontology and Egyptology were digging up ancient body fragments, animal and human, to carry away the remains for further examination or reconstruction. Many of the discoveries, for example of fossil crocodiles, were taking place around Honfleur and Caen; the Muséum d'Histoire Naturelle in Rouen, for example, boasted extensive collections of both Egyptian and local palaeontology.[23] Like the Lares represented as 'cire peinte' in domestic niches, museums similarly 'housed' and displayed real remains, but also wax models.[24] If religion's intermediaries between man and the gods, humans and animals, are centred in the 'soul', the most major debates in French nineteenth-century natural science, namely fixity of 'règnes' versus their 'transformisme', depended on finding intermediate types. The lemur, like the Egyptian *bichir* 'discovered' for French ichthyology by Geoffroy Saint-Hilaire, is an important case in point. As with the *Bel* detail as prefiguration of discoveries in the macrocosm (nineteenth-century astronomy) in the sixth tableau of the *Tentation*, the 'lémures' augur discoveries in the seventh tableau's 'microcosm' of Nature and nineteenth-century natural sciences. Hilarion's mocking of the science of comparative religion is also the magic conjuring trick that turns polytheistic religions into natural science and zoology. For the logic of Flaubert's *Tentation* from tableau five also to tableau seven, Maury's *Magie* has once more provided the missing links.

Intermediaries are therefore essential to understanding any hierarchy or classification of (super)natural realms, and to effecting metamorphoses (translations) between levels of the similar, or from one end of a scale to another. Maury's *Magie* thus has a configurative function for tableau five, beyond offering a key (the term 'magie') to its temporal sequence and structure of the 'gods' or the details of specific pantheons. The nub is the way that 'magic' and the magus (scientist) can be at once religious and scientific and, more importantly for a fictional work on belief(s), draw equally on superstition and empirical reason. To recall Maury's introductory sentence: 'Les sciences physiques n'étaient à l'origine qu'un amas de superstitions et de procédés empiriques.... Cette science avait pour but d'enchaîner à l'homme les forces de la nature et de mettre en notre pouvoir l'œuvre de Dieu.' Tableaux six and seven will indeed look at this 'œuvre', macro- and microcosmically and, following Maury's conclusions, will reserve judgement as to its provenance by not referring to the God of Genesis. Within the context of the death of all the naturalistic, astrological, and anthropomorphic 'gods', and the 'voix du Seigneur' of the Old Testament, Maury leaves psychology as the site of the new versions of these antique and antiquated psychic phenomena. It seems to me that Flaubert rejects this narrowing into science, albeit a modern version of Gnosis or of the goddess Psyche, because his *Tentation* must for the purposes of avoiding anachronism hold on to fourth-century religious world views. However, his trickery of palming off modern science through Hilarion's mock-Christianizing gloss of comparative religions borrows its central configurative turn directly from Maury. A bigger intermediary than Antoine's familiar other and fellow creature is necessary to hold in tension all the mythological, religious, and also scientific worlds of magic. Who better to take forward the magic of tableau five into both six and seven than the 'Ahriman juif' in the form of Satan or 'le Diable'? While the Devil is not an evil god in either the Greek or the Roman pantheons, equivalent supernatural personifications of evil and destruction are found in Indian, Babylonian, Persian, Egyptian, and Druidic religions and importantly hold (almost) equal with the chief god of their respective systems. By ending the fifth tableau with classical culture in its 'French' and modern forms, defamiliarization of this same toppled empire (in religious, but not scientific terms) can occur only by its most preposterous opposite, the Devil Scientist arriving with dramatic irony after the dying voice of God. Magus of magi, Flaubert's 'Diable' (like Goethe's Mephistopheles) is not so much interested in questions of evil and good, but in superstition, reason, and disbelief as the stuff of science as much as religion. Magic and modern science can thus head out together into the sixth tableau in the completely ludicrous, but eminently logical, form of the Devil as winged 'god' (like Jupiter), monster 'Lémure' ('qui sont des fantômes, étendent leurs ailes de chauve-souris'), the Prince of Darkness (astronomy and outer space are next on the agenda), and anti-classical (and anti-Enlightenment) 'vehicle' to take Antoine, but not Hilarion, with him. In Flaubert's 'comédie surnaturelle', it is the supreme devilment of the Devil who has the last laugh at the reader's credulity or pat ideas that superstition and 'gods' (or devils), whether in anthropomorphic form (like Hilarion) or disembodied voice, are dead.

HILARION'S EGYPTIAN DOUBLES

However close are Hilarion's roles as tempter and deceiver of Antoine to those of the Devil, Hilarion as Science is not however the Devil himself. We have suggested why for reasons of the *Tentation*'s overarching structure above. Flaubert's careful elision of Hilarion with paradigmatic *human* figures in history as we saw in Chapter 3 also tempers his innately mythological functions as Trickster or mediatory figure between natural and supernatural realms.[25] While he himself swells to superhuman proportions at the same time as he choreographs metamorphoses and transformations across tableaux three to five, why he must leave the work where and how he does so needs to be addressed. As cynical interlocutor and cross-questioner of all of Antoine's beliefs about heaven and earth by scientific method (culled as we saw from Renan in tableau three and from Maury in tableau five), Hilarion's zenith is aptly the tableau where he is powerfully the purveyor and manipulator of the *science* of nineteenth-century comparative religion (the *Vie de Jésus* and *La Magie*), and its authority. Mocking the 'normal' basis and direction of comparative religious analogies—from Western Christendom to its others, or that Christianity is but another version of more ancient others—he inverts religions' comparative orders by pressing hard on their inherent bid for superiority over rival systems (astrology/sciences). By such turning upside down of the surety of their value systems (such as a chronology of 'before' and 'after', a scale of simple to complex forms), Hilarion challenges neat hierarchical orders, whatever their larger classification by geographical, historical, theological, cultural, or scientific sophistication. Whether in the realm of the

abstract (the strictly Egyptian Gnostic section of tableau four) or in
the realm of the material and multiform (polytheistic representations
in their entire plethora in tableau five), his authority as polymath
comes from his razor-sharp reason, mockery, irony, and rhetorical *mise
en question* of fixed structures and classifications of belief. Hence, we
have his (mocking) claim to fame in his own mouth: 'On m'appelle
la Science' (*Tent*, 206), whereas his stance proves everywhere always
Janus-like, one face to religion, the other to science. Having established
Hilarion's religious substitutions in chapter 3, his final transformation
into a figure that could also be called 'Science' (in enormous guise
to boot) yet not the Devil needs to be established. This link is what
is missing from Peter Starr's persuasive argument for the wonderfully
punning double for Hilarion as the nineteenth-century natural scientist
Geoffroy *Saint-Hilaire* (1984, 1074). Beyond the latter's 'transformiste'
theories, Starr's equation between them is moreover problematic and
reductive, because anachronistic. If 'Hilarion has profited from the
nineteenth-century's continued interest in comparative religion, historical anthropology and ... natural history' (1073),[26] Starr's modern
delineation paradoxically makes it more difficult to account for the
following. Why does the Devil take Hilarion's place? How does Geoffroy
Saint-Hilaire's 'science' link to tableau *six* in subject matter (astronomy),
and to both six and seven when 'Hilarion' is absent from the text? How
does the Geoffroy Saint-Hilaire incarnation graft onto a *religious* Hilarion, let alone a fourth-century one? Despite flagging Geoffroy Saint-
Hilaire's ' "unity of organic composition" (the "theory of analogues" [to
which] Flaubert's letter of July 7–8, 1853 implicitly refers)' (1075),
Starr's wonderfully provocative article inherently points to answers to
these questions, but rushes too quickly to its conclusions by ignoring
the evidence of the *Tentation* as everywhere a series of analogical and
inductive steps. For analogues and analogies to work on the level that
Geoffroy Saint-Hilaire and Flaubert's *Tentation* in fact demand, multiple
contexts and delineated constants are all, as Flaubert's original letter to
Louise Colet quoted only very partially by Starr implies:

Les matérialistes et les spiritualistes empêchent également de connaître la
matière et l'esprit, parce qu'ils scindent l'un de l'autre. Les uns font de l'homme
un ange et les autres un porc. Mais avant d'en arriver à ces sciences-là (qui seront
des sciences), avant d'étudier bien l'homme, n'y a-t-il pas à étudier ses produits,

à connaître les effets pour remonter à la cause? Qui est-ce qui a, jusqu'à présent, fait de l'histoire en naturaliste? A-t-on classé les instincts de l'humanité et vu comment, sous telle latitude, ils se sont développés et *doivent* se développer? Qui est-ce qui a établi scientifiquement comment, pour tel besoin de l'esprit, telle forme doit apparaître, et suivi cette forme partout, dans les divers règnes humains? Qui est-ce qui a généralisé les religions? Geoffroy Saint-Hilaire a dit: le crâne est une vertèbre aplatie. Qui est-ce qui a prouvé, par exemple, que la religion est une philosophie devenue art, et que la cervelle qui bat dedans, à savoir la superstition, le sentiment religieux en soi, est de même matière partout, malgré ses différences extérieures, correspond aux mêmes besoins, répond aux mêmes fibres, meurt par les mêmes accidents etc.? Si bien qu'un Cuvier de la Pensée n'aurait qu'à retrouver plus tard un vers ou une paire de bottes pour reconstituer toute une société et que, les lois en étant données, on pourrait prédire à jour fixe, à heure fixe, comme on fait pour les planètes, le retour des mêmes apparitions.   (*Corr,* ii. 378, emphasis in the original)

Failure to account for any of the multiple comparisons here, let alone their remapping or morphologies, will cause Starr's stimulating hypothesis—Hilarion as Geoffroy Saint-Hilaire *is* nineteenth-century science—to disintegrate, as the 'gods' of tableau five everywhere demonstrate. Reading Hilarion as a very definite double of Geoffroy Saint-Hilaire is however possible if this analogy is read against the many others in Flaubert's dense and scientifically well-informed letter. This is therefore a blueprint methodology for our remapping of nineteenth-century French science in the *Tentation,* particularly tableaux five to seven. A satisfactory explanation for Hilarion's many transformations, then, needs on the one hand to adhere to the internal logic of his (changing but also similar) role in the three central tableaux of the *Tentation* as summed up in his ever increasing *physical* form from 'un nain . . . sa tête prodigieusement grosse' (*Tent,* 86) to colossus of enlightenment, 'transfiguré, beau comme un archange, lumineux comme un soleil,—et tellement grand, que pour le voir ANTOINE se reverse la tête' (*Tent,* 205). On the other hand, Hilarion's transformations need to hold in tension the equivocations between fourth-century Alexandria and nineteenth-century France without dispensing with or overplaying the one or the other.

The all-important missing link is again provided by Maury's *Magie,* in a passage immediately issuing from the discussion (quoted above) of the advanced astronomical and astrological knowledge of Egyptian priests, exemplified by the zodiacs sculpted on temple ceilings. The zodiac discovered at Dendera, illustrated and described in the *Description d'Égypte* and widely circulated, would have been immediately identifiable by Maury's French reading public. Flaubert's reuse of Maury is evident in Isis's speech about the 'Dendera' zodiac in tableau five (*Tent*, 184), already prepared by 'Sheba's' dress and footwear in tableau two. From zodiacs, Maury's attention turns to the sacred books of the Egyptians

dont on faisait remonter la rédaction au dieu Thoth ou Tat...l'inventeur de l'écriture, et identifié plus tard par les Grecs à leur Hermès. Ces livres d'Hermès égyptien surnommé Trismégiste, c'est-à-dire *très-grand*, comprenaient des traités de toutes les sciences dont l'étude était réservée à la caste sacerdotale. Les égyptologues en ont retrouvé des fragments écrits sur papyrus, en caractères hiératiques. A l'époque alexandrine, on les traduisait en grec, en y introduisant sans doute de nombreuses interpolations et leur faisant subir un remaniement sous l'influence des idées platoniciennes.   (*Magie*, 44–5)

Hilarion we recall was born of pagan Egyptian parents and was educated in the Alexandrian Neoplatonic schools before converting to Christianity and eventually becoming St Anthony's disciple. As Egyptian and Greek, he grows visibly *greater* in knowledge, authority, and stature in the *Tentation*—it is part of the black comedy of tableau five—but this is because he literalizes the stature of his model. As new Thoth or Hermes *Trismégiste*, Hilarion's roles as Egyptian priest and scientist versed in all the mysteries (Gnosis) and sciences of the ancient (and fourth-century) Egyptian worlds are now in place. Indeed his 'rouleau' in tableau three may also be a proleptic signpost to his Hermes persona in tableau five.[27] In line with the densely comparative analogy at work in Hilarion's religious metamorphoses across fourth- and nineteenth-century Egyptian and French contexts in tableau three, there only remains to be found a specifically nineteenth-century *Egyptian* scientific link between Hilarion as Thoth/Hermes and Geoffroy Saint-Hilaire. This missing piece which Starr nowhere mentions is Étienne Geoffroy Saint-Hilaire's pivotal place as natural scientist on Napoleon's Expédition d'Égypte, and his many contributions to empirical science at the Institut d'Égypte in Cairo.

Starr's omission is readily excusable insofar as historians of nineteenth-century French science and biographers of Étienne Geoffroy Saint-Hilaire have largely glossed over his early Egyptian career.[28] At best this is mentioned briefly in an initial chapter to preface the 'important' synthetic work to come (the theory of the unity of composition) and once Geoffroy Saint-Hilaire had returned to Paris permanently as established Muséum, not field-based, scientist.[29] What remain crucial and critical for these studies are the increasingly acrimonious differences thereafter between Cuvier and Saint-Hilaire culminating in the famous 'querelle des analogues' of 1830 to which we will return in Chapter 7. A notable exception to such histories of science is Théophile Cahn's more pedantically chronological biography of Geoffroy Saint-Hilaire of 1962 which devotes a whole chapter (5) to the Expédition d'Égypte. Quoting extensively from Geoffroy Saint-Hilaire's correspondence to various scientific colleagues back at the Jardin des Plantes, but especially Cuvier, Cahn understands Geoffroy Saint-Hiliare's richly varied scientific work undertaken in Egypt as pivotal in shaping all his subsequent thinking and ideas. The rich collections of Egyptian fauna (contemporary and mummified) that Geoffroy Saint-Hilaire brought back added significantly to the material and scientific importance of the collections at the Jardin des Plantes, as Cuvier himself warmly attested in his role as perpetual Secretary. Recent republication of Geoffroy Saint-Hilaire's *Lettres d'Égypte* allows fascinating insights into his intense, vital, and necessary dialogue with Cuvier regarding discoveries of various species in Egypt. While germs of the later quarrel are indeed to be found here, suffice it to say for tableau five of the *Tentation* that it is the Hilarion–Antoine, master–disciple relationship of profoundly differing similarities that Flaubert aligns with their nineteenth-century *scientific* but also arguably religious successors, Geoffroy Saint-Hilaire and Cuvier.[30] Hilarion is not therefore a Geoffroy Saint-Hilaire of *nineteenth-century science* or devil's advocate for it. He is however the '*très*-grand' Egyptian magus figure to orchestrate its many parts in tableau five by comparative *religious* analogy and parallelism. As the final part of the chapter will demonstrate, it is thanks to Hilarion that ancient zoology and natural science may metamorphose into recognizably nineteenth-century forms. How this process operates lies in remapping his guided tour of comparative religions *on display* in tableau five as so many cabinets of pertinent artefacts in a museum of ideas. For the larger 'unités de composition' to become manifest in each display case (the sections of the tableau), the 'collection' as a whole, and for the rest of the *Tentation* from which Hilarion the guide is absent, his very appearance and disappearance need explanation. Their structural symmetry and perfect logic in the work (at the end of tableaux two and five) encapsulate his powerfully double-faced persona—as Janus-like manipulator of religious and scientific analogy and as figure of deceptive likeness.

Hilarion the dwarf-to-become-angel-of-Science emerges in the text from the extraordinary train of possessions of the 'Queen of Sheba' which rival any of the mighty collections of the (biblical) kings, including Solomon's, as encapsuled in Antoine's readings in tableau one. Amid the incredible list (the Queen's 'j'ai..., j'ai..., j'ai...') is a veritable menagerie, but introduced, importantly, by intermediaries in the human, animal, and monstrous worlds:

> J'ai des... *eunuques* de quoi faire une armée. J'ai des armées, j'ai des peuples! J'ai dans mon vestibule une garde de *nains* portant sur le dos des trompes d'ivoire.... J'ai des attelages de gazelles, des quadriges d'éléphants, des couples de chameaux par centaines, et des cavales à crinière si longue que leurs pieds y entrent quand elles galopent, et des troupeaux à cornes si larges que l'on abat les bois devant eux quand ils pâturent. J'ai des girafes qui se promènent dans mes jardins, et qui avancent leur tête sur le bord de mon toit... Assise dans une coquille, et traînée par les dauphins, je me promène dans les grottes écoutant tomber l'eau des stalactites. Je vais au pays des diamants, où les magiciens mes amis me laissent choisir les plus beaux; puis je remonte sur la terre, et je rentre chez moi.   (*Tent*, 82–3, emphasis added)

At this point the mythical Simorg-Anka also returns to the Queen to disrupt her list of past possessions for the conquest of Antoine as her latest one. While all critics have read the 'Je suis un monde' as sexual (we have argued why in Chapter 2), her person and menagerie is extremely evocative and prefigurative of the pan-creational goddess *figures* of tableau five—Diana of Ephesus, Cybele, Isis—who all embody nature's diversity of life forms. Against Sheba's overwhelming spirit of 'prostitution' and generation, theirs is however a litany of *degeneration* and casting off of (sexual) parts and monstrous coupling. Sheba's phoenix-like Simorg-Anka (of Egyptian name and whose attributes the god Horus borrows) is not the only exotic, 'Egyptian' creature in her menagerie. The giraffe(s) 'qui se promènent dans mes jardins' surely signal a specifically nineteenth-century wink to the fantastic as real. Until the arrival in 1827 of a giraffe, the gift of the Egyptian Pasha (which both Cuvier and Geoffroy Saint-Hilaire officially received into the menagerie of the Jardin des Plantes), no French person had ever seen a living one. Similarly, where a monkey lifted the hem of 'Sheba's' skirts in tableau two, we meet 'Isis' in tableau five in a pose not only redolent of a Virgin *lactans*, but also accompanied by 'un grand singe'. This is her pet Cynocephalus, who squats, sphinx-like, beside her, and by analogy with medieval iconography like a unicorn beside a Virgin Mary. Both these 'mythical' animals will appear again in the final tableau in the so-called parade of the monsters. Like the other gods and goddesses above, however, the Cynocephalus 's'est *évanoui*' (*Tent*, 185, emphasis added) in prefiguration of the death of her son Harpocratus (or Horus the child).[31] Monstrous births and arrivals (divine, incestuous, natural) do indeed shake the orders ('règnes') of the animal/(super)human world as we will discover in Chapter 7. But like the intermediary creatures in Sheba's train, those in Isis's speech also replicate the abstract creations (anti-trinities) of tableau four by giving them more recognizable, comparative, and hybrid forms: 'triades particulières des Nomes, éperviers dans l'azur, sphinx au bord des temples, ibis debout entre les cornes des bœufs, planètes, constellations, rivages, murmures du vent, reflets de la lumière' (*Tent*, 182). What we have here is a 'creation story' told as an Egyptian version of the biblical Flood to mesh ancient Egypt via Hilarion with its 'Geoffroy Saint-Hilaire' face. If he visited the Nileometer in Napoleon's party, and participated in the annual festival to release the Nile flood water onto the land to irrigate and render it fertile, 'Isis' only describes this 'real' event in more mythological language: 'Autrefois, quand revenait l'été, l'inondation chassait vers le désert les bêtes impures. Les digues s'ouvraient, les barques s'entrechoquaient, la terre haletante buvait le fleuve avec ivresse' (*Tent*, 183). Geoffroy Saint-Hilaire would find no species of Nile fish that were not like their fossil relatives, only some that provided evidence that the Mediterranean and the Red Sea had once been connected.[32] He would discover in his dissections of Egypt's common silurid species of fish (including the catfish) his missing link between 'l'organisation des quadrupèdes et de la seiche'.[33] Isis's description of this 'regular' flood is however a comparative (and distorting) mirror of the altogether 'unique' event in which Noah famously saves animal species in his floating menagerie. The flood, singular or annual, therefore humorously marks the distinction in tableau five of 'gods' ante- and post-Deluge with which it began. In scientific terms it is the watershed between natural scientists who are 'transformistes' like Geoffroy Saint-Hilaire, or believers like Cuvier in cataclysm, Neptunism, and the extinction of certain monstrous creatures who belonged to the fantastic yet very real worlds of palaeontology of which the nineteenth-century French father was Cuvier.

After the disappearance of Isis, Hilarion's role is to blur the lines of equally dogmatic truths revealed in comparative religions, as in science, to show monster gods (Titans) and monster 'caravans' of gods with their centaurs, empusas, Stymphalian birds (*Tent*, 198) who all disappear because '[u]ne ravale de givre les enveloppe' (*Tent*, 199). Even if this may at a structural level enable linkage to the Latin and hence 'northern' gods culminating in Crepitus, this peculiar end for hot Mediterranean pantheons forces an end to Hilarion's chameleon 'Egyptian' personae in their transformations and 'transformismes'. This comparative religious and scientific scene brings Hilarion face to face with his master Antoine (as saint and Cuvier figure in his creationist beliefs) in ways similar to the 'sexual' confrontation with Sheba at the end of tableau two.[34] When Antoine refuses to bow down to this new 'god' of comparative or Egyptian natural sciences, just as Cuvier adamantly defended his position in the 'querelle des analogues' against Geoffroy's unity of composition, the impasse is the raising of the stakes to bigger (meta)physical propositions and beliefs. If the Devil was resting as giant caricature against Antoine's 'cabane' (at the beginning of tableau two), his moment to reveal his positions has now come. Hilarion, superlative human monster of oversized brain, needs replacement by something even more supernaturally cerebral, the Devil as mastermind of a religion without any necessity of God. Flaubert is then also able to rework the new natural scientific debates (embodied in those of Geoffroy Saint-Hilaire) that challenge older scientific beliefs (Cuvier's catastrophism) because tableau five has set them up allegorically in 'myth' language (Isis's 'flood', Buddha's birth). For the wider issues of the Étienne Geoffroy Saint-Hilaire–Georges Cuvier quarrel to continue unabated in tableau seven through Antoine's ironic and scientific discovery of an 'Origin of Species', Hilarion has to depart because his nineteenth-century alter ego is only one of the French 'Egyptian' magician scientists that Flaubert employs in the final two tableaux of the *Tentation*.

The jokes which Antoine and Hilarion share at the beginning of tableau five are ultimately then at the expense of what readers 'see' and will believe. Degeneration and regeneration are indeed inextricably linked in the 'creation' stories of both comparative religion (world mythology) and comparative anatomy (palaeontology) interpreting the same old primary matter of life and death. Much can in fact be reconstructed from the most insalubrious of remains from old gods such as 'Crepitus' in the scientific study of coprolites (fossil faeces of extinct species). The final substructure that tableau five remaps as fantastic comparative anatomy of myth is the story of the new 'gods' of geology as modern science of prehistory.

MATTERS OF LIFE AND DEATH: NEW GENERATIONS IN GEOLOGICAL TIME

In the series of exhibits of myths of (re)creation in world religions of tableau five, what is comparable between pantheons is inflected by what is significant by its *absence*. If the disembodied 'voix de Dieu' is the destructive and jealous God of wrath in the Old Testament, his claims to fame are Sodom and Gomorrah, the Flood, the drowning of Pharaoh's armies (and the might of Egyptian civilization including its magicians). His creation claims are however limited to writing (like Hermes) on the stone tablets of the Law (*Tent*, 204). The Lord God ('le Seigneur, le Seigneur Dieu') is therefore not the Creator God of Genesis 1–2 walking in the Garden or discovering Adam hiding his new-found nakedness because of eating from the Tree (of knowledge). Creation stories frame the tableau, however, in the 'cycles' (or 'révolutions du globe' in Cuvier's terms) of creation and destruction behind the time of civilizations. It seems hugely important that the opening of the tableau specifically dates the period of 'earliest gods' as 'antérieures au Déluge' (*Tent*, 161), the first being Indian 'gods' in a valley which becomes 'une mer de lait, immobile et sans bornes' (*Tent*, 163), and out of which the 'dualité primordial des Brachmanes' emerges, and from the navel of its god sprouts a lotus. While Antoine's response—'quelle invention!'— presents this story of creation as pure myth, geological discoveries of the earliest visible life forms—fossil plants and small crustaceans— belong to epochs where warm, shallow (milky) seas covered vast tracts of the earth, and which were transformed into limestones and chalks by pressures and cataclysms in the earth's crust. Comparative philology and comparative religions were also discovering India (beyond the

Himalayas) as the 'birthplace' of civilizations. Oannès, similarly, is the challenging contemporary of these antediluvian geological events, those earliest creatures which inhabited the waters, in what is now called 'primordial soup':

> J'ai habité le monde informe où sommeillaient des bêtes hermaphrodites, sous le poids d'une atmosphère opaque, dans la profondeur des ondes ténébreuses,— quand les doigts, les nageoires et les ailes étaient confondus, et que des yeux sans tête flottaient comme des mollusques, parmi des taureaux à face humaine et des serpents à pattes de chien...j'ai surgi de l'abîme pour durcir la matière, pour régler les formes; et j'ai appris aux humains la pêche, les semailles, *l'écriture et l'histoire des Dieux*.
>
> Depuis lors, je vis dans les étangs qui restent du Déluge... —et je meurs sur ma couche de limon regardant les étoiles à travers l'eau. J'y retourne.
>
> (*Tent*, 171, emphasis added)

As a geological remapping of ancient forms in mythological time, Oannès's account ceases to be fantastical and becomes strikingly accurate in its emphasis on ancient and modern science by analogy (and the 'querelle des analogues'): Pliny's observations about birds' wings and fins, fingers, and feet as all serving the same function transform into the more sophisticated comparative anatomy of a Buffon or a Cuvier, and thence return via Geoffroy Saint-Hilaire's idea of the unity of composition to a law ('règlement') of formal development. It was also in reading the scientific 'tablets of stone', rock strata, that Cuvier and Brogniart in France and Lyell in England were able to ascertain which species existed or became extinct prior to the appearance of humans on the earth. Nature's generations, de-, and regenerations at a more profound level than climate zones with their specific flora or fauna are in play here, so that the striking 'rafale de givre' quoted above now takes on a wonderfully geological meaning. The transformation of the earth's waters into ice and hence a Cuvieresque suggestion of the planet's dark pre-human epochs through which many species failed to survive is picture language for Ice Ages. Degeneration in fact becomes extinction in other words, whether through natural cold or darkness (Hilarion's identification of the seemingly redundant Nortia, Kastur and Pulutuk, Summanus and Vesta (*Tent*, 199–200)), prefiguring the passage already discussed about the 'Lémures' and the 'Larves' of intermediary species, bringing the reader to the contemporary 'home' gods (Lares), and the

Manes of scientific 'civilization' which one can call 'Science'. Brach-Manes which open and close the tableau are then one and the same in this cycle of geological remapping of the religious roots of mythology, just as the family gods (Lares) become the science of HiLARion/HiLAiRES. Peter Starr's vital understandings of Flaubert's punning on names and the magic this works on the significance of the *Tentation* is thus proven by extending the range of Flaubert's wicked dressing up of the absurd human imagination as the very heart of science itself. If there is no Garden of Eden in Flaubert's *Tentation*, readers are left very squarely back in the Jardin des Plantes as the new Muséum of Alexandria in another guise. Sexual generation and the fantastical couplings of the 'gods' are but stories for the generations of hybrid and new forms of life in all its abundance, mystery, and complexity long before the advent of human forms. The geological stories of the 'gods' in tableau five are therefore the perfect opening up of cosmological and zoological significance in the remaining two tableaux.

The old gods, especially the Greek and Roman ones, have a perdurance for modern nineteenth-century geology, if not religious practice. Neptune and Vulcan, those gods on the destructive and dark sides of the creative pantheons, are reinvested with new 'clothes', nineteenth-century debates about the fundamental chemistry and physics of the earth and its creative forces residing primarily in the power of water (Neptunism) or fire (Vulcanism).[35] The old gods may be dead in one form, but this tableau adamantly supposes that their new disguise will be another way of conforming to the old stories, of conflict and jealousy between two rivals of very similar 'religions', the truth of which can be neither proved nor disproved to end the cycle of fundamental ideas about first causes returning to haunt the rational world of enlightened science. In terms of (in)credible theories, there is also no Geoffroy Saint-Hilaire without a Cuvier, no Darwin without a Lamarck, and no Laplace without a Pascal.[36] And like the heresiarchs of tableau four, all scientists need adherents and worshippers to give their ideas credence and authority and the power to persecute opponents and 'heretics' pronouncing rival creeds.

Flaubert's remapping of the myths of nineteenth-century French science as a geological farce is a virtuoso comedy of human errors in the guise of science as comparative religion. Hilarion, the enigma machine in Sheba's train, effects this huge and glittering joke thanks to his complex *Egyptian* disguises; he is false Saint(-Hilaire), pseudo-Hermes Trismégiste, and Scientist. When Hilarion tries to step outside his humanity to become a god, Antoine necessarily refuses to worship him as he has refused to bow down to any other anthropomorphized gods. This choice in what to believe is not only a religious one. Antoine's refusal to countenance any but the Christian God is the same as his refusal to countenance one civilization or race as being superior to any other.[37] If there is any 'syncretism' in tableau five, it is arguably Flaubert's 'postmodern' attitude to the new science of anthropology especially its French colonial, nineteenth-century guises. Gobineau, Cuvier, and Renan, for example, were peddling fixed hierarchies of civilizations by colour, brain size, ability to write, and cultural prowess. With Caucasians at the top, yellow races (Semites) or red in the middle, and black peoples at the bottom, these unshakeable 'règnes' were enforced by climatic conditions.[38] Contrariwise, Flaubert's 'trans-formism' of the gods in tableau five is more cynically arguing against any (positivist) view of 'civilization' as progress, let alone any superiority in modern Caucasian (read Greek and Latin) cultures.[39] Unlike Balzac's 'Comédie humaine' the *Tentation* does not take Geoffroy Saint-Hilaire's unity of composition as its model either. The lesson of tableau five (as also implied in Flaubert's letter to Louise Colet quoted above) is surely that it is from the most ancient (black) cultures and religions such as ancient Egypt that we still have much to rediscover when it comes to the life sciences of death, however they are couched in modern religious, mythological, or new geological fields of knowledge. Hilarion's physical enormity as Trismégiste and as near-devouring rational spirit of empirical science when it comes to Antoine's faith embodies all the power of Egypt's counterparts to the belated wisdom of Anthony the Great of Egypt. The horror and magnitude of Hilarion's bid to make Antoine confess his own error of faith (apostasy) can now only be outstripped by the Devil, his non-Egyptian alter ego of Omni-science.

6

The Devil in the Detail

The dark night (of Antoine's soul and religious mind) that ends tableau five merges with the empty enormity of the black cosmos beyond the kingdoms of the globe in tableau six. Indeed, the immense proportions of the Devil's body (and gaping maw) seem to signify Antoine's now vastly increased state of doubt, especially on surveying the (godless) cosmos, and on hearing the Devil's demolition job of the existence of any benign creator, first cause, or architect upholding earth and man at the centre of the universe. Hilarion's hybrid enormity (as dwarf and angel of science) has likewise turned into the Devil's even more fabulous stature and monstrous form (complete with horns, cloven hooves, and wings). His powers which blot out the sky symbolize his figurative status in Antoine's mind, but are also reminiscent of his space in paintings of St Anthony by Brueghel, Bosch, or Cazotte.[1] What Antoine experiences on his 'Devil's ride' then seems a reflection of the macro-microcosm, but more in keeping with medieval orders of things (and Flaubert's earlier versions of the *Tentation*), so that they follow one another here and in tableau seven. Despite the tableau's obvious interest therefore to psychoanalytic and genetic criticism, let alone its intertextuality— flights into space have a long precedent in French literary production such as *Cyrano de Bergerac*, Voltaire's *Micromégas*, and Lesage's *Le Diable boîteux* let alone Flaubert's early work, *Smahr*—it has surprisingly evinced the slightest of comment from specialists on the *Tentation*.[2] Moreover, although Flaubert's protagonist is a further remake of Alfred Le Poittevin's Bélial, or the Satan of Byron's *Cain* central to the modern 'mystère', he is explicitly called 'le Diable', *not* the 'démon' or evil spirit of Eastern religions, nor yet Satan, the fallen angel of the Book of Job. Such reversion to macro- and microcosmic worlds,[3] and medieval orders of the universe, instead of the fourth- or nineteenth-century ones that have been in parallel in our reading thus far, could then be interpreted in the 1874 *Tentation* as a preposterous caricature, except that the Devil's near-swallowing up of Antoine at its end is no laughing matter. In the light of the Devil's place in tableau six after the death of all the gods, it has also escaped critical notice that he appears to *imitate* the many mythological gods in tableau five such as Jupiter who took on animal forms as bird and beast to carry off and violate women to produce monster progeny. Given Antoine's unquestioned maleness, the Devil's abduction of him is a much more 'monstrous' seduction than 'Sheba's' attempt in tableau two. As mocking inversion of a theological Satan or the Serpent of Genesis or the trappings of popular superstition and belief as underpinned by Maury's *Magie* set up in tableau five (demon possession, out-of-body experience, etc.), Flaubert's Devil cannot but shock the rational reader by his new personification as *Science*. A case in point is his rhetorical question to suggest a Copernican (and hence anachronistic) view of the place of the earth to Antoine: 'Elle ne fait donc pas le centre du monde? Orgueil de l'homme, humilie-toi!' (*Tent*, 208). This clever form of denial by doubt is arguably then in keeping with a modern 'Mephisphelean' devil who always denies, or with the *meta*physical reverberations of the ideas of Spinoza.[4] While Spinoza (and Newton of the *Optics*) is undoubtedly part of the lineage being explored by analogy, his ideas do not readily explain how Flaubert's Devil is 'La Science', let alone how this fantastical trip into space remaps nineteenth-century, Newtonian French astronomy and physics, or where Egyptian scientific parallelisms lie to match the religious ones of Part I. If we are to argue for the whole of the second part of *La Tentation* as Flaubert's remapping of nineteenth-century French *science* through the ambits of fourth-century religion, tableau six and its Devil necessarily play a crucial part. How can such clashing world views be explained satisfactorily?

Some imagination and help from twentieth-century computer language gets to the heart of the figure of Antoine's flight into space of tableau six. As macro (instruction) 'that initiates a set of instructions to perform a certain task' (*Collins English Dictionary*), it operates the literal and metaphorical instruction of the Devil (as computer wizard) and mode of conveying to Antoine an understanding of cosmo*logy* (explanation of the laws of the emergence of the universe by means of science and astronomy), *and* hence cosmo*gony* (explanations of the creation of the universe). Cosmology and cosmogony take forward the theogonies treated in tableaux four and five (creators and orders of creation in Judaeo-Christian and Eastern religions) to the measure of the cosmic. For verisimilitude on this scale of things, no human vehicle (such as Hilarion) is then possible. A Devil-Scientist as opposing force to God or the gods is one neat solution, but one that also has Gnostic and Greek scientific merit and even fourth-century credibility if we see this Diable as a magus of magi. From there it is a small step from cosmology/cosmogony to astrology/astronomy and their very similar ancient history as discussed briefly in Part II.[5] If the science and arts of astrology-astronomy were birthed and began to be recorded in ancient Babylon among its priestly class (*c.*550 BC), Flaubert has already transported Antoine to Babylonian observatories in tableau five, and had Hilarion give him his astronomy lesson on the seven known planets of our solar system in readiness for the sixth tableau.[6] The core belief and tenet in the early history of astronomy was that the earth was the centre of the solar system (and universe). This had not changed in the fourth century, or in 'medieval' astronomy. It would take the Polish *Churchman* Nicolaus Copernicus (1473–1543) to overturn fifteen centuries of astronomical 'fact' with his heliocentric view of our solar system. More crucial to the Alexandrian contexts of Antoine, one of the reasons for the long stability of the earth-centred view was the unsurpassed work of the Greek Alexandrian astronomer Ptolemy (*c.*85–165) whom we introduced in Part II.

A contemporary of the Gnostic Valentinus, Ptolemy was the most important figure in Egyptian science in the Greek Alexandrian schools. He made numerous astronomical observations from Alexandria during AD 127–41, recorded in his 'system of the world', the *Almagest*.[7] Building on centuries of ancient Babylonian, Egyptian, and Greek (including Aristotle's) observations of the planets and their motions, Ptolemy's aim was to prove that the earth was the centre of the universe and, by intricate mathematics, to calculate the motions of the planets. This early modelling work was matched by his *astrological Planispherium*, his *Geography* (the attempt to map places by latitude and longitude coordinates since maps were notoriously difficult to copy), and the *Optics* (studies of colour, refraction, and reflection). Careful reading below of the short descriptions which organize the sixth tableau into phases of distance from the earth demonstrates Flaubert's punctilious adherence to a Ptolemaic understanding of the cosmos, via Antoine, but as a 'visionary' like priests of old (including Daniel) 'observing' the heavens of a present, but also future nineteenth-century 'Copernican' universe thanks to the laws of cosmic time.[8] Anachronism is thus avoided, provided that the reader suspends *disbelief* in the supernatural (a Devil) as vehicle to understand the scientific super-natural. We will discover that Flaubert's French Mephistopheles also turns out to be a speculative nineteenth-century mathematician-physicist rather than metaphysician, and a strategically (post)Enlightenment Devil, not only French but Norman. First, the preposterousness of the vehicle for these analogies, and the intensely shocking scientific and religious debates they raise, needs to be examined more closely. Was 'space' travel realized only in imaginative science fiction (of a Jules Verne for example), before Yuri Gagarin (1934–68) became the first man to orbit the earth and marvel upon it from space on 12 April 1961?

TRANSPORTS OF THE IMAGINATION

The life and times of the original Anthony and Flaubert's Antoine as a nineteenth-century remake are conjoined afresh and launched out into this tableau by the same two kinds of Egyptian narrative, Athanasius' hagiography and early nineteenth-century history that propelled the first tableau. For the hagiography, Flaubert seems to have returned afresh to Voragine's abridged version, first for the verifiable size of his 'Diable' 'dans un corps d'une taille si haute que sa tête semblait toucher le ciel' (*LD*, 89), and for Anthony's 'flight into space' as form of religious rapture in the manner of a Daniel or a St John of Revelation.

Un jour qu'il était ravi en esprit, il vit le monde tout couvert de filets étroitement unis. Et il s'écria: 'Oh! Qui pourra s'échapper hors de ces filets?' Et une voix lui répondit: 'L'humilité!' Une autre fois, comme les anges l'emportaient dans les airs, les démons voulurent l'empêcher de passer en lui rappelant les péchés qu'il avait commis depuis sa naissance. Mais les anges: 'Vous n'avez pas à parler de ces péchés, que la grâce du Christ a déjà effacés. Mais, si vous en connaissez qu'Antoine ait commis depuis qu'il est moine, dites-les!' Et comme les diables se taisaient, Antoine put librement s'élever dans les airs et en redescendre.

(*LD*, 88–9)[9]

Flaubert interestingly used the final turn of phrase here for the departure of his Apollonius of Tyana in tableau four. The transports that Antoine has already experienced—'in the spirit' to Constantinople (the new Jerusalem on earth) in tableau two—logically and structurally preface this one, but to take Antoine beyond the earth to an even greater degree. If the *Arabian Nights* clearly attests to flights on magic carpets, Ptolemy's *Geography* and the *Almagest* plot similar flights of mathematical, rather than spiritual or literary, imagination by attempting to designate a shape to the known earth (plotting its longitude, that is, it cannot be flat!) and the place of the earth at the centre of the solar system. Antoine's flight in tableau six is, however, an astronomical and 'scientific' leap of faith *à la lettre*, to complete Flaubert's play on involutions and metamorphoses of religion and science as two coexistent terms on the Möbius strip of his *Tentation*. But the flight also allows various nineteenth-century *clins d'œil* to new inventions permitting human flight, especially in balloons. Those that Joseph Louis Guy-Lussac (1778–1850) undertook in 1804 were specifically to study magnetic forces and to measure the differing air temperatures at higher altitudes.[10]

Less successful were the launches of Montgolfier balloons that Napoleon I hoped to be successes in his self-publicity campaigns in Europe, but more importantly from the very outset of his career, and for our necessary Egyptian connections, in Cairo, to mark the 'Fête de la République' in 1798. Publicity was posted for the Egyptian populace to witness the marvels of French science in the launch of a large red, white, and blue balloon, with alleged flight capacities across national borders. On the day itself, the balloon only lifted off a few hundred paces to crash down into the crowd. It was the eyewitness account of al-Jabarti that has so famously recorded the flop, and the pretensions of the French, when he suggested that any servant at a wedding could make a 'kite', such as this giant one, fly.[11] A later launch was marginally more successful, but did not achieve anything near the height and range promised on the brochure. Like the building of a Channel Tunnel, air travel was among the engineering ambitions of the young Napoleon, who was a radical advocate and supporter of scientific and technical innovation throughout the first Empire, but more crucially in his vision for his Egyptian campaign with its secular missions of mapping and enlightening it. Flaubert's Antoine is therefore experiencing 'modern' aero- or more properly astronautics,[12] but in a manner wildly beyond the best hopes of France's inventors of the Montgolfière or Garnerin's parachute. The Montgolfiers' hot air balloons had prior to this campaign been a subject of caricature.[13] Antoine's ride on the Devil's giant wings as his 'para-*chute*' upwards is, of course a potentially monstrous anti-religious joke about the Fall. The nineteenth-century 'flop' of French science in Egypt cloaked under the guise of Flaubert's fourth-century Antoine then turns the joke back onto nineteenth-century history of science and explorations of the universe, which deny the existence of God, and of course the Devil, but which have complete faith in the laws of gravity.

The famous 'être la matière' passage concluding tableau seven is not the only highly lyrical moment of the *Tentation*. The whole flight of tableau six is narrated through Antoine's wonderment at the view of earth and heaven, an 'eyewitness' response which maps onto Flaubert's own admiration for the new aerostatic technology and its beauty when he went to Rouen to see a flight on 25 July 1852.[14] Antoine's wonderment modulates from the initially positive (amazement, pleasure, joyful liberation) to negative (horror, fear, terror), as the Devil undermines any glorious story of the creation of the heavens from Scripture (Genesis 1–2), or the paradises of the ancients, by correcting them with the brutal realities of 'science'. The Devil is then Hilarion's magnification (in optical terms) in his role to undermine and cast doubt on Antoine's dearest beliefs. Where the Devil differs from Antoine's 'disciple' is his destruction and demolition of belief and false 'truths' by the use not of religion, but of undeniable visual and empirical evidence to assert the truth of science. Concomitantly Flaubert transforms religious 'visionary' experience (from Antoine's historical point of view) into a science textbook lesson on a heliocentric universe of the 'future', our solar system and its place in the Milky Way. If this tableau constitutes an example of 'literary science' in ways which have not been recognized, there is more to the tableau than the fictional inversion of speculation (understood as literary-theological imagination and scientific hypothesis) into facts that turn out to be larger and more marvellous than science fictions. Like the geological ideas of tableau five dressed up as mythologies, tableau six is employing major (French) discoveries in astronomy and mathematics to discount myths about God and (ancient) science. The Devil's proofs here are not for the existence of God, but for proof as truth independent of him. The careful scattering of strategically positioned descriptive reference points (to complement Antoine's naive discoveries of the empty soullessness of the universe in dialogue with the Devil) underscores the following (in chronological order):

Cependant la terre prend la forme d'une boule; et il l'aperçoit au milieu de l'azur qui tourne sur ses pôles, en tournant autour du soleil.   (*Tent*, 207)

Le Diable
l'emporte au milieu des étoiles.

    Elles s'attirent en même temps qu'elles se repoussent. L'action de chacune résulte des autres et y contribue,—sans le moyen d'un auxiliaire, par la force d'une loi, la seule vertu de l'ordre.   (*Tent*, 209)

Les astres se multiplient, scintillent. La Voie lactée au zénith se développe comme une immense ceinture, ayant des trous par intervalles; dans ces fentes de sa clarté, s'allongent des espaces des ténèbres. Il y a des pluies d'étoiles, des traînées de poussière d'or, des vapeurs lumineuses qui flottent et se dissolvent.
    Quelquefois une comète passe tout à coup.   (*Tent*, 209)

Il distingue l'entrecroisement de leurs lignes, la complexité de leurs directions. Il les voit venir de loin,—et suspendus comme des pierres dans une fronde, décrire leurs orbites, pousser leurs hyperboles.
    Il aperçoit...Jupiter avec ses quatre satellites, et le triple anneau du monstrueux Saturne ! toutes les planètes, tous les astres que les hommes plus tard découvriront[138]! Il emplit ses yeux de leurs lumières, il surcharge sa pensée du calcul de leurs distances.   (*Tent*, 210)

Gothot-Mersch can only note (number 138) that this sentence constitutes Flaubert's most obvious narrative intervention. It is surely the clearest signal to his reader (as one of these same 'hommes') to link Antoine's vision to contemporary astronomy and its concurrent theological and scientific debates. The four passages above are a remarkable literary résumé of the key scientific discoveries that challenged the world view of astronomy and creation in Genesis and the works of the ancients. We need to read the first again from the viewpoint of Antoine's amazement to capture its startling (factual) truth: the world is neither flat (it is a 'boule'), nor the *centre* of the solar system, let alone the universe. This little description sums up the first two paradigm shifts in astronomy. The flat world of the ancient Babylonians was challenged by Aristotle (384–322 BC) in three proofs that the earth was round (but the centre of the universe); Copernicus' *Revolution of the Celestial Spheres* (1543) would promote a heliocentric cosmology long after the time of Anthony the Great to birth modern scientific astronomy as epitomized

Sciences of the Gods

in the work of Kepler (1571–1630) and his three laws of planetary motion which enabled more accurate prediction than Ptolemy's of the positions of planets.

Flaubert's modern, double-voiced discourse then intervenes (to avoid anachronism at the point noted by Gothot-Mersch) in the fourth description, so as to take Renaissance astronomy—the four moons ('satellites') of Jupiter were plotted by Galileo thanks to his invention and the development of telescopes—into the modern era. William Herschel (1738–1822) would discover Uranus in 1781 (on 13 March corroborated by the Finnish mathematician Anders Lexell) and, by use of even larger telescopes, two new satellites of Saturn and two for Uranus itself. His theory and then discovery of the hitherto 'invisible' Uranus was due to observations of the 'pull' on the rings of Saturn, leading him to postulate the action of another planetary body in space. In poetic language, Flaubert puts it thus: 'Elles s'attirent en même temps qu'elles se repoussent. L'action de chacune résulte des autres et y contribue.'[15] Moreover, in Flaubert's own lifetime, a planet even further out than Uranus in our solar system was calculated to exist and then discovered, Neptune. The year was 1845, and involved the calculations of John Couch Adams (1819–92) for the probable existence of a planet which was affecting the orbit of Uranus. George Airy, the English Astronomer Royal, failed to investigate these claims passed on to him by Adams's professor, John Challis, who was charged by Airy later in the year to mount a search. On the other side of the Channel, Urbain Jean Joseph Le Verrier (1811–92) published his prediction about a similar planetary body. Having failed to mount a search for the planet at the Paris Observatory, he approached Johann Galle at the Berlin Observatory. With his assistant he found the missing body thanks to the precise calculations of Le Verrier, and it is thus Galle who is on record as having discovered the planet.[16] The importance of observation and calculation (mathematics) is thus the intrinsic motor of this tableau and mode of discovery, in spite of its seeming lyricism, for example in the use of astronomical poetic tropes like the comet in the third description. If comets have long been seen as 'signs and wonders', it was William Herschel's sister and helper, Caroline (1750–1848), who discovered no fewer than eight (in 1786, 1788, 1790, 1791, and 1797).[17]

But the Norman, nineteenth-century Devil is also in the detail of these descriptions as he is in the interpretation of the cosmic phenomena as their enlightened (calculating and reasoning) scientist. The initial, seemingly superfluous, focus on the earth's axis in the first description as it circles the sun is the clue, matched by a moment rather like Antoine's 'becoming' Nebuchadnezzar in tableau two: Antoine's mind is filled up with a 'pensée de calcul de leurs distances' ending description four. Pierre Simon Laplace (1749–1827) would calculate this tilt from those of all the other known planets as within a surprisingly small range of difference, and thence predict a determined stability of planetary orbits and the universe, even as it was expanding by laws of gravitation ('les astres se multiplient'). Surely Flaubert's 'sans le moyen d'un auxiliaire, par la force d'une loi, la seule vertu de l'ordre' is another poetic way of describing gravity? It is therefore not so much Spinoza as Laplace who is the 'meta-physician' behind tableau six, and the main protagonist behind the macro-cosmological import of the *Tentation* as exploration of beliefs, religious and positivist scientific.[18] What better a nineteenth-century French match with Ptolemy within the Alexandrian schools and his work on mapping longitudes could Laplace be, not only as a founding member with Lagrange in 1795 of Napoleon's Bureau des Longitudes,[19] but also chair of geometry in the mathematics section of the Muséum d'Histoire Naturelle?

SELECTIVE INFINITIES

The 'French Newton', Pierre-Simon Laplace, was born in Normandy in Beaumont-en-Auge and went to the Collège des Arts at the University of Caen in 1765 to read humanities and thus enter the Church.[20] In the quirks of fate for this future mathematician of probability theory and determinism, there was no faculty of sciences at Caen, but there were chairs of mathematics and experimental physics (which included chemistry) within the Arts Faculty. Laplace rapidly found that his real interests lay in the Abbé Gadbled's classes on mathematics, geometry, and navigation, so he never completed his degree. His connections with D'Alembert and then Lagrange, with whom he soon worked, brought Laplace rapidly to the Institut de France, where he became a fellow of the first class (mathematical sciences) in geometry.[21]

If Laplace 'was among the most influential scientists in all history',[22] his mathematical astronomy and the theory of probability are two

main fields among many to which he made major and innova-
tive contributions.[23] Those of immediate import and connection to
Flaubert's descriptive details highlighted above include work on the
inclination of planetary orbits, and on how planets were moved by their
moons, which led to his recognized masterpiece on the stability of the
solar system. As early as 1786 'he had proved that the eccentricities and
inclinations of planetary orbits to each other always remain small, constant and self-correcting'.[24] In 1796 he presented what is his 'Almagest',
the *Exposition du système du monde*, which modern historians of science
and specialist astronomers agree might be called an Ur-version of the
Big Bang, his nebular hypothesis.

Laplace ne considère pas le chaos de l'Univers décrit par Descartes, mais à
la certitude d'un proto-soleil, c'est-à-dire une nébuleuse contenant un noyau
fortement condensé avec une température élevée. Cet ensemble tournant d'une
seule pièce autour de son axe. Par la rotation, le refroidissement des couches
extérieures aurait provoqué dans le plan équatorial de la nébuleuse des anneaux
successifs (à l'image de ce que sont les anneaux de Saturne), le noyau central
formait le soleil. Par condensation, chaque anneau aurait donnée, en certains
points, naissance à une planète qui elle-même, à son tour, aurait donné naissance à un satellite, en suivant le même processus.[25]

If Laplace saw the solar system as originating from the contracting
and cooling of a slowly revolving cloud of glowing gases, the 'fourth-
century' poetic reference above to the 'immense ceinture' with its
'vapeurs lumineuses' is highly suggestive of Laplace's ideas. His study
on the movement of the tides (in Normandy) had convinced him of
the apparent motions yet stability of celestial bodies, while his theory of
universal gravitation allowed him to find in this a determined order to
the universe as a whole. It was because he could envisage bodies of sufficient size to have a speed greater than that of light that Laplace was able
to determine in 1794 what is considered a very modern phenomenon,
the black hole. A tacit allusion to this can again be read in the seemingly
most lyrical and second of the descriptions from the *Tentation* above,
the 'trous' and 'fentes' in the huge nebula that is the Milky Way.

Laplace's *Exposition*, which was largely non-mathematical, prefaced
his *Traité de mécanique céleste* in five volumes, the first two published in
1799. In what seem a bewildering starburst of numbers and calculations
to the non-specialist,[26] Laplace set out in differential equations general

laws for the movements of planets in the universe, based on the Newtonian keystone, gravitation. This universal law was also the theological
rub for Laplace. Either God was omniscient, creator of perfect laws to
which he would then be subject (and then not God), or as God the
omnipotent, he could intervene in these laws, which could then not be
perfect, which made his handiwork not omniscient.[27] Laplace resolved
the issue (for which science has no definitive answers) by the fact that
one cannot know with any certainty, only probability, the nature of
matter and its universal laws (like gravitation); nothing of any certainty
whatever can be said about the nature of God. It is a short step to say
that he might as well not exist since he is not necessary to explain first
causes of the universe. It was Laplace's 'faith' in the power of probability
theory in his *Mécanique céleste* that was behind his famous reply to
Napoleon's comment on it, that the work had given the laws of the
whole of creation but not once talked about the existence of God: 'Sire,
répondit Laplace, je n'avais pas besoin de cette hypothèse.'[28] We are now
getting very close to Flaubert's 'Diable'.

What interested Laplace, apart from the discovery of universal laws,
was the ability to use probability theory to reduce error in observation,
and to uncover mathematically grounded determinants that could predict among other things the presence of planets in relation to those
already observed (as was the case with Uranus and Neptune), or determine their relative masses. If Laplace (like Cuvier with Neptunism)
would remain a staunch supporter of one side of a major cosmological theory that has later proved erroneous—in this case a corpuscular
theory of light rather than one of waves (which Fresnil would promote
in 1821[29])—his introduction to his *Théorie analytique des Probabilités*
(1812) underlines his belief that 'les questions les plus importantes de la
vie ne sont en effet, pour la plupart, que des problèmes de probabilité',[30]
and marks the course for all his later work. The Manichean determinism
of the orders of things thus returns not in supernatural form, but as
differential equations, which can be expressed as simple algebra problems so that a solution can readily be obtained. The operator from the
difficult differential equation to the simpler algebraic one is known as a
Laplace Transform ('Transformation de Laplace' in French); the inverse
Laplace transform then retrieves the solutions of the initial problem
from the simpler one. Probability and mathematics, not God, thus
determine the movements of the spheres, and the actions of men.[31]

While inverse metamorphoses (transforms) might have been a tempting vehicle for Flaubert to exploit in tableau six after the many 'évanouisse-ments' of the gods of tableau five, the Devil is not interested in solving the problems of life and death, only undoing faith as the solution to them.

In his introduction to his analytic theory of probability, Laplace wrote:

Nous devons envisager l'état présent de l'univers comme l'effet de son état antérieur et comme la cause de celui qui va suivre. Une intelligence qui, pour un instant donné connaîtrait toutes les forces dont la nature est animée et la situation respective des êtres qui la composent, si d'ailleurs elle était assez vaste pour soumettre ces données à l'analyse, embrasserait dans la même formule les mouvements des plus grands corps de l'univers et ceux du plus léger atome: rien ne serait incertain pour elle, et l'avenir, comme le passé serait présent à ses yeux.[32]

This famous quotation is also known as 'Laplace's Demon'. This 'super-computer' of differential equations can determine all elements of the future and past because of calculability itself. Flaubert's Devil wonderfully characterizes and literalizes Laplace's Demon by repackaging its 'super'-determinism of the universe in pseudo-theological arguments to prove to Antoine the non-existence of his God as exemplified by the cold cosmos. In a wonderful balancing act of dual time frames (fourth and nineteenth century), Flaubert's Devil inverts all the famous (philosophical) proofs for the existence of God from his properties (such as first cause, prime mover, perfect creator, omniscient, omnipotent). However, from the second half of the tableau on, the analogous and predictable interplay of past and future worlds exemplified in Laplace's Demon is replicated in the very language of Flaubert's Devil. His barrage of calculations to disprove God from his properties is also poeticized *geometry* ('the branch of mathematics concerned with the properties, relationships and measurement of points, lines curves and surfaces' (*Collins English Dictionary*).

Contemple le soleil! De ses bords s'échappent de hautes flammes lançant des étincelles, qui se dispersent pour devenir des mondes;—et plus loin que la dernière, au-delà de ces profondeurs où tu n'aperçois que la nuit, d'autres soleils tourbillonnent, derrière ceux-là d'autres, et encore d'autres, indéfiniment...

(*Tent*, 211)

Flaubert's Devil is not envisaging the plurality of other imaginary worlds like Fontenelle,[33] but mathematical ones based on those we know. Moreover, the succession of predictable creations along geometrical lines and points denies one that is complete (*Tent*, 210). As the beginning and end of time in the expanding universe collapse into infinity, Flaubert's Laplacean Devil also knocks down Antoine's ideas of nothingness as the opposite of what God may be, since Antoine has before his eyes space in all its fullness and emptiness (*Tent*, 211) which also challenges any notion of the eternal substance (let alone will) of God (*Tent*, 211, 212). Argument by the stable law of infinity (whether infinite regress or magnitude) then also destroys any part of God's providence or, in the face of evidence, the perfection of his universe (*Tent*, 214). 'Comment Dieu aurait-il un but? Quelle expérience a pu l'instruire, quelle réflexion le déterminer? Avant le commencement il n'aurait pas agi, et maintenant il serait inutile' (*Tent*, 210). The Devil's clinching calculation for God's non-existence (from what looks like a mathematics of multiplying nought or the power ^{n}), is thus 'Puisque l'infini seul est permanent, il y a l'Infini;—et c'est tout!' (*Tent*, 214).[34] Not content with this, the Devil swells to gigantic proportions as if to demonstrate this 'infini' and blot out the heavens. If Antoine momentarily experiences an 'outer darkness' beyond even the darkest night of the soul of his spiritual precursors, only then can Flaubert's Devil mock the puny humanity of Antoine when compared to his 'Intelligence' as Laplace's Demon. At this apogee of differential equation at the end of the tableau, Flaubert then uses the only trick in the book that can thwart Laplace's Demon: 'Antoine lève ses yeux, par un dernier movement d'espoir' (*Tent*, 215).[35] His 'irrational', mathematically incalculable hope in God demonstrates that human choice and faith (neither of which can be factored into probability theory) are all that can paradoxically decide whether or not God is, and whether of course this Demon exists. The Devil's final challenge to Antoine to worship him is now explained, since Pascal's wager (thanks in part to anachronism) is the least of Antoine's positions of faith. But it is precisely because Antoine has a very strong faith in spite of his huge doubts, to confront what appears indubitable in this tableau, that the Devil is forced to flee.[36] Moreover, Antoine's decision for his unknowable God is also his choice to believe in the great mysteries that neither theology nor science has as yet resolved. No Laplacean Demon can explain why, in the expanding cosmos with its primeval matter and clouds of toxic gas, life on earth, let alone human life, has developed in the manner that it has. The point of exhaustion or near annihilation of Antoine then pre-empts, and with dramatic irony determines, the finale of the whole. Antoine has not seen God or a first cause of Life, but it is his free will that allows him to discover life under his nose in all its richest possible variety and diversity of form in tableau seven.

TRANSFORMING THE DEMONS: RETHINKING THE GENESIS OF FLAUBERT'S *TENTATION*

By cloaking grotesque 'medieval' devils in modern, Laplacean, and Norman ones, Flaubert brings Antoine and his *Tentation* right back to home, nineteenth-century France, its religious, scientific, and super-stitious present. But if tableau seven can now launch exploration of the microcosm (and a return to 'Genesis' to reflect the macrocosm), so too can we read in this inter-space Flaubert's figurative, mon-strous, confrontation with his own demons in the writing of the first *Tentation*. Like the mythical, phoenix-like Simorg-Anka in tableau two, the Devil's form as gigantic pterodactyl seeking to devour Antoine operates a fabulous (and palaeontological) return of the dead.[37] In the Devil's ride scene, Flaubert's *Tentation* is very much a dialogue with its dedicatee beyond the grave. Alfred Le Poittevin's Bélial had also taken his protagonists, the Duvals, to hell (and death) and back in a fantastic carriage ride. Le Poittevin's hell, like Flaubert's cosmos, envisages no traditional (medieval, Catholic) view of hell, just as Bélial and Flaubert's (Laplacean) Devil are not used to discuss the problem of evil.[38] In terms of tableau six, then, Brueghel's *St Anthony* (like that of Hieronymus Bosch) is therefore a pictorial *recognition* of a subject, but not the main inspiration of Flaubert's Devil who needs to be *Science* (to encompass Laplace) yet merge credibly with Antoine's religious world view. Goethe's Mephistopheles and Le Poittevin's Bélial as modern cynic, Enlightenment devils come closer, but only go so far as models for Flaubert's more chilling *religious* and metaphysical speculations on the problem of *knowledge* (science) and human existence in the universe.[39] Quinet's *Ahasvérus*, seen by Bouilhet and Du Camp as Flaubert's over-predominant source for the first *Tentation*, also fails to furnish this figure. However, the early inspiration of the *Tentation* and specifically Flaubert's ongoing dialogue with Le Poittevin about 'mystères' immediately throws up the candidate, Lucifer, the Angel of Enlightenment, of Byron's *Cain*, the second act of which is a two-part devil's ride. One of Byron's letters concerning his conception for Cain's flight into space states that

the object of the Demon is to *depress* him [Cain] still further in his own estimation than he was before, by showing him infinite things and his own abasement, till he falls into the frame of mind that leads to the Catastrophe... from the rage and fury against the inadequacy of his state to his conceptions, and which discharges itself rather against Life, and the Author of Life, than the mere living.[40]

In contrast to the biblical, if just post-Edenic, world of Genesis in scene i of *Cain*, Act II constitutes the devil's ride: 'Scene I: The Abyss of Space. Scene II: Hades.'[41] As in the sixth tableau of the *Tentation*, Cain is given a lesson in Science by Lucifer. He is shown earth (and Eden) as tiny specks in a universe that is not only infinite, but infinite in its replications of other worlds with their 'Fall'. This does not however depress Cain. It is on the second part of the ride to Hades, which is made up of former worlds (especially extinct ones with prehistoric monsters before the dawn of human existence), that Cain then becomes depressed by the abyss of time without first causes or the advent of man in Genesis. When he returns to his 'biblical' world, it is this knowledge that is unbearable, and so he kills Abel as a re-enactment of the (rebellious) Fall of his parents.[42]

Antoine's experience of lost civilizations in tableau five and of space in tableau six is a direct structural reversal of the two rides in *Cain*. Antoine is no Cain, however, and only acts as an 'homme révolté' ironically against the Laplacean Demon into faith. It is Hilarion who inherits Cain's rebellion, cynicism, knowledge of the things of God (and Scripture), and human 'raisonneur' status of uncannily devilish intent. He has also been noted by Antoine at the end of tableau five as shining, like Lucifer.[43] But this is Flaubert's solution to the 'earthly' spheres of Gnosis and science after the long revision period between the first and final *Tentation*. Concerning cosmic-microcosmic spheres, it is Byron's Lucifer who is altogether more useful to enable Flaubert to hold together the Devil's presence in tableaux two and six for the metaphysical questioning of knowledge (lying behind Antoine's gloss of the biblical Queen of Sheba) and its potential limits let alone good or evil:

Byron had jotted in this diary that the story of Cain was a metaphysical subject ... metaphysical because freighted with a certain kind of abstract meditation—psychological, analytical introspection and speculation of the nature of God and the individual's relationship to divinity and society, and on the baffling problems of mortality, eternity, and human destiny.[44]

Against the panorama of 'eternity' on the Devil's ride, Antoine will contemplate his mortality and human destiny in tableau seven through his mother and Ammonaria returning in the guises of the Vieille and la jeune Femme. But death and extinction, the known absence of man on the face of the earth, and the much greater age of the planet than the story of Genesis (as Antoine has seen from the cosmos) are all encapsulated in the lessons of Byron's Lucifer to Cain in his trip to Hades, conjured up through the palaeontological and geological discoveries of Cuvier. Byron's preface is quite clear yet deeply ironic about his choice of the Serpent in Genesis, the rhetorical mode for his Lucifer, and Cuvier's *Discours sur les révolutions de la surface du globe* to convey Lucifer's ideas, yet parry theological and scientific (positivist) objection to his work alike:

With regard to the language of Lucifer, it was difficult for me to make him talk like a Clergyman upon the same subjects; but I have done what I could to restrain him within the bounds of spiritual politeness.

If he disclaims having tempted Eve in the shape of the Serpent, it is only because the book of Genesis has not the most distant allusion to any thing of the kind, but merely to the serpent in his serpentine capacity.

Note—The reader will perceive that the author has partly adopted in this poem the notion of Cuvier, that the world has been destroyed several times before the creation of man. This speculation, derived from the different strata and the bones of enormous and unknown animals found in them, is not contrary to the Mosaic account, but rather informs it; as no human bones have yet been discovered in those strata, although those of many known animals are found near the remains of the unknown. The assertion of Lucifer, that the Pre-adamite world was also peopled by rational beings much more intelligent than man, and proportionally powerful to the mammoth etc. etc., is, of course, a poetical fiction to help him make out his case.[45]

Karkoulis has recently investigated the contribution of these deeply ambivalent elements to the epistemic break and asymmetrical structure of *Cain*, to take forward Steffan's earlier work on the huge importance for Byron's dramatization of his own aversions and pessimism, first in the 'speculations in geology, cosmology, and astronomy of such scientists as Fontenelle and Cuvier' and, second, in 'a bifurcation in ontology that went back to Plato and Zoroaster [to provide] a cosmic stage, with pre-adamite worlds, and with an everlasting warfare between body and soul, between good and evil spirits'.[46] Flaubert's Laplacean Devil has now found his blueprint and his *raison d'être* within a dialogue with Alfred on 'mystères' with *Cain* as the principal model. Tableau six in the 1874 *Tentation* is then Flaubert's 'Egyptian Book of the Dead' in that he has thus bested Le Poittevin's demons (literally and metaphorically) by his own more creative resurrection of Le Poittevin's *Bélial* as a Laplacean Lucifer. Flaubert's Hilarion as science in tableau five and his Devil as Science in tableau six both herald this 'transform' of ideas. It will be their nineteenth-century French alter egos, Étienne Geoffroy Saint-Hilaire and Georges Cuvier, who will be left to speak by comparative analogy in tableau seven.

The fixity of determined worlds in the deepest past and in the furthest future that Laplace, and to a certain extent also Cuvier, investigated now permits the 'monstrous' world of prehistoric and fantastical creatures to be remapped in tableau seven because *Cain* and Byron's Lucifer-Cuvier have set them up. One tiny link is missing in the chain of logic to explain how Flaubert's Devil-Laplacean Demon is subsumed and returned in the Cuvier that is essential to the Saint-Hilaire debates about creation that are to come. Both Cuvier and Laplace were adamant believers in proof by fact and by meticulous comparative method (knowledge of comparative anatomy for the one, differential equations for the other). Whereas Laplace had dispensed with God as an unnecessary hypothesis, Cuvier stopped short of first causes (and hence in displacing God from his beliefs) by saying that these were unknowable. Religious humility may go further than positivist faith, and chance meetings than predetermined fate. It is then in the serendipity that brought Laplace to mathematics, Flaubert to Byron's *Cain* as our inverse transform of Le Poittevin's *Belial*, that dedications can prove transforms in disguise. Flaubert's dedication to Alfred in the final *Tentation* is therefore a just reflection of the importance of his long-dead friend to the writing of the *final* as much as to the first version of the *Tentation*. It is homage of such personal master—disciple relationships that is also Cuvier's in his *Recherches sur les ossemens fossiles de quadrupèdes*, dedicated to Laplace:

Mon cher et illustre confrère,
C'est à bien des titres que cet Ouvrage vous est offert. Lorsque jeune encore, je vous en communiquai les premières idées, vous m'engageâtes à les suivre; admis depuis à m'asseoir à côté de mes maîtres, j'ai trouvé, dans la Classe des Sciences à l'Institut, conseils, encouragemens, secours de tous les genres; j'ai pu surtout m'y pénétrer de cet esprit sévère, fruit de l'heureuse association établie dans son sein entre les Mathématiciens et les Naturalistes. Vous, Monsieur, qui, après avoir achevé de soumettre le Ciel à la Géométrie, l'avez appliquée avec tant de bonheur aux Phénomènes terrestres, vous contribuez plus que personne à entretenir cet esprit: c'est donc pour mon livre un grand avantage de voir votre nom à sa tête; c'en sera, dans tous les tems, un inestimable pour l'auteur, d'avoir reçu publiquement cette marque de l'estime·et de l'amitié de l'un des plus heureux génies de son siècle.
Cuvier.[47]

7

Bones of Contention

Strangers, gods and monsters represent experiences of extremity which bring us to the edge. They subvert our established categories and challenge us to think again.... Monsters show us that if our aims are celestial, our origins are terrestrial.... But where monsters arise from underworlds, and strangers intrude from hinterworlds, gods generally reside in otherworlds beyond us.... Divine monstrance was not infrequently an occasion of terror. *Fascinans et tremendum*, as the mystics said.[1]

Antoine's journeys with the 'stranger' Hilarion, to explore Gnosis in its myriad forms (tableaux three to five), and with the Devil (tableau six), to discover the 'extremities' of the universe's outer godless darkness, have indeed brought him recurrently 'to the edge'. It also configured the position of his puny faith in confrontation with their greater science, embodied in their gigantic size at the ends of tableaux five and six, but where paradoxically they were forced to flee. At the beginning of tableau seven, Antoine's return to earth finds him once more on the edge, literally this time. On the brink of the cliff beside his hut, situated topographically between the 'celestial' and the 'terrestrial', he contemplates the sublimely human possibility of taking his life as solution to the problem of (im)mortality.[2] Like and unlike the stylized setting with which the *Tentation* opened, its physical geography will now force the reader through Antoine to rethink 'established categories' and, as this book has everywhere argued, contemplate the very monstrousness of Flaubert's remapping of the fantastic real of his own epoch.[3] For even before Antoine meets the parades of monster creatures on which the 1874 *Tentation* ends, he has already witnessed the potentially more monstrous forms of the human imagination issuing from Gnostic, comparative religious, mythological, astrological, cosmological, and mathematical

'hinterworlds' and 'otherworlds'. What further functions can the iden-
tifiably 'authentic' monsters in tableau seven then fulfil given that
Flaubert specifically moved them in his final revision of the *Tentation*?
Seznec (1949) among others has noted but not stopped to question why
the so-called 'tableau of the monsters' no longer precedes the episode of
the gods. What is the importance of the monsters' new place succeeding
the gods as well as the more incredible Devil or his ride? Has this
strategic move, radically changing the order and structure of the final
Tentation, further ramifications for reinterpreting the much-studied set
pieces of tableau seven which are usually read in isolation? Do the
'monsters' endorse or arbitrate between critics' conflicting readings of
the impasse depicted by the Sphinx and the Chimera?[4] Does it matter
that the monsters preface and might hence inform the 'être la matière'
epiphany, which critics ever galvanize to clinch pantheistic, syncretistic,
or undecidable readings of the *Tentation*, or Flaubert's anti-clericalism?[5]

We have argued thus far that Antoine's 'fantastical' hallucinations
invoke not so much an overwrought imagination or his psychic or erotic
repressions, although they undoubtedly do both.[6] Rather as almost
cinematic projections they offer 'accurate' visions of the world views
of nineteenth-century France, whereby a critique of its beliefs may
be configured retrospectively by analogy. The peculiar forms of their
similar excess and enormity (monstrosity) have arisen precisely from
the seemingly alien, 'unreal' beliefs of ancient and fourth-century Egypt
when these are transformed into the religious and scientific 'real' of the
parallel worlds of the Egypt of nineteenth-century France. In Flaubert's
careful collation, intercalation, and layering of dogmas and heresies in
their concepts and details, the fantastic of hallucination and vision thus
proves more realistic than the 'effet du réel' of realism. In this final
tableau which speaks to and concludes the *Tentation* as a whole, the
monsters need prising out of the fixed categories identified by even their
best and least challenged critics to date such as Seznec.[7] By seeing and
reading the monsters as supremely the subversion of orders of things, we
will be arguing for their fitting place in the *Tentation*'s virtuoso fourth-
and nineteenth-century ending, its still open questions for religion but
especially science. From there, critical blocks about final interpretations of the *Tentation* can better be reviewed, whether the responses of
Bouilhet and Du Camp, or exhaustive genetic studies (such as Séginger's). The no less modest proposal here for the *Tentation* is that, as

modern *mystère*, it is Flaubert's religiously scientific and scientifically religious masterpiece.

FAMILY RESEMBLANCES

Antoine's opening recall in tableau seven of his mother and Ammonaria appears a somewhat forced, mirror-image connection to their intro-duction in tableau one.[8] Their roles as frames of reminiscence or echo chambers for this tableau are however essential to the piecing together of its three seemingly disjointed movements. The parade of mythical monsters is the middle sequence between that of Antoine's 'mère' culmi-nating in the strange 'vision' of the hybrid 'goddess' of re-decomposition (*Tent*, 224),[9] and that of the 'bêtes de la mer' and Mother Nature's other multifariously wondrous creations which herald Antoine's final words of the text.[10] While the reappearance of his mother (let alone Ammonaria) is absent from Athanasius' (or Voragine's) version of the story of St Anthony and hence far-fetched, this opening scene is however completely true to Hieronymus Bosch's 'St Anthony': on either side of him two women figures, young and old, accompany the saint.[11] After Antoine's view of the empty macrocosm in tableau six, and the no less tempting abyss opening tableau seven, these figures therefore frame and reground him in the microcosmic particularity of his altogether human existence and unexceptional mortality. They confront him directly with his own generation (his mother), but chosen ending of his line (in spite of a soul-mate, the probably dead virgin-martyr Ammonaria). Together the two female figures force Antoine to contemplate the solitude (rather than the exceptionalism) of man as the centre of his universe imbued with God-given free will, whether employed for suicide, procreation, or higher vocations, but no different in his human condition or end from all other creatures and their mortal coils. The generic Old Woman and the Young Woman metamorphosing into the symbolic concepts, 'La Mort' and 'La Luxure', finally to become one in the composite goddess of re-decomposition, undercut any higher end for human veneration of Nature in its economies of death and regeneration, especially as a god(dess). Most of all they mock any lofty human notions about noble death by suicide (or martyrdom) as some individualizing gesture of defiance in the face of the universe and its laws (*Tent*, 219), or about human powers through sexuality or its transcendence to immortalize the flesh (*Tent*, 223). By inference, St Anthony the Great as exceptional yet utterly mortal being is thus ever caught between historical reality, legend, the *Vita,* and artistic representation,[12] not least through being downplayed in Flaubert's further incorporation of him into his Antoine.

The deceptive similarities of these two female figures to all the women in the *Tentation*, especially as 'Mort' and 'Luxure' with medieval notions of the seven deadly sins as recast in the 1849 *Tentation*, have led critics to miss their point. Not least, their mockery of human worship of Nature as any kind of god(dess) surely reiterates the message of tableau five and militates very strongly against reading Antoine's final epiphany as 'pantheistic'. Although their enlacement and choric 'dissolution de la matière' and 'renouvellements' (*Tent*, 223) herald the vocabulary of Antoine's famous 'être la matière' exclamation, his culminating articulation of desire is couched in the past conditional, and hence situates him as subject outside absorption into creation as some 'Grand Tout'.[13] More importantly, they are supremely principles of re-collection in the 1874 version, as their final 'monstrous' embodiment surely suggests 'C'est une tête de mort, avec une couronne de roses. Elle domine un torse de femme d'une blancheur nacrée. En dessous, un linceul étoilé de points d'or fait comme une queue;—et tout le corps ondule, à la manière d'un ver gigantesque qui se tiendrait debout' (*Tent*, 224). Conjoining 'family' resemblances (Antoine's mother and Ammonaria in tableau one), the description of Sheba's departure (tableau two), the shadowy women visiting graves (tableau four), other goddess figures as described in tableau five, but particularly Isis or a feminized Oannès (*Tent*, 171), or even constellations in tableau six, this creature could be the synthesis of Antoine's overwrought imagination or a 'real' 'Feejee mermaid'.[14] Although clearly sexed, and with all the attributes of monstrous fin-de-siècle femininity or of Baudelaire's 'la charogne', this 'creature' remains nameless or unnameable. Yet Antoine very clearly identifies it by breaking down its combined form of re-decomposition into separate parts or complementary opposites: 'Encore une fois c'était le Diable, et sous son double aspect: l'esprit de fornication et l'esprit de destruction' (*Tent*, 224). While his vocabulary is 'saintly'—he is discerning the spirits masquerading in physical forms as does St Anthony—his method and tone could not be more 'scientific'; identification comes through classification of parts. What this hybrid 'monster' of (Mother) Nature therefore importantly encapsulates at the very outset of the parades of 'monsters', large and small, is observable transformation. Since time immemorial observing changes in the earthly and heavenly spheres has triggered the human religious and scientific spirit of enquiry. This 'spirit' in turn has undergone constant metamorphoses and provoked unending conflicts in what constitutes authoritative categorization in human ordering of things.

If these two 'women' figures call forth the fundamental properties of 'transformisme' and conflicting categorizations of 'monster' creatures to come, not least the Sphinx and the Chimera, they also return the *Tentation* specifically to fourth- and nineteenth-century considerations of more ancient Egyptian religion and sciences of the dead that we explored in Chapter 5. Thanks to ancient Egyptian religious 'science' of embalming and mummification, whether of nobles, Ruler-Gods, or temple animals (such as monkeys and crocodiles) to preserve their living forms, the sciences of Egyptology and palaeontology in nineteenth-century France came properly into being. The all-important choreography of Hilarion as also an Étienne Geoffroy Saint-Hilaire proved pivotal to the (Egyptian) moves of tableau five so that comparative religion turned into Egyptology, natural history, and geology (in the guise of myths of origins). Tableau seven now takes up these stories in their even more ancient forms. This strange amphibian is thus no medieval monster but some ancient being between the humanoid Mort and Luxure (on two legs), the animal-monster hybrids such as the Sphinx and Chimera (of uncertain sex, and number of legs to wings), and the marine creatures that will complete the series of strange creatures of the tableau. Mineral, vegetable, animal, and human parts are complemented with hybrid elements between these distinct 'classes' such as 'nacre'. How such a composite should be classified let alone named then raises the spectres of French nineteenth-century successes, progress, and bones of contention for its major comparative anatomists and zoologists.[15] Moreover, this 'female' creature of Mother Nature also embodies the forces of extinction and re-creation of life forms in the earth's longer history. Understanding and remapping genealogies of the dead and of the living, their scientific family resemblances, or non-transcendence of classes is therefore the overarching problem posed by the opening frame of tableau seven. The seemingly fabulous genealogies (parades) of creatures on display before Antoine's discerning eyes must now be seen not for what they seem or have been made to symbolize, but for what they are, lessons in the fabulous real of nineteenth-century French comparative anatomy and palaeontology. Antoine as Flaubert's remake of the father of monasticism now turns into the necessary religious and scientific antagonist to continue the Hilarion/Étienne Geoffroy Saint-Hilaire debate in the latter's absent presence. As fitting completion to the *Tentation*, Antoine's visionary calling holds up the mantle to confer on his prospective nineteenth-century French double, the father of palaeontology (and the Protestant Churches of France), Georges Cuvier.

Antoine's raw confrontation with his own mortal coil at the beginning of the tableau thus heralds the appearance on his cliff of 'family resemblances', the myriad other strange, monstrous, infinitesimal, terrestrial, marine, extinct, or extant mortal coils. These apparitions (to parallel the nineteenth-century French sightings of the Virgin Mary lying behind tableau two) sublimely recall Cuvier's public demonstrations where he reconstructed fabulous, but scientifically verifiable, extinct creatures from the evidence of a single fossil bone. Chapter 5 has already quoted Flaubert's letter to Louise Colet specifically referring to Cuvier's consummate skill as a comparative anatomist. Interpretation based on accumulated knowledge is all, as Antoine's has proved for each tableau, whether his biblical exegesis in tableau one, or his own words at the vital moment between the hybrid creature and the arrival of the Sphinx and the Chimera in tableau seven. This time they set up the scientific rather than religious bones of contention in the remainder of the tableau, chiefly the intense 'querelle des analogues' of 1830 between Cuvier and Geoffroy Saint-Hilaire, and their very different views on classification, teratology, 'transformisme', and the beginnings and extinctions of life:

Ainsi la mort n'est qu'une illusion, un voile, masquant par endroits *la continuité de la vie.*

   Mais la Substance étant unique, pourquoi les Formes sont-elles variées?

   Il doit y avoir, quelque part, *des figures primordiales*, dont les corps ne sont que les images. Si on pouvait les voir *on connaîtrait le lien de la matière et de la pensée, en quoi l'Être consiste*!

   Ce sont ces figures-là qui étaient peintes à Babylone sur la muraille du temple de Bélus. ... Moi-même, j'ai quelquefois aperçu dans le ciel comme des formes d'esprits. *Ceux qui traversent le désert rencontrent des animaux dépassant toute conception* . . .

Et en face, de l'autre côté du Nil, voilà que le Sphinx apparaît.

(*Tent*, 224–5, emphasis added)

Antoine's first thought here is not so much an oblique reference to the idea of a 'Great Chain of Being' (explored in tableaux four and five concerning metempsychosis and transmigration of souls); it spearheads questions in nineteenth-century palaeontology about the gaps ('la mort') in the fossil record or animal series and how they should be explained. The sentence wonderfully and ambiguously covers the gamut of theories in comparative anatomy from (Lamarckian) transformism of creation as a gradual, uninterrupted mutation as opposed to one which entails changes in climate and hence forms (Geoffroy Saint-Hilaire) or, more radically, catastrophe and extinctions and thus distinct re-creations (Cuvier). Note that no (divine) Creator or (mechanistic) Law of Nature is designated as first or second cause of creation. Nor is creation delineated as transcendent or material, singular or multiple, spontaneous, epigenetic, or arrested.[16]

Antoine's second thought then calls into question the fit between a unity and diversity of life forms, and why the plethora of creatures has turned out as they have. Is there one plan for all (Geoffroy Saint-Hilaire's 'unity of composition'), or four irreconcilable 'règnes' precluding missing links or leaps of nature (Cuvier), or five main classes (Blainville)? And is the diversity of forms due to function and fit purpose (Cuvier) with or without a Designer, or due to causes such as adaptation to climatic or niche habitats (Lamarck), or to generational laws whereby parts become wholes across all orders or hierarchies of creatures (Geoffroy Saint-Hiliare), or via arrest at various stages of complexity of the embryo (Serres)? Captured here and in Antoine's third main thought is then most obviously the question whether some blueprint exists for all creation (Geoffroy Saint-Hilaire's 'unity of composition', Lamarck's law of gradual 'transformisme'), however unlike are the ensuing kinds of creatures. These theories in fact smack more of 'Platonic' forms than Cuvier's empirical comparative anatomy and inductive method applied to prehistoric creatures that had never been witnessed by humans. Even though his demonstrations conjured up 'images' from 'figures primordiales', Cuvier's knowledge as comparative anatomist of living organisms allowed him accurately to predict the configuration of extinct forms from a particular kind of tooth or claw. Any whole organism depends for its viability ('pensée') and existence on material constraints and interconnected function—mobility, nutrition, reproduction. Antoine's 'Si on pouvait les voir on connaîtrait le lien de la matière et de la pensée, en quoi l'Être consiste!' surely refers proleptically to Cuvier's inductive art, to match the future tense discovery of new planets so clearly flagged in tableau six.

Antoine (like Cuvier) nevertheless draws a veil over what can be known beyond empirical observation, especially the question of what brings beings to be. He will maintain this stance even in his final exclamation of fascination and wonder at life itself. Yet his position (like Cuvier's) is not purely materialist. Matter is not all there is to make it 'alive'. Antoine's use of 'la pensée' here avoids the idea of a Gnostic, Manichean divine spark, but points to the problems for both religion and science of explaining definitively how 'life' is generated from inert stuff. Does this 'transformation' come about by the will or 'breath' of God (Genesis 1), spontaneously (Aristotle), by laws of predetermina-tion or pre-formation (Lamarckian 'transformisme'), or by life forms generating further life forms (epigenesis[17])? To explain the inexplicable, as Cuvier does for the appearance or demise of prehistoric 'monsters', the closest that can be got is the dynamic at work in Antoine's final thought, use of analogy or analogues from the known to the unknown. Hypotheses or arguments from first causes or design cannot establish proofs for either God or the cause of life as it is scientifically observed. Ultimately the riddle of life cannot be resolved, which helps to explain the logic on Flaubert's part why the parade of monsters is fronted by the Egyptian monster of riddles par excellence, the Sphinx. Where Seznec has viewed its necessary relationship of conflict, opposition, and completion by its other, the (Greek) Chimera, as the 'impossible conciliation de la fantaisie et de la pensée logique—problème déchirant pour Flaubert, perpétuel tourment de son âme et de son art',[18] it is time to read their dialogue outside the bounds of literary aesthetics. Rather than medieval or imaginary creatures, these 'fabulous' monsters offer a literary-scientific 'shape' for the most heated debate in early nineteenth-century French science, the 'querelle des analogues' of 1830. By ironically portraying real scientific impasse in monstrous animal forms, the subsequent parades of monsters in the two further main sections of the tableau then also configure the wonders befitting and vexing enlightened nineteenth-century French natural science. We may then find ourselves not far from specimens of all kinds on display in the galleries and showcases of the Muséum National d'Histoire Naturelle. The textual logic of the monstrous real then allows the (in)famous 'être la matière' finale to offer controversial questioning through the mouth of a 'saint' of the marvels of nineteenth-century French natural science.

MARVELLOUS AND (M)ANY-HEADED MONSTERS

Throughout this book, Egyptian intermediaries have been essential to the strategic order, dynamic, and metamorphoses of one layer of signification into its others in tableaux two to six for both religious and scientific ends, to bring into stark parallel fourth-century Egypt and nineteenth-century France. Where the geographical and historical exposition of tableau one about Antoine's Egypt provided all the necessary parallels for remapping the worlds of Napoleon's Expédition, tableau seven appears to lack any overtly Egyptian intermediary figures such as gods, let alone scientists, between Antoine and his visions of the monsters apart from the Sphinx. To return to the above epigraph and the role of the monster as that which shows, it is of course the monsters themselves—by their very nature they *are* intermediary or grotesque amalgams of recognizable forms—which serve as the mediators most fit for purpose in tableau seven between Antoine as 'saint' and 'scientist', and his final response to them as 'matter' and wonder. Monsters have always carried enormous allegorical freight.[19] The four great beasts of Daniel or Revelation for example serve as precedents for this tableau so that it may also mesh with the religious remits of the *Vita Antonii*. For the scientific real of tableau seven, however, the monsters need ideally to demonstrate specifically fourth- and nineteenth-century, Egyptian morphologies. The missing link comes with telling which monsters are truly monsters within this double context, as Antoine himself reminds us in his final thought above: 'Moi-même j'ai quelquefois aperçu dans le ciel comme des formes d'esprits. Ceux qui traversent le désert rencontrent des animaux dépassant toute conception' (*Tent*, 24–5). Recalling the mirage of the Nile/serpent in tableau one, and the tall tales of travellers

in Ptolemy the Astronomer's time, it is also an oblique reference to
Pliny the Elder's *Natural History*. Its thirty-seven books were completed
around AD 76–*c*.78 and constituted a first, encyclopedic compendium
of entries (real and fantastical) about the flora, fauna, physics, chemistry,
crystallography, and wonders of the natural world.[20] As representative
of the science of the times of the *Roman* Empire of the early Egyptian
Christian Church and Alexandrian schools, Pliny's *Natural History* (lost
in its entirety) remained a major intertext for medieval bestiaries as
for later Renaissance and Enlightenment texts about the natural world.
While Seznec's identification of Flaubert's faithful reuse of Pliny and
Elien for the *Tentation*'s 'monsters' seems a remarkable piece of classical
detective work in literary source studies (which has not been challenged
or surpassed), his whole 1949 essay on the 'monsters' looks at best
merely descriptive and derivative from the viewpoint of nineteenth-
century French history of (natural) science. Georges Cuvier was its most
eminent and most copied exponent. He also commented at length on
the science of Pliny's *Natural History* among many others in his writings
and public lectures at the Collège de France on the history of science
in all its ancient and modern spheres.[21] A new translation into French
of Pliny's *Zoologie*, notably with a full commentary and annotations by
Cuvier, was published in 1831 by the same editor as the massive *Description d'Égypte*, Panckouke. Cuvier's work as historian as well as polymath practitioner of natural sciences was then the nineteenth-century
model to be emulated by later science populizer-practitioners such as
Félix Andromède Pouchet, Flaubert's teacher, friend of the family, and
director of Rouen's Muséum d'Histoire Naturelle.[22] In the genealogy
of science, therefore, Antoine's visions of the 'monsters' arising from
the desert (the Sphinx and the Chimera) mediate Pliny and Cuvier
via Étienne Geoffroy Saint-Hilaire's Egyptian natural history collections
brought back to the Jardin des Plantes.

    Critics have commented endlessly on the symbolic and artistic
significance of Flaubert's Sphinx and Chimera as uncomplementary
opposites.[23] They have failed to note the detail of the language or
construction of the Sphinx-Chimera set piece as reflecting the dialogue
between Antoine and Hilarion in tableau three. This time strong repulsions (like two north poles of magnets), prohibitions, and naming of
differences are in operation: 'Arrête-toi', 'Non jamais', 'ne cours pas si
vite', ne m'appelle plus', 'Cesse de ...'. These stichomythic challenges

work against any modern scientific theory of 'elective affinities' such as Goethe's. Couched in the negative, to demarcate the limits and boundaries of the other's sphere of action or operation, they very clearly mirror the catalogue of papers in reply and retort read throughout the main 1830 Cuvier–Saint-Hilaire 'querelle des analogues'.[24] Flaubert is wonderfully encapsulating in these two monsters the impasse of two major modes of scientific method and thought. On the one hand there is the surety, fixity, rigidity, and logic of empirical analysis, the 'hard', granite, solid, and immovable Sphinx; on the other hand there is the range, heights, and mobility of synthetic thought in the flighty, fire-breathing, but circular-moving Chimera. Cuvier's empirical method, his four 'règnes' classifying all species according to evidence not hypothesis— 'mon regard, que rien ne peut dévier, demeure tendu à travers les choses sur un horizon inaccessible'—cannot be more opposed to Geoffroy Saint-Hilaire's 'philosophical' and speculative method: 'Je découvre aux hommes des perspectives éblouissantes avec des paradis dans les nuages et des félicités lointaines' (*Tent*, 226). Both Sphinx and Chimera are of course *the same*, monstrous compositions of hybrid parts resembling no 'real' living creature, but representing how 'Egypt' and 'Greece' tackle the same fundamental questions. The irony is that neither monster can see itself in or as the other, or that both invoke more ancient and extinct forms of their current bodies. Replace the 'bandelettes sur son front' by the horns of some prehistoric bison or mammoth-like creature for the Sphinx; and replace the dragon-like Chimera with the giant flying lizards, pterodactyls, or gavids, and both monsters are the kind of creature which Cuvier was able to reconstruct from his discoveries in the excavations of Montmartre, or which Geoffroy Saint-Hilaire exploited in his teratology, that monsters are normal creatures arrested from full growth often in the womb. The art of comparative anatomy is then the genius of both these 'creatures' like a Cuvier (the Sphinx) and Geoffroy Saint-Hilaire (the Chimera), but their modes of employing comparative method are diametrically opposed. The 'horizon inaccessible' of Cuvier's four 'règnes', to put all living things into these categories without exception, would be most challenged by where the human might fit vis-à-vis simians: Cuvier quite specifically made no bridge between his work on human races and on animal classification.[25] Geoffroy Saint-Hilaire's bid to find one plan to explain the developmental pattern from embryo to adult or the reordering of the same numbers of bones in all vertebrates without respect to functional similarity are indeed 'éternelles démences' which can never finally be proved. The place of man is equally a problem (as it also proved for Darwin). As neither monster may budge from its predispositions or impossible objectives, their impasse is indeed never to couple two complementary modes of scientific thought which, together, might better crack the enigmas of prehistory or the development of life in all its forms. It is not without irony that both figures disappear fittingly into the milieu of their own making. The granite Sphinx disappears into the sand of its own micas, solid yet enigmatically fluid matter like its empirical thought; the Chimera's fire and breath become the smokescreen fog of abstract thinking which obliterates solid shape.[26] In both ends, these composite monsters of intangible conception and tangible form (science) prove their lack of difference from the gods of tableau five. All adhere to the same law of death in their 'défaillances' or 'épanouissements', and law of life in their reappearances in other guises. Such reappearance is indeed the operating principle for the 'imaginary' monsters of the middle section of the tableau headed up by humanoid species as by the more formless 'bêtes de la mer' which conclude it.

Since its very inception, critics have been attempting to categorize and classify the *Tentation*. The same is true of the parades of monsters in tableau seven.[27] Seznec's demonstration of Flaubert's reliance on Pliny's *Natural History* as source for its bizarre creatures did not consider why this model was so vital. As exemplary encyclopedic work of *science*, it takes over where Hilarion and the Devil left off, to allow Antoine to compare the best book of nature and scientific knowledge available in the fourth century with his observations of the Book of Nature. Pliny's work is therefore vital for the structure and order of the tableau, as well as to its overall questioning of how things come to be (re)ordered. Antoine therefore confronts creation according to Pliny's ordering, classificatory systems, and naming of it, from lesser human forms to sea creatures via land species. The initial, strange 'apparences de corps humains', so like Hilarion's first appearance as 'nain' in tableau two and Isis's Cynocephalus in tableau five, then serve as the very Egyptian cues to nineteenth-century French natural science. The 'Astomi', 'Nisnas', 'Blemmyes', 'Pygmées', 'Sciapodes', and 'Cynocéphales' all seem utterly incredible, because unviable living forms. At stake, however, is their nineteenth-century scientific reality. Apart from the fact that the

Astomi are recreated in the same way that Monge had scientifically demonstrated to explain mirages (as discussed in Chapter 1), the Blemmyes were a real Nubian tribe (seen as 'barbares' by Roman and other occupants of Egypt) as Pygmies are indubitably African. Ethnographical veracity or nineteenth-century race theories to which Cuvier also contributed however come second to the big debates in natural science. The similarity of these humanoid monsters to the norm immediately summons Geoffroy Saint-Hilaire's work on teratology, but read as if through Antoine's fourth-century eyes and familiarity with Pliny's accounts. They ironically challenge classification by any of the functions by which animals will have been classified by the nineteenth century; by respiratory organs (lacking in the Astomi), digestive tracts (lacking in the Blemmyes), symmetrical cohesions of complementary parts (lacking in the Nisnas), or backbones (it is unclear whether the Sciapods are invertebrates or vertebrates). The Pygmy and Cynocephalus then appear less monstrous and more familiar, but do not belong to the species *homo sapiens/erectus*, the former because of undeveloped size yet sheer proliferation, the latter because not bipeds (they 'courent à quatre pattes'[28]), although their delight in wantonly cruel acts inflicted on other beasts and women makes them very 'human'. In the unfolding orders of creation before Antoine's eyes which will go back to the simplest forms in his final epiphany—and hence operate a reverse 'transformisme' to Lamarck's simple-to-complex order of things—the big underlying question is where and how 'man' fits in the fossil record let alone in religious accounts. Geoffroy Saint-Hilaire's *Considérations générales sur les monstres* neatly resolves the temporal and structural problems with the anomalous in tableau seven, because the history of monsters from antiquity to the Middle Ages frames his own theories of regular and arrested (monstrous) development. There is only one, normal, 'plan' for all life, but different external conditions determine normal development, particularly in the womb: 'Acephales', for example, are complete beings and function perfectly in amniotic fluid, but not without it.[29] Geoffroy Saint-Hilaire then concludes his defence of the 'normal monster' by challenging (religious) ideas about monsters as 'punishment' from God, or as outside his 'providence', when they should more properly be seen as a 'témoignage à la bonté et aux sages prévisions de l'Intelligence suprême'.[30] Superstitions about monsters thus need to be replaced by nineteenth-century science. This same science which can devise a 'plan' of the unity of composition cannot however prove the non-existence or un-viability of other planners, superhuman or human.

Geoffroy Saint-Hilaire's understanding of the inherent symmetry of forms and the adherence of all types of creature to one 'plan' potentially covers the differing parades of creatures which ensue with more specific detail from the Cynocephalus to the Unicorn. The use of 'monsters' to explain the gaps in animal series rather nicely allows Geoffroy Saint-Hilaire's ideas to be modulated by those of Blainville, who saw fossils as intermediary forms between non-recurrent and extant versions of species.[31] Blainville's siding with Lamarckian transformism against his patron, Cuvier, and the latter's theory of 'catastrophism' begins to put in place the synthetic nineteenth-century scientific reordering of this tableau. The many 'fantastical' extinct creatures that Cuvier reconstructed for his public of course offer a 'real' precedent for the apparitions of prehistoric monsters in this tableau. This section of it (like the last) is particularly indebted to his commentary on Pliny's *Natural History* and on his *Anatomie des catastrophes*. Cuvier was as versed in the history of science as in comparative anatomy,[32] and the latter text is richly footnoted with the many classical sources that Seznec claims for the tableau as the stuff of the medieval bestiary.[33] In his notes on Pliny, Cuvier takes apart the 'mythical', 'fabulous' nature of the Cynocephalus, 'Martichoras', and 'Catoblépas' as in fact the ancients' (mis)identification of natural history. In the *Anatomie*, Cuvier examines the *stylized* representation of these creatures as found in Egyptian hieroglyphs and monuments, not as imaginary but real.[34] As everywhere in Cuvier's work, it is wrong classification (through ignorance, false report, or exaggeration) that arrests good science (modelled after his own).[35] We might therefore better recognize the 'Catoblépas' as a gnu (not to be mistaken for a hippopotamus), the Cynocephalus in simians still extant in Egypt, and the 'Martichoras' as a kind of rhinoceros.[36] Although Cuvier does not deal with the Basilisk at this juncture, its multithected career in fantastic tales has in medieval times mistaken it for the crocodile.[37] And as a joking aside in this section of the *Anatomie*, Cuvier also dismisses the devil, because he is an impossibility of comparative anatomy: 'car la nature ne combine ni des pieds forchus, ni des cornes, avec des dents tranchantes'.[38]

It will be Cuvier's own mis-classification of species of fossil crocodiles found in the Caen area of Normandy that later brought him into contention with Geoffroy Saint-Hilaire over detailed comparative anatomy and the 'querelle des analogues', but it is Saint-Hilaire's rich haul of Egyptian species (mummified remains and his preservation of those he collected during the Expédition) that gave the Muséum collections of comparative anatomy their real fillip. For the first time, Cuvier and other comparative anatomists could prove the links or not between prehistoric and modern species, just as Geoffroy Saint-Hilaire excitedly wrote to Cuvier from Egypt that he had seen a Cynocephalus with his own eyes : 'J'ai trouvé le vrai *cynocéphale*, précisément l'espèce d'après lequel Linné a basé son *simia cynocephalus*. Brogniart a donc eu tort de rapporter le papion à cette espèce, et vous, mon très habile maître, de le supprimer tout à fait'.[39] The right naming and classifying of creatures (cloaked or unmasked behind their fabulous or scientific Latin) was precisely the bone of contention in the science world that suddenly looks so very like the designation of 'heretics' in tableau four, especially when so many components in their beliefs are the same. That is partly the *comparative* point about heresy in this section of tableau seven, just as ultimate authority in science is equally moot.

The exotic Latin, behind which are very ordinary 'real' (and Egyptian) animals before us in the scientific showcases of this scene, is ultimately used to the same end as the disorientation and reorientation of 'gods' in tableau five, to remap 'mythological' creation stories in the language of geology and palaeontology. The Sadhuzag ('cerf noir') has many of the features of the giant fossil elks being discovered in the peat bogs of Ireland and northern Europe.[40] From contemporary real time, Antoine is again being taken back into prehistory, because these fantastic monsters also belong to the 'worlds' of antiquity, as also to the 'real' of Cuvier's discoveries with Alexandre Brogniart of extinct fossil creatures in the quarries of Montmartre, formed at the same time as such animals also roamed what is now Egypt.[41] The troupe of creatures issuing from the monster 'rameaux' of the Sadhuzag's antlers therefore permits the turning of the ensuing menagerie of extinct 'fantastic' forms of 'Egypt' back into those in the museums of nineteenth-century Paris. The wonderful 'hybrids' in the conflation of all animal kinds and forms in the seemingly gratuitous extravaganza encircling Antoine prior to the arrival of the Unicorn operate a fictional graft of Cuvier's mammoths, elks, bison, and porcupines, and 'Egyptian' (desert) Mirag, the 'lièvre cornu', alligators, and for this tableau the aptly named chameleon.[42] Their spikes, claws, quills, and horns all lead to the anomaly of anomalies, the singular one-horned 'monster' for Geoffroy Saint-Hilaire's theory of symmetry that otherwise accounted for normal animal development to *include* monsters.

The Unicorn's allegorical and iconic status is of course essential to the religious and doctrinal implications of the *Tentation*, not least our discussions in Chapter 2 of nineteenth-century sightings of the Virgin and the enshrining of the dogma of the Immaculate Conception by Pope Pius IX as implied by the Unicorn's last words ('Une vierge seule peut me brider'; *Tent*, 235).[43] This creature was also demolished by Cuvier in his *Anatomie* as another example of human imagination taking precedence over observed reality on the one hand—only the rhinoceros and the narwhal have one horn in nature—and on the other of the practices of human representation. He cites cave paintings and also the 'style raide' of Egyptian hieroglyphics, where the oryx in profile has only one horn. Cuvier's 'unicorn' thus turns out to be a kind of antelope. He also reports that images of 'unicorns' have also recently been found in Tibet.[44] Human propensity to inflate and deform reality may be more *contra natura* than nature herself. There is then some 'reality' behind Flaubert's Unicorn in its habitat from Babylon to the Steppes and from the Ganges to Mesopotamia, but there is also a large dose of artistic licence to ensure that this range of habitat reconnects with the 'bubal' accompanying both an antelope and the Gymnosophist behind that strange branching tree of tableau five (*Tent*, 129–30).[45] If we follow the inverse logic of comparative religion that Hilarion deployed in tableau five to work from its others to Christianity, this 'Indian' version of the 'tree' of the Sadhuzag posits the creation story of Genesis (and its Tree of Knowledge) as mythical, geological, and of course monstrous, analogue. We are now ready for the *Tentation*'s final lessons in the religious science of geology, questioning of 'in the Beginning...' from the authority of nineteenth-century French natural science and hence Christianity.

Sand of the desert becoming the seashore makes for a logical analogy whereby the final section of the parade of life can unfold its marine beginnings in time. Pliny's *Natural History* follows the same logic. Geologically speaking, however, the very rocks on which Antoine is now lying are made (like the limestones of Normandy[46]) from marine microorganisms formed in the warm, shallow seas, described later in the scene: 'des débris d'éphémères font sur le sol une couche neigeuse' (*Tent*, 236).

The cover of this book gives an illustration of such foraminifera. We discussed myths of the birth of Indian gods as 'geology' in tableau five, where Antoine laughed at such things: 'Les plus vieilles [idoles], antérieures au Déluge, disparaissent sous des goémons qui pendent comme des crinières' (*Tent*, 161). While the 'Breton' etymology of the word 'goémons' (used as fertilizer) may be one of the jokes at the reader's expense in a tableau that ends with Crepitus, this 'petit détail qui fait vrai' prefigures with the same geological conjuring power the seascape,[47] which the matching 'varechs' conclude in tableau seven (*Tent*, 236). If we recall Flaubert's letter to Louise Colet quoted in Chapter 5 (pp. 178–9), Flaubert is doing with art what he hopes his future Cuvier-anthropologist could reconstruct from a pair of boots. Even before the 'être la matière' finale, renowned for its lyricism, the speech of the 'bêtes de la mer' is a virtuoso swash and backwash of verbal construction, mythological, lyrical, geological, and 'real'. On the one hand, this speech blends legends of the lost world of Atlantis or Breton folktale, just as it recapitulates a geological rewinding in time from 'peuples' (all things on one plan), to strange 'sea-cows' ('broutent comme des bœufs les plaines de corail, aspirant par leur trompe...') so that they become, in turn, like Indian myths depicting the world on an elephant's back. On the other hand, the alliterations and assonances meld with the very sentence structure pivoting around balancing parts for this flux as 'reflux des marées' (*Tent*, 235) to formulate visionary (and real) scientific discovery. Milne Edwards, for example, would be instrumental in studying living marine forms *in situ*, to take such expeditions into the 'immensite où personne encore n'est descendu' (*Tent*, 235). This phrase thus echoes the prolepsis in tableau six concerning future discovery of the planet Neptune.

But this 'poetry' of the wonder and fantastical forms of marine life that is the long description prefacing the 'être la matière' finale is no poetic invention on Flaubert's part. Although the first proper name in the list of strange (prehistoric) sea creatures, the 'cornes d'Ammon' (*Tent*, 236, 'ammonites'), allows punning exuberance across the *Tentation* to conflate orders of things, poetry like science is more about producing multiple significance through analogues and analogies. The Egyptian god Amon, Antoine's disciple Ammon, Ammonaria, and an important extinct geological species are thus all rolled and unrolled into one thanks to prefiguration as 'unicorne'.[48] We recall Antoine's longing in tableau one to undertake journeys, like Ammon (*Tent*, 55), to exotic shores. Those 'submarine' worlds Antoine is now observing are surely more exotic than any 'real' Mediterranean countries of the earth's current geophysical surface thanks to fossil evidence. Such working together of an assortment of scientific, fantastical, and common names to describe things that can be verified from the optic of palaeontology in this final description in the *Tentation* thus transforms the unnameable, like the female 'monster' composite above, into living (or extinct) worlds of identifiable forms. The metamorphoses of all orders—the animate and inanimate, vertebrates and invertebrates, molluscs, sea plants that are animals, fronds of plants that are corals—issue from life's simplest 'éphémères'. While these are prefigured in Antoine's 'Il doit y avoir, quelque part, *des figures primordiales*, dont les corps ne sont que les images' (*Tent*, 224, emphasis added), this geological allusion requires all the components of these descriptions to be read literally. For example, 'les plantes se confondent avec les pierres' are fossil plants, while '[d]ans des fragments de glace, il distingue des efflorescences, des empreintes de buissons et de coquilles – à ne savoir si ce sont les empreintes de ces choses-là, ou ces choses elles-mêmes' (*Tent*, 236) are fossilized imprints of species, such as indeed are ammonites, whether or not discovered beneath literal ice. Just as the mirror of the lighthouse of Alexandria acted as a 'telescope' to see 'Constantinople', so these 'fragments de glace' act as 'microscopes', not just to view these infinitesimal creatures, but to identify them. Through their discoveries of fossils in various strata in the limestone quarries of Montmartre, Cuvier and Brogniart (1811) were able to date extinct (and living) species by the known geological time of the rock formation.[49] Cuvier also held to catastrophe and cataclysm, such as ice ages, to explain the definitive extinction of certain species. There is then no mistaking over which side of the debate about origins or 'révolutions' of the globe, Neptunist or Vulcanist, Antoine with Cuvier presides, and that its foundations are at once richly scientific and 'biblical'.

At the end of this 'geological' passage, and in the same manner as a diver waiting to plunge, Antoine now takes a deep breath and sees the 'cells' (thanks to those 'contact lenses' of 'fragments de glace'), formed like an eye reflecting his.[50] If critics agree that his gaze is as through a microscope, it is precisely this scientific analogy that has been seen as anachronistic, but which indubitably underpins the reading of this book, that Flaubert's Antoine throughout the *Tentation* is a fourth-century visionary seer looking at the 'wonders' of nineteenth-century French science, but always with the contexts of fourth-century AD religion and science. While critics have noted the 'petites masses glob-uleuses, grosses comme les têtes d'épingles, et garnies de cils tout autour' (*Tent*, 237) into which the 'éphémères' turn as connoting Virchov's theories of the cell,[51] and as the inspiration to Odilon Redon's wonderful illustrations for the *Tentation*,[52] the geological significance of cellular biology, microfossils, has not been considered or analysed. Georges Pouchet (1833–94), Cuvier's successor as chair of comparative anatomy at the Jardin des Plantes in 1879, would be instrumental in further development of micropalaeontology at the end of his career. However, much of the 'poetic' contents and lyricism of this microscopic world (the concluding passage before the 'être la matière' finale), and the fact that it could only be viewed thanks to the microscope, comes directly from a 'real' science intertext, Alexander von Humboldt's *Cosmos*:

la mer contient dans son sein *une exubérance de vie*. ... car la mer aussi a ses forêts; ce sont les longues herbes marines qui croissent sur les bas-fonds, ou les bancs flottants de fucus que les courants et les vagues ont détachés, et dont les rameaux déliés sont soulevés, jusqu'à la surface, par leurs *cellules gonflées d'air*. ... *Là pullulent les animalcules phosphorescents*, les mammaria de l'ordre acalèphes, les crustacés, les peridinium, les néréides rotifères, dont les innombrables essaims sont attirés à la surface par certaines circonstances météorologiques, et transforment alors chaque vague en une écume lumineuse. *L'abondance de ces petits êtres vivants, la quantité de matière animalisée qui résulte de leur rapide décomposition* est telle, que l'eau de mer devient un véritable liquide nutritif pour des animaux plus grands. *Certes, la mer n'offre aucun phénomène plus digne d'occuper l'imagination que cette profusion de formes ani-mées, que cette infinité d'êtres microscopiques dont l'organisation, pour être d'un ordre inférieur, n'en est pas moins délicate et variée; mais elle fait naître d'autres émotions plus sérieuses, j'oserai dire plus solennelles, par l'immensité du tableau qu'elle déroule aux yeux du navigateur.* Celui qui aime à créer en lui-même un monde à part où puisse s'exercer librement l'activité spontanée de son âme, celui-là se sent rempli de l'idée sublime de l'infini, à l'aspect de la haute mer libre de tout rivage.   (1846, i. 365–6, emphasis added)[53]

In tone, however, this passage is the inverse mirror image of Antoine's 'cool' (Cuvieresque) observation as scientific observer 'navigateur'. Science intertexts may then prove to be more effusive and religious ('pantheistic') than Flaubert's reworking of *Cosmos* as a carefully crafted and grafted piece of literary science. Only a saint outside his cell may thus 'literally' be privy to the vision of splitting cells envisaged but not verified by transformistes (such as Lamarck or Geoffroy Saint-Hilaire) or by their imaginary doubles, Hilarion or the Devil. Paradoxically too, a vision of the mystery of the beginnings of life itself is more the stuff of catastrophists (such as Cuvier) than those opting for gradual change without extinctions since even more marvellous are *plural* re-creations of life as if from nothing. The 'être la matière' finale can now be investigated for what it is, a virtuoso amalgam of the two main components of the *Tentation*, the world of Gnosis and science, combined in the 'religions' vision of its natural supernaturalist protagonist.

REVELATIONS OR ANALOGUES IN DIALOGUE

Like all of Flaubert's wonderfully doubled conclusions, the 'être la matière' finale is a direct invitation to return to the text's beginnings as it points directly to, but also conceals, origins or final arbitrations.[54] Antoine's geological vision of the waters being commanded 'to teem with living creatures' has taken him back from the Book of Nature (and Pliny) to the Book he commented upon in tableau one, but right to its beginnings in Genesis I: 20, and God's fifth day of creation. His single breath response here (exhalation after the inhalation above) also configures one of the ends of man from the catechism, to magnify (God). With superlative condensation of both sides of the 'querelle des analogues' in Antoine's final response to Life, 'Je voudrais avoir des ailes, une carapace, une écorce...être la matière', Cuvier's catastrophism and fixity of 'règnes' nicely sits beside Geoffroy Saint-Hilaire's unity of composition. At the same time, this exclamation is a bowdlerized condensation of the title of Darwin's watershed contribution to natural science, *The Origin of Species* (1859), but only by analogy. French 'transformisme' remains the emphasis, to complete the *Tentation*'s many temptations as metamorphoses in the guises of Hilarion, the Devil, and Pliny as 'Science'. A reason why the monsters now succeed 'strangers' and the 'gods' in the final *Tentation* is that modern Science is perhaps the greatest 'temptation' of all. As the epigraph to the chapter states, '*Fascinans et tremendum*, as the mystics said'. Whereas

Antoine repelled his previous (super)natural antagonists, he appears here to embrace this 'temptation' to become one with creation. Yet the use of the pivotal verb of volition (and free will) in the conditional in this final epiphany, 'Je voudrais avoir...' to which the verb 'être (la matière)' is in apposition has exactly the same effect as the final sentence of *Un cœur simple*, 'et, quand elle exhale son dernier souffle, elle *crut* voir...' (*OC*, ii. 177, emphasis added). Belief in God and/or in Science is left open, optional or complementary. As nineteenth-century refiguration of his superlative model in Athanasius' *Vita Antonii*, Antoine only confirms his incarnation in his mortal coil. From a 'religious' point of view, he is then ready to 'see' the face of Christ Incarnate as reward for his perseverance against the monsters of the mind and body before him.[55] Yet he does not see the earlier days of Creation, or its Ancient of Days, just as he cannot as seer-scientist 'see' 'creation' behind even the earliest cellular forms, living or extinct, recorded in the fossil record.[56] The final passage thus encapsulates the *Vita* (*Antonii*) as *Vita*, that is description of models of conceiving (a) life, whether for hagiographical or scientific human ends. Antoine's 'J'ai vu naître la vie' therefore also pokes fun at belief in spontaneous generation (posited by Aristotle among many of the ancients). This theory was not definitively disproved until 1864, when Pasteur discovered that microbes were responsible for the emergence of 'life' from inert matter (such as worms from dead carcasses, or plagues of frogs after rain).[57] A heated argument for spontaneous generation against Pasteur was spearheaded by the natural historian Félix Andromède Pouchet. While the 'spontaneous generationists' lost to science, science was lost to explain how microbes came to be 'in the beginning'. August Weismann (1834–1914), the first theoretician of heredity and a founder of modern genetics, had to side with Pasteur, but only because he saw the logic of spontaneous generation unfounded by proof.[58] In him is perhaps a synthesis of the Cuvier–Saint-Hilaire anti-magnetic attraction and figure behind Antoine's final statement of religion as mystic science. Georges Pouchet would then succeed his father (and his unrelenting beliefs in 'spontaneous generation') by combining expeditions with laboratory research—he joined the Comte d'Estayrac de Lauture's expedition to find the source of the Nile in 1856–7, and undertook new experimental work in marine biology in Brittany (of the 'goémons' and 'varechs') to develop histology and work on microfossils. Like Cuvier, he was a polymath and historian of science, as well as Flaubert's consultant on matters scientific.[59] In Antoine's final observations, emerging from the physical rocks under his nose, Normandy comes back as the inspiration for 'fourth-century Alexandria' and Parisian science as its parallel term.

Earlier prehistory, like the precise 'evolution' of man from the many families of species that preceded him in the sea or on the land, evades definitive empirical description. Flaubert's finale thus end stops the *Tentation* to subsume the discovery of Neanderthal man in 1865, and creationist versus evolutionist (Darwinian) hypotheses about human origins. The mysteries of the universe for saint and scientist therefore remain intact. In the end, Antoine's personal expression of belief remains precisely that of the religious or anti-religious reader, since neither religion nor science has adjudicated finally on first things. Antoine's climactic undersea and microscope visions thus richly express the '*œuvre* de toute LA vie'. We with him have witnessed its 'Jardin des Plantes', 'Muséum' galleries of mineralogy, comparative anatomy, and palaeontology, with Antoine himself as a human specimen on display. His final epiphany is then not so much pantheistic as pan-creational, to bring the wonders of natural science and the ecstatic experience of mystics into one work, a modern *mystère*.

To match the cosmologies of tableaux four and five, homage to the Pouchets, father and son, therefore completes Flaubert's scientific 'trinity' of modern Norman 'gods' of the sciences, Laplace and Cuvier, writ large in the final tableaux of the *Tentation*.[60] All were firm believers in empirical method and the displacing by science of former superstitions, but not private religious conviction as in Cuvier's case. If the Pouchets, Cuvier, and Laplace bring the 1874 *Tentation* firmly back to Flaubert's Normandy disguised as 'fourth-century Egypt', this '*œuvre* de toute LA vie' also in its ending remains very personally Flaubert's '*œuvre* de toute [s]a vie'. Macro- and microcosm can inter-reflect by analogies and analogues in dialogue through carefully ordered and structured suggestion and the poetry of language. We saw in Chapter 6 how the first and final dedication of the *Tentation* to Alfred Le Poittevin allowed Flaubert to finish his dialogue with his long-dead friend concerning the validity of the *mystère* as a thoroughly modern form. When Flaubert was working on the major revisions in 1869 that transform the *Tentation* into its restructured final version, his lifelong aesthetic critic and collaborator Louis Bouilhet died.[61] Flaubert was actively seeking recognition of Bouilhet's art when the *Tentation* was finally published, in matter (a monument of Bouilhet to be erected in Rouen), and in form (publication of Bouilhet's late works with a preface). The ending of the *Tentation* has never been read as a deeply personal homage to Bouilhet's poetry, especially *Les Fossiles* (published in 1854), of which Flaubert wrote to Louise Colet: 'C'est une œuvre, *Les Fossiles*! mais combien y a-t-il de gens en France capables de la comprendre?' (*Corr* ii. 541). The reverberations between the 'être la matière' passage and the first section of Bouilhet's poem are striking:

> Le sable, cependant, fermente au bord de l'onde,
> La nature palpite et va suer un monde.
> Déjà, de toutes parts dans les varechs salés
> Se traîne le troupeau des oursins étoilés;
> Voici les fleurs d'écaille et les plantes voraces,
> Puis tous les êtres mous, aux dures carapaces.
> Et les grands polypiers qui, s'accrochant entre eux,
> Portent un peuple entier dans leurs feuillages creux.
> La vie hésite encore, à la sève mêlée.
> Et, dans le moule antique, écume refoulée!
>
> . . .
>
> Au bruit des vents lointains, parfois la bête énorme
> Tourne son museau grêle et sa tête difforme;
> Hérissant leur poil dur, ses naseaux dilatés
> Semblent humer le monde et les immensités,
> Pendant que ses yeux ronds, bordés de plaques fortes,
> Nagent, lents et vitreux, comme des lunes mortes,
>
> . . .
>
> Elle pousse avec force un long mugissement,
> Qui s'élargit au loin sous le bleu firmament!
> Par les monts, par les bois aux mornes attitudes
> La clameur se déroule au fond des solitudes,
> Et le vaste univers écoute, soucieux,
> Ce grand cri de la vie épandu dans les cieux!
>
> (1974, 222–4)[62]

If Flaubert permits Antoine the 'grand cri' of human joy and ecstasy, he also leaves his saint ambiguously expressing his religious faith in a science of life, unlike the final section of *Les Fossiles* where Bouilhet discusses 'l'homme futur'. Antoine's lesson is the more Cuvieresque to Bouilhet's beliefs with Saint-Hilaire about the future of *homo scientificus*.

By revisiting his earliest development of the *Tentation* in dialogue with Le Poittevin and Bouilhet in its final version, Flaubert aesthetically recreates and remaps in the 'être la matière' finale the 'stuff' of his past and nascent artistic talent. The *Tentation*'s final breath then only repeats Fluabert's ebullient words to Ernest Chevalier in 1841:

Quant à moi je deviens colossal, monumental, je suis bœuf, sphinx, butor, éléphant, baleine, tout ce qu'il y a de plus énorme, de plus empâté et de plus lourd au moral comme au physique.... Je ne fais que souffler, henner, suer et baver, je suis une machine à chyle, un appareil qui fait du sang qui bat et fouette le visage, de la merde qui pue et me barbouille le cul. (*Corr,* i. 83)[63]

The *Tentation* is then a wonderful unity of composition: of its three versions, of religion and science as the Janus-headed dialogues of the ages, and of the analogues of micro- and macrocosm. Its final fusion is also a rejection of both fideism and pantheism, to side with faith exercised *in* science patterned on the model of the *Stromata* (book 4) of Clement of Alexandria.[64] Antoine has indeed overcome all his monstrous 'temptations' and their harbingers, Hilarion and the Devil, by deciding to carry on with his spiritual exercises in the science of prayer at the dawn of a new day. Whether he is any the wiser for having been 'à quatre pattes' in tableaux two and four, or reviewing 'Peter's tablecloth' of unclean (monster) quadrupeds on his belly in tableau seven, will be for the reader to decide.

When it comes to belief in the final truth claims of religion or science, Flaubert's *Tentation* makes clear through the Sphinx and the Chimera, however allegorized or interpreted, that it is folly for the one to deny the other. It has taken a lifetime's work on St Anthony for Flaubert to visualize through Antoine's 'hallucinations' the revelations of divine science. The Book of Life needs to include Nature and the Book remapped as 'géognosie' through the fantastic nineteenth-century libraries of religion and the natural science and geological induction of a polymath such as Cuvier. Science is not the Devil, merely science, but no less fascinating and potentially all consuming for all that. Only religiously scientific art, as arguably Brueghel's and Bosch's 'Anthony' paintings exemplify, can capture the modern imagination and show it something of the wonders ('mystère') of its past and present in apposition or opposition to God. In its seven tableaux, the *Tentation* of 1874 is therefore a marvellous work about the fantastic real of nineteenth-century French religion and science. Puncturing the notions of 'progress' in nineteenth-century French religious and scientific beliefs, the final *Tentation* of Flaubert is a virtuoso remapping that exposes the nothing new under the sun from time immemorial.

Conclusions

Ils dirent tout ce qu'ils voudront. *Saint Antoine* est un chef-d'œuvre, un livre magnifique. Moque-toi des critiques. Ils sont *bouchés*. Le siècle actuel n'aime pas le lyrisme, attendons la réaction, elle viendra pour toi, et splendide. Réjouis-toi des injures, ce sont de grandes promesses d'avenir.

(Corr, iv. 797, emphasis in the original)

The main contention set out in the introduction of this book as its rationale was that the 1874 *Tentation* is far from meaningless, undecidable, interminable, or boring when earlier critics' blocks are challenged, and when it is understood as if through the vision and viewpoints of its unlikely main protagonist. The *Tentation*'s intrinsic and interrelated parts have everywhere proved in this study to constitute a virtuoso, modern 'mystère'. There is then no better place to conclude this book than to follow Flaubert's own penchant in his endings, so supremely encapsulated by the 1874 *Tentation* itself, the return to beginnings. This time, George Sand's words in her letter of 4 May 1874 to Gustave Flaubert quoted above replace those of the *Tentation*'s first critics. With her characteristic directness, she fulsomely praises the 1874 *Tentation*'s qualities, and just as fulsomely castigates its critics for their blocks. In the light of the last chapter on tableau seven's poetic, intertextual, and highly allusive 'être la matière' finale to the whole work, we can only echo Sand's critical evaluation. Flaubert's *Tentation* is indeed a magnificent 'chef-d'œuvre', but one moreover 'de toute *la* vie'. Unlike its earlier versions, the 1874 text closes on the stunning diversity and nature of creation, and on the question of how to respond to it. By analogy, our concluding response to the *Tentation* is for it as Flaubert's masterpiece of dazzling literary creativity. In the manner of his literary Cuvier recreating worlds from a pair of boots (see p. 179), the *Tentation* represents Flaubert's exuberant, tongue-in-cheek reconstruction of his own epoch. Flaubert's creativity thus remakes the dusty tomes in libraries into the fantastic stuff of the nineteenth-century religious, scientific, and archaeological real, providing readers often take literally what is before their eyes. Flaubert's 'fantastic' library (Foucault) in the *Tentation* has also reconstructed in Antoine's imagination lost collections of the Great Library of Alexandria.

These concluding reactions to the 1874 *Tentation* stem directly from the contexts we set out in this book in the two overarching frames (religious and scientific), and close analyses of its seven tableaux-chapters. We have everywhere demonstrated that while the *Tentation* is indeed richly a fiction of the life and times—religious, philosophical, political, and scientific—of St Anthony the Great, and in ways that hitherto have not been investigated, his *Vita* is also the springboard enabling Flaubert to remap similar ideas, debates, and questions of immediate pertinence to nineteenth-century France. In this regard, we took seriously as a starting point Bouilhet's expectations of the first *Tentation*, namely that it would be 'about' the history of fourth-century Alexandria. This book understood this brief however in a larger sense, both as critical and comparative anatomy, and as literary geology. Thus it was not by looking deeper into the psychoanalytical ramifications of the *Tentation* (Du Camp's expectations of it as a psychological work), or into specialist source and genetic criticism (the combined criticism by Bouilhet and Du Camp of Flaubert's poor copying of Quinet), that the text could be prised from previous critical terrains or blocks. Rather it was by looking beyond specialist critical scrutiny *en bloc* that the fascinating worlds of nineteenth-century French doctrinal debate, comparative religion, astronomy, and natural science came into view. From these intercalated contexts, the bigger picture of the *Tentation*'s significance (plan) could emerge, unshackled also from psycho-biographical baggage surrounding the text, such as Flaubert's marvelling at Brueghel's *St Anthony*. We could then uncover the microcosm of Antoine's unfolding experiences and 'hallucinations' as visions of, and deeper analogical reflection (meditation) on, the 'fantastic real' macrocosm of Flaubert's own times. Antoine then turned out to be the model commentator on the longer history in the making of post-revolutionary France as a new ('Roman') empire and world power in terms of trade, colonization, culture, civilized society, knowledge, and science.[1]

Moreover, understanding the 1874 *Tentation* as a geo-theological remapping of nineteenth-century France allowed the individual strata (tableaux), the folds and fractures in the narrative (Hilarion's role in the three central tableaux, his 'break' with the worlds of the Devil in tableau six), or indeed its genetic reordering, to be newly looked into as well. Analyses in individual chapters have thus been able to show fresh ways of resolving what critics have previously regarded as incoherencies in the narrative structure or orders of protagonists: Seznec's problems with the tableau of the 'heresies' to describe tableau four, or tableau seven as the tableau of the 'monsters', are examples. By challenging an overly 'classical' priority in critics' understandings (Greek/Roman Enlightenment and rational value systems and culture references), the analyses also further refined more imaginatively ground-breaking readings, such as Starr's on Hilarion as double of (Geoffroy) Saint-Hilaire, by finding the necessary intermediary steps to make a logical whole of analogies that went only so far.[2] Additionally, individual chapter analyses could then offer major new readings of those tableaux which have never properly been considered in the critical literature, such as the 'Devil's ride' in tableau six, or which have not been revisited because of the seemingly definitive appraisals by critics such as Seznec (on heresies, gods, and monsters) or Gothot-Mersch (on the Queen of Sheba). By contrast, analyses of the most famous sections, not least Antoine's elegiac expression in the famous 'être la matière' epiphany, have revealed by way of Humboldt's *Cosmos* and other 'scientific' intertexts even more layers of analogy and meaning than have previously been identified by critics applauding the *Tentation*'s 'syncretism' or 'pantheism'. By reclassifying Antoine's 'hallucinations' as multivalent observations and visions befitting 'Gnostic' (in Part I) and nineteenth-century French natural scientific ideas epitomized by 'géognosie' (in Part II), more precision has been brought to umbrella concepts such as 'syncretism', 'heresies', and 'monsters' as well.

Understanding tableau seven's Sphinx and the Chimera episode as a remapping of the Cuvier–Saint-Hilaire 'querelle des analogues' however demonstrates the impasses in reading the *Tentation* solely through one optic or methodology. With Cuvier alias the Sphinx, analysis and naming of parts are but arid catalogues, classifications, or lists (source or genetic studies) if they are without overarching hypotheses or syntheses to explain, revivify, or challenge orders of meaning. Equally, the blue-skies ideas of the Chimera alias Geoffroy Saint-Hilaire go round in the higher terms of their own theoretical circles (psychoanalytic, post-modern approaches) unless they are empirically grounded by verifiable and specific contexts. The title and overarching concept of this book, like its argument for Flaubert's *Tentation* as a literary-geological 'remap-ping', might then be categorized more on the side of the Chimera, since application of this geological metaphor elucidates and unifies the text in ways that differ markedly from previous critical approaches. How-ever, the chapter analyses and their attention to comparative anatom-ical 'proofs' and close reading deliver the necessary 'earthing' for our hypothesis that the *Tentation* is really about nineteenth-century French religious and scientific ideas (and their heresies), as well as how to write about them *heretically*. Artful disguise in the analogous life and times of a fourth-century saint provided Flaubert's best window of criticism on his own epoch. Yet such imaginative remapping after the geological model of Smith's 'map that changed the world' comes about only by empirical, inductive method, and attention to the detail of previous mappings, as the notes and bibliography to this book amply demon-strate.

To the ends of combining the Sphinx and Chimera, and of avoid-ing their respective one-sidedness, prejudice, or dogmatisms, the book overall has ordered its analyses and syntheses within a two-part, dialogic structure already intrinsic to the dynamic of the text itself, but partic-ularly visible in the Antoine–Hilarion/Devil debates of tableaux three and six. By adopting these debates 'simply' as the larger overarching orders of Religion and Science for the whole work, this book has set out how Flaubert's *Tentation* reclassifies these two coextensive dynamics of human understanding. As with any ideological conflict, the two main arenas of debate needed first to be polarized (to identify their parts) and represented, the better then to demonstrate their surprisingly analogous, interrelated concerns about those larger human questions regarding the meaning and provenance of life and death. Artful recomposition and an art of the composite are then the aegis best able to combine or challenge seemingly antagonistic belief systems. Although Flaubert achieves this textually in the *Tentation*, his art remains supremely visual. Its tableaux operate at once as a religious icon or triptych, a mosaic or frieze, and as anatomical plate, scientific collection, or display of specimens labelled in a cabinet.

Over-separation of the 'religious' and 'scientific' spheres, topics, and representatives in the two discrete parts of this book then allowed their striking and paradoxical similarities to emerge. Central to this paradox is the 1874 *Tentation*'s investigation of heterodoxy in both spheres by means of its protagonist observer, Antoine, based on the father of orthodoxy. The 'heresies' of the text proved not only to be the overtly religious debates *en abyme* in tableau four. We saw in tableau two how the doctrinal status and Christian theology of the Virgin Mary was spearheaded by the 'pagan' Queen of Sheba, but in terms that are no less sacrilegious or comparative religious. She was seen also to prefigure the older goddesses of Mediterranean civilizations in tableau five, but in the form of an 'Isis *lactans*'. But science too in the latter tableaux of the *Tentation* proved rife with heresies and bones of contention. In similar vein to earlier questioning of 'Virgin Birth', Immaculate Conception, or (re-)incarnation, the finale of the text debates the doctrines of 'spontaneous generation' and 'transformisme'. Creationism versus evolution put contemporary terms upon them. Nineteenth-century religions and sciences in the *Tentation* therefore prove to have remarkably similar institutions, knowledge bases, 'priesthoods', and laws for interpretation of 'truth', and thus to exchange the same spaces in their bid for final authority and infallibility.

This paradox can then be exploited as the tacit 'moral' or 'lesson' of the *Tentation* in its final version. 'Religion' and science' are not left as mutually deconstructive or undecidable discourses. That Flaubert reordered the tableau of the 'monsters' to succeed that of the 'gods' in the 1874 *Temptation* represents no victory for science over religion either. The final tableau's emphasis on 'querelle(s) des analogues' suggests that the 'new religion' of nineteenth-century science, its heresies and wrangles over interpretative authority, only looks very 'déjà vu' when understood through the eyes of Antoine from the 'heretical' times of the early Church of St Anthony the Great. Antoine's final 'observations' as prophetic 'seer' of nineteenth-century science then 'retrospectively' demystify it (and the modern scientist) of its pretensions. Our investigation of the heresiarchs of new 'churches' only discovered rather old questions repackaged by newly founded disciplines such as Egyptology and palaeontology. As a modern 'mystère' Flaubert's *Tentation* thus encapsulates the truth for religion as much as for science that the great mysteries will nevertheless remain. Allegorical and empirical realities can then tell us much about human puniness in the greater scale of things. Only if we as readers are prepared to suspend belief in our critical prejudices are we able (like Antoine) to address the inexplicable questions concerning the nature of man [*sic*] that religion and science continue to ponder. Antoine—eccentric, ecstatic, wise fool, seer (scientist and prophet), curiously agnostic of final truth statements— is therefore the linchpin of the 1874 *Tentation* rather more than his disciple Hilarion, important though this figure is to drawing out the paradoxes of the *Vita Antonii*'s (creative) fixities of form.[3] Antoine is no muscular Christian or model saint, good ascetic or natural theologian.[4] Rather it is his uncertain openness as against dogmatic inflexibility, his enquiring observations pressing against passive acceptance of final authority (institutional, textual, or doctrinal), that make him a very human foil for the confident, scientific, rational demolition of personal religious faith by Hilarion, the Devil, or their historical duplicates, such as Renan, Geoffroy Saint-Hilaire, Byron, or Laplace. The unexpected epitome of a figure against the grain, Antoine also sits among the pantheon of Flaubert's unlikely, anti-heroic central male protagonists— Charles Bovary, Frédéric Moreau—as vital mouthpieces of their times.[5] Antoine's anticlimactic final return to his daily routine of prayer and contemplation is indeed the other side of the same coin of Frédéric's return to diurnal inactivity and narcissistic reminiscence that concludes *L'Éducation sentimentale*. The same motor of compositional circularity, endless repetition, and distorting symmetry operates in both works to return their respective protagonist anti-heroes to beginnings. Antoine's retrospection as productive resilience to acedia has, however, turned imaginary, fantastic visions into proleptic equivalents of modern, identifiable scientific discoveries. In its definitive version, the *Tentation* thus bespeaks a bigger lesson about nineteenth-century France than any sentimental education. As aesthetic 'mystère' of the art and science of (literary) creation, Bouvard and Pécuchet may only ultimately imitate, bowdlerize and mock such work by being its uncreative male copyist doubles.

Yet what the two-part structure of this book has perhaps shown more clearly than has previously been acknowledged of the *Tentation*'s supremely 'orientalist' interest is Flaubert's remapping of *Egypt* as the concerted interspaces and forum for critiques of nineteenth-century French 'progress' and enlightenment. Napoleon's invasion of

Egypt as military and scientific mission in 1798–1801 marks the pivotal historical moment between ancient Egypt and the 'medieval' feudalism of modern Egypt he conquered, and between Flaubert's Antoine as nineteenth-century St Anthony the Great grappling with the final vestiges of the rich culture of ancient Egyptian civilization. The implicit value judgement the *Tentation* contains of both fourth-century AD Alexandria (or Constantinople) and the new 'Alexandria' of nineteenth-century Paris (or Napoleon's Institut d'Égypte in Cairo) is that probably neither can compare with the extraordinary civilization that was ancient Egypt in its religious, scientific, cultural, and artistic sophistication.

We did not however limit our rereading to the 1874 *Tentation*, following Foucault, as a 'bibliothèque *fantastique*' or, indeed, as some 'archaeology' of knowledge. By looking at the wealth of verifiable details that make up the 'Egyptology' of the text as an intricate and complex literary mosaic of 'stones' from an even more diverse geology of knowledge (and wonderful adventure in the intertextual), this study has also sought to show the capaciousness of Flaubert's creative art as literary-scientific endeavour, but one acknowledging overtly spiritual roots. This capaciousness was exemplified in discussions of some of the nineteenth-century religious and 'scientific' intertexts in Flaubert's library—such as Renan's *Vie de Jésus*, Maury's *Magie*, or Humboldt's *Cosmos*—which critics have ignored. Remapping nineteenth-century French religious and scientific ideas through the prism (and reaches) of the final version of the *Tentation*, therefore, offers a model text and method whereby other 'literary-scientific' creations of the period in France (or indeed in Germany or England) might be (re)evaluated. As we have seen in the fantastic, 'future' discoveries of Neptune in tableau six as 'science fiction', Flaubert does much more than represent science and its possibilities in the manner of a Jules Verne. He also does more than borrow one scientific theory as metaphor to structure his work in the manner of a Balzac (whose preface to the 'Comédie humaine' acknowledging Geoffroy Saint-Hilaire's Unity of Composition as literary model is the endlessly cited example).[6] Flaubert's own interests, family background in medical science, social circle including scientific friends, do not countenance a single theory (dogma or set of beliefs) as providing all the answers. The role of Hilarion and the Devil as Antoine's key interlocutors also demonstrates that for hidden middles to come to light, strong polar opposite positions (often uncovered as homologous relations) are needed for understanding to deepen. What is arrived at in the in-between is always closer to truth than either polarity or its dogmas. Consequently, the remits of Flaubert's *Tentation* and the character of his ever-curious Antoine contrast strikingly with other nineteenth-century literary-scientific works which deliberately ignore key religious or other antagonists in their debate, or claim they do not exist.[7]

In the Introduction, we highlighted Flaubert's early discovery via Alfred Le Poittevin of St Anthony, the 'mystère' and Byron, and in Chapter 6 of Byron and Le Poittevin's important developments of a religious genre with eminently secular and scientific impact, particularly by means of thoroughly modern devils who were wizards at science. Through Antoine, an altogether paler, more human version of his precursor, the (arch) conservative St Anthony the Great *and* his history as paradigm *Vita*, Flaubert shows how the hagiography and the summum could indeed be remapped to speak about 'Gnostic' science. His final *Tentation* as modern 'mystère' however challenges any ultimate belief in science, when it is compared with other strong rival beliefs. Balzac's *Louis Lambert* of course brings nineteenth-century religious and scientific fanaticisms of its age together in a figure who is both a Gnostic and an alchemist, but Balzac's novels of the fantastical human imagination are put second to his realist, 'sociological', and more 'scientific' descriptions of arriviste nineteenth-century bourgeois France. This book suggests that such critical hierarchies—realist/sociological/scientific versus romantic/fantastic/imaginary—might be thought otherwise through the possibilities of the modern *vita* using Flaubert's 1874 *Tentation* as paradigm. His creative imitation of the grand models of both the hagiography and the summa extends their appeal to universal truths about what is (divinely and scientifically) human in the human condition. As Flaubert was exploring in his letters to Louise Colet (written during the same period as his rethinking of the second *Tentation*), Art(s), religion(s), and science(s) prove to share the same spirit of the nineteenth-century age of modern beliefs because

[O]n ne fait rien de grand sans le fanatisme. ... Le fanatisme est la foi, la foi même, la foi ardente, celle qui fait des œuvres et agit. La religion est une conception variable, une affaire d'invention humaine, une idée enfin; l'autre

un sentiment. Ce qui a changé sur la terre, ce sont les dogmes, les *histoires*
des Vischnou, Ormuzd, Jupiter, Jésus-Christ. Mais ce qui n'a pas changé, ce
sont les amulettes, les fontaines sacrées, les ex-voto, etc., les brahmanes, les
santons, les ermites, la croyance enfin à quelque chose de supérieur à la vie et
le besoin de se mettre sous la protection de cette force. Dans l'Art aussi, c'est le
fanatisme de l'Art qui est le sentiment artistique. La poésie n'est qu'une manière
de percevoir les objets extérieurs, un organe spécial qui tamise la matière et qui,
sans la changer, la transfigure. Eh bien, si vous voyez exclusivement le monde
avec cette lunette-là, le monde sera teint de sa teinte et les mots pour l'exprimer
votre sentiment se trouveront donc dans un rapport fatal avec les faits qui l'ont
causé. Il faut, pour bien faire une chose, que cette chose-là rentre dans votre
constitution. Un botaniste ne doit avoir ni les mains, ni les yeux, ni la tête
faits comme un astronome et ne voir les astres que par rapport aux herbes. De
cette combinaison de l'innéité et de l'éducation résulte le *tact*, le *trait*, le *goût*,
le *jet*, enfin l'illumination.... La conclusion, la plupart du temps, me semble
acte de bêtise. C'est là ce qu'ont de beau les sciences naturelles: elles ne veulent
rien prouver. Aussi quelle largeur de faits et quelle immensité pour la pensée!
Il faut traiter les hommes comme des mastodontes et des crocodiles. Est-ce
qu'on s'emporte à propos de la corne des unes et de la mâchoire des autres?
Montrez-les, empaillez-les, bocalisez-les, voilà tout; mais les *apprécier*, non.
Et, qui êtes-vous donc vous-mêmes, petits crapauds?

                                          (*Corr*, ii. 291–2 and 295, emphasis in the original)

UNITIES OF COMPOSITION

If Du Camp's expectations that the 1849 *Tentation* would be a psychological work were unfulfilled, the approach of this book also appears
to have sidelined psycho-critical approaches to the text. Yet we chose to
end Chapter 7 by considering the personal reverberations in content and
form between Antoine's final words and Bouilhet's poem of 1854, *Les
Fossiles*, as a retrospective intertextual dedication and literary-aesthetic
dialogue with a dead friend. In this, Bouilhet's work operated in the
same manner as the *Tentation*'s direct acknowledgement and debt to
Le Poittevin (the dedication to the first and final versions), which we
highlighted in Chapter 6, to argue for Flaubert's rewriting of *Bélial* into
tableau six of the 1874 text. The intervening, 'objective' reshaping of the
Tentation may then also be inductively reconstructed with hindsight, if

we assume that strongly personal configurations might also have been at work. The paradigmatic passage just quoted from Flaubert's intense correspondence with Louise Colet in the early 1850s offers such an arena. The complex sentiments in this letter of 1853 are prophetic in their summing up of the remits, roles, objects, and finale of the final *Tentation*, as elucidated in the chapters of this book.[8] Through the same retrospective-prospective optic which we everywhere argue comprises the principal critical dynamic of the final *Tentation* as a whole, this period of Flaubert's correspondence allows rare insights into the radical self-critical processes he was undergoing as he meditated upon, and rethought, the *Tentation's* first (and also second) versions. Not least it offers insights into Flaubert's own later definition of the importance of the *Tentation*—'l'œuvre de toute ma vie'—that critics have taken as read. How and why its significance was so central to his aesthetic output derives as much from his resilience about the first *Tentation's* artistic worth (his figuration of the resistant Antoine), as from the radical revision of it that assured its final version as an 'œuvre de toute LA vie'. The dialogue of opposites and paradoxes that are science and religion in the 1874 *Tentation* are at the heart of his letters to Colet. One can then speculate that Flaubert found a more workable aesthetic *modus vivendi* for his final *Tentation*, as for his whole artistic output, thanks to the 'glasses' ('cette lunette-là' in the quotation above) borrowed co-equally from the material writing of *Madame Bovary* (as 'antidote' to the *Saint Antoine* fiasco), and from his intense dialogue about the role of art and the artist with his lover-antagonist-Muse. His critic friends Bouilhet or Du Camp continued to be too closely, and negatively, associated with the *Tentation* project. Where we began to unpack the *Tentation* by examining the latter critics' blocks as paradigmatic 'monocles' of later critical tendencies, Flaubert's own self-critical reappraisals of his *Tentation* rely on seeing it *correctively* through the double lens of this vital period of intense emotion and conviction, energetic research, and stylistic effort, summed up in the composite image of a *woman*'s pearl necklace. It cannot be a necklace, pearl or otherwise, without the essential ordinariness, yet orderliness, of its thread:

Mais les perles ne font pas le collier; c'est le fil. J'ai été moi-même dans *Saint Antoine* le saint Antoine et je l'ai oublié. C'est un personnage à faire (difficulté qui n'est pas mince).... j'ai mis là beaucoup, beaucoup de temps et beaucoup d'amour. Mais ça n'a été assez mûri. De ce que j'ai beaucoup travaillé les éléments matériels du livre, la partie historique je veux dire, je me suis imaginé que le scénario était fait et je m'y suis mis. *Tout dépend du plan. Saint Antoine* en manque; la déduction des idées sévèrement suivie n'a point son parallélisme dans l'enchaînement des faits. Avec beaucoup d'échaudages dramatiques, le dramatique manque.... j'en ai passé une bonne (jeunesse) avec Alfred. Nous vivions dans une serre idéale où la poésie nous chauffait l'embêtement de l'existence à 70 degrés Réaumur.... Jamais je n'ai fait, à travers les espaces, de voyages pareils. Nous allions loin sans quitter le coin de notre feu. Nous montions haut quoique le plafond de ma chambre fût bas.

(*Corr*, ii. 40–1, emphasis in the original)[9]

Where we argued for the principle of disorientation in the first chapter of this book as its vital dynamic, Flaubert has just returned from his personal experience of Egypt in 1851 when writing this. It marks a first stage in the disorientation and reorientation of the first *Tentation*, where his deromanticized observations grounded some of the 'chimerical' flights stated above with Alfred, not least Flaubert's experience of blacking out in the Pyramid of Giza guarded by its sphinx. The unpublished 'La Spirale' would work on this material.[10] Physical remove and double-distancing go some way to positing the unknowable route whereby Flaubert arrived at the final *Tentation* as exploration of 'Egypt' in terms of a unity of *plan*, yet fascinatingly returning it to his own Normandy in the fictional representations of the discoveries of Cuvier, Laplace, and Pouchet. It is more difficult to surmise how he came upon his redrawing of Antoine as quintessentially a modern saint and visionary-cautionary eyepiece for his times. Being too symbiotically involved with one's subject is precisely Flaubert's own assessment in his letter quoted above. 'Saint Antoine, c'est moi, d'après moi' is surely as valid as the more apocryphal 'Madame Bovary, c'est moi, d'après moi'? Both works are in evolution in the early 1850s, refractions of 'Normandy' and 'Egypt' as their mutually creative impetus. Flaubert had then to resolve the creative problem of redrawing his *Tentation* and Antoine with self-critical force and a *distance* which did not contradict intimate involvement. The complex relationship (including its eventual break) with Louise Colet, particularly where Flaubert explores his aesthetic and affective priorities, allows us to deduce how Flaubert disengaged from his first, 'Byronic' 'St Anthony' to look on himself through a less idealized Antoine of greater insight and awareness. The solution was Flaubert's creation of Hilarion as distorting mirror image protagonist/antagonist to the Antoine of the final version.[11] At the same time, Flaubert's adoption of the viewpoint of the natural scientist within his domain and way of looking at the world (the 'botanist' above, or Hilarion as 'science' in the *Tentation* itself) avoids uncritical 'appreciation'. Antoine as primary viewer of the work is also its chief religious and scientific object on display. In the final *Tentation* he is more and less than a reconfiguration of St Anthony the Great of Egypt: he is a specimen of ideological contentions in a cabinet of human curiosities in the bell jar of human civilization. Art, then, like the anatomist examining samples, sifts the evidence and transfigures the form, but not its substance, into words. Precision combined with artistic insight by style and wit surely brings Flaubert to the only authentic solution (within his 'unity of plan' or pearls on their thread) whereby a fourth-century Alexandrian Christianizing world view can be at once a nineteenth-century de-Christianized and scientific one.[12] Antoine as a visionary observer-seer of the 'real' science of nineteenth-century France is also the very unextraordinary human being in the bigger, *palaeontological* (scientific) scale of things.

We also noted Flaubert's thoroughgoing reflections on the future for art in tableau five in the long quotation from another important letter of the same period to Louise Colet, of 7 July 1853 (see pp. 178–9). Here, his contemplation of art was at once the ability to unify (with Saint-Hilaire) and to reconstruct a whole from a single part (*pars pro toto*) in the manner of a Cuvier. Yet what Flaubert also wanted was not just a science model for his art or narrative point of view (the impassibility of the natural scientist observing), but an ecstatic effect of such a viewpoint, homologous to God's in the universe:

L'auteur, dans son œuvre, doit être comme Dieu dans l'univers, *présent partout*, et *visible nulle part*. L'art étant une *seconde nature*, le créateur de cette nature-là doit agir par des *procédés analogues*: que l'on sente dans tous les *atomes*, à tous les aspects, une impassibilité cachée et infinie. L'effet, pour le *spectateur*, doit être une espèce d'ébahissement.   (*Corr*, ii. 204)

While this familiar passage is often quoted to illustrate Flaubert's famous narrative impersonality, no critic has remarked upon the intensity of its scientific vocabulary and empirical viewpoints, which the emphasis added above highlights. The final effect required hypothetically here, 'ébahissement', is realized magnificently in Antoine's stunned amazement and exclamation in the 'être la matière' finale. How to understand such sentiments comes once more in retrospective reading of Flaubert's correspondence with Louise Colet as the locus of his articulation of a transformative art of science to include the 'transfigurative'. The artist's model of the natural scientist as observer-narrator absorbed by, but detached from, his objects of study[13] needs to be inflected by a Cuvier, who caused wonderment in his audience from his scientific reconstructions. Flaubert's 'science' of writing thus boils down to the most careful handling (stylistic transformism) of metamorphoses, of the virtuoso kind that remapped the 'gods' and myths of tableau five into the stories of prehistory and geology, or the Sphinx and the Chimera into the Cuvier–Geoffroy Saint-Hilaire 'querelle des analogues':

> Je suis dévoré maintenant par un besoin de métamorphoses. Je voudrais écrire tout ce que je vois, non tel qu'il est, mais transfiguré. La narration exacte du fait réel le plus magnifique me serait impossible. Il me faudrait le *broder* encore.... Il faut à la fois ne pas perdre l'horizon de vue et regarder à ses pieds. Le détail est atroce, surtout lorsqu'on aime le détail comme moi. Les perles composent le collier, mais c'est le fil qui fait le collier. Or, enfiler les perles sans en perdre une seule et toujours tenir son fil de l'autre main, voilà la malice.
>
> (*Corr*, ii. 416–7, emphasis in the original)

Flaubert's need to reach beyond the best of previous and contemporary models thus transposes itself into his Antoine as artist-scientist-visionary before the works of nature as if its creator, because words are the only form of *creative* self-expression. Where Beauty might become an idol for art, Flaubert finally eschews this old religious stance for his own art of tranfigurative imitation (the world of identifiable microfossils in tableau seven, dressed up in others' lyrical terms) in defiance of such *bêtise humaine*. The truly moral role for the artist, then, is saintly *and scientific* amorality—embodied in Antoine's 'curiosity' and refusal to judge by doctrinal lights—and attention (his final words) to expressing his observation of truths beyond their surfaces with as much authenticity (and as little self-attention) as possible:

> Depuis la fin du xvi* siècle jusqu'à Hugo, tous les livres, quelque beaux qu'ils soient, sentent la poussière du collège.... Il faut faire de la critique comme on fait de l'histoire naturelle, *avec absence d'idée morale*. Il ne s'agit pas de déclamer sur telle ou telle forme, mais bien d'exposer en quoi elle consiste,

comment elle se rattache à un autre et *par quoi* elle vit (l'esthétique attend son Geoffroy Saint-Hilaire, ce grand homme qui a montré la légitimité des monstres). Quand on aura pendant quelque temps, traité l'âme humaine avec l'impartialité que l'on met dans les sciences physiques à étudier la matière, on aura fait un pas immense. C'est le seul moyen à l'humanité de se mettre un peu au-dessus d'elle-même. Elle se considérera alors franchement, purement, dans le miroir de ses œuvres. Elle sera comme Dieu, elle se jugera d'en haut. Eh bien, je crois cela faisable. C'est peut-être, comme pour les mathématiques, rien qu'une *méthode* à trouver. Elle sera applicable avant tout à l'Art et à la Religion, ces deux grandes manifestations de l'idée. . . . Donc, de degré en degré, on peut s'élever ainsi jusqu'à l'Art de l'avenir, et à l'hypothèse du Beau, à la conception claire de sa réalité, à ce type idéal enfin où tout notre effort doit tendre. Mais ce n'est pas moi qui me chargerai de la besogne, j'ai d'autres plumes à tailler.

(*Corr*, ii. 450–1)

The final version of the *Tentation* is Flaubert's unacknowledged undertaking of such a brief for the future of a 'scientific', transfigurative art (including the mathematical as our exploration of Laplace in Chapter 6 suggested), but without its positivist thrust or belief in progress as the ultimately knowable or predictable. The finale of the 1874 *Tentation* as a work of retrospection, personal and structural, thus fittingly ends with hypothetical reconstruction ('j'aurais voulu . . . '), not a future perfect, and defies the teleological thrust of positivism by going backwards into historical, mythological, biblical, and geological time in order to understand and remap the present.

One cannot prove Flaubert's recollections of his earlier correspondence with Louise Colet when he was completing the 1874 *Tentation*. However, a rereading of the Louise Colet correspondence as the *Tentation's* vital and *impossible* aesthetic other (her effusive lyricism) goes far in explaining why 'misogyny' suffuses the 1874 *Tentation* as indicative of most of Flaubert's later works. While not exonerating his violent break with his 'Muse', such absolute rejection of essential female creativity (biological, intellectual, aesthetic, and spiritual) finds strangely analogous, almost obsessive refiguration in the *Tentation's* almost overwhelming female protagonists in their sexually proactive, mortal power, and Antoine's rejection of it. In this reponse, Flaubert's saint of course follows his ascetic precursor to the letter. St Anthony the Great had to eschew the world and women to embrace a completely defeminized universe (and desert landscape) to become the father of

monasticism. Yet Flaubert surely misplaces artistic vocation in the space
of his ascetic saint as martyr to the higher cause of his art? Consequently
Woman, especially purely imaginative creations of her as in Ammonaria
or Salammbô, returns with a vengeance, and always in superlative guises
throughout the *œuvre*. 'Louise' perhaps finds her reconstruction psycho-
biographically as the pivotal, negative dedicatee effecting the many
transformations ('temptations') of the final *Tentation*. She can only be
contained as a rejected 'Sheba', a dis(re)membered, superlative female
form such as Ammonaria, the composite female creature of tableau
seven or its Old Woman. Antoine's overcoming of these monster female
figures is potentially suicidal, but once slain in *his* flesh, a universe in
his own male creative image—hermaphroditic monsters, spontaneous
generations, asexual matter, and a face of Christ in a sun disc—may
ultimately be restored. Science and gender readings must then take forward the *incomplete* images, preoccupations, and description of the text's
finale to comment on its 'divine science'.[14] After his climactic vision as
hero-saint or seer-scientist, Antoine merely returns to the solitude of his
diurnal work of prayer and meditation. While completely in keeping
with his sainthood to be after the manner of the father of monasticism,
this final position is also redolent of the scientist's work of 'discovery'
at Napoleon's Institut d'Égypte or the Muséum National d'Histoire
Naturelle. Such science in the masculine (whether in the form of the
Sphinx or Chimera) also prohibits the admission of women into its
spaces.[15] Yet Antoine himself reminds us in tableau two that the Queen
of Sheba, wisest woman of the East, came to seek Solomon's wisdom
and knowledge. Whether the context is third-century AD Alexandria or
nineteenth-century Paris, Museums quintessentially require Muses for
their establishment and *raison d'être*.

LITERARY TRANSFORMISMS

As unity of aesthetic composition and 'embranchements', as a geology
of theology, Flaubert's *Tentation* is very much more than Foucault's
'bibliothèque fantastique' or 'archaeology' of knowledge. To return to
Sand's term, this *chef d'œuvre* encompasses within its superimpositions,
folds, and fault lines the accretions of the history of the globe regarding
its species and civilizations, the religious and scientific mysteries of

the origins of the planets and of life, incarnation and creation, the alpha and the omega, the Book of God and the Book of Nature. In these, it is therefore also very much more than the pale imitation of Quinet's *Ahasvérus* that both Du Camp and Bouilhet identified it to be. As *Gesamtkunstwerk* defying the very limits of this 'multi-media' genre as envisaged by the Romantics, or sociological and encyclopedic remits as explored by the Realists and Naturalists, the *Tentation* posits the modern *mystère* as on a par with the discoveries and wonders of the hard and natural sciences, because it can also enfold them. In the light of what in this study can only be a selective cross-section of its many strata, Flaubert's *Tentation* proved undoubtedly to be a micro-macrocosmic work encompassing an 'œuvre de toute *LA* vie'. Its fictional remapping of nineteenth-century France ironically then proved the latest achievements to be no more than another 'révolution du globe'. Such raising of aesthetic stakes to achieve this—'transformism' of genres such as the *vita*, the summa, the *mystère*, the novel to match a subject matter of metamorphosing forms—then raises the old critical chestnut about how to classify Flaubert's art. Is he the precursor of the modern novel, a quintessential realist, or ultimately an unrepentant Romantic? With Sand in the opening quotation, Maxime Du Camp in his *Souvenirs littéraires* published shortly after Flaubert's death was unequivocal:

C'était un colosse fait pour vivre cent ans....La mort de Gustave Flaubert fit vibrer pour moi une de ces heures solennelles; elle secoua les torpeurs de ma mémoire, elle évoqua les fantômes...On a dit de Flaubert qu'il était un réaliste, un naturaliste; on a voulu voir en lui une sorte de chirurgien de lettres disséquant les passions et faisant l'autopsie du cœur humain; il était le premier à en sourire: c'était un lyrique.... Flaubert était romantique, ai-je besoin de le dire?...il était ouvert à l'enthousiasme.

(Du Camp 1993, 1, 2, 168, and 172 respectively)

In his unenviable but remarkable task of summarizing Flaubert's critical reception so concisely as an encyclopedia entry, Lawrence Porter sees Flaubert criticism evolving 'through three over-lapping stages: first normative criticism, which called Flaubert a realist; next, thematic criticism, which considered him an idealist; and finally, structuralist and post-structural criticisms, which consider him an indeterminist, a writer who resists conclusions.'[16] He goes on to put in table form the two extremes of Flaubert's writing output as shuttling from 'Romantic excess' (the *Tentation* of 1849, *Salammbô*, the *Tentation* of 1874) on the one side, to 'Realistic restraint' (*Madame Bovary*, *L'Éducation sentimentale* of 1869, *Bouvard et Pecuchet*) on the other. The attempt to challenge this schema emerged for Porter only in post-1970s criticism, with 'the psychological realism of the *Tentation* and the relevance of the history of *Salammbô*'. What this book has argued in terms of the *Tentation*'s disorientations and geological remapping of its subjects so that their contemporary significance may then emerge the more clearly chimes with a synthetic view of the two 'affres' of Flaubert's style as a 'post-1970s' response, but it is also a very belated one when we return to Flaubert's self-critical summation of his art, which again emerges in that period of vital correspondence with Louise Colet in 1852–3 when he was reworking the *Tentation*:

Il ya en moi, littérairement parlant, deux bonshommes distincts: un qui est épris de *gueulades*, de lyrisme, de grands vols d'aigle, de toutes les sonorités de la phrase et des sommets de l'idée; un autre qui fouille et creuse le vrai tant qu'il peut, qui aime à accuser le petit fait aussi puissamment que le grand, qui voudrait vous faire sentir presque *matériellement* les choses qu'il reproduit; celui-là aime à rire et se plaît dans les animalités de l'homme. *L'Éducation sentimentale* a été, à mon insu, un effort de fusion entre ces deux tendances de mon esprit... J'ai échoué.... *Saint Antoine* en est un autre. Prenant un sujet où j'étais entièrement libre comme lyrisme, mouvements, désordonnements, je me trouvais alors bien dans ma nature et je n'avais qu'à aller. Jamais je ne retrouverai des éperduments de style comme je m'en suis donné là pendant dix-huit grands mois. Comme je taillais avec cœur les perles de mon collier! Je n'y ai oublié qu'une chose, c'est le fil. Seconde tentative est pis encore que la première. Maintenant je suis à ma troisième. Il est maintenant temps à réussir ou de se jeter par la fenêtre.... le style étant à lui seul une manière absolue de voir les choses. (*Corr*, ii. 30–1)

His synthesis of styles (as Chimera and Sphinx), not their polarization, will emerge in a paradox that underpins the whole of final *Tentation* and his other works, perhaps most fully visible in the late works outside Porter's schema, the *Trois Contes* (1876) on early drafts of which Flaubert had been working in the late 1850s, especially *Saint Julien*. The motor of these inter-reflecting *contes* is the interchange of fantastical and real, so that what appears the most fabulous bespeaks a biting social critique, and what appears most real transcends any one reality by the layering of description and use of the 'petit détail qui fait vrai'. Heroic anti-heroes abound beside lyrical banalities so that cliché and human pomposity can be resoundingly punctured. Flaubert takes equally to task the excesses of Romanticism *and* Realism by imitating and metamorphosing their antagonisms into one another. His incorporation of his two 'bonhommes' as the Chimera and the Sphinx in *Le Tentation* as preface to the parade of monsters and Antoine's paean to creation as plastic and multiform, lyrical and scientific, religious and profane, is proof of Flaubert's already sure art of remapping the excesses of imagery and scientific precision as two parts of the same whole. But lest this be understood as avant-garde and pre-postmodern, Flaubert is not opting for aesthetic undecidability either when it comes to representing the unrepresentable (of prehistory or mystic ecstasy). When harmonized, the two seeming extremes of lyrical/ideal vs. scientific/real details can depict illumination of revelations beyond human grasp.

Deeps may be discerned none the less by consultation of geological maps, literal and figurative. The text and consequently Flaubert's art is thus Cuvieresque in its conservative appraisal of what one might know of first causes or the Creator, traditional in its veiling of what is not undecidable but unknowable, and fixed in its vision of human civilization as essentially the same in slight variations down the epochs, with major cataclysm (political rather than natural) explaining the fall (extinction) and rise (regeneration) of empires because this is a law of (human) nature. Flaubert is therefore a realist when he is at his most lyrical, and an idealist in what his realism might attempt to encapsulate. In this, his *Tentation*'s science is the wonderful world of other's monsters. It all depends through which glasses one is looking, religious or scientific.

REMAPPING NINETEENTH-CENTURY FRENCH LITERARY-CRITICAL TERRAINS

Major paradigm shifts only take place in practice with the aid of seeing through glasses less darkly. Although it is a truism that Renaissance and nineteenth-century advances in science came about by the right minds behind the new eyepieces of the telescope and the microscope respectively, Flaubert's *Tentation* also benefited from the new mechanical 'eye-pieces' that transformed its initial and disastrous first version into its final one. The Egypt of his Antoine as viewer of the panoramas of the ruins of its great civilizations, including nineteenth-century *French* occupation and its aftermath in the founding of 'Egyptology', are richly served by contradistinction to the camera of Maxime Du Camp. As among the first French photographer–ethnographers of Egypt's antiquities and modern life, Du Camp's work was acknowledged by a medal at the 1855 Exposition Universelle and the *Légion d'honneur*. As the illustrative, scientific, medium and 'Muse' of science replacing the lithograph and painting of the *Description d'Egypte* for example, Du Camp's photography would help transform public appreciation of the new wonders of Egyptology and travel as later displayed at the 1867 Exposition Universelle, where ancient Egypt was brought 'to life' in reconstructions of 'real' temples, and in the public unwrapping and dissection of mummies. The ending of the *Tentation* surely conjures real life forms as if seen under the microscope in imaginative guise in ways that the camera lens attempted to capture subjects in real life in black and white albumen print.

Maxime Du Camp's *Un voyageur en Égypte vers 1850* includes a photograph of Flaubert. While rather indistinct because swathed in native clothing, he is the subject in profile framed by the courtyard garden in the Quartier Frank in Cairo, indubitably a 'colosse' captured for posterity in a collection featuring ruins of temples and giant statues of Egyptian gods.[17] Flaubert had a surprisingly different, and very personal, response to Du Camp's work when he was sent a copy on its appearance as his letter to Louise Colet records:

Voici pourquoi je lui ai écrit: j'ai reçu aujourd'hui la dernière livr[aison] de ses photographies, dont jamais je ne lui avais parlé.... Sais-tu ce que j'ai vu aujourd'hui dans ses photographies? La seule qui ne soit pas publiée est une représentant notre hôtel au Caire, le jardin devant nos fenêtres et au milieu duquel *j'étais* en costume de Nubien! C'est une petite malice de sa part. Il voudrait que je n'existasse pas. Je *lui pèse* et c'est toi aussi, tout le monde. L'ouvrage est dédié à Cormenin, avec une dédicace-épigraphe latine. Et le texte a une épigraphe tirée d'Homère: toujours en grec! 'Encore le crocodile!' Ce bon Maxime ne sait pas une déclinaison, n'importe. Il s'est fait traduire de l'allemand l'ouvrage de Lepsius et il le pille impudemment (dans ce texte que j'ai parcouru) sans le citer une seule fois. J'ai su cela par Fouard, que j'ai rencontré en chemin de fer, tu sais.—Je dis: il le pille, car il y a toute sorte d'inscriptions qu'*il* n'a nullement prises, qui ne sont pas non plus dans les livres dont nous nous sommes servis en voyage, et qu'il rapporte comme ayant été prises par lui.

(*Corr*, ii. 364–6, emphasis in the original)

This seems strangely to contradict an early reference to receiving Du Camp's photographs a year earlier (*Corr*, ii. 110), and to make of himself a 'fantôme' with paradoxical 'weight'. It is tempting to (psycho)analyse Flaubert's amnesia regarding Du Camp in the light of the latter's criticisms of the first *Tentation*, coolness in friendship after the *Voyage en Orient* in 1849–50, or (jealous?) disbelief that photographers were now decorated with the *Légion d'honneur* over poets in this new technological age.[18] The existence of this photograph of Flaubert is also not the question. Rather, the two modes of representation of 'reality' seem altogether what are aesthetically at stake for Flaubert as he is working out his third *Tentation*. Positive artistic realism comes from proper use of detail reworked (that is not pillaged) from myriad sources, whereas Du Camp's photographic realism (which openly pillages as did the Egyptologists) is a *negative* realism of limiting and exacting imagination. For Flaubert, dealing with fantastic forms not real ones always takes art closer to the real than any photographic reproduction of an alleged reality. Eyewitness accounts are then also suspect because of the subjective viewpoint of the diarist, traveller, or correspondent choosing to write for a particular audience.[19] Over-romanticized Orients are however also to be avoided. It will take the finale of the *Tentation* of 1874 to work through Du Camp's 'camera' images of France's Egypt—political, archaeological, and scientific—and Redon's reworking of these micro-organisms as drawings of the imaginary to find that *juste milieu*, of science becoming properly artistic:

Plus il ira, plus l'art sera scientifique, de même que la science deviendra artistique. Tous deux se rejoindront au sommet après avoir s'être séparés à la base. Aucune pensée humaine ne peut prévoir, maintenant, à quels éblouissants soleils psychiques écloront les œuvres de l'avenir. (*Corr*, ii. 76, to Louise Colet)

A fictional 'saint' of visionary and ecstatic bent paradoxically proves to be the best qualified for having real insights into a future for art, pictorial, scientific, and literary. The 1874 *Tentation*'s remapping of the *vita* of the fantastic real proves indeed to be a 'future' form of sufficiently

creative vision to make Flaubert not only a first modernist, but also a
first magical realist before his time.

For newcomers to the *Tentation*, as for specialist researchers, this book
has thus everywhere sought to elucidate Flaubert's fascinating, challenging, stunning, and absorbing text as prism whereby to reinvesti-
gate the religious and scientific contexts of nineteenth-century France,
and as a model whereby to compare other literary-scientific works of
the period.[20] The analytic and synthetic methodology of geological
remapping—whether applied to the text's parameters, challenges to the
best critical wisdom and received ideas about it, debates specific to
the tableaux taken individually and collectively, mode of investigat-
ing biographical, generic, historical, religious, scientific, and aesthetic
implications—serves as a model for *dix-neuviémistes* tackling the important *œuvres* of poets, playwrights, novelists, artists and photographers
fascinated with representing the histories of ideas of their times. In
terms of the *Tentation* itself, space has not permitted fuller investigation
of several territories which others may wish to remap. For example,
there is more work to be done on the many parallels between the
multifarious Gnostic heresies and sects of fourth-century AD Alexandria
and the many new cults and religious doctrines circulating outside
the official Churches in nineteenth-century France. Similarly, further
development of this book's new theses—that the 'metamorphoses of the
gods' in tableau five is the conversion of 'mythology' picture language
into (pre-human) geological epochs, and that palaeontology and natural
histories illuminate the final chapter—will uncover additional layers of
nineteenth-century scientific interest and authenticity. Chapters 5 to 7
focused on key scientific players in Geoffroy Saint-Hilaire, Laplace, and
Cuvier, but at the expense of others who also fit Flaubert's picture such
as Lamarck, Arago, and Claude Bernard.[21] Last but not least, critics
need to return to what seem particularly arcane, but specifically religious
texts in Flaubert's bibliography (and mentioned in his *Correspondance*)
to be surprised by his intertextual refashioning of them. The anti-clerical
Flaubert would be the first to signal in his reading and rewriting that the
theological cannot be ignored in his comparative religious and scientific
age. Indeed, as his Antoine everywhere showed, *doxa*, the doctrinal, and
entrenched received ideas are the very matter of it.

Antoine's final response to the amazement of creation and to other visions of his world is then the fitting place to conclude. He simply returns to the altogether banal and daily act of meditation. By analogy, may new and specialist readers in the light of this book go back in similar vein to (re)reading the 1874 *Tentation*, but with an eye now to its wonderfully provocative questioning of received ideas, and as a text which richly remaps nineteenth-century France.

Endnotes

INTRODUCTION

1. Ecclesiastes 6: 10a; 6: 11; 8: 17b; 12: 8; 12: 12b.
2. See for example Wall (2001), although Starkie (1967 and 1971) arguably remains essential to study of Flaubert behind his *œuvre*.
3. For an account of the trial of *Madame Bovary* see LaCapra (1982).
4. The mystery play perhaps best known today is that of Oberammergau.
5. See Du Camp (1993, 313–15), also cited by Gothot-Mersch (*Tent*, 11).
6. See Isbell (1994).
7. As Flaubert admitted to Bouilhet, 'l'histoire de *saint Antoine* m'a porté un coup grave, je ne le cache pas' (*Corr*, i. 601).
8. Du Camp (1993, 315): 'nous ne devions pas le laisser se prolonger, car il s'agissait d'un avenir littéraire dans lequel nous avions eu une foi absolue.'
9. See Flaubert's letter of 15 Jan. 1850 to Louis Bouilhet and his letter of 23 Feb. 1850 to his mother (*Corr*, i. 567–76, 589–93).
10. Flaubert's correspondence to Bouilhet is also a return critical response. Copious editorial comments on Bouilhet's *Melaenis* intersperse the travelogue accounts, especially the sexual and erotic encounters. See Orr (1998b).
11. Porter (1975–6) argues for 'A Fourth Version of Flaubert's *Tentation de saint Antoine* (1869)'.
12. Letter to Mlle Leroyer de Chantepie, 5 June 1872: 'j'achève mon *Saint Antoine*. C'est l'œuvre de toute ma vie, puisque la première idée m'en est venue en 1845, à Gênes, devant un tableau de Breughel et depuis ce temps-là je n'ai cessé d'y songer et de faire des lectures afférentes' (*Corr*, iv. 531).
13. Nebuchadnezzar's feast and the Queen of Sheba (21 Dec. 1856), the Courtisane (28 Dec. 1856), Damis and Apollonius (11 Jan. 1857), the dialogue between the Sphinx and the Chimera and the fabulous beasts (1 Feb. 1857). See *Tent*, 245–6 for details of the editions and manuscripts of the text, and *Tent*, 12–13 for Gothot-Mersch's emphasis, from Flaubert's correspondence, on the first version as a 'déversoir'.
14. See Green (1982, 1986).
15. For a succinct overview of the work's genesis, see Porter (1975–6), especially the schema of the various episodes of the *Tentation*, their

reworking, reordering, or omission in the 1849, 1856, 1869, and final 1874 (56–7).

16. For a résumé of the immediate reception of the *Tentation* in reviews in *L'Univers*, the *Revue des deux mondes*, caricatures, and the mixed praise and censure of advocates such as Zola and Renan, see Harter (1998).

17. See for example Neefs (1987).

18. The only other monograph-length study of the *Tentation* in English is Neiland (2001), a genetic reading of the three versions of the text across key themes and their intertextuality with Flaubert's other fictions. Cuthbert (2003) also examines the final version of the *Tentation* but as an exploration of the question of knowledge ('myth' and 'metaphysics') alongside the *Trois Contes* and *Bouvard et Pécuchet*.

19. See Seznec (1949), Séginger (1997a), and Gothot-Mersch's edition of the text. Bem (1979a) and Bowman (1990) bring further scholarship from the angles of Freudian psychoanalysis and history of religions respectively.

20. After 1856 and 1869, Flaubert expressed his anxiety concerning the overall plan and the personality of his Antoine. As Porter (1975–6, 62–3) states, 'since the work consists in a series of the saint's hallucinations, the coherence of the portrayal of his personality determines the coherence of the overall structure'.

21. See Williams and Orr (1999).

22. See Foucault (1983) and Porter (2001).

23. Sartre (1971), Reik (1912), Bem (1979a), Gendolla (1991), Gothot-Mersch (1983), Dünne (2003).

24. Bowman (1981, 1985, 1986, 1990).

25. Seznec (1949), Neefs (1981), Séginger (1997a).

26. Orr (2000b) and Pasco (2002).

27. According to Du Camp (1993, 168), Flaubert knew Chateaubriand's *René* and Quinet's *Aashvérus* [*sic*] by heart so that he reproduced them without suspecting what he was doing.

28. See for example Carmody (1958), Seznec (1949), Demorest (1967) and also Bart (1977). For biographical questioning of the extent or nature of Flaubert's own religious or anti-religious position see Guillemin (1963). Cuthbert (2003) has returned to this issue.

29. See for example Foucault (1983), Neefs (1981), Séginger (1997a), and Neiland (2001).

30. See for example Lapp (1966), Olds (1998), and Thiher (2001) who see the temptations as 'hallucination'.

31. See Orr (1998a).

32. See for example Culler (1974) and Schehr (1997).

33. An exception is gender criticism. See Schor (1985) or Orr (2000a).
34. See for example Charlton (1963).
35. A recent counter-current is rectifying this position in literary criticism. See Jefferson (2007), which does not however include Flaubert.
36. Flaubert thought that the subject would make excellent theatre, but written by someone better qualified than himself (*Tent*, 8) and Raitt (2005, 52).
37. See the unsurpassed study of Flaubert's art by Tooke (2000). For excellent studies on Flaubert's *Tentation* and Redon's figural interpretations of it, see Müller-Ebeling (1997) and Harter (1998).
38. Guillemin (1963) remains the only monograph study recuperating a 'Catholic' Flaubert.
39. See Porter (2001, 321–33) for an overlapping view of 'temptation'.
40. Hence the more medieval first version of the text (based on the Brueghel) is what critics implicitly expect from the work. See Flaubert's own comments on the nature of '*la* tentation' in a letter to Louise Colet: 'A la place de saint Antoine, par exemple, c'est moi qui y suis. La tentation a été pour moi et non pour le lecteur.—*Moins on sent une chose, plus on est apte à l'exprimer comme elle est* (comme elle est *toujours*, en elle-même, dans sa généralité, et dégagée de tous ses contingents éphémères. Mais il faut avoir la faculté *de se la faire sentir*. Cette faculté n'est autre que la génie' (*Corr*, ii. 127–8, emphasis in the original).
41. Gothot-Mersch's essay on the Queen of Sheba (1986), discussed below in Chapter 2, outlines this method. She sees the three versions and the *brouillons* of the text as an 'interprétation conjointe'. 'En étendant le système de la comparaison ou de la superposition à l'ensemble du dossier, on peut considérer celui-ci comme un "super-texte", ou "métatexte"— assez fascinant—qui invite à substituer à la lecture linéaire une perspective mouvante, qui fait jouer l'œil à travers les divers strates, qui déborde et enrichit tout commentaire d'une des versions. Ici, plus que jamais le lecture est une construction. . . . La *Tentation de saint Antoine* apparaît alors comme un palimpseste: sous la dernière couche de texte subsistent les traces invisibles des couches précédentes. Mais ce qui fait l'intérêt de la chose, c'est qu'ici les couches successives sont en relations les unes avec les autres, et que la prise en compte des versions primitives peut avoir pour effet de réactiver un thème (dans l'exemple choisi, la magie) affaibli dans le texte final, quoique toujours présent. . . . Avec ses avantages et ses inconvénients—et un problème supplémentaire, particulier aux études de genèse: le danger de confondre *intentions* et *effets*' (1986, 144–5, emphasis in the original).

42. That Religion and Science are personified by Antoine and the Devil is one of the critical 'idées reçues' of the text, but this book is the first to work through the larger structural and ideological implications of this duality.

43. See note 12. The word 'idée' is not necessarily only the very first inspiration, but the first aesthetic translation of the subject into art. For a study of recognition, see Cave (1990) and for intertextual recognition more broadly, see Orr (2003).

44. Du Camp (1993, 162) is unequivocal. For a recent example see the cursory reference in Leclerc (2000, 13) in his preface to the Flaubert–Le–Poittevin–Maxime Du Camp correspondence. The critical exception which proves the rule is Descharmes (1924), as editor of Le Poittevin's works.

45. Desportes (2002, 70). Desportes sees Le Poittevin as Flaubert's 'bon et mauvais génie', 'le guide spirituel, l'initiateur et le mentor', a personal 'bibliothèque fantastique', but with little qualification.

46. See Descharmes (1924, 205), henceforth *LP*.

47. *Bélial*'s sacrilegious subject matter is of course framed by the biblical reference in 2 Cor. 6: 14–16.

48. Published in *La Revue de Rouen et de Normandie* (1836), *Le Colibri* (18 Sept. and 27 Nov. 1836), and *LP*, 55–8, 71–3, 64–6 respectively.

49. *LP*, 67–70, 74–5, 116–18, and 135–9 respectively.

50. These subjects return in Flaubert's correspondence with Louise Colet for example in *Corr*, ii. 283 and 450–1.

51. There is also a poem entitled 'A Gustave Flaubert' (*LP*, 110–11). The *Tentation* would then be a return compliment.

52. See for example Descharmes (1924, pp. xxxix and lx); Raitt (2005, 39).

53. Le Poittevin wrote a poem 'A Goethe' which refers to 'Faust' in line five (*LP*, 105–8). His poem 'Comme perce le jour' has a direct reference to Byron. Leclerc (2000, 13) notes that Le Poittevin was instrumental in introducing Flaubert to Byron's work, quoting Flaubert's letter of 24 Mar. 1837 as proof.

54. For Descharmes, 'Quand Le Poittevin n'aurait d'autre mérite que d'avoir préparé Flaubert à écrire *la Tentation de saint Antoine*, en orientant sans doute son esprit vers l'étude des religions et des hérésies, ce serait encore assez pour sauver son nom de l'oubli' (1924, p. lxii).

55. See Fabre d'Olivet's letter to Byron (as translator of the French edition of 1823) in which he refutes the blasphemous elements of *Cain*.

56. Quinet's work dramatizes the essential tenets about the person of Christ and also man's ultimate end found in various Gnostic world views, especially Jewish Kabbalah.

57. Byron (1822). For a succinct critical survey of the mystery as drama of evil, see Lima (2005).
58. Foucault (1966 and 1969) respectively.
59. 'Lectures de Flaubert' (*Tent*, 273–85).
60. See also Leclerc (2001).
61. See the indebtedness to other critics of Séginger (1997a) or Gothot-Mersch (1983).
62. Frye (1957).
63. See Flaubert's letter to Louise Colet: 'L'élément *réaliste* t'a blousé dans cette œuvre. Je sais ce que c'est, va! et je l'ai payé cher. J'en puis parler. Les notes de *Saint Antoine* m'ont bouché saint Antoine' (*Corr*, ii. 271).
64. These retorts are usually dismissed or ridiculed by bookish critics. See Starr (1984) for example.
65. Green (1982).
66. Important literary histories include Hollier (1989), Kay, Cave, and Bowie (2003), Farrant (2006).
67. Within Flaubert's corpus it is compared to early works such as *Smarh*, or late works such as *La Légende de saint Julien* in the *Trois Contes*. Dünne (2003) offers an interesting account of *Hérodias* in relation to the *Tentation*. See Todorov (1970) on the fantastic as literary genre.
68. See Raitt (2005, 61).
69. See Bartelink's edition of the *Vita Antonii* (1994), henceforth *VA*. Bartlelink (1994, 47) distinguishes between the exemplary lives of extra-ordinary heroes (Neoplatonic figures such as Apollonius of Tyana as recorded by Philostratus) and ' "l'homme de Dieu" [qui] a succédé à "l'homme divin", et l'homme héroïsé . . . qui se suffit à soi-même a cédé la place à l'homme de Dieu Chrétien guidé par la grâce et qui n'est qu'un instrument dans la main de Dieu'.
70. See Cuvier and Brogniart (1811).
71. See Winchester (2002).
72. Gothot-Mersch (1986, 141) and note 41 above. My 'remapping' now takes up her metaphors of 'couches' and 'strates' in their properly geological contexts.

PART I

1. This includes reading of Spinoza, whose philosophy has been seen as a major influence on Flaubert and the *Tentation*. See Brown (1996).
2. On the spiritual significance of the inner and outer desert with direct reference to St Anthony, see Davy (1985).

3. See Flaubert's extensive bibliography to authenticate these contexts, especially the sections 'Topographie ancienne' (*Tent*, 275) and 'Christianisme (exégèse)' (*Tent*, 276–8).

4. The skeleton of this appendix draws on the 'Conspectus' in Hazlett (1991, 317–22). This appendix and the four other timelines of this study are found in electronic form as part of a different project, 'Visualising the arts of the sciences', on my home page <http://www.soton.ac.uk/profiles/ Orr.html>.

5. For a recent study of Nicaea and its legacy, see Ayres (2006).

6. Chadwick (1999, 198), henceforth *EC* and page reference.

7. See also Ware (1993, ch. 2, 'Byzantium 1: the Church of the Seven Councils').

8. See Ware (1993, 50–1), henceforth *W* and page reference.

9. See 1 Corinthians 12 and 14 for the list and exercising of spiritual gifts.

10. For the history of the Antonines at Saint-Antoine d'Abbaye, see Baudat (1994). For a study of the medical 'realism' of Antoine's hallucinations, see Orr (1998b).

11. Flaubert will later seek to develop this insider orientalism with his reworking of *Hérodias* from a non-biblical and non-Christian viewpoint.

12. See Flaubert's letter to Alfred Baudry of 10 Feb. 1874: '*Saint Antoine* est imprimé et paraîtra comme poisson le 1er avril' (*Corr.* iv. 767).

13. Cannuyer (2000, 11).

14. See Gen. 37–48; Exod. 2; Acts 7: 22; Matt. 2: 13–20.

15. Armenia became the first Christian country in AD 310.

16. What follows is not a synopsis of nineteenth-century history of French Catholicism, for which readers should consult Gibson (1989) or Cholvy and Hilaire (2000). As argued above, Antoine's Coptic perspective visualizes but does not actualize Roman Catholicism.

17. See Tallet and Atkin (1991, ch. 1) for the short history of the cult of reason, the Revolutionary Calendar, and the bid to eradicate Christian names of people and places.

18. See Gibson (1989, 30): 'There is no doubt that the French Revolution was a watershed in the history of Catholicism in France.'

19. See Cholvy (2001) and Cholry and Hilaire (2000).

20. See for example Charlton (1963).

21. See for example Crossley (1993).

22. The skeleton of this timeline is based on the 'repères chronologiques' in Cholvy and Hilaire (2000), although the many additions and translation are mine, and obviously targeted towards specific issues of relevance in subsequent chapters. Readers may however find it a useful starting point

to see the less clear-cut separation of religion and politics, reactionary and reformist progress, than is usually presented.

23. See for example Bowman (1973 and 1987).

24. See for example Mours and Robert (1972).

25. See for example Gibson (1989), but also more recently Surkis (2006).

26. See Erdan (1855). Both volumes of Erdan's work are included in Flaubert's bibliography for the *Tentation*. Victor Hugo is among notable French writers who attended and hosted many séances in his home in Guernsey.

27. See Flaubert's 'prophetic' comments in his letter to Louise Colet of 4 Sept. 1852 (*Corr*, ii. 151): 'je tourne à une espèce de mysticisme esthétique (si les deux mots peuvent aller ensemble), et je voudrais qu'il fût plus fort.... Si la société continue comme elle va, nous reverrons, je crois, des mystiques, comme il y en a eu à toutes les époques sombres. Ne pouvant s'épancher, l'âme se contentera. Le temps n'est pas loin où vont revenir des langueurs universelles, les croyances à la fin du monde, l'attente d'un Messie? Mais la base théologique manquant, où sera maintenant le point d'appui de cet enthousiasme qui s'ignore? Les uns le chercheront dans la chair, d'autres dans les vieilles religions, d'autres dans l'art; et l'humanité, comme la tribu juive dans le désert, va adorer toutes sortes d'idoles.—Nous sommes, nous autres, venus un peu trop tôt. Dans vingt-cinq ans, le point d'intersection sera superbe.'

28. Similar but later response came from with the Catholic Church in the form of the Society of St Vincent de Paul founded in 1833 specifically to address urban poverty. In 1837 and 1839 respectively the Benedictine and Dominican orders with their rule of poverty were re-established.

29. Histories of nineteenth-century French Catholicism note the decline in numbers of priests after the Revolution, thanks to persecution and then secularization of clergy to fill the gap, and because celibacy obviously had only limited appeal. See for example Gibson (1989, ch. 3).

30. Maxime Du Camp and George Sand were adherents. See also *Corr*, ii. 91 (letter to Louise Colet), which mentions Enfantin by name. For a more comprehensive study and overview of the scientific contributions of the Saint-Simonians see Coilly and Régnier (2006) although there is no treatment of the religious importance of the movement.

31. For the importance of the Saint-Simonians in France and Egypt, see Régnier (2006).

32. See *W*, 37. St Benedict would use Pachomius' rule in the West. Basil the Great emulated it in Eastern monasticism.

33. For a fuller study of popular religious expression in France of the period, see Gibson (1989, ch. 5).

34. As Warner (1985, 93) notes: 'As early as the fifth century, the "woman clothed with the sun" was understood to be the Virgin.'

35. Kaufman (2005, 2). This comprehensive study of the Lourdes pilgrimage explores its intertwining of religious and mass cultures.

36. See for example Bem (1979a) and Olds (1988).

37. Similar debates over the authenticity of 'stigmata' manifesting on women's bodies were also raging between the Church and medical science. See Maury (1860). This may indeed be an allusion so deliciously immortalized by Flaubert in the wake of Emma Bovary, where neither Bournisien nor Homais correctly read the 'stigmata' issuing from her body.

38. Flaubert was allegedly enthralled as a child by Père Legrandin's puppet show retelling the story of St Anthony at the Foire Saint-Romain in Rouen. Gothot-Mersch (*Tent*, 9) is particularly sceptical of the weight earlier critics such as Maynial and Dumesnil placed on this 'influence' on Flaubert.

39. Muhammad was born *c*.570 to found the latest oriental religion, Islam. Although much of the first half of the *Tentation* takes place in 'Constantinople', Islam is a future event that may only be compared to the advent of Christianity by inference.

40. For a fuller account of the Saint-Julien claims on Anthony's bones, see Baudat (1994).

41. The Catholic Order of the Assumptionists was founded in 1845 by Emmanuel d'Alzon.

42. The problem of course does not go away within the lineage of mothers of the Virgin Mary.

43. See Guillemin (1963). Flaubert's correspondence with Louise Colet offers a more interesting observation on his position of belief (*Corr*, ii. 88): 'La débauche me plaît et je vis comme un moine. Je suis mystique au fond et je ne crois à rien.'

44. *Corr*, i. 558–9: '[L'évêque des Coptes] m'a reçu avec moult politesses;... je me suis mis à lui pousser des questions touchant la trinité, la Vierge, les évangiles, l'eucharistie. Toute ma vieille érudition de *Saint Antoine* est remontée à flot.... le vieux bonhomme ruminait dans sa barbe pour me répondre, moi à coté de lui, les jambes croisées, gesticulant et prenant des notes... La religion copte est la plus ancienne secte chrétienne qu'il y ait, et l'on n'en connaît presque rien.'

45. See Said (1978) and more recently Moussa (2004).

46. See Solé (1998, 43–4). The Muslim leaders call Napoleon's bluff and invite him and the French army to convert. Napoleon employs due casuistry by laying out the impossibility of circumcising 35,000 Frenchmen and depriving an army of alcohol. In return for not having full access to all the joys of the Muslim hereafter, the French are allowed to convert without circumcision and abstaining from alcohol. The subject was never taken further although General Ménou did in fact convert and married a Muslim.

47. See El-Enany (2006).

48. Laurens (1999, 3) notes the irony of the fact that the wasteland of modern Egypt was the direct result of Egypt's despots (whether the Pharaohs or the Mamelukes). The Pharaohs' despotism was also the acme of rule by absolutist divine right since Pharoahs saw themselves as kings and queens and gods and goddesses in one.

49. The helpful 'chronologie' at the end of Solé (1998) directly informs Appendix 3, translated and amended to include additional events relevant to later chapters.

50. This appendix is based on elements from the chronology of Solé (1998) not used in Appendix 3, and also Solé (1997), again translated and changed for the needs of this book.

51. My thanks here to the useful 'chronologie' in Moussa (2004, 1047–52).

52. There was a very clear demarcation between the explorer doing science in the field and the expert scientist in his laboratory-cabinet in a major institute to whom he was sending collections back. See Bourguet (1999, 31).

53. See Annexe 1 in Solé (1998) for the almost complete list of the 167 savants who constituted the Commission des Sciences et des Arts, drawn largely from the publication by Jean-Édouard Goby in the *Bulletin de l'Institut d'Égypte*, 38 (1957).

54. *La Description de l'Égypte*, prefaced by Fourier, sets out the ideology of the whole mission and expedition in Egypt. Its three main parts are (1) 'Antiquités' (2) 'Etat moderne', and (3) 'Histoire naturelle'. 1:1 'Le Zodiaque de Dendera'; 1:2 history of glassmaking first in Egypt (by Bondet); 2:1 topology of Alexandria area and of 'ville d'Alexandrie' find direct remapping in Flaubert's descriptions.

55. For example Edward Lane and Frederick Kreuzer.

56. See Edmond (1867).

57. For a recent study of 'phantasmagoria', including time travel and 'fancy's images', see Warner (2006).

CHAPTER 1

1. Du Camp (1993, 388).

2. *The Description d'Égypte*, often described as a 'monumental' work, the first part published in 1809 but not completed until 1828. Part II will discuss its contents and significance in more detail.

3. Even Foucault's advocacy of the *Tentation* as a 'bibliothèque fantastique' (1983) has failed to make this plethora less baffling because reading of its contents has largely not been undertaken.

4. Volney (1799) aimed to overturn 'picturesque' ideas about the Middle East (such as the *Lettres sur l'Égypte* by Claude-Étienne Savary (1749–88)) with rigorous descriptions of among other things Egypt's physical landscape, politics, racial mix of inhabitants, history of the Mamelukes.

5. See *Corr*, ii. 320 (letter to Louise Colet of 30 Apr. 1853). It may be from Volney that Flaubert gleaned information about the Copts. See Volney (1799, 65–7, Volney's emphasis): 'On prétend que le nom des Coptes leur vient de la ville de *Coptos* où ils se retirèrent, dit-on, lors des persécutions des Grecs; mais je lui crois une origine plus naturelle et plus ancienne. Le terme arabe *Qoubti*, un Copte, me semble une altération évidente du grec *Ai-goupti-os*, un Égyptien . . . les *Coptes* sont donc proprement les représentans des Égyptiens . . . tous ont un ton de peau jaunâtre et fumeux, qui n'est ni grec ni arabe; tous ont le visage bouffi, l'œil gonflé, le nez écrasé, la lèvre grosse; en un mot une vraie figure de Mulâtre. J'ai tenté de l'attribuer au climat, lorsqu'ayant été visité le Sphinx, son aspect me donna le mot de l'énigme. En voyant cette tête caractérisée *nègre* dans tous ses traits, je me rappelai ce passage remarquable d'Hérodote, où il dit *Pour moi j'estime que les Colches sont une colonie des Égyptiens, parce que, comme eux, ils ont la peau noire et les cheveux crépus*. . . . Quel sujet de méditation, de voir la barbarie et l'ignorance actuelles des Coptes, issues de l'alliance du génie profond des Egyptiens, et de l'esprit brillant des Grecs; de penser que cette race d'hommes noirs, aujourd'hui notre esclave et l'objet de nos mépris, est celle-là même à qui nous devons nos arts, nos sciences, et jusqu'à l'usage de la parole.'

6. See *Tent*, note 23. Gothot-Mersch is referring here to the Alexandrian geographies in the second, not the first tableau. See also Flaubert's descriptions of Egypt in *Corr*, i.

7. The cadences and triplicate qualifiers of this opening description are also highly reminiscent of the famous and much-noted opening of

Salammbô, but critics have again missed the connection here in the *Tentation*.

8. As noted in Part I, the heretic Nestorius also ends his days in the Thebaid. There is latent irony in Flaubert situating his Antoine there.

9. Foucault (1983, 106) argues that 'l'imaginaire se loge entre le livre et la lampe'. 'Real' twilights play a large part in the *Tentation* as well as metaphorical ones.

10. Antoine's opening words, 'Encore un jour! Un jour de passé' (*Tent*, 52) further connect this text with Beckett (1952). See Kenner (1962) for a study of Flaubert, Joyce, and Beckett.

11. See Davy (1985).

12. For the perspective on cities from a high point in nineteenth-century literature, see Neiland (2001, 58).

13. Thomas (1994) is not alone among critics for bringing his own prejudices, misinformation, and imprecision about the desert of the New Testament (let alone the Old) to his reading of the text.

14. See Laurens et al. (1989, 372–3).

15. Thomas (1994, 158) rightly connects these opening 'mirages' with the ensuing tableaux and their 'hallucinations' of sex, wealth, and power, and with the latest progress of nineteenth-century, industrial France.

16. Foucault (1983, section 3), also notes the futurity of Antoine's 'hallucinations', but does not particularize them to nineteenth-century science let alone religion.

17. Part I has already discussed Flaubert's removal of the medieval elements from earlier versions as evidence that a mock-medieval parody was not the 'end' of the work. We will be qualifying the dramatic ironies of Flaubert's treatment of the *Vita* in the seventh tableau/ chapter.

18. The spiritual nature of acedia is also noted by Chastel (1936), who studies the art historical representation of 'saturnism' or melancholia often symbolized in a saint and in St Anthony in particular. Chastel reads both the Brueghel and the Bosch 'St Anthonys' as pictures of the depths and heights of the melancholic imagination. Flaubert's representation of acedia is Catholic to the letter here. For Antoine's 'ego-defences', see Porter (1979). For recent studies of melancholia and abjection, see Kristeva (1980, 1987).

19. Tableau one obviously treats spiritual sloth, tableau two *spiritual* lusts, tableau three spiritual pride, and so on.

20. Withstanding is the most exemplary kind of spiritual warfare as outlined in Ephesians 6, especially verses 13–14 and 18. 'Tenir ferme', 'persévérance' are the French words used.

21. Biblical prophets and the Psalmist are renowned for their groaning and sighing as prayer responses to their worlds. See the Book of Job. This exhalation will be matched by the text's final one, the 'être la matière' outpouring.

22. *Correspondance d'Orient*, Lettre 123, in Moussa (2004, 585): 'Parmi tous ces débris des anciens peuples, le plus considérable est la nation des Coptes; on en compte encore cent soixante mille en Égypte... les Coptes ont toujours été chargés de mesurer les terres, de lever les impôts... Quoique les Coptes aient été persécutés, ils ont conservé en Égypte quarante-cinq églises, vingt-six dédiées à la Vierge, dix-neuf à saint Georges.... L'Égypte n'a point d'habitants plus patients, plus souples et plus dociles que les Coptes. Ils passent pour descendre des anciens Égyptiens; ils en ont le caractère triste et mélancolique; leur langue est devenue pour les savants comme la clef des hiéroglyphes.'

23. See *VA*, 43–4: 'Ses parents étaient des Coptes de bonne famille et des chrétiens;... l'ascèse est comme un métier qu'il faut apprendre graduellement... où on avance par la voie de la prière et de l'abnégation.'

24. Voragine (1998), henceforth *LD*.

25. Although Gothot-Mersch notes the reference from a modern translation of the *Vita Antoinii* to this 'enfant noir' in note 15 (*Tent*, 293), Voragine's text here names him specifically as 'luxure'. Hilarion will have some of the features of this 'enfant'.

26. There may also be a further layer to these Egyptian signs and symbols on the walls of a 'Temple'. After the Egyptian campaign, Bonaparte actively encouraged the 'Grand Orient' as a particularly French branch of Freemasonry to wrest its domination from the Scottish rite. Monge, Saint-Hilaire, and others on the expedition were all involved in Freemasonry on their return. See Solé (1997, 55): 'Une deuxième influence est exercée par la franc-maçonnerie qui reprend ses activités en France à partir de 1801. Napoléon souhaite contrôler et la détacher de l'Angleterre. Il s'y emploie avec l'aide de Cambacérès, grand maître du Grand Orient qui contribue à diffuser l'égyptomanie dans les loges. On voit se multiplier les temples du style pharaonique, les "diplômes de maître" illustrés par les sphinx ou les pyramides, les tabliers "retour d'Egypte".' See also Laurens (1999, 1): 'Cet ésotérisme dans lequel puise abondamment la franc-maçonnerie, fait de l'Égypte la terre des origines

de la civilisation et le lieu d'élection de la sagesse.' Étienne (1991) and Collaveri (1986) analyse the masonic 'missions' of Bonaparte in Egypt.

27. See also Davy (1985, 11): 'Les ermites extérieurs doivent abandonner leur famille, leur patrie, leur demeure. Les ermites intérieurs sont aussi affrontés à une séparation. Ils s'évadent de l'omnitude, de la conscience commune, des formes scléroses, des anti-humanismes et parfois de certaines formulations religieuses aliénantes.'

28. See *LD*, 90: 'Et un jour…les frères lui demandaient quel était ce malheur, il répondit, avec des larmes et des sanglots: "J'ai vu dans le ciel l'autel de Dieu entouré par une multitude de chevaux qui foulaient aux pieds les choses saintes; et j'ai entendu la voix du Seigneur disant: 'Mon autel sera souillé!' " Et, en effet, deux ans après, les ariens hérétiques rompirent l'unité de l'Église, souillèrent les choses saintes, et foulèrent aux pieds les autels chrétiens.'

29. See Luoni (1994, 152): 'Ce croyant dans l'Un, le seul risque qui demeure pour l'anachorète, c'est de s'exiler dans sa propre particularité.' Flaubert reserves for his Hilarion figure an 'Enlightenment Self'. From the perspective of the nineteenth-century French reader of the text, St Anthony was frequently quoted as the exemplary overcomer of the temptations of the world and for his celibacy and steadfastness to the true faith by the Pope and French cardinals alike.

30. See for example *LD*, 88: 'Un jour qu'il était ravi en esprit, il vit le monde tout couvert de filets étroitement unis. Et il s'écria: "Oh! Qui pourra s'échapper hors de ces filets?" Et une voix lui répondit: "L'humilité!" ' Section 2 of this hagiography ends with 'Antoine put librement s'élever dans les airs et redescendre' (*LD*, 89).

31. No critic has noted how the repeated 'J'ai + past participle' construction resonates with the Queen of Sheba's famous list of wondrous material possessions in tableau two, 'J'ai…j'ai…' (*Tent*, 82).

32. See *LD*, chs. 19, 107. Pachomius was an exact contemporary of Anthony and another Coptic desert father. The tiny detail concerning his insomnia directly relates spiritual matters with 'real' nineteenth-century scientific treatises on the subject (and on hallucination). See Maury (1848), also cited in Flaubert's bibliography for the *Tentation*.

33. Maunoury (1858, 5–6).

34. Orr (2009c) offers a study of the significance of the Maunoury text in Houbert's *Légende de saint Julien L'hospitalier*.

35. Given the final statement in Antoine's mouth above about self-martyrdom, Ammonaria's censure by the nameless elder only the more confirms her status of virgin martyr as a new type. See Warner (1985,

69): 'The shift from the rabid violence of the circus to the world of the hermitage or nunnery is a most important one to recognize in moral attitudes towards women, for it created one of Christianity's most important and enduring mythological types: the virgin martyr.'

36. See for example the story of the 'Onze mille vierges' which has firmly Breton roots and protagonists. Warner (1985, ch. 5) has also noted the peculiar sadomasochistic delight in the graphic accounts of torture and humiliation meted out to virgin martyrs.

37. Flaubert eliminates the love interest except as retrospective 'regret' since Antoine is at the end of his life and therefore in a place of great spiritual maturity thanks to overcoming the 'flesh'.

38. The Circoncellions (*Tent*, 112–13) saw in martyrdom the furthering of the apocalypse. Suicide bombers retain exactly this kind of reasoning in its excessive spirituality and ultimate self-annihilation.

39. See Orr (2000a, ch. 4) for further comment on these master–disciple relations and Chapter 3 below.

40. We will be returning to Seznec's major articles on the heresies and the problems for him of the Gymnosophist among them in Chapter 4.

41. For Didymus' central place in pro-Nicene and anti-Arian debates, see Ayres (2006).

42. See <www.newadvent.org> for the entry on 'Didymus the Blind'.

43. Denon (1802, 43–4).

44. See Gothot-Mersch (1986, 126). Here and in her edition of the *Tentation* she gives the biblical reference as 1 Kings 10: 1–13. She seems unaware that there is a second version of the story (with interesting differences as to its ending) in 2 Chron. 9: 1–12.

45. Leclerc (1997) fails to note this all important detail which clears Antoine of the 'bibliomancie' he rightly mentions.

46. Flaubert has also fully exploited the horror of killing one's own in *Salammbô* in his reworking of the Massacre of the Innocents in the Carthaginians' sacrifice of their children to Moloch.

47. See Hilaire (2003, chs. 16, 17).

48. See note 28 above.

49. Anthony the Great (250–356) was not present at the Council. However his dates show that Flaubert's reworking is quite within historically possible frames even though it is purely fictional. Here is perhaps his solution to presenting prophecy as the fulfilment of history which can only be seen with the hindsight of the longer future looking back. This is also one of the few episodes where Antoine judges and condemns, with a reaction strangely similar to the radical reactions of the Jews in the Scripture from Esther that Antoine has just glossed.

50. See Claude Mondésert's introduction to *Les Stromates: Stromate 1* (1954, 6–8).
51. Minois (1990, i. 72–3).
52. Alchemical and other attempts to find 'deep' meanings were particularly prevalent within Gnostic and Jewish Kabbalistic sects of the life and times of Anthony the Great, but were also pursued in medieval times. There is a tradition among the Antonines that is alchemical, but lies outside this study. See Tarade (1999).

CHAPTER 2

1. I am eschewing Freudian readings as anachronistic to the medical under-standings of the unconscious that Flaubert's text is so richly exploring, although see Bem (1979a) as the main Freudian reading of the *Tentation*. The Jungian reading Porter (1979) proposes sits more neatly than Freud with early nineteenth-century French psychology.
2. See Esquirol (1838) (in the 'calepin rouge' of the bibliography of the *Tentation*), Garnier (1852), and Maury (1848), whose works Flaubert much admired, as we will see in Chapter 5.
3. Flaubert himself suffered from both and so had first-hand experience of the mental effects of these illnesses. Some critics have seen Flaubert's *crises*—epilepsy is not the only diagnosis—as a source of Antoine's 'visions'.
4. Bem (1979a, ch. 8, 'La Tentation de la science et les voies du savoir') explores medical representation in Flaubert's novels, but not in *La Tentation*.
5. Leclerc (1997, 63) mentions these various intertexts of hells in very general terms and only with reference to later tableaux.
6. Unlike other key scenes these two have remained juxtaposed in the same order in all versions of the text.
7. Taine (letter to Flaubert of 1 Apr. 1874), quoted in *Tent*, 295. See for example Bem (1979a), Gothot-Mersch (1986), and Neiland (1998 and 2001). When much of the 1874 *Tentation* differs from its earlier versions, the latter are quick to point out that the juxtaposition (and importance) of Nebuchadnezzar and Sheba remains unchanged.
8. Neiland (2001) sees the seduction of the reader as a particular effect of this set piece.
9. Flaubert's penchant for food in excess and in pyramids in his works is well known, but taken to comic levels here which are almost self-mocking.

10. The 'disque d'argent' becomes the all important mirrors in tableau two that transport Antoine to two different epochs in the history of civilizations, via the giant mirror of Alexandria (*Tent*, 72) although it is of copper, and the mirror effect of the white sand in Constantine's hippodrome, the 'plaques d'orfèvrerie' (*Tent*, 74).

11. This parable is recorded in all four Gospels, Matt. 14: 13–21, Mark 6: 30–44, Luke 9: 10–17, and John 6: 1–14.

12. No critic to my knowledge has focused on Antoine's (imagined) violent orgy of revenge or its specifically religious motivations in the light of the text from Esther. A contemporary nineteenth-century parallel is the Muslim uprising in Cairo during the French occupation, where the Institut and its adjacent buildings were sacked and the books, instruments, collections, and boxes of specimens 'dont ils ignorent l'usage, et qui, à cause de cela, les exaspèrent' were destroyed (*Tent*, 72). The scene also shows in personal terms the destruction of pagan temples and relics that Antoine and Constantine discuss later in the scene.

13. The history of science also accords the lighthouse of Alexandria a giant mirror 'telescope', whereby ships on the horizon could be viewed. See Arago (1854, i. 155), a work in Flaubert's library according to Leclerc (2001).

14. Seznec (1949) and Heuzey (1953) explore modern intertexts which Flaubert grafted into Strabo's *Geography* to make his Alexandria 'ancient'.

15. See for example Neiland (2001). A further source that has never been explored by Flaubert critics is in fact the *Expédition d'Égypte*. A reproduction of 'Le Zodiaque de Dendera', offers a visual key to the whole. And Bondet's history of glassmaking as discovered first in Egypt provides Antoine's 'glasses'.

16. See Étienne (1991) and Collaveri (1982, 1986).

17. Edmond (1867, 19). This modern Egypt is at once nineteenth-century European, and the vision of Mohammed Ali.

18. The Samaritaine would open in 1871. See Crossick and Jaumain (1998) for more on these 'Cathedrals of Consumption' and Miller (1981) on the Bon Marché. Zola's *Au bonheur des dames* would first fictionalize this department store/story.

19. Edmond (1867, 74–5).

20. Gothot-Mersch (*Tent*, note 25) cites Seznec's identification of Labarthe as the intertext that operates this shift, but the text itself carefully makes the necessary 'geographical' links.

21. This image will return in *Un cœur simple* (*OC*, 169), but with the more familiar St Michael slaying the dragon.

22. There is a probable wink to the later Muslim rule in this crescent moon, but any link here with Islam would of course be anachronistic as far as Antoine is concerned.

23. It lies outside this study to explore in more detail Flaubert's attention to the art he saw in Constantinople at the end of his *Voyage d'Orient*, a text which Tooke (2000, ch. 4) discusses. She only mentions mosaics in Rome and does not deal with Constantinople. For illustrations of the Constantinople mosaics of the Virgin, see Cronin (1968, ch. 2).

24. Again, Constantine's throne is more than a comic copy of those of more illustrious rulers. In the sequel to the story of the arrival (and departure) of the Queen of Sheba in 1 Kings 10 is a section on Solomon's splendour and all the objects he makes of his massive amounts of gold, including 'a great throne inlaid with ivory and overlaid with fine gold. The throne had six steps...On both sides of the seat were armrests, with a lion standing beside each of them. Twelve lions stood on the six steps, one at either end of each step. Nothing like it had ever been made for any other kingdom' (verses 19–22). Flaubert's description is in fact an almost verbatim copy of the description of the throne room in Labarthe (1861). Orr (2009b) investigates this in more detail.

25. See also the mission statement of Champollion's mission to Egypt of 1828–9 (1868, 14). His finds in projected excavations were already allocated to the Louvre collections.

26. This is a trademark fantastic detail begging a 'real' referent. See the duc de Préval's remarks in *Bélial*: 'La matière est dans un éternel mouvement...Pourquoi n'en serait-il ainsi de l'homme? Aujourd'hui roi, pâlefrenier demain, cheval peut-être bientôt après' (*LP*, 5–6).

27. The full context is that this act by the Jews inaugurates the feast of Purim, a remembrance and thanksgiving for release from the persecution (and indeed decreed extermination) had Esther not interceded on behalf of her people at the risk of her own death. Flaubert seems to be making direct links between Old Testament persecutions and those by Roman emperors.

28. A work Flaubert read in his teens, it is cited in the bibliography of the *Tentation* (*Tent*, 283). Quotations from Apuleius' text (henceforth *GA*) are from the translation by Robert Graves (1950). The final transformation in *GA* is not only the return of Lucius' mortal frame after his numerous adventures as an ass, but also his initiations into the mysteries of Isis, the goddess who enables his return to 'normal', and the cult of Osiris.

29. *Tent*, note 27, and Daniel 2. Flaubert is clearly setting Antoine in the spiritual lineage of Daniel in other ways since Daniel's spiritual training also included rejection of choice foods for vegetables, and prayer and

fasting to seek God's revelation about Nebuchadnezzar's dream. Daniel is also set up as a seer greater than any magician or sorcerer of Babylon as Antoine will be framed against the arcane magic powers of Apollonius in tableau four.

30. Flaubert has already explored these themes in the first chapter of *Salammbô*, the Festin where the Mercenaries eat the Barca sacred fish.

31. Flaubert again copies Labarthe (1861) and his descriptions of the Emperor's Triclinium here.

32. See Daniel 4: 32–3, where Nebuchadnezzar 'ate grass like cattle'.

33. Even in the early *Correspondance*, Flaubert is fascinated with Nero and Sade (see for example *Corr*, i. 47–8).

34. See 2 Kings 24: 12b–14.

35. The translation of Edward Gibbon's *The Decline and Fall of the Roman Empire* is cited in the bibliography (*Tent*, 277) but specifically ch. 15, 'Progrès de la religion chrétienne . . .'.

36. Display of wealth to one's nobles and officials seemed customary for Eastern potentates as an unequivocal self-endorsement. King Xerxes (Esther's husband) throws a banquet for just such an occasion (Esther 1: 5–9). This may be a further intertext in Flaubert's mind given Antoine's exegesis from this book.

37. The verse is incomplete. Flaubert has omitted reference to Solomon's fame concerning the name of the Lord after his wisdom.

38. In her definitive article on the Queen of Sheba, Gothot-Mersch (1986) raises the dilemma that there is no sexual interest in the Bible story, but explains the enigma by precisely this move, seeing Flaubert's reworking as his incorporation of lust (*luxuria*) in all forms previously depicted by Luxure's daughters in earlier versions of the *Tentation*. Gothot-Mersch also admits that Antoine's emphasis on secret rather than carnal knowledge poses another intrinsic problem (127–8). To resolve it, she calls on the Queen of Sheba of Arabic legend, the Oriental Woman epitomizing 'à la fois—ou successivement—celle de la magie, du sexe, et des richesses' (133), rather than the scriptural quotation as her final point of reference. Her argument for this choice is that it also explains the clearly sexual connotations of the 'petite boite' (*Tent*, 81).

39. Gothot-Mersch (1986, 140) quoting fo 91r°. She comments that 'si elle représente toutes les femmes, tout le mystère féminine . . . Flaubert a même jusqu'à envisager d'en faire le symbole de toute la sexualité, mâle et femelle'.

40. Both Gothot-Mersch and Neiland point out the similarities between this box and Marie Arnoux's 'coffret'. Neither critic mentions Pandora's box.

41. Neiland (2001, 130).

42. Bem (1979a, 286) concludes unequivocally on the importance of the Bible as 'source, modèle, miroir, objet fascinant', and Flaubert's ambivalence to it. What follows is not ambivalence.

43. See Tournier (1980). See also Orr (2009a).

44. This dress is highly reminiscent of Salammbô's when she sets out on Schahabarim's orders as the Priestess of Tanit to overcome Mâtho. Sacred and earthly seduction and power play combine here as they seem to do in *Tentation*.

45. See also the fantastic description of Isis's dress and accoutrements in *GA*, ch. 17, 227–8. There are too few overlaps with Flaubert's description for this to qualify as a rival text to Revelation, however.

46. Gothot-Mersch (1986) documents both creatures and moreover contends that Sheba's legs are hairy because she has depended too much on the non-biblical, legendary versions of Sheba with her magical powers synonymous with the Land of Sheba.

47. See for example Kselman (1983, 92). Roman Catholic theology has also always interpreted Revelation 12 as a reference to the Virgin Mary.

48. See Cronin (1968) and Warner (1985, 115): 'The image of the Virgin as queen is scored so deep in western imagination that many Catholics will think of her as a medieval monarch. When she appeared in visions in Knock in Ireland in 1879 and at Pontmain in France in 1871, she wore the long dress, sash, veil, and crown of the thirteenth-century feudal lady.'

49. See Bem (1979a, ch. 5).

50. Warner (1985, 249) again gives the details of the Virgin's attire: 'veiled, an azure sash, barefoot except for two roses.... Bernadette always maintained that the parade of Raphaels and Botticellis shown her did the Virgin little justice.'

51. Renan (1992, 19, italics in the original), henceforth *VJ*. In the note which immediately follows, Renan adds 'La devotion de Lourdes semble prendre les mêmes proportions' (*VJ*, 319).

52. This is another instance where Gothot-Mersch challenges the 'authenticity' of Flaubert's remake of Antoine, note 30 (*Tent*, 295).

53. There may be some overlap with Fotis, the slave-girl/lover in *The Golden Ass*.

54. Or a 'Gretchen' equivalent by Bem (1979a), who notes the absence of any 'femme-ange' (90–1).

55. See Warner (1985, ch. 15, 'The Penitent Whore'). There is also the story in Voragine of Mary of *Egypt*, which counterbalances the many

hideously martyred virgins, a 'penitent whore' who is clothed only in her own hair (*LD*, ch. 56).

56. Antoine's rejection of Sheba and the Devil as Possession behind this whole scene also endorses his chastity. The shift or substitution of Hilarion for Sheba points also to homosexual dynamics at work. Flaubert was very familiar with Diderot's *La Religieuse*, for example.

CHAPTER 3

1. Seznec (1949, 34) draws from Du Camp's *Souvenirs littéraires* the cautionary remark by Bouilhet regarding Flaubert's too erudite an Antoine: 'Voyant les livres empilés sur sa table... il lui disait: *Prends garde! Tu vas faire de Saint Antoine un savant, ce n'etait qu'un naif...*'. If evidence is needed that Flaubert in fact heeded this warning, tableau three exemplifies it. Hilarion remains the 'savant' throughout. Surprisingly for a critic so attuned to Flaubert's massive intertextual project, Seznec barely mentions Hilarion or his roles.

2. Note 39 (*Tent*, 296).

3. Lilley (1981). Without Hilarion (as the 'clef du mystère'), the *Tentation* 'resterait, comme la première version, un lieu de désorganisation, d'anarchie, où temps et espace ont perdu leur valeur humaine, où la frontière entre notions opposées est confuse, où des combinaisons monstrueuses acquièrent une permanence effrayante. Hilarion suggère une méthode d'organisation des thèmes et une interprétation nouvelle des faits et des connaissances' (21).

4. Orr (2000a) investigated the *Vita Hilarionis* of Jerome and the historical Hilarion in more depth than any prior critics had undertaken to counter the non-theological arguments presented by Lilley (1981) and Starr (1984).

5. Starr (1984). Orr (2000a, 129) dismissed Starr's reading of Hilarion/Geoffroy Saint-Hilaire as 'fanciful' because of Flaubert's clear adherence to the Hilarion in church history. All Flaubert critics have blocks and this was mine. Part II and Chapter 5 will return to Starr's foundational study concerning the 'science' of the *Temptation*, a study not referred to by Wulf (2004) (<http://flaubert.univ-rouen.fr/revue/revue4/03wulf.pdf> (accessed 4 Nov. 2007)).

6. Flaubert's other novels also rely heavily on often shady go-betweens. See Orr (1999) on Lheureux in *Madame Bovary* as another 'devilish' figure, or the many 'transfuges' in *Salammbô*, including Spendius. Hilarion is *not* the Devil, and it is equally questionable that he is as Seznec claims

a 'personnification *satanique* de la Science' (1949, 14), since the Devil takes this role fully in tableau six. Hilarion's science is altogether the acme of its *human* faces.

7. Also bowdlerized in this tableau is the question and answer form of the catechism, which had of course not as yet been formulated. See Ware (1993, ch. 3) for further discussion of the longer-standing developments of the widening theological differences between Orthodox and Roman Catholic Churches from the end of the fourth century which lies outside the time that concerns Flaubert.

8. See Orr (2000a). Ironically, of course, Damis merely fulfils the (biblical) role of a disciple not becoming greater than his master, a position which Hilarion is obviously testing by his onslaught on all of Antoine's positions as his former master. Damis as echo of Apollonius (and the mocking effect thereby created) is reminiscent of the final refrain of *L'Éducation sentimentale*.

9. See Luke 22: 24–7. Flaubert will come back to the idea of the greatest being the least, and the least the greatest, with his reworking of John the Baptist in *Hérodias*. Hilarion's increasing size matches his increasingly powerful bid to demoralize Antoine totally. Space does not permit a psychological analysis of this onslaught, but Hilarion's roles in blowing apart Antoine's religious beliefs (as examined in this chapter), and then 'scientific' world view (investigated in Part II), are embodied in his increasing monstrous form.

10. In his preface to the *Vita Hilarionis*, Miniac (1992) uses the word 'pastiche' of Jerome's approach: 'il "excède": il irrite et il dépasse' (7), and, regarding the life of Hilarion, that it is difficult to 'démêler d'un nombre important de données légendaires ou imaginées' (9).

11. This donkey-like braying laughter further connects with the Midas/*Golden Ass* intertexts of tableau two. In the iconography of St Hilarion, he is often depicted astride a donkey because his severe fasting and poverty so decimated his health and strength that he needed a form of transport to allow him to fulfil his missionary journeys. The famous lion in the hagiography of Jerome also *contra natura* befriends a donkey.

12. There is probably a very sly wink to the 'science' of craniology here, not least the alleged superior size of the Caucasian and of course male brain as 'proof' of greater intelligence.

13. As Lilley (1981, 11) has noted.

14. See Miniac (1992, 65), henceforth *StJ*: '(Ses parents) l'envoyèrent à Alexandrie où il fut confié aux soins d'un professeur de lettres, et là, autant que le permettait son jeune âge, il donna des preuves éclatantes de ses qualités intellectuelles et morales.'

15. There is perhaps a 'homosexual hermeneutics' also at work, to borrow the title term from Schehr (1995), but historically grounded within the 'master–disciple' educative relationships of ancient Greek male schooling.

16. The historical Hilarion was the pioneer of Palestinian monasticism (building on St Anthony's Egyptian model) before he planted monasteries in Sicily, Dalmatia, and Cyprus. See Farmer (1992, 229). Like Anthony, Hilarion was not martyred for his faith, but experienced similar 'persecutions' from other bishops and the many who sought him out for miracle cures and deliverance from evil spirits so that his solitude was constantly denied him. Jerome's *Vita* informs his readers that Hilarion's monastery in Palestine was destroyed by Julian the Apostate in 362–3 (*StJ*, 102).

17. My emphasis. See the whole story in *StJ*, 63–116. Jerome uses the term 'enfant' after a section describing Hilarion's body as 'gracile et menu' (*StJ*, 67). Hilarion was also known as having very frail health.

18. See *W*, 39: 'A characteristic figure in Orthodox monasticism is the "elder" or "old man" (Greek *gerōn*; Russian *starets*, plural *startsy*). The elder is a monk of spiritual discernment and wisdom, whom others— either monks or people of the world—adopt as their guide and spiritual director. He is sometimes a priest, but often a lay monk; he receives no special ordination or appointment to the work of eldership, but is guided to it by the inspiration of the Spirit.... The elder sees in a concrete and practical way what the will of God is in relation to each person who comes to consult him; this is the elder's special gift or *charisma*. The earliest and most celebrated of the monastic *startsy* was St. Anthony himself.' Hilarion of course also represents the *puer senex* archetype and is an oxymoronic figure *par excellence* throughout the *Tentation*.

19. This is especially true of the *Vita Hilarionis'* accounts of Hilarion's wrestling with evil spirits, the devil, sorcerers (of Aesculapius in Memphis, Egypt), and with a hideous serpent in Epidaurus in Dalmatia. The 'authentic' detail behind Hilarion's foreknowledge of who has recently visited Antoine (*Tent*, 88) is the famous episode where the Hilarion of the *Vita Hilarionis* 'sees' his master Anthony's death. As ascetics and individuals at the work of faith against the tide of their times, both Anthony and Hilarion took on their adversaries in matters material, political, and spiritual, including involvement in rebutting Arianism. Hilarion in fact experienced even more difficult circumstances than Anthony before him by having to contend with the Emperor Constantius, who was an overt supporter of Arian bishops.

20. See Panagia (2006).

21. For an English account, see Farmer (1992, 230). It may also be significant that the Battle of Poitiers marked the turning point of Islam's sweeping invasion of Spain and France, about one hundred years after the Prophet Muhammad's death in 632. Flaubert is very careful in the *Temptation* to avoid all analogy with Islam by turning further east to the Levant and India.

22. There is also Hilary's challenge of Pope Leo as 'juge suprême' who had fallen to Arian heresy. Although Hilary was not invited to the Council, the Pope goes off to relieve himself, but dies of dysentery. The earth rises under Hilary's seat and he leads the other bishops back to true faith. The year is AD 340, in the reign of Constantine.

23. Farmer (1992, 229–30), which also records Hilary as a Western Athanasius. The 'one substance' is in Greek the *homoousios*, Athanasius' central contribution to the Nicene Creed and the pivotal term against which all heresies may be judged 'unorthodox'.

24. Flaubert will elide various saints (drawn from Voragine) for similar ends of comparison and contrast in his *Trois Contes*. See my discussion of St Hubert as particularly French variant of St Julian in Orr (2000a, ch. 5).

25. Whether Geoffroy Saint-Hilaire is Étienne or Isadore then becomes a moot point that Starr also elides.

26. Matt. 4: 5–7 (where it is the second temptation); Luke 4: 1–12 (where it is the third and final temptation).

27. See for example the contemporary review of the *Vie de Jésus* by Réville (1864).

28. Seznec's blindness is probably the most serious since he specifically mentions Renan's (and Strauss's) *Vie de Jésus* as principal intertexts (1949, 16–17) and dwells on Flaubert's use of Renan's *Marc Aurèle* and dialogue with Renan concerning the finished *Tentation* (38–9). Seznec the classicist obviously won out over Seznec the critic in Renan's scientific sense.

29. With the exception of Guillemin (1963), French critics in the main have eschewed every vestige of the religious in Flaubert to emphasize his religious syncretism. Personal faith is however very different from profound intellectual interest in matters religious and spiritual, a premiss that non-French critics such as Bowman (1990), Pasco (2002), and Orr (2000b) have been able to exploit in more nuanced studies.

30. Lilley (1981, 11) notes the following characteristics in the tone of Hilarion's words: 'clarté, rigueur étonnante, autorité mêlée d'affection, sévérité tempérée d'amour'; but makes no intertextual attribution to any real source for this voice.

31. In an editor's note to the Folio edition of the *Vie de Jésus* Jean Gaumier underscores a major theme of the work, 'le contraste entre Judée aride et la souriante Galilée' (note to p. 128 on p. 503). Renan's words on martyrdom may also be those behind Hilarion's: 'Le martyre ne prouve pas la vérité d'une doctrine, mais il suppose une telle concentration d'énergie, il donne une telle intensité de joie! "Je ne pense pas qu'il y ait au monde de joie plus vive que celle du martyr. Que de fois… j'ai maudit notre critique de nous avoir rendu le martyre impossible."

Cette nostalgie de la spontanéité qui fait croire et affirmer, sera celle encore de l'historien du Peuple d'Israel: "Vivent les excès, vivent surtout les martyrs! Ce sont eux qui tirent l'humanité de ses impasses, qui affirment quand elle ne sait comment sortir du doute" ' (vi. 1205, quoted by Retat (1977, 115)).

32. *VJ*, 20: '*Gardons-nous d'appliquer nos distinctions consciencieuses, nos raisonnements de têtes froides et claires à l'appréciation de ces événements extraordinaires, qui sont à la fois si fort au-dessus et si fort au-dessous de nous. Tel voudrait faire de Jésus un sage, tel un philosophe, tel un patriote, tel un homme de bien, tel un moraliste, tel un saint. Il ne fut rien de tout cela. Ce fut un charmeur. Ne faisons pas le passé à notre image*' (italics in original).

33. This is precisely the move Flaubert also makes regarding his Antoine who works no miracles in the *Tentation*, but who thus also fails to offend believing readers since his sanctity is taken as read.

34. Renan also highlights the distinctively philosophical language in the Gospel of John (which appears later than the Synoptic Gospel accounts) in his *Vie de Jésus*.

35. Note that Flaubert's Antoine is very correct in his terms and does not use either the word 'Anathema' or 'Hérésies' for example.

36. In the extensive bibliography for the *Tentation*, there is only slight but very intriguing evidence that Flaubert read up on Eastern Orthodox theology alongside that of the Church Fathers. The opening 'Calepin noir' contains the work of 'Saint Basile le Grand' who is venerated by the Orthodox as a founding Church Father.

CHAPTER 4

1. See Queffelec (1988, 275).
2. See Seznec (1949) and Bowman (1990). Unless otherwise stated, all references to Seznec below are to this work.

3. Séginger (1997b). Extensive examination of the 'critique génétique' has not included following up Flaubert's references in the manuscripts concerning particularly 'religious' subject matter.
4. Orr (2000b) and Pasco (2002).
5. Cunningham (2006, 1).
6. Seznec also states clearly where his own critical lacuna lies, in ecclesiastical history (religion in another guise). As everywhere in his scholarly *œuvre*, Seznec reads primarily as a classicist and humanist.
7. Neither Lilley (1981) nor Starr (1984) picks up on Hilarion's absence.
8. See Orr (2000a).
9. Parisot (2002, 8) squares the circle rather well: 'les hérésies pouvaient provoquer des schismes; la peur des schismes faisait convoquer les conciles, et les conciles établissant le dogme, permettaient de dénoncer des hérésies.'
10. While identification of specific intertexts in Seznec is a daunting act to follow, there are many which can in fact be traced to several sources, since the regular practice of Creuzer-Guigniaut and others in the nineteenth century was to quote at length from various Greek sources which were themselves already based on multiple sources.
11. In spite of the authority of Foucault's famous reading of the *Tentation* as a 'bibliothèque fantastique' (1983), it is debatable whether he in fact consulted any of the works he lists from Flaubert's bibliography.
12. Seznec (1940–1).
13. See Heilbrun (1999) for a fascinating study of cathedrals as observatories.
14. Labarthe (1861). Orr (2009b) examines the importance of Labarte's text for the authentifiable details of the basilica, not least as the 'real' source of the Ophites' room.
15. Augustine's famous work of the same name strictly speaking has as yet to be written although it appears under the 'mythologies' section of Flaubert's bibliography.
16. This scene in tableau four is therefore set up by the 'hippodrome' descriptions in the Labarte intertext used by Flaubert in the second tableau, linked to the roaring lions decorating Constantine's throne. His throne then transforms into that of Mani as first speaker of tableau four.
17. Two possible intertexts lie behind the 'figuier' reference here. In the *Vita Hilarionis*, ten figs eaten at sunset constituted Hilarion's meagre diet. He is also known to have constantly suffered from ill health! In an article in the *Dictionnaire des merveilles et curiosités de la nature et de l'art*, vol. 44 of the Abbé Migne's *Nouvelle Encyclopédie théologique* (of which

other volumes are in Flaubert's bibliography), its huge mythological and comparative religious significance is underlined. Offerings of figs were made to Ceres, to Saturn, to Mercury, to Bacchus, to the Charybdis, in the mysteries of Isis and Osiris. The etymology of the word 'sycophant' (fig-bearer) and hence its meaning as 'calomniateur, délateur' is also discussed (412). The Gynosophist is therefore the antithesis of all the gods of fertility and plenty that people tableau five as the dry stick of the fig tree from which their offerings come.

18. See Leclerc (1988).

19. See for example the Albigensian heresy of medieval France promoted by the Cathars, or the Protestant heresy of the Reformation launched by Luther but which rapidly splintered into various groupings not unlike the many in tableau four, all with their 'heresiarch'.

20. Seznec's authority and erudite solutions have therefore stood, only to be endorsed by other very specialist evidence such as that provided by Gothot-Mersch (see *Tent*, note 38, where she further resorts to the structure of Flaubert's first *Tentation* to explain Simon and Apollonius as 'rivaux du Christ, comme des incarnations de la sagesse et des êtres doués de pouvoirs surnaturels. Le sage de l'Inde, émule de l'ermite égyptien, nous paraît faire la transition entre les martyrs...et les deux figures de la fin').

21. Indeed, the further specialist question for theologians is the definition of a belief system as a 'heresy' rather than as a 'schism', a 'sect', or another and separate 'religion'.

22. Seznec does note that Manicheism is not a Christian heresy, but resolves the problem by enlisting works on Mani in the 'heresies' subsection in Flaubert's bibliography. He does the same for Apollonius.

23. Only a very few of the texts under this specific rubric (by Pluquet, Sts Augustine and Epiphanus) strictly fit the bill, while other relevant works on heresy, by for example Tertullian, are listed under by far the largest category, 'Christianisme (exégèse)', in which Beausobre's *Histoire critique de Manichée et du manichéisme* is also found.

24. There were in fact Egyptian Gymnosophists as well, but the Indian provenance of Flaubert's is a vital link with the Buddha in tableau five.

25. This order would resolve another major problem that has escaped critical notice concerning Mani's opening position in the tableau, namely that historically Mani founded his sect *after* the heresiarchs Marcion and Montanus.

26. Given his final word, 'L'Anéantissement', his religion is rather that of 'le Grand Rien' and hence arguably a better bridge with the cold emptiness of space Antoine discovers in tableau six.

27. (1817) henceforth *DH*. Seznec does not put this work on his key list of Flaubert's reading for tableau four, although arguably he mentions it *en passant* via Maxime Du Camp's *Souvenirs littéraires,* where Flaubert is described as lost in 'lectures excessives, dont il eut trouvé un résumé suffisant dans le *Dictionnaire des Hérésies* et dans la *Légende dorée*' (15). What follows shows that Pluquet was more than merely 'suffisant'.

28. His moralizing tone is exemplified ten pages later: 'les principes religieux de ces Mages ne conduisaient ni à la piété, ni à la vertu, et ne rendaient les hommes, ni bons, ni religieux, mais superstitieux et méchans. Par-tout où la croyance du bon et du mauvais principe a été un dogme religieux, on a fait beaucoup de mal pour plaire au mauvais principe, et fort peu de bien pour plaire au bon' (62).

29. His *De Prescriptionibus* is cited in Flaubert's bibliography. Alternative terms for 'hérésies' are precluded by such fanatical and pejorative usage.

30. While these are all 'doctrinal' texts, 'rouleaux' were a cheap and easily portable medium, running to tens of metres in length. In the exhibition 'Livres d'Arménie: collections de la BNF' (Feb.–Mar. 2007), the rouleaux on display were 'Phylactères': ' En Arménie, le livre rouleau est presque exclusivement réservé à la confection de livres de prières aux vertus talismaniques et magiques. Pouvant atteindre huit mètres de long, de faible coût et se transportant facilement, il est souvent destiné aux marchands. On y trouve mêlées des prières plus sulfureuses contre le diable et les démons ainsi que des histoires édifiantes. Il est souvent illustré de peintures naïves.' For a longer version of this text, see the catalogue of the exhibition (Vernay–Nouiri 2007, 96). This function as talisman seems fortuitous in the position Flaubert inserts his rouleaux in the *Tentation*.

31. 'Mensonges' is an interesting development of the 'songes' which prefaced tableau two.

32. Matter (1843).

33. See Collin de Plancy (1846). See also Bardeau (1977, 8): 'Il faut rapporter à la Gnose alexandrine la totalité des sectes dérivées et secondaires dont les adeptes ont reçu le nom d'*Ophites* en raison du rôle donné dans leur système au serpent primitif d'Eden, le fameux *Ouroboros* des hermétistes grecs.'

34. St Anthony the Great will himself go on to become the father of monasticism (in Eastern Orthodox and Western Christendom), with his legacy continuing to live in the twenty-first century.

35. See Didyme l'Aveugle (1992). If the useful introduction also mentions the importance of St Hilary of Poitiers (see Chapter 3) in the Council of Constantinople and the theology of the Holy Spirit, Didymus' 'sérénité'

and 'ton irénique' are specifically mentioned (p. 36 and on pp. 38–9): 'Mais ce qui frappe, c'est à la fois sa tranquilité pour défendre, discuter, argumenter, couper, en somme, les mailles du filet hérétique enserrant le Saint Esprit, et ses efforts lucides pour déployer les états et les richesses de l'Esprit, fixer son origine et ses relations divines, pour proclamer ses charismes, le montrer l'œuvre dans l'âme des fils de Dieu, et agiter au besoin les sanctions redoutables.' Flaubert of course does not show the work of the Spirit any more than he did Christ, except by default and counterpoint through Antoine.

36. The Gymnosophist's seemingly monotheistic 'Grand Tout' swallowing up all creation is like Mani's by also being completely (pre-) deterministic.

37. See Parisot (2002, 26–7): 'Iranien d'origine, poète, peintre, médecin,...surtout prophète inspiré passa en son temps, pour une manifestation du Paraclet.... hétéroclite en apparence, cette doctrine était en fait bien unifiée (et) combinait des éléments judéo-chrétiens, gnostiques, voire hindouistes ou bouddhistes, comme le thème de la transmigration des âmes, au traditionnel dualisme iranien réformé par Zoroastre, en enseignant que, tels Ormuzd et Ahriman, deux principes antagonistes, l'un de lumière et de bien, créateur du monde spirituel et des choses invisibles, assimilés au Dieu Père du Nouveau Testament, l'autre de ténèbres et du Mal, créateur du monde matériel et des choses visibles, assimilé au Yahvé de l'Ancien Testament.' We will be returning to the God of the Old Testament who concludes the 'twilight' of the gods in tableau five.

38. On the contrary God, the no less ineffable 'I Am' of the Old Testament, retained a remnant of his *people* the Jews in exile, whether under Pharaoh, Xerxes, or Nebuchadnezzar.

39. For the impact of Arianism and Nicaea on Trinitarian theology, see Ayres (2006).

40. For a recent study on Arianism, see Wiles (1996).

41. See Bardeau (1977, 7–21). The *Pistis* was 'découvert dans quelque cachette de l'immense nécropole thébaine où se réfugièrent, bien après l'extinction du paganisme antique, les magiciens de toute tendance.... Il appartient a'abord à la bibliothèque du docteur Askew (d'où son appellation de Codex Askiewianus), puis il fut acheté par le British Museum en 1785.... Une première version latine fut éditée en 1851 à Berlin par un orientaliste allemand, M. G Schwartze. C'est à la traduction française de J-P Migne à laquelle nous nous rapportons ici, parue sans sons *Dictionnaire des Apocryphes* en 1856 à Paris' (7–8).

42. For an English translation of the *Pistis Sophia*, see Schmidt (1978). The further significance of Sophia regarding Hilarion's 'Désires-tu connaître

la hiérarchie des Anges, la vertu des Nombres' is that she was the thir-teenth eon, an 'ange' and a 'nombre', a 'germe' and a 'métamorphose'.

43. His *Tentation* could also not be further from the genre of 'Catholic writing', to which Mauriac and Bernanos belong, or writers such as Chateaubriand in the nineteenth century defending Catholic values.

44. See Flaubert's letter to his mother of 5 Jan. 1850 (*Corr*, i. 558–9) quoted in Part I n. 44.

45. See for example Erdan (1855) and Réville (1870). Other references on 'mystiques' include Görres and St Theresa. Both figures are writ rather large in another dictionary in the Abbé Migne's huge, 60-volume *Encyclopédie théologique*, the *Dictionnaire de mystique chrétienne ou essai d'encyclopédisation historique et méthodique* (vol. xxxvi, Paris, 1858), where for example the article on 'ascension extatique' (there are a num-ber in *La Tentation*) is cross-referenced to 'extases'. Under 'extase', the 'real' variety (of saints) is clearly distinguished from 'ce degré culminant d'hypnotisation qu'on a nommé l'extase magnétique' (421). It is likely that this dictionary provided Flaubert with information for the fetid smell discussed above, for under 'Discernement des Esprits' (335 and quoting Görres) St Anthony's smelling of 'une odeur insupportable' turns out to be a demon-possessed stowaway. When exorcised, he loses his foul smell. This story takes up the whole entry.

46. Chapter 2 in Erdan (1855, i) deals with 'Magnétiseurs'.

47. By Collin de Plancy (1846, 96–122). I am convinced that Flaubert con-sulted these volumes to recrystallize particular speeches by heresiarchs once he had read longer specialist works such as Matter or Beausobre, since there are striking similarities in turns of phrase or replications of certain details. See for example the entries for 'abraxas', 'Basilide', 'Circoncellion', 'Oannès'. This also seems to me the source for the Simorg-Anka in tableau two.

48. See Buisset (1984, 12 and 154).

49. See Charlton (1963).

50. See Juden (1984).

51. The quotation inside the quotation is from Schelling in Juden (1984, 183).

PART II

1. See Cuthbert (2003) for a closer engagement with both these terms in the late works of Flaubert.

2. Antoine very much reflects Clement of Alexandria's 'true' Gnostic (the subject of *Stromates VI*), the portrait of which is put in a nutshell in

Camelot's introductions to *Les Stromates II* (1954, 9): 'Le gnostique, seul véritable philosophe, s'exerce à la contemplation, en même temps qu'à la pratique des commandements, et il forme les autres à la vertu. Il cherche Dieu et s'efforce de parvenir à la plus haute contemplation, science véritable, connaissance de la sagesse, inséparable de l'activité vertueuse. Cette gnose, ou science véritable, n'est pas la fausse gnose déjà condamnée par saint Paul, elle est une "démonstration scientifique" des vérités révélées et l'on entrevoit qu'ici le terme "gnose" recouvre deux activités de l'esprit nettement différentes: la contemplation dont il vient d'être parlé, et le raisonnement théologique.'

3. Seznec (1949).
4. Carmody (1958), Starr (1984) and Cuthbert (2003, ch. 1).
5. Vacherot (1846–54), subsequently *HCEA* with volume and page number. In volume i, book 1 (chs 1–2) covers Plato and his disciple Aristotle, ch. 3 stoicism; book 2 ch. 1 deals with the establishment of Greek philosophy in the 'Orient' (Egypt), ch. 2 looks at the Jewish Alexandrian school and particularly Philo, ch. 3 focuses on the importance of Christianity and its theology. Book 3 considers the Eclectic tendencies of the Greek schools. Volume ii, book 1 looks at Potamon, Ammonius Saccas, Origen, and Longinus; book 2 the successors of Plotinus (of his Enneads). Flaubert may have been drawn to p. 124 and syntheses of 'cosmic' gods in the Enneads and polytheism listed as 'Dieux créateurs' (Jupiter, Neptune, and Vulcan), 'Dieux animateurs' (Ceres, Juno, and Diana), 'Dieux organisateurs' (Apollo, Venus, and Mercury), and 'Dieux conservateurs' (Vesta, Pallas Athene, and Mars) to order his fifth tableau. Book 3 examines the School of Athens (and its uptake of the three Nicene 'hypostases'. Volume iii (publication was interrupted by the 1848 revolution) covers the closure of the pagan schools, and their legacy into the modern era.
6. Bowman (1986, 20) is the only critic to my knowledge who discusses these works as context for Flaubert's 'discours sur le mythe' in the *Tentation*. Bowman contrasts Matter's 'pavé érudit et catholique' with Simon's 'éclectisme cousinien'. Vacherot's work is 'un des monuments de l'humanisme romantique'.
7. Simon (1845, i. 1–2).
8. Seznec (1949, ch. 3) asserts that Chassang is the principal source for Flaubert's Apollonius section.
9. Simon (1845, i. 97). I suspect Simon (and also Flaubert) to have in fact drawn this directly from one of his main sources for the period, Clement of Alexandria's *Stromata* and specifically book 1 (1954, 99–101): '(67, 3) Il saute aux yeux que les Barbares ont rendu des

honneurs exceptionnels à leurs législateurs et instructeurs; ils les ont appelés "dieux". (68,1) C'est, à mon sens, parce qu'ils ont senti l'immense bien qui leur venait par le canal des sages que le peuple entier des Brahmanes, des Odyrses, les Gètes, la race Égyptienne, ont vénéré ces hommes, fait de la philosophie une institution d'État, étudié leurs écrits comme des textes sacrés. De mêmes des Chaldéens...(69, 2, 6b) Zoroastre, le mage Perse a eu Pythagore comme émule et les tenants de la secte de Prodicos se vantent de posséder les livres secrets de ce Mage....(71, 3) Ainsi donc, la philosophie, ce trésor si fructueux...rayonna parmi les nations; plus tard seulement elle arriva chez les Grecs. (71, 4) Ses maîtres furent en Égypte les prophètes, en Assyrie les Chaldéens, en pays Gaule les Druides...en Perse les Mages...en Inde les Gymnosophistes et d'autres philosophes barbares; (71, 5) car il y en a deux sortes, dites Sarmanes et Brahmanes. Parmi les Sarmanes, les Hommes des bois, comme on les appelle, n'habitant pas les villes, n'ont pas de maison. Ils s'habillent d'écorces d'arbres, se nourrissent de fruits sauvages, boivent de l'eau dans le creux de leur main, ignorent le mariage et la procréation...(6) Il y a aussi dans l'Inde ceux de tendance qui obéissent aux préceptes de Bouddha, qu'ils vénèrent, vu son extrême sainteté, comme un dieu.'

10. See for example Simon (1845, i. book 2 'La Philosophie de Plotin'). The second chapter is 'De la dialectique', and ch. 3 'La Trinité de Plotin' (266–87).

11. Matter (1844, ii. p. v) (italics in the original), henceforth *École* 2 and page reference. 'Alexandre' is the final word of this quotation.

12. Addison (1996) is the only critic to deal seriously with the 'numerology' of Flaubert's works, on elisions of dates and times, but she rarely deals with the *Tentation*.

13. Note that Ptolemy is allegedly from the Thebaid where Flaubert specifically situates his Antoine at the very beginning of the *Tentation*.

14. See <http://www-groups.dcs.st-and.ac.uk/~history/Biographies/Ptolemy.html>, 'Grasshoff writes... *Ptolemy's "Almagest" shares with Euclid's "Elements" the glory of being the scientific work longest in use. From its conception in the second century up to the late Renaissance, this work determined astronomy as a science'* (2, italics in original).

15. See Levy (1995, 19).

16. For a history of the Jardin des Plantes contemporary to Flaubert, see Cap (1854). For modern histories (which seem to ignore Cap), see Blanckaert et al. (1997). See also Yanni (1999), Spary (2000), Deligeorges et al. (2004), Jaussaud and Brygoo (2004). For a discussion of the 'Culture of Science in France' see Fox (1992).

17. See Cuvier (1864) for his 'scientific' report on his ethnographical findings and of course on her unusually long genital labia. See also <http://news.bbc.co.uk/2hi/africa/1971103.stm> for the coverage of the event.
18. See the chapter on her in Bondieson (1999), henceforth B.
19. Barbarians of indiscriminate kinds produced monsters and anomalies of all shapes, colours, and sizes, whereas Greeks were the civilized norm in all aspects.
20. Guides were available to these explorers on how to preserve and pack specimens collected over lengthy journeys. See for example Pouchet (1893).
21. See Juden (1984, 195–6).
22. Foucault (1969). See also Laurens (1989) and Laurens et al. (1989).
23. See Geoffroy Saint-Hilaire (2000).
24. The Institut was tasked for example with producing gunpowder, finding fuel to replace wood to mass produce bread, and the making of beer without hops.
25. Quoted in Solé (1998, 38).
26. See ibid. 49–50.
27. See for example Solé (1998, 47–49) and Ortega (1999).
28. Moreh (1975) and Cuoq (1979).
29. See Orr (2008a).
30. Gray (2004, 13–14).
31. See *HCEA*, ii. 425–6.
32. See Gray (2004, 47).
33. Appendix 5 has as a basis some of the scientific developments of nineteenth-century France listed by Thiher (2001).
34. *EC*, 227–8. See also Hazlett (1991, 156–7).

CHAPTER 5

1. Seznec (1940). The standard secondary-school curriculum for boys included Virgil, Homer, and Horace.
2. Creuzer (1825, 1829, and 1838) and Burnouf (1844). These gods are largely transposed into the parade in tableau five of the 1874 text.
3. Seznec (1993) draws hugely on his previous work on the *Tentation* in its first and final versions, but does not return to these questions either. For a recent classicist contributor to Flaubert studies see Laüt-Berr (2001).
4. I am grateful for Lawrence Porter's reminder that Haig (1986) investigates 'theolocutives' (aphorisms) and hence that the 'voice of God' at the end of the scene can of course be read in this vein as self-parodic. We

will discover a more precise source for Flaubert's inclusion of the voice of God below.

5. See Séginger (1987, 1988). Bowman (1981, 1985, 1990) has always argued against syncretism by exploring Flaubert's more properly eclectic portrayals of God and the gods based on understanding of the *Tentation*'s Alexandrian contexts and also nineteenth-century Eclectics such as Cousin. Although the *Légende de saint Julien* not the *Tentation* illustrates his study, Bart (1973) remains one of the best critical appraisals of Flaubert's pantheism.

6. Starr (1984, 1074) and by contrast to 'Hilarion's brilliant display of erudition'. All further references to Starr below are to this article.

7. The work of Helein-Koss (1991) is the exception. It is Hilarion's role to link the 'lisible', the 'risible', and the 'visible' that concerns her, rather than Antoine's laughter. Flaubert's exploration of the 'grotesque rire' emerges from the invented alter ego of his youth, le Garçon, and is redolent of the 'Rabelaisian' Crepitus for example.

8. Hence we have only the 'voix de Dieu' at the end of the tableau.

9. See Du Camp (1987).

10. Flaubert's *Salammbô* pivots around the worship of Moloch.

11. Among few critics to discuss Crepitus (who participates in all three versions of the *Tentation*) see Bem (1979a, 81–2): 'Crépitus enfin est *un dieu qui n'existe pas!* et Flaubert le savait depuis 1849' (82).

12. Tignor (1995, 157).

13. Maury (1860).

14. Maury's work (henceforth *Magie*) is referenced in the famous bibliography to the *Tentation* under the 'Mythologie' rubric. Flaubert's reliance on Maury on all manner of subjects is evident from this bibliography as I have also argued (Orr, 2005). It also goes without saying the date of Maury's study precludes its use in versions of the *Tentation* before the final reworking.

15. Solomon was also a scientist in the more modern sense. See 1 Kings 4: 20 ff.: 'God gave Solomon wisdom and very great insight, and a breadth of understanding as measureless as the sand on the seashore. Solomon's wisdom was greater than the wisdom of all the men of the East and greater than the wisdom of Egypt. He was wiser than any other man, including Ethan the Ezrahite—wiser than Heman, Calcol and Darda, the sons of Mahol. And his fame spread to all the surrounding nations. He spoke 3000 proverbs and his songs numbered a thousand and five. He described plant life, from the cedar of Lebanon to the hyssop that grows out of the walls. He also taught about animals and birds, reptiles and fish. Men of all nations came to listen to Solomon's

wisdom, sent by all the kings of the world, who had heard of his wisdom.'

16. See Leclerc (2001, 78) where Flaubert's copy of Maury's *Magie* has 'annotations' noted against it.

17. Maury in fact quotes some of the same sources that Flaubert used to authenticate this historical melting pot, namely Vacherot (1846–54).

18. 'En Italie, S. Antoine a de son côté pris la place de *Consus* ou de *Neptunus Equester*, le dieu des courses de cirque; il est devenu le patron des chevaux' (154). Flaubert's Antoine of course visits Constantine's palace in tableau two and in a very 'odd' passage watches the Fathers of Nicaea brushing the horses' manes, painting their hooves, or removing their droppings (*Tent*, 75). As replacement saint of horses for *Neptunus Equester* the following in the text becomes clear: 'Antoine passe au milieu d'eux. Ils font la haie, le prie d'intercéder, lui baisent les mains.' Maury's *La Magie* is therefore not confined in its reworking to tableau five.

19. See Maury (1848, 1857).

20. The word 'apotèlesmatique' refers to the 'science of influences'. This Babylonian 'observatory' is an earlier version of tableau four's 'basilique'.

21. Flaubert's ambiguous punctuation in this single sentence is semantically rich, the commas after each element suggesting both equivalence and apposition, to elide the ancient and early modern world view, Hilarion's 'le ciel, comme l'éternité, reste immuable!', with proven nineteenth-century scientific observation.

22. It would be tempting to include the word 'theodicy' here—it comes originally from Leibniz's *Théodicée* (1710)—particularly with reference to Hilarion's role as herald of science and the Devil in tableau six, Leibnizian elements to Hilarion's science, and Flaubert's interest in Leibniz's thought. We have however been careful throughout to preclude terms that are 'anachronistic' to the life and times of Sts Anthony and Hilarion.

23. See Pouchet (1859). For discussion of this guide and the Rouen collections, see Orr (2008a).

24. Rouen was in fact a national centre in the nineteenth century for the production of wax models for use in anatomy lessons for trainee midwives and *officiers de santé*, but also for the display cases of natural history where original pieces were too fragile, or where cross-sections were required. See Blanckaert et al. (1997).

25. While Hilarion's mythical, shaman-like status and functions as intermediary between life and death are eminently behind Flaubert's reworking of him, especially here in tableau five as study of comparative

mythography, his 'real' 'human' faces are what most significantly distinguish him from the Devil.

26. While Starr states that he neither wishes to use reference in the *Correspondance* to natural historians, nor 'Hilarion as a thinly veiled Geoffroy Saint-Hilaire' (1075), the article in the end does the latter by flitting too lightly over its mass of ideas and connections.

27. Space does not permit a study of the gods Flaubert interestingly *omits* from tableau five, but Hermes is one of them. Mercury is inserted instead for his equivalence as part of the Greek pantheon, but only in the description of astrological clocks (*Tent*, 188) and somewhat humorously as a statue atop one.

28. See for example Guyader (1998).

29. After the Expédition Geoffroy Saint-Hilaire undertook a further scientific mission to Portugal to set up a national Museum of Natural Science in 1807.

30. Cuvier was the head of the Protestant Churches throughout his long career at the Jardin des Plantes. See Rudwick (1997). Geoffroy Saint-Hilaire never denied the need of God (as first mover or cause). This scientific aspect of the master–disciple relationship in the *Tentation* also further complements my own earlier study of Hilarion (Orr, 2000a).

31. This segment of the *Tentation* is larded with Flaubert's own experience of Egypt, his fainting fit in the Pyramid of Giza, his observation of the bird droppings on the ancient monuments (and link to Crepitus to come). A psycho-biographical reading of this scene is ripe for further investigation, especially when so much of Flaubert's reflections on revisions to his first *Tentation* come on the back of his trip with Du Camp and stormy affair with Louise Colet.

32. See Geoffroy Saint-Hilaire (2000, 120). The former link was somewhere along the line chosen across the Isthmus of Suez for the Suez Canal, opened in 1871 by the Empress Eugénie. It was for this event and its new Egyptian Queen that Verdi wrote *Aida*.

33. Geoffroy Saint-Hilaire (2000, 86–92 and letter of 16 Aug. 1799 to Cuvier) puts this phrase as a rhetorical question to the master of ichthyology as if it were a monstrous suggestion. It is the real evidence of the moment when Geoffroy Saint-Hilaire begins seriously to question Cuvier's fixity of 'règnes' or theories of cataclysm pre and post-diluvium.

34. In his bid to possess Antoine here, Hilarion's seductions bespeak a veiled but no less homosexual force.

35. For a potted history of geology, see Pouchet (1868, section 3).

36. For a cogent study of Lamarck and the differences between Lamarckian 'transformisme' and Darwin's theory of evolution, see Jordanova (1984).
37. See *Corr*, iii. 131 (to Edma Roger des Genettes): 'Vous vous étonnez de ma rage antireligieuse, en voici la raison immédiate: c'est qu'à chaque moment dans mes études, je touche à la Bible, et dans la Bible, au Dieu actuel, à celui des Catholiques, qui m'exaspère de plus en plus par son côté restreint, borné, oriental, monarchique. C'est un Louis XIV, un sultan, je ne sais quoi d'humain, qui me semble, en définitive, très piètre et dont la conception me paraît très impie.... Quand la concile de Trente a eu décidé qu'il ne fallait plus s'occuper de la question de *Grâce*, de ce jour-là, le christianisme a commencé son suicide; il s'est jugé lui-même: il a reculé devant la philosophie.'
38. See Gobineau (1984) and Cuvier (1864). For a recent study of nineteenth-century French doctrines of race, see for example Taguieff (1998) and Moussa (2004).
39. See Bem (2006) and Ogane (2006) among few works that investigate Flaubert's 'anthropologies'.

CHAPTER 6

1. For Lecuyer (1967, 47), the Devil's giant form is part of 'l'immense, le gigantesque, le démesuré même, [qui] font partie intégrante du "baroque" ' and the baroque of the *Tentation* itself.
2. Seznec's silence on it probably explains the dearth of more recent work. The blank is particularly surprising in Séginger (1997a), and is tantamount to footnotes in Neiland (2001) and Gothot-Mersch's edition of the 1874 *Tentation*, which only mentions links between the 'Devil's ride' and *Smarh*. For a recent assessment of *Smarh* as a reworked *Faust* see Seabrook (2007–8). For dedicated articles on the sixth tableau, see the short pieces by Koskimies (1972) and Leclerc (1997).
3. See Wright (1995) for a study of cosmology in antiquity, and Chapter 4 for the history of the terms 'macrocosm' and 'microcosm'.
4. Gothot-Mersch's edition of the *Tentation* references the ideas of Spinoza to explain such conundrums of this tableau. Spinoza is undoubtedly an intertext, one Flaubert was reading as Alfred Le Poittevin was dying. See also Brown (1996) on Flaubert's Spinozism.
5. For the omission of the word 'theodicy' see Chapter 5 n. 22. See also Juden (1984, 205–6): 'Tous les dieux étant des attributs de la divinité suprême, avaient le serpent pour symbole, rappelant sous la forme d'un

cercle le monde de la création, l'âme universelle et même le temps éternel. Signifiant tour à tour le génie du bien et celui du mal, le serpent présidait à la vie et à la mort.... Le titre de *grand conducteur* désigne les fonctions du dieu-serpent qui parcourant toute la nature, y régit la vie et la mort.' Flaubert's Devil is certainly a 'grand conducteur'. Juden also notes the importance of the 'dieu-serpent né de la vase déposée au fond de l'eau' in Matter (1843) in Gnostic sects, not least the Ophites (211), whom Antoine has visited in tableau four.

6. See Chapter 5, pp. 172–3. See also Swerdlow (1998) for the Babylonian theory of the planets.

7. See <http://www-groups.dcs.st-and.ac.uk/~history/Biographies/Ptolemy.html>.

8. Flaubert may also have consulted Pouchet (1853) on the medieval monk-scientist Alfred Le Grand.

9. This section comes immediately after the cup of gold coins reworked in tableau two.

10. Gillispie (1997, 195) notes Laplace's very dry report of this event that Guy Lussac ascended to 6,000 metres. Laplace was more interested that 'the proportions of oxygen and nitrogen in the atmosphere turned out to be about the same as at ground level'.

11. See Cuoq (1979, 87) and Moreh (1975, 112–13).

12. Interestingly, the opening descriptive phrase of tableau six, 'Il vole sous lui [Antoine], étendu comme *un nageur*' (*Tent*, 207, emphasis added), underlines the 'nautical' and hence 'astronautical' implications or what is to follow.

13. See Poniatowski (1983) and Perrin (2000). The Montgolfiers' hot air balloons had prior to this campaign already been a subject of caricature. See Gillispie (1989) and Faure (1983).

14. See *Corr*, ii. 139 (to Louise Colet): 'Hier j'ai été voir à Rouen une ascension aérostatique de Poitevin; c'est fort beau. J'ai été dans une vraie admiration.'

15. Antoine's gloss of Solomon's science in tableau one further prefigures this law of attraction and repulsion that is played out in sexual terms in tableau two.

16. The 'Archi-Galle' in tableau five seems to play little part except for the reverberations of his name, which are equally pertinent to the discovery of Neptune by Galle. Airy then tried to have Adams named as co-discoverer. Adams and Le Verrier remained aloof from the controversy and became close friends.

17. Because clearly visible with the naked eye, the comet of 1843 was much discussed in France.

18. Cuthbert (2003, 12) sets out the Laplacean outlook (gradual elimination of God) as 'the epistemological foundation for the positivists for the nineteenth century and for the modern sense of science' as only what can be proven by observation. Although one of very few critics to moot Laplace in connection with Flaubert's late works, Cuthbert does not take further the Laplacean allusions.

19. Laplace went on to lead this Bureau, as well as the Paris Observatory.

20. For a biography of Laplace see Sochon (2004).

21. Sochon (2004, 249). Lagrange, Boussuet, Legendre, Biot, and Lacroix were also members of section one, Geometry.

22. Gillispie (1997, p. vii).

23. For a very full list of the many fields in modern science which are indebted to Laplace's geometry, see <http://cerebro.xu.edu/math/Sources/Laplace/index.html>.

24. See <http://www-groups.dcs.st-and.ac.uk/~history/Biographies/Laplace.html>, 3.

25. Sochon (2004, 97).

26. See Laplace (1776). They have the same bewildering effect as the Gnostic systems in the *Tentation*.

27. See Hahn (2004, 59–60).

28. <http://www.math.unicaen.fr/~reyssat/laplace>, 8. See also <http://www.mahs.tcd.ie/pub/HistMath/People/Laplace/RouseBall/RB_Laplace.html> (3) for the anecdote expanded to include Napoleon's retelling of Laplace's reply to Lagrange 'who exclaimed, "Ah! c'est une belle hypothèse; ça explique beaucoup de choses." '

29. See Gillispie (1997, 243). Laplace did not support the new chemical atomic theory, since Berthollet's chemistry of affinities and his notion of chemical forces between bodies in proximity looked much more like gravitation.

30. <http://www.math.unicaen.fr/~reyssat/laplace>, 4.

31. 'Il pousse l'approximation à un degré bien supérieur aux travaux de ses prédécesseurs, permettant ainsi d'expliquer et prévoir des phénomènes secondaires par rapport aux modèles de l'époque et de les confronter à une observation de plus en plus précise et rigoureuse.' <http://www.math.unicaen.fr/~reyssat/laplace>, 6.

32. <http://www.math.unicaen.fr/~reyssat/laplace>, 7.

33. Fontenelle (1973).

34. This clinching argument 'c'est tout' is recurrent in Flaubert's works and as I have suggested elsewhere (Orr, 2004, 114–15) always implies an 'encore'.

35. For a refutation of mechanistic implications of Laplace's Demon see Green (1995). Green contends that 'a fully "demon-computable" world...would be incompatible with the nature of animal and human intelligence' (7).

36. Antoine here then also prefigures a Cartesian method of proposing doubt as the way to reconstruct what is (including a God).

37. The pterodactyl was one of the most important 'intermediary' forms in the fossil record to explain the transformation of creatures from land to air. Intermediaries are thus not the same as the hybrid monsters of the imagination but 'normal' forms.

38. See Minois (1998, 3): 'Loin d'être une créature irrationnelle, il résulte des efforts de l'esprit humain pour trouver une explication logique au problème du mal.'

39. For a more detailed reading of Flaubert's Devil as a French Mephistopheles see Thiher (2001, 85–8).

40. Steffan (1968, 9).

41. Bem (1979a) references this scene in Byron, but does not analyse or expand upon her observation.

42. See Karkoulis (2007, 279) for a fuller discussion of Cain's motives and motivations.

43. In *Cain* there are several moments when characters have 'flashing eyes', for example in Act II. Flashing eyes have been a trope to link the episodes in tableau four.

44. Steffan (1968, 6–7).

45. Byron (1822, pp. vii–viii). This edition was published in Paris.

46. Karkoulis (2007, 273) and Steffan (1968, 29). Steffan also quotes a more concise version of Byron's preface to *Cain* in a letter of 19 Sept. 1821 with a more precise elaboration of the 'notion of Cuvier', 'that the world has been destroyed three or four times, and was inhabited by mammoths, behemoths and what not, but *not* by man till the Mosaic period, as, indeed, proved by the strata of bones found' (8).

47. Cuvier (1812, 1–2).

CHAPTER 7

1. Kearney (2003, 3–6).

2. In this Antoine also reflects the moment where Christ was tempted by the devil to throw himself from the Temple mount so that the angels might rescue him, and the moment on the Cross where he experienced

abandonment by God and then accepted the death that is also God's redemption of mortality itself.

3. See Žižek (2002) and his questioning of Barthes's 'effet du réel'. Although Žižek is talking of the horror of the images of the collapse of the Twin Towers, 'the Real itself, in order to be sustained has to be perceived as a nightmarish unreal spectre. Usually we say that we should not mistake fiction for reality . . . the lesson of psychoanalysis here is . . . *we should not mistake reality for fiction.*' This is the lesson of the *Tentation* that this book is proposing.

4. See for example Pohle (1965), Vadé (1977), Evrard and Valette (1999, 15–17), and Paré (2001, 123–6).

5. See for example Starr (1984), Séginger (1987), Nancy (1994). Testa (1991–2, 139) considers the end a desexualized 'Unio Mystica'.

6. As argued by for example Bernheimer (1976–7), they suggest the mind of Flaubert.

7. Of note are Seznec's detailed source criticism from the classics to support the 'medieval' quality of the monsters including the Unicorn, or their allegorical meanings as 'modern' psychologies by Digeon (1946), Feyler (1977), and Porter (1979).

8. Potentially this is a more forced structural 'mirror' than the one previous critics noted in tableau two, the mirror of the lighthouse of Alexandria that beams Antoine to Constantinople.

9. While much ink has been spilled on the Sphinx and the Chimera, Leclerc (1997) is the only critic to my knowledge who has commented on this figure, remarking on its ambiguous and composite nature.

10. In the Introduction, we chose not to renegotiate a key fact galvanized by psychoanalytic critics, that Flaubert's mother had recently died as he was completing the final version of the *Tentation*. Space does not permit the more interesting intertextual engendering at work here, the obvious links between Goethe's Faust, part I and the first *Tentation*, and Faust, part II (especially the Mothers) and the final *Tentation*.

11. See Chastel (1936).

12. See Walter (1996), Tarade (1999), and Bricault (1992) for the wider ramifications of the St Anthony legends.

13. It again lies outside this study, but Antoine's confrontations in tableau seven, with 'woman', 'death', the other (the monsters), and his epiphany of ontology illustrate in fiction Levinas's steps in the discovery of 'être' as distinct from 'l'existant' and hence not an absorption by the other. See Levinas (1979).

14. See Bondeson (1999, 48).

15. See also Feyler (1977, 162–3) for his attempt to classify the monsters of tableau seven in five orders of 'fables': first, monsters 'par confusion de règne et de genre', second, monsters of 'transformations de grandeur', third, monsters 'par modification d'organes', fourth, 'monstres composantes', and finally, 'par indétermination'.

16. All these possibilities, and also 'panspermie', were being debated in the famous Pouchet–Pasteur debates about growths of organisms in so-called sterile conditions. See Pouchet (1861).

17. The most famous definition of epigenesis was Rudolf Virchow's (1821–1902) theory of cells published in 1858 epitomized in the epigram, 'omnis cellula e cellula' (every cell originates from another living cell like it), coined by Raspail. Pouchet turned this to his advantage in his ongoing arguments for 'hétérogénie' against the new 'chemical' theories of Pasteur.

18. See Seznec (1949, 75).

19. For a 'fantasmatic' reading of the monsters see Bem (1979b).

20. See for example French and Greenaway (1986) or Healy (1999) for studies in English on Pliny's contributions to science.

21. See for example Cuvier (1841), the first of eight volumes completed posthumously by M. Magdeleine de Saint Agy.

22. Although *Smarh* is frequently cited by critics as an early version of the *Tentation*, Flaubert's *Une leçon d'histoire naturelle genre commis* (*OC*, 100–2) presents an equally if not more important early work for the conception of the final *Tentation*.

23. For example Feyler (1977, 72) sees the Sphinx as a 'figure de mystère, de volupté' and the Chimera 'le symbole de labour'; Evrard and Valette (1999, 15) see them as masculine and feminine principles respectively. For Paré (2001, 123), the sphinx is the 'idéal flaubertien d'impassibilité muette' whereas Séginger (1987) sees the Chimera's openness to the ideal as the model for the Flaubertian artist.

24. See Tort (1983).

25. See Beyls (1999, 70) for a discussion of Cuvier's adamant refusal to engage with human fossil remains, some of which were discovered in Germany in the early 1820s. Gabriel de Mortillet (1821–98) was a strong critic of Cuvier's antediluvian ideas and the holding back of human palaeontology. His own work was devoted to studying flint implements and hence human origins.

26. See Deligeorges et al. (2004, 30). Geoffroy Saint-Hilaire went blind in 1840 and suffered from 'desert blindness' during the Expédition.

27. See for example Seznec (1949, ch. 4) and Feyler (1977).

28. The technical term and classification is 'quadrumanes' as opposed to 'bimanes'.
29. Geoffroy Saint-Hilaire (1826, 20–1). 'Acephales' are also a classification of micro-organism. See Pouchet (1841).
30. Geoffroy Saint-Hilaire (1826, 48).
31. See Jaussaud and Brygoo (2004, 80).
32. See Flourens (1858).
33. For example Cuvier (1999, 57) for the 'Martichoras'.
34. Cuvier (1999, 54–8).
35. It lies outside this discussion, but Cuvier's demolition of the myth of the ibis by his careful reclassifications of living ibises is a case in point. The appendix to Cuvier (1999) provides the full account.
36. Reading via Cuvier also puts paid to the symbolic readings of Helein-Koss (1992) following Butor (1970a), that these are all monstrous representations of the vices.
37. See Bondeson (1999, 162–7).
38. Cuvier (1999, 58).
39. Geoffroy Saint-Hilaire (2000, 64). There are other reverberations concerning the domestication of the 'Temple' 'Cynocéphales'. Acclimatization of species was part of the mission and programme of the Jardin des Plantes in which Frédéric Cuvier and Geoffroy Saint-Hilaire were actively involved.
40. See Orr (2005) for Flaubert's reworking of Irish elks in the stag in *Saint Julien*.
41. See Cuvier and Brogniart (1811). Some of the larger creatures in the lengthy description of monsters before the arrival of the Unicorn are reminiscent of the *Megatherium* or *Megalonyx* that Cuvier discovered and classified.
42. This scene is Flaubert's reworking of onslaughts of the demon-animals in the Egyptian tombs in the *Vita Antonii* to 'prepare' the final appearance of Christ in the disc of the sun. It is also reminiscent of the second hunt in *La Légende de saint Julien l'Hospitalier*.
43. See Cuthbert (2003, ch. 3).
44. Cuvier (1999, 59–60).
45. See Pouchet (1841, 204) on 'bubals'.
46. George Pouchet's guide to the Rouen Musée collections (1859) specifically draws attention to the importance of fossil planktons in the formation of limestones.
47. Flaubert may also be poking fun at creationist interpretation of marine fossils found in rocks at the tops of mountains as belonging to the time of

Noah's ark. Pliny the Elder more scientifically understands small marine fossils in the Pyramids as lentils.

48. Flaubert may very well have borrowed heavily from Pouchet (1841, 316–20) on 'Ammonites', and not only the fact that they are the 'moules de ces animaux' (317). Pouchet also discusses Cuvier's discovery in 1802 of another kind of ammonite called the 'spirule'—'Dans les siècles d'ignorance on les a souvent prises pour des serpents pétrifiés' (319) and notes that 'Pline et Solin . . . les nomment Pierres sacrées, les comparant à la forme des cornes d'un Bélier . . . et qu'on les trouvait près du temple de Jupiter Ammon. . . . On apprend par les lettres de Père Calmette . . . que les Indiens révéraient les Ammonites et leur rendaient une sorte de culte' (320). All of these elements are richly entwined in the *Tentation* as we have seen.

49. The English 'Cuvier', Lyell, also used a similar inductive method to 'read' life forms by the rocks in which their fossils were embedded.

50. Emerson's famous 'transparent eyeball' passage in 'Nature' is an interesting parallel description of life, especially since Emerson experienced a moment of epiphany in the Jardin des Plantes in 1833 on seeing Cuvier's gallery collections.

51. See for example Cuthbert (2003).

52. See the particularly strong German criticism of Müller-Ebeling (1997) and also Harter (1998).

53. In Leclerc (2001), the inventory lists *Cosmos*, beside which is the word 'annotations'.

54. See Orr (2004). While I did not treat the *Tentation* in this essay, its finale presents a geological 'post mortem' *par excellence*, Cuvier fashion.

55. See Bartelink (1994, sections 9 and 10). Flaubert's use of this passage and inversion of demons back into animals is, as I argue elsewhere, a key intertext for his *Légende de saint Julien l'Hospitalier*, Orr (2009c).

56. It is not perhaps without some small irony that some of the simplest structures of zoophyte have 'star' or aureole shapes. See Pouchet (1841, 516), which deals with 'Animaux intermédiares ou transitionnels. 1° articulés rayonnés'. In a later subsection, the 'Classe des Zoophytaires' comprise 'Animaux rayonnés, pourvus d'une simple couronne de tentacules ordinairement pinnés. Presque toujours un polypier calcaire ou corné' (576).

57. See Latour (1999, ch. 5).

58. See Maurel (1999, 8–12).

59. See the biography of Georges Pouchet in Jaussaud and Brygoo (2004). They mention Pouchet as adviser concerning Flaubert's *Bouvard et*

Pécuchet. This study amply proves that its 'diptych' is as vitally scientific and perhaps the more so for its aesthetic challenge in maintaining ancient and modern scientific perspectives in balance to avoid anachronism in either direction. See also Fischer (1997).

60. Dord-Crouslé (2000, 12) mentions Flaubert's indebtedness to, and friendship with, George Pouchet, but dates this around 1875 and for Flaubert's science in *Bouvard et Pécuchet*.

61. For a study of Bouilhet see Raitt (1994).

62. Although it lies outside this study, there is very strong evidence from the vocabulary of the whole of Bouilhet's *Fossiles* that he had read the same books as Flaubert, namely Humboldt's *Cosmos* and Pouchet (1841).

63. See also Flaubert's letter to Louise Colet of 21 Aug. 1853 (*Corr*, ii. 404): 'L'autre jour, en plein soleil, et tout seul, j'ai fait six lieues à pied, au bord de la mer.—Cela m'a demandé tout l'après-midi. Je suis revenu ivre.— Tant j'avais humé d'odeurs et pris de grand air. J'ai arraché des varechs et ramassé des coquilles.—Je me suis couché à plat dos sur le sable et sur l'herbe.—J'ai croisé les mains sur mes yeux et j'ai regardé les nuages. Je me suis ennuyé. J'ai fumé. J'ai regardé les coquelicots.'

64. See Minois (1990, i. 74). See also Hello (1897, 183): 'Pour connaître la création, il faut ne pas l'adorer. Il faut la voir telle qu'elle est. L'œil qui la perce comme un voile peut aller plus loin qu'elle.'

CONCLUSIONS

1. The realism of the *Tentation*, namely that civilizations fall as well as rise, is particularly poignant in the light of the 1870 Franco-Prussian War.

2. This assertion also includes my own earlier work on the importance of master–disciple relations as model for the deeper structures of the text (Orr, 2000a).

3. See Lilley (1981).

4. The two senses of natural come together insofar as Flaubert's Antoine offers no theological leadership (whereas St Anthony did fulfil this role regarding Arian and other heresies) and his final paean to the wonder of creation is not in the least an apology for English Natural Theology as part of evolutionary debate.

5. See Orr (2000a).

6. For a more searching study from the same received ideas see Thiher (2001).

7. Rather narrow critical anti-clericalism disguised as 'scientific' critical theories has relegated important religious contexts, themes, and literary texts to specialist corners of nineteenth-century French studies. Flaubert's *Tentation* is a particularly overt challenge to its critics to read the theology and church history that Flaubert read. It seems no small coincidence that the most recent work on religious topics in the *Tentation* has come from Anglo-American, not Francophone critics.

8. We examined Flaubert's reworking of debates about just such a 'corne' (three lines from the end of the quotation) for example in tableau seven (the 'Unicorne' and the ammonite as 'unicorne').

9. The image and discussion issues directly from Flaubert's earlier letter of 16 Jan. 1852 (*Corr*, ii. 30–1).

10. See Leclerc (1988).

11. Colet as female 'Hilarion' to Flaubert as 'Antoine' also proves in the fullness of her mind and body to be an eminently modern, overwhelming, 'Queen of Sheba'. Like Flaubert's fictionalization of this figure in the *Tentation* she too must be eradicated decisively from the text at an early stage. See also *Corr*, ii. 283, a further letter to Louise Colet: 'On a compris jusqu'à présent l'Orient comme quelque chose de miroitant, de hurlant, de passionné, de heurté. On n'y a vu que des bayadères et des sabres recourbés, le fanatisme, la volupté, etc. En un mot, on en reste encore à Byron. Moi je l'ai senti différemment. Ce que j'aime au contraire dans l'Orient, c'est cette grandeur qui s'ignore, et cette harmonie de choses disparates.'

12. See *Corr*, ii. 137 (letter to Louise Colet): 'Tout le talent d'écrire ne consiste après tout que dans le choix des mots. C'est la précision qui fait la force.'

13. See Dord-Crouslé (2000, esp. 15–20).

14. For further reading on gender and science see for example Harding and O'Barr (1987), Keller (1985), Keller and Longino (1996), Schiebinger (1993), and Spary (2000).

15. See Orr (2007) for a counter-claim to the accepted verities about male-only science at the Jardin des Plantes in the early 1820s (thanks to women's legal position under the Code Napoléon, exclusion from his new university, and from schooling that included classics and science subjects).

16. Porter (2001, 77–8). The further quotations in the next sentence from this article are from pp. 79–80

17. This black and white photograph may also be viewed on the internet at <http://www.eastman.org/ne/cromer/m197900300003_ful.html>.

18. *Corr*, ii. 239 (to Louise Colet) on the subject of Du Camp's *Légion d'honneur*: 'Admirable époque (curieux symbolisme! comme dirait le père Michelet) que celle où l'on décore les photographes et où l'on exile les poètes (vois-tu la quantité de bons tableaux qu'il faudrait avoir fait avant d'arriver à cette croix d'officier?).'

19. Flaubert's letters variously recount the same 'facts' about Egypt to his mother, Bouilhet, or other male friends.

20. Bem (1979a, 165) intriguingly posits Flaubert 'dans la lignée d'un Balzac "zoologiste", d'un Zola "biologiste", d'un Jules Verne "ingénieur". Il est l'héritier de Cuvier, le contemporain de Darwin et de Claude Bernard', but never follows up her intuitions.

21. Flaubert's famous bibliography as recorded by Leclerc (2001) does offer some signposts, some of which I have followed up here, including Humboldt's *Cosmos*. My other hunches have been richly rewarded by lateral thinking about Flaubert's science friends, including the Pouchets.

History of the Early Christian Church; Egypt as Part of the Roman Empire

64	Nero, Great fire of Rome; persecution of Christians in Rome
70	Mark's Gospel
c.85	Gospels of Matthew and Luke
c.85/90–c.165/168	Ptolemy (Claudius Ptolemaeus)
c.90	Gospel of John
90–5	Domitian demands worship as a god; persecution of Christians; Revelation of John
97–117	Trajan; growth of Gnosticism
c.100–c.160	Valentinus
c.127–41	Ptolemy is making astronomical calculations in Alexandria; production of his *Almagest*
c.140–202	Irenaeus (his *Against Heresies* written c.197)
144–	Marcion active in Rome; Marcion's expurgated *New Testament*
c.150	Apuleius' *Golden Ass*
c.150/160–c.230/240	Tertullian
c.150–211/216	Clement of Alexandria
c.156	Emergence of Montanism, the new Phrygian sect of prophets
c.160	Martyrdom of Polycarp
161–80	Marcus Aurelius (emperor and Stoic philosopher); persecution of Christians; growth of Montanism
168	Death of Justin Martyr (his works included *Against Heresies, Against Marcion*)
177	Massacre of Christians at Lyon; growth of Sabellianism
c.185–c.254	Origen of Alexandria
c.197	Quartodeciman (Easter controversy)
205–70	Plotinus
c.215	Tertullian becomes a Montanist
c.216–77	Mani
218	Origen, teacher in catechetical school of Alexandria

History of Nineteenth-Century France: State and Religion

First Republic

1792	Law granting divorce
1793	Cult of Reason established along with the Revolutionary Calendar
1794	(7 May) Cult of the Supreme Being established
1794	(18 Sept.) Suppresson of the budget for religious practices (the Budget des Cultes)
1795	Freedom granted for religious expression
1798	Malthus, *Essai sur le principe de population*
1800	Bank of France created
1801	(15 July) Concordat between Napoleon and the Pope
1802	Chateaubriand's *Génie du Christianisme*; (Apr.) law concerning the equal status of other recognized churches (Reformed Churches, the Confession of Augsburg (Lutheran))
1804	Code Napoléon (Code Civil)
	(2 Dec.) Coronation of Napoleon by the Pope in Notre-Dame Cathedral
1805	End of the Revolutionary Calendar.

First Empire

1804–15	Napoleon I Emperor of France
1806	Imperial University created
1808	Jews were allowed to practise their religion with leadership by rabbis (but synagogues were not given any financial subsidies until after the July Monarchy)
1809	Conflict between the Pope and Napoleon
1814	(6 Apr.) first abdication of Napoleon

The Restoration (1814–30)

	Reign of Louis XVIII (brother of Louis XVI)
1814	(August) Pius VII re-establishes the Jesuits, the Inquisition, and the Index

100 Days

1815	(1 Mar.) Napoleon returns from Elba; (18 June) Waterloo; (22 July) second abdication of Napoleon

1815	(July) Return of Louis XVIII to Paris
1816	Suppression of divorce
1817	Joseph de Maistre, *Du Pape*; Lammenais, *Essai sur l'indifférence en matière de religion*
1821	5 May: Death of Napoleon I
1822	Société des Missions Évangéliques set up in Paris. Œuvre de la Propagation de la Foi set up in Lyon
1824	Death of Louis XVIII

Reign of Charles X

1825	Coronation of Charles X at Rheims
1830	(27–9 July) The 'Trois Glorieuses'

July Monarchy (Bourbons-Orléans Dynasty)

1830–48	Louis-Philippe succeeds Charles X
1830	Visitation of the Virgin Mary to Catherine Labouré and her vision of the Miraculous Medal
1830	(16 Aug.) *L'Avenir* founded
1832	The encyclical *Mirari Vos*
1833	The Loi Guizot; the Society of Saint-Vincent-de-Paul set up
1834	Lammenais, *Paroles d'un croyant*
1837	Dom Guéranger re-establishes the Benedictines
1839	Lacordaire restores the Dominicans
1845	Emmanuel d'Alzon founds the Assumptionists and M. Le Prévost the Brothers of Saint-Vincent-de-Paul
1846–78	Pope Pius IX
1846	Appearance of the Virgin Mary at La Salette

Second Republic

1848	(24 Feb.–10 Dec.) Louis-Napoleon elected President of the Republic
1850	Loi Falloux
1851	(2 Dec.) *Coup d'état* of Louis-Napoleon
1852	Comte, *Catéchisme positiviste*

Second Empire

1852–70	Napoleon III
1854	Dogma of the Immaculate Conception
1854–55	Crimean War
1858	Bernadette Soubirous's visions of the Virgin Mary at Lourdes
1859	Darwin's *Origin of Species*
1862	The encyclical *Gravissima*, 'Nous ne pouvons tolérer que la raison envahisse pour y semer le trouble le terrain réservé aux choses de la foi'
1863	Renan, *Vie de Jésus*

1864	The encyclicals *Quanta Cura* and *Syllabus Errorum*
1867	Mgr. Lavigerie Archbishop of Algiers
1869–70	Vatican I
1870	The infallibility of the Pope vs. heresies of pantheism, naturalism, rationalism, positivism, and socialism

Third Republic

1871	(Mar.–May) The Commune
1871	Visions of the Virgin Mary at Pontmain
1871	Albert Le Mun founds the Circles of Catholic Workers
1872	National Synod sets in opposition 'orthodox' and 'liberal' Protestants
1873	Law declares the public utility of the erection of the Sanctuary of Montmartre (Sacré Cœur)
1875	Law on the freedom of higher education
1878–1903	Pope Leo XIII, 'Pope of the Rosary'
1880	Law suppressing Sunday as an obligatory day of rest; decrees against unauthorized congregations.
1882	Public primary schools no longer under the control of the Church
1883	Death of Louis Veuillot, founder of *La Croix*
1884	Law re-establishing divorce
1891	The encyclical *Rerum Novarum*
1905	Separation of Church(es) and the State in France
1907	The encyclical *Pascendi* on 'modernism'

History of Napoleon's Egyptian Campaign, 1798–1801

1798   14 Feb. Talleyrand recommends to the Directory that France occupy Egypt to curb British trading and colonial interests and expansion in the Far East.

9 May. The General in Chief Napoleon arrives in Toulon.

19 May. Embarcation of the fleet at Toulon.

28 June. Official announcement on board ship of the expedition to Egypt.

2 July. Troops disembark at Alexandria.

4 July. 167 'savants' and artists on the mission disembark at Alexandria, but vital scientific instruments are lost when the *Patriote* sinks.

7 July. Monge and Berthollet leave Alexandria for Cairo with Napoleon's army.

8 July. 20 members of the Commission des Sciences et des Arts leave for Rosetta.

13 July. First combat against the Mamelukes near Chebreis.

21 July. Mamelukes defeated at the Battle of the Pyramids.

24 July. Bonaparte enters Cairo.

25–7 July. Institution of the Conseil de Notables (the Divan) in Cairo and in each province.

1–2 Aug. French fleet destroyed by the English at Aboukir.

22 Aug. Creation of the Institut d'Égypte in Cairo.

23 Aug. First meeting of the Institut d'Égypte.

25 Aug. Start of the campaign of Upper Egypt let by General Desaix.

29 Aug. First issue of the *Courrier de l'Égypte* published.

9 Sept. Turkey declares war on France.

22 Sept. Celebrations in Cairo of the Fête de la République.

24 Sept. Bonaparte and a group of savants visit the Pyramids at Giza.

1 Oct. First issue of *La Décade égyptienne* published.

7 Oct. Mamelukes are defeated by Desaix at Sediman; first meeting of the Divan in Cairo.

21–4 Oct. Muslim insurrection in Cairo.

24 Oct. British attack on the fort at Aboukir aborted.

Nov. Vivant Denon leaves for Upper Egypt.

10 Dec. Bonaparte is President of the Institut d'Égypte.

25 Dec.–3 Jan. Bonaparte and party of savants explore the Isthmus of Suez.

1799   5 Jan. Anglo-Turkish treaty of military alliance signed.

14 Jan. (Disastrous) launch of a Montgolfier hot air balloon in Cairo.

22–7 Jan. Exploration of the Nantron Lakes.

2 Feb. Vivant Denon arrives at Aswan with Desaix's troops.

10 Feb. Start of Napoleon's Syria campaign.

20 Feb. Capture of the fort at El-Arich.

24 Feb. Capture of Gaza.

7 Mar. Capture of Jaffa.

10 Mar. Dolomieu (a geologist) leaves Egypt for France.

19 Mar. Commission des Sciences leaves under Girard for Upper Egypt to undertake hydro-geological investigations.

20 Mar. Siege of Saint-Jean-d'Acre begins.

16 Apr. French victory at Mount Thabor.

27 Apr. Death of General Caffarelli.

20 May. Lifting of siege of Saint-Jean-d'Acre.

29 May. Jollois and Viliers du Terrage arrive in Dendera.

14 June. Bonaparte returns to Cairo.

19 July. Discovery of the Rosetta Stone by a French general.

25 July. Turkish disembarkation rebuffed at Aboukir.

16 Aug. Two 'Commissions Scientifiques' led by Fourier and Costaz leave Cairo for Upper Egypt.

23 Aug. Bonaparte leaves Egypt leaving Kleber in command.

23 Oct. In Paris Bonaparte reports to the Institut de France on the scientific work of the Egyptian expedition.

10 Nov. Kleber becomes President of the Institut d'Égypte in Cairo.

19 Nov. Kleber creates the Commission des Renseignements sur l'État Moderne de l'Égypte.

22 Nov. Kleber invites the savants and artists to join forces on a collaborative publication of their work (the *Description d'Égypte*).

13 Dec. Bonaparte becomes First Consul.

15–18 Dec. Mission Scientifique visits Giza, Saqqara, and Memphis.

1800   20 Mar. Turks defeated at the Battle of Heliopolis.

20–1 Mar. Second insurrection in Cairo.

25 Apr. French retake Cairo.

27 Apr. Group of savants on the *Oiseau* remain in Alexandria.

14 June. Assassination of Kleber by a Syrian. Menou is commander of the French army.

1801   8 Mar. 18,000 British soldiers disembark at Aboukir.

21 Mar. Menou's troops are routed by the British at the Battle of Canopus, leaving thousands dead on the beaches.

22 Mar. Last meeting of the Institut d'Égypte in Cairo.

1 Apr. British forces break the dyke at Aboukir.

6 Apr. Most of the savants leave Cairo for Alexandria.

9 June. Last edition of the *Courrier de l'Égypte*.

27 June. Capitulation of General Belliard in Cairo.

14 July. French evacuate Cairo.

Aug.–Sept. Repatriation of the French savants on British vessels.

Key Dates for Franco-Egyptian Relations, 1802–1876

1802   Denon publishes the *Voyage dans la Basse et la Haute Égypte*.
(6 Feb.) Decree that the *Description de l'Égypte* is published at French government expense.

1804   In rivalry to the British Consul Salt, Bernardino Drovetti (French Consul to Egypt) encourages the organization of archaeological digs and collects ancient Egyptian antiquities (part of his collection was bought by the Louvre).

1805   Mohammed Ali is governor of Egypt.

1810   The first volume of the collaborative results of the findings of the 167 academics and artists, *La Description de l'Égypte*, published. It would run by 1826 to nine volumes with plates, detailing 'Antiquities', 'the modern state', and 'natural history'. Panckoucke edited the second, more user-friendly, edition in 1821.

1811   Mohammed Ali's troups occupy Medina and Mecca.

1817   (1 Aug.) In the service of Britain, Belzoni makes his way inside the temple at Abu-Simbel. In October, he discovers the mummies of Rhamesis II and Seti I in the Valley of the Kings.

1818   Belzoni finds the opening of the Pyramid at Giza. The 'Egyptology' race begins in earnest.

1820   Louis XVIII authorizes the second edition of the *Description de l'Égypte* published by Panckouke.

1820   Beginning of the Egyptian conquest of the Sudan.
'Egyptian' cotton produced for export by Jumal.
Colonel Sève creates the first military school at Aswan after the French model.

1822   (27 Sept.) Major coup for France: Jean-François Champollion writes his famous *Lettre à M. Dacier relative à l'alphabète des hieroglyphes phonétiques* read to the Académie d'Inscriptions et Belles-lettres. The code is cracked.

1825   Gift of a giraffe sent to France from Mohammed Ali, the first seen in France and exhibited at the Ménagerie of the Jardin des Plantes after it had walked from Marseille.

1826   J.-F. Champollion becomes Curator of the Musée Égyptien of the Louvre.

1827   (15 Dec.) Charles X inaugurates the Musée Égyptien of the Louvre. Creation of the École de Médecine of Cairo by Clot Bey and a veterinary school.

1828   J.-F. Champollion arrives in Alexandria as part of a Franco-Tuscan archaeological mission directed by the Italian Egyptologist Rosellini and stays over a year.

1831   Mohammed Ali sends his troops to conquer Syria.

        (10 May) J.-F. Champollion gives his inaugural lecture at the Collège de France.

1832   (4 Mar.) Death of J.-F. Champollion.

1833   (30 Apr.) Arrival of first group of Saint-Simonians led by Cayol in Alexandria followed on 24 May by a group under Barrault and 23 Oct. a group under Prosper Enfantin with the 'mission' of founding a utopian community and the dream of piercing the Isthmus of Suez.

1834   (10 Jan.) Enfantin and Saint-Simonians start exploring the Isthmus of Suez.

        (3 Feb.) Mohammed Ali commissions Linant de Bellefonds to construct a dam at the neck of the Nile Delta.

        Publication in Paris of the novel *L'Or de Paris* by the Egyptian Rifaa el-Tahtawi.

        Creation of the École Polytechnique of Cairo by the Saint-Simonians.

1835   Creation of the École des Langues in Paris under the direction of el-Tahtawi.

1836   The Trappist Ferdinand de Géramb publishes *Le Pèlerinage à Jérusalem et au Mont-Sinaï*.

        (25 Oct.) The Luxor obelisk (gift of Mohammed Ali) is transported by boat and erected in the Place de la Concorde in Paris.

        Departure of most of the remaining Saint-Simonians ravaged by the plague of 1835, shattering dreams of building a dam across the Nile.

1839   (Oct.) First French photographers in Egypt.

1840   (Dec.) Egyptian troops evacuate from Syria.

1842–45   Scientific expedition of the German Egyptologist Richard Lepsius.

1844   Exhibition of the 'Kings' Chamber' from Karnak at the Bibliothèque Nationale, rue Richelieu.

1845   Visit of Ibrahim Pasha to France and the Duke of Montpensier to Egypt.

1846   (27 Nov.) Prosper Enfantin creates the 'Société d'Études pour le
            Canal de Suez' in Paris.
1849   Death of Mohammed Ali.
1849–50   *Voyage en Orient* of Gustave Flaubert who accompanied Maxime
            Du Camp.
1851   Discovery of the entrance to the Serapeum of Memphis by Auguste
            Mariette. Nerval publishes his *Voyage en Orient*.
1852   Maxime Du Camp publishes the first collection of photographs of
            Egypt, *Egypte, Nubie, Palestine, Syrie*.
1854   (15 Feb.) First Collège des Frères des Écoles Chrétiennes opened in
            Cairo.
            (13 July) Assassination of Abbas. His uncle Saïd rules in his place.
            (30 Nov.) Saïd grants Ferdinand de Lesseps the concession of the
            Suez Canal.
1857   (1 Jan.) The Alexandria–Cairo railway opens its service.
1858   (1 June) Directorship of the Egyptian Antiquities given to Auguste
            Mariette.
            (5–30 Nov.) Subscriptions open for shares in the Suez Canal com-
            pany.
            (15 Dec.) Constitution of the 'Compagnie universelle du Canal de
            Suez' drawn up. Gautier publishes *Roman de la momie*.
1859   Alexandria–Suez railway opens.
            (25 Apr.) Opening of work on the Suez Canal at Port Said.
            (6 May) Foundation and first meeting of the Institut Égyptien in
            Cairo in the manner of Napoleon's earlier Institut d'Égypte.
1862   (18 Nov.) Water from the Mediterranean flows into Lake Timsah.
1863   Auguste Mariette is the first Director of the Egyptian Museum of
            Cairo.
1867   (June) Ismail arrives in France for the Exposition Universelle in
            Paris inspired by Egyptology and Egyptomania.
1868   (15 Aug.) Suez–Ismailia railway inaugurated.
1869   (15 Aug.) Waters from the Mediterranian and Red Sea flow into the
            'lacs amers'.
            (17 Aug.) Inauguration of the Suez Canal by the Empress Eugénie.
1870   Decree ordering the use of Arabic (not Turkish) for administrative
            purposes in Egypt; Turkish and French at the Palace and the
            Ministries of Finance and War; Arabic and French by the police
            and regional governments.
1871   Verdi's *Aida* (composed for the inauguration of the Suez Canal) first
            performed in Cairo.
1875   (25 Nov.) Britain buys the Egyptian holdings of shares in the Suez
            Canal Company.
1876   (8 Apr.) Declaration of bankruptcy by the Egyptian government.

History of Nineteenth-Century French Sciences and Scientific Institutes

1778	Mesmer arrives in Paris with his medical theory based on animal magnetism.
1781	William Herschel discovers Uranus.
1785	Coulomb publishes his research on the inverse square laws of electrical and magnetic attraction.
1789	After years of research including discovery of oxygen, Lavoisier publishes his *Traité élémentaire de chimie* containing the law of mass conservation, and is ironically himself guillotined.
1793	The Jardin du Roi becomes the Jardin des Plantes (Muséum National d'Histoire Naturelle de Paris).
1800	Bichat's *Traité des membranes* results from research that founds histology and experimental physiology.
1801	Pinel's *Traité médicophilosophique sur l'aliénation mentale ou la manie*, perhaps the first work of modern psychiatry.
1803	Académie de Pharmacie de Paris founded.
1804	Reconstitution of the Académie d'Agriculture de France (est. 1761).
1809	In his *Philosophie zoologique*, Lamarck proposes that species emerge gradually and from the simple to the complex.
1811	Jöns Jacob Berzelius states that electrical and chemical forces are one and the same.
1812	Sir Humphrey Davy publishes *Elements of Chemical Philosophy* to oppose Dalton's theory of atoms as basic elements.
1815–17	Cuvier's *Le Règne animal* founds palaeontology.
1819	Fresnel undertakes work on a wave theory of light (following work by Young on light interference) against Newton's theory.
1821	Société de Géographie and Société d'Histoire Naturelle de Paris (reconstituted in 1833) both founded.
1822	Birth of Pasteur.
	Magendie confirms Bell's work on nerves by showing that spinal nerves have separate paths controlling movement and sensation.
	Société Asiatique founded.

1824 Carnot's *Réflexions sur la puissance motrice du feu* first describes the relation of work and heat, later developed in thermodynamics.

1826 Comte begins his *Cours de philosophie positive* (published 1830–41), a work crowning humanity's coming of age with the age of science.

1827 After Oersted's discovery of the magnetic field generated by an electrical field, Ampère's work results in a mathematical formulation of electromagnetism.

Société d'Horticulture de France founded.

1829 Coriolus publishes *Du calcul de l'effet des machines* giving definitions of work and kinetic energy.

1830 The 'querelle des analogues' between Cuvier and Geoffroy Saint-Hilaire, famously reported by Goethe (on Saint-Hilaire's side).

Lyell's *Principles of Geology* and the doctrine of uniformitarianism, that is that geological change occurs slowly.

Société Géologique de France founded.

1832 Société Entomologique de France founded.

1833 Müller's *Handbuch des Physiologie des Menschen*, confirming that each nerve responds to a stimulus in a specific way and suggesting that human beings perceive only the effects of their sensory systems.

1835 Dumas appointed to the École Polytechnique, where he develops his theory that organic compounds exist as types.

Quételet's *Sur l'homme* advances the theory of probabilities to describe the average man.

1836 Édouard Lartet uncovers first fossil anthropoid in the Miocene deposits near Sausan.

1838 Esquirol's *Des maladies mentales* published in the same year that France undertakes reform of care of the insane and mandates an asylum in every département.

1839 Schwann working with the botanist Scheiden lectures on cellular theory in research on microscopic structures of animals and plants.

1841 Remak describes cell division and works throughout the decade with Müller to develop modern embryology.

1843 Loi d'Ohm on sonic vibrations.

Société de Chirurgie founded.

1845 Boucher de Perches uncovers prehistoric discoveries near Abbeville.

Discovery of Neptune by Johann Galle, but thanks to the mathematics of Josephe Le Verrier.

1848 Société de Biologie founded.

1850 Helmholz, studying physiological optics and colour vision, invents the ophthalmoscope.

1851   The experiment of Foucault's Pendulum which demonstrates the rotation of the earth.
1852   Société Météorologique de France founded.
1854   Société Zoologique d'Acclimatation and Société Botanique de France both founded.
1855   Claude Bernard appointed to Collège de France for work on gastric juices and hormonal functions.
1856   Discovery of Neanderthal man.
1857   Gas lighting in the Grands Boulevards of Paris.
1858   Pasteur and Félix Andromède Pouchet begin polemics on spontaneous generation.
        Claude Bernard publishes *De la méthode expérimentale*.
1858   Following Schwann, Virchow decrees that every cell is derived from a pre-existing cell and says that disease originates in singles cells, thus founding cellular pathology.
1859   Darwin's *Origin of Species*.
        After Joule's work on the principle of the conservation of energy, Clausius publishes a paper showing the energy of a system remains constant while its entropy strives towards a maximum.
        Broca founds the pioneering Société d'Anthropologie de Paris.
1861   Sub-marine expeditions led by Milne-Edwards.
1865   Pasteur studies silkworm disease and conceives that micro-organisms are agents in pathology.
        Claude Bernard publishes the *Introduction à la médicine expérimentale*.
1869   Mendeleyev works out his first version of the periodic table tabulating the elements in terms of atomic weight.
1871   Darwin's *The Descent of Man* explores paths of human evolution from other animal species having avoided the topic in the *Origin*.
1872   Broca starts the *Revue d'anthropologie*.
1873   Société Française de Physique and the Société Mathématique de France both founded.
1876   Société Zoologique de France founded.
1878   Société Française de Minéralogie et de Cristallographie founded.
1887   Société Astronomique founded
1897   Société d'Océanographie de France founded.

References

PRIMARY WORKS

Flaubert, Gustave (1964). *Œuvres complètes*. Ed. Bernard Masson. 2 vols. Paris: Seuil.

——(1973–98). *Correspondance*. Ed. Jean Bruneau. 4 vols. Paris: Bibliothèque de la Pléiade.

——(1974). Preface to *Louis Bouilhet: Œuvres*. Geneva: Slatkine Reprints.

——(1983). *La Tentation de saint Antoine*. Ed. Claudine Gothot-Mersch. Paris: Gallimard.

SECONDARY CRITICISM ON *LA TENTATION DE SAINT ANTOINE*

Allenspach, Max (1923). *Gustave Flaubert*: *'La Tentation de saint Antoine' eine literarische Untersuchung*. Zurich: Dissertation Philosophique de l'Université de Zurich.

Barbe, Norbert-Bertrand (1994). 'Introduction à l'étude des tentations de saint Antoine', *Revue de la Bibliothèque Nationale de France*, 4: 10–15.

Bem, Jeanne (1979a). *Désir et savoir dans l'œuvre de Flaubert: étude de* La Tentation de saint Antoine. Neuchâtel: La Baconnière.

——(1979b). 'La Fonction des bêtes dans la *Tentation*', *Cahiers de l'Association des Études Françaises*, 31 (May): 35–44.

Bernheimer, Charles (1976–7). ' "Etre la matière": Origin and Difference in Flaubert's *La Tentation de saint Antoine*', *Novel*, 10: 65–78.

Blanchard, Émile (1874). 'L'Origine des êtres', *Revue des deux mondes*, 44 (1–6 May): 837–67.

Bowman, Frank Paul (1981). 'Flaubert et le syncrétisme religieux', *Revue d'histoire littéraire de la France*, 4–5 (July–Oct.): 621–36.

——(1985). 'Symbole et désymbolisation', *Romantisme*, 15/50 (Religions et religion): 53–60.

——(1986). 'Flaubert dans l'intertexte des discours sur le mythe', in Bernard Masson (ed.), *Gustave Flaubert 2: mythes et religions 1*. Paris: Lettres Modernes, Minard: 5–57.

——(1990). 'Flaubert's Temptation of Saint Anthony', in *French Romanticism: Intertextual and Interdisciplinary Readings*. Baltimore: Johns Hopkins University Press: 182–200.

Butor, Michel (1970a). 'La Spirale des sept péchés', *Critique*, 26: 387–412.

——(1970b). 'La Forme de "La Tentation"', *Esprit créateur*, 10: 3–12.

Carmody, F. J. (1958). 'Further Sources of the *Tentation de saint Antoine*', *Romanic Review*, 49: 278–92.

Chastel, A. (1936). 'La Tentation de saint Antoine ou le songe du mélancholique', *Gazette des beaux arts*, 15: 218–29.

——(1949). 'L'Épisode de la reine de Saba dans *La Tentation de saint Antoine*', *Romanic Review*, 40/2: 261–7.

——(1978). 'L'Épisode de la reine de Saba dans *La Tentation de saint Antoine*', in *Fables, Formes, Figures*. Paris: Flammarion: 123–30.

Cuthbert, Andrew (2003). 'Les Champs des connaissances: Myth and Metaphysics in the Late Works of Flaubert'. Exeter: unpublished Ph.D. thesis.

Danger, Pierre (1979). 'Sainteté et castration dans *La Tentation de saint Antoine*', in Charles Carlut (ed.), *Essais sur Flaubert*. Paris: Nizet: 185–202.

Demorest, Donald (1967). *L'Expression figurée et symbolisme dans l'œuvre de Gustave Flaubert*. Geneva: Slatkine.

Digeon, Claude (1946). *Le Dernier Visage de Flaubert*. Paris: Aubier: ch. 1.

Dusmesnil, René, and Demorest, Don L. (1937). 'Bibliographie de Gustave Flaubert', *Bulletin du bibliophile et du bibliothécaire*: 395–401, 452–60, 498–505, 549–55; and (1938): 25–32, 75–82, 134–42, 168–75.

Duthie, E. L. (1951). 'The Conclusion of Flaubert's *Saint Antoine*', *Contemporary Review*, 157–61.

Evrard, Franck, and Valette, Bernard (1999). *Gustave Flaubert: thèmes et études*. Paris: Ellipses.

Feyler, Patrick (1977). 'Les Monstres dans *La Tentation de saint Antoine*', *Eidôlon*, Oct: 59–90.

Foucault, Michel (1983). 'La Bibliothèque fantastique', in Gérard Genette and Tzvetan Todorov (eds), *Travail de Flaubert*. Paris: Seuil: 103–22.

Gendolla, Peter (1991). *Phantasien der Askese: Über die Entstehung innere Bilder am Beispiel des 'Besuchung des Heiligen Antonius'*. Heidelberg: C. Winter Universitätsverlag.

Gothot-Mersch, Claudine (ed.) (1983). *Flaubert: La Tentation de saint Antoine*. Paris: Gallimard.

——(1986). 'Flaubert, Nerval, Nodier et la reine de Saba', in Bernard Masson (ed.), *Gustave Flaubert 2: mythes et religions 1*. Paris: Lettres Modernes, Minard: 125–60.

Griffin, Robert B. (1990). 'The Transfiguration of Matter', *French Studies*, 40/1 (Jan.): 18–33.

Guedes, Tereza Moura (1984). '*Bouvard et Pécuchet "le pendant de" La Tentation de saint Antoine*', *Ariane*, 3: 99–113.

Haddad, Michèle (1992). 'Une image "déversoir": la *Tentation de saint Antoine* dans la deuxième moitié du dix-neuvième siècle français', in Stéphane Michaud, Jean-Yves Mollier, and Nicole Savy (eds), *Usages de l'image au xixe siècle*. pref. Maurice Aguilhon. Paris: Éditions Créciphis: 100–13.

Harter, Ursula (1998). *Die Versuchung des Heiligen Antonius: Zwischen Religion und Wissenschaft – Flaubert, Moreau, Redon.* Berlin: Dietrich Reimer Verlag.

Helein-Koss, Suzanne (1991). 'Le Risible Dans *La Tentation de saint Antoine*', *Romantisme*, 74: 65–71.

—— (1992). 'Les Avatars prosodiques du martichoras dans *La Tentation de saint Antoine*: du "visible" au "grotesque triste"', *Romance Review*, 83/2 (Mar.): 193–206.

Heuzey, Jacques (1953). 'Quelques sources inédites de *La Tentation de saint Antoine*', *Revue d'histoire littéraire de la France*, 53: 62–85.

Huss, Roger (1979). 'Nature, Final Causality and Anthropocentrism in Flaubert', *French Studies*, 33: 288–304.

Jasper, Gertrude (1933). 'Influence of Flaubert's Travel on the Last Version of Saint Anthony', *Modern Language Notes*: 162–65.

Kanasaki, Haruyuki (1987). 'Apollonius ou un rival de Jésus-Christ: étude génétique de *La Tentation de saint Antoine*', *Equinoxe*, 1 (Autumn): 92–105.

Kim, Yong-Eun (1990). '*La Tentation de saint Antoine*', version de 1849: genèse et structure. Chuncheon: Kangweon University Press.

Koskimies, Rafael (1972). 'Le Voyage dans l'espace dans *La Tentation de saint Antoine*', *Neuphilologische Mitteilungen*, 73: 153–61.

Lapp, John (1966). 'Art and Hallucination in Flaubert', *French Studies*, 10: 322–4.

Leal, R. B. (1990). 'The Unity of Flaubert's *Tentation*', *Modern Language Review*, 85: 330–40.

—— (1991). 'La Réception critique de la *Tentation de saint Antoine*', in *Œuvres et critiques: critique contemporaine et littérature du xviie siècle*. Tübingen: Gunther Narr: 115–34.

Leclerc, Yvan (1997). '*La Tentation de saint Antoine* de Flaubert: scènes infernales', *Magazine littéraire*, 356: 61–4.

Lecuyer, Maurice (1967). 'Triple Perspective sur une œuvre', *Cahiers de la Compagnie Madeleine Renaudin et Jean-Louis Barrault*, 59: 46–65.

Levin, Harry (1948). 'The Artist as Saint', *Kenyon Review*, 10 (Winter): 28–43.

Lilley, Lily Ann (1981). '*La Tentation de saint Antoine* de Flaubert: Hilarion la clef du mystère', *Nottingham French Studies*, 20/2: 9–24.

Lombard, Alfred (1934). *Flaubert et saint Antoine.* Paris: Éditions Victor Attinger.

Luoni, Flavio (1994). 'Saint Antoine et les deux voies vers la matière', in Raymonde Debray-Genette, Claude Duchet, Bernard Masson, and Jacques

Neefs (eds), *Gustave Flaubert 4: Intersections*. Paris: Lettres Modernes, Minard: 135–53.

Macherey, Pierre (1990). 'L'Irréalisme de Flaubert', in *A quoi pense la littérature: exercices de philosophie littéraire*. Paris: PUF. 155–76.

Mandiargues, André Pierre de (1967). 'Une hallucination merveilleuse', *Cahiers de la Compagnie Madeleine Renaudin et Jean-Louis Barrault*, 59: 3–5.

Mazel, Henri (1921). 'Les Trois "Tentations de saint Antoine"', *Mercure de France*, 15: 626–43.

Müller-Ebeling, Claudia (1997). *Die 'Versuchung des hl. Antonius' als 'Mikrobenepos': Eine motivgeschichtliche Studie zu den drei Lithographiefolgen Odilon Redons zu Gustave Flauberts Roman*. Berlin: Verlag für Wissenschaft und Bildung.

Munch, Marc-Matthieu (1986). 'Présentation de Creuzer', in Bernard Masson (ed.), *Gustave Flaubert 2: mythes et religions 1*. Paris: Lettres Modernes, Minard: 59–67.

Nancy, Jean-Luc (1994). *De l'écriture qu'elle ne révèle rien*. Paris: Albin Michel.

Neefs, Jacques (1981). 'L'Exposition littéraire des religions (la *Tentation de saint Antoine* de 1874)', *Revue d'histoire littéraire de la France* (July–Oct.): 637–47.

Neiland, Mary (1998). 'The Three Daughters of Lust: From Allegory to Ambiguity in Flaubert's *La Tentation de saint Antoine*', *Romance Studies*, 31 (Spring): 57–68.

——(2001). *'Les Tentations de saint Antoine' and Flaubert's Fiction: A Creative Dynamic*. Amsterdam: Rodopi.

Olds, Marshall C. (1988). 'Hallucination and Point of View in *La Tentation de saint Antoine*', *Nineteenth-Century French Studies*, 17/1: 170–85.

——(2001). Foreword, Glossary, Notes, Appendix, and revisions to the text of Gustave Flaubert, *The Temptation of Saint Anthony*, trans. Lafeadio Hearn, introd. Michel Foucault. New York: The Modern Library: pp. ix–xxii.

Orr, Mary (1998a). 'Stasis and Ecstasy: *La Tentation de saint Antoine* or the Texte bouleversant', *Forum for Modern Language Studies*, 34/4: 335–44.

——(2000a). *Flaubert: Writing the Masculine*. Oxford: Oxford University Press.

——(2000b). 'East or West? Flaubert's *La Tentation de saint Antoine* or the Question of Orthodoxy', in Paul Cooke and Jane Lee (eds), *(Un)faithful Texts: Religion in French and Francophone Literature from the 1780s to the 1980s*. New Orleans: University Press of the South.

——(2008c). *'La Tentation de saint Antoine* by Gustave Flaubert', in *The Literary Encyclopedia* at <http://www.LitEncyc.com>.

——(2009b) 'Les Animaux "parlants" comme signe de la vérité…'.

Paré, François (2001). 'Silence et poésie chez Gustave Flaubert: une étude de *la Tentation de saint Antoine*', *Études françaises*, 37/1: 117–32.

Pasco, Allan (2001). 'Anthony, Saint', 'Apollonius of Tyana', 'Arius and Arianism', 'Athanasius', 'Catoblépas', 'the Devil', 'Hilarion', 'Pantheism', 'Pig', 'Queen of Sheba', 'les sept péchés mortels', '*La Spirale*', '*La Tentation de saint Antoine*', 'Thebaid', 'Voyage en enfer' in Ed. Laurence Porter (ed.), *Encyclopedia of Flaubert*. Westport, CT: Greenwood Press: 6, 11–13, 13, 16–17, 51–52, 101–2, 169, 246, 256, 262, 302, 309, 323–8, 331, 344.

—— (2002). 'Trinitarian Unity in *La Tentation de saint-Antoine*', *French Studies*, 56/4: 457–70.

Pohle, Almut (1965). 'Sphinx und Chimäre: Zu einer Episode der "Tentation de Saint Antoine" ', in *Aufsätze zur Themen und Motifgeschichte: Festschrift für Hellmuth Petriconi zum 70. Geburtstag*. Hamburg: De Gruyter: 135–49.

Porter, Lawrence M., (1975–6). 'A Fourth Version of Flaubert's *Tentation de saint Antoine* (1869)', in Frank P. Bowman (ed.), *Patterns of Inquiry: Essays in Honor of Jean Seznec. Nineteenth-Century French Studies*, 4/1–2 (Fall-Winter): 53–66.

—— (1979). *The Literary Dream in French Romanticism: A Psychoanalytic Interpretation*. Detroit: Wayne State University Press.

Queffelec, Henri (1988). *Saint Antoine*. Paris: Librairie Séguier.

Reff, Theodore (1974). 'Images of Flaubert's Queen of Sheba in Later Nineteenth-Century Art', in Francis Haskell, Anthony Levi, and Robert Shackleton (eds), *The Artist and the Writer in France: Essays in Honour of Jean Seznec*. Oxford: Clarendon Press: 126–33.

Reik, Theodor (1912). *Flaubert und seine Suchung des Heiligen Antonius*. Minden: JCC Bruns.

—— (1986). 'Flaubert and his Temptation of Saint Anthony', in Laurence M. Porter (ed.), *Critical Essays on Gustave Flaubert*. Boston: Hall & Co.: 145–50.

Séginger, Gisèle (1987). 'L'Artiste, le saint: Les Tentations de saint Antoine', *Romantisme*, 17/55: 79–90.

—— (1988). 'L'Ontologie flaubertienne: une naturalisation du sentiment religieux', in Bernard Masson (ed.), *Gustave Flaubert 3: mythes et religions 2*. Paris: Lettres Modernes, Minard: 63–85.

—— (1994a). 'Une version apocryphe de la *Tentation de saint Antoine*', in Raymonde Debray-Genette, Claude Duchet, Bernard Masson, and Jacques Neefs (eds), *Gustave Flaubert 4: intersections*. Paris: Lettres Modernes, Minard: 189–203.

—— (1994b). 'Écriture et ascèse chez Flaubert, de l'inspiration à l'aspiration', in *Éthique et écriture: Actes du Colloque internationale de Metz, 14–15 May 1993*. Paris: Klincksieck.

—— (1994c). *Le Mysticisme dans 'La Tentation' de Flaubert: la relation sujet: objet*. Paris: Archives des Lettres Modernes 215/5.

—— (1995) 'La Chimère, figure de l'écrivain libéré: éthique et fantastique dans *Les Tentations* de Flaubert', in Joseph-Marc Bailbé (ed.), *La Fantaisie*. Rouen: Presse de l'Université de Rouen: 49–56.

—— (1997a). *Naissance et métamorphoses d'un écrivain: Flaubert et* Les Tentations de saint Antoine. Paris: Honoré Champion.

—— (1997b). 'Fiction et transgression épistémologique: le mythe de l'origine dans *la Tentation de saint Antoine* de Flaubert', *Romanic Review*, 88/1: 131–44.

Seznec, Jean (1940). *Les Sources de l'épisode des dieux dans 'La Tentation de saint Antoine' (première version 1849)*. Paris: J. Vrin.

—— (1940–1). 'Flaubert and India', *Journal of the Warburg and Courtauld Institute*, 4: 142–50.

—— (1945a). 'Flaubert historien des hérésies dans *La Tentation*', *Romanic Review* (Oct): 200–21.

—— (1945b). 'Flaubert historien des hérésies dans *La Tentation*', *Romanic Review* (Dec): 314–28.

—— (1945c). 'Flaubert and the Graphic Arts', *Journal of the Warburg and Courtauld Institute*, 8: 175–90.

—— (1947). 'The Temptations of Saint Anthony', *Magazine of Art*, 40: 86–93.

—— (1949). *Nouvelles Études sur* La Tentation de saint Antoine. London: The Warburg Institute, University of London.

Sherrington, R. J. (1965). 'Illusion and Reality in *La Tentation de Saint Antoine*', *Journal of the Australasian Universities Modern Language Association*, 24 (Nov.): 272–89.

Sonnenfeld, Albert (1971). '*La Tentation de saint Antoine*', *Cahiers de l'Association Internationale des Études Françaises*, 23 May: 311–26.

Starr, Peter (1984). 'Science and Confusion: On Flaubert's *La Tentation de Saint Antoine*', *Modern Language Notes*, 99/5: 1072–93.

Testa, Carlo (1991–2). 'Representing the Unrepresentable: The Desexualization of Desire in Flaubert's "etre la matière"', *Nineteenth-Century French Studies*, 20/1–2 (Fall–Winter): 137–44.

Thomas, Yves (1990a). 'Luxe et désert dans *La Tentation de saint Antoine*', *Letters romances*, 44/3 (Aug.): 181–92.

—— (1990b). 'La Valeur de l'Orient: l'épisode de la reine de Saba dans *La Tentation de saint Antoine*', *Études françaises*, 26/1: 35–45.

—— (1991). 'La Tour au Rat: un épisode oublié de *La Tentation de saint Antoine*', *Romance Notes*, 32/1 (Fall): 19–22.

Thomas, Yves (1994). 'La Tentation du désert chez Flaubert', in Raymonde Debray-Genette, Claude Duchet, Bernard Masson, and Jacques Neefs (eds), *Gustave Flaubert 4: intersections*. Paris: Lettres Modernes, Minard: 155–67.

Vadé, Yves (1977). 'Le Sphinx et la Chimère'. *Romantisme*, 15: 2–17 and 16: 71–81.

Valéry, Paul (1945). 'La Tentation de (saint) Flaubert', in *Variété V*. Paris: Gallimard.

NINETEENTH-CENTURY WORKS CONSULTED

Arago, François (1854, 1855, 1856). *Astronomie populaire*. Vols. i–iii. Paris: Gide et J. Baudry Éditeurs.

—— (1857). *Astronomie populaire*. Vol. iv. Paris: Gide Éditeur.

Burnouf, Eugène (1844). *Introduction à l'histoire du bouddhisme indien*. Paris: Imprimerie Royale.

Byron, Lord (1822). *Cain: A Mystery*. Paris: A. & W. Galignani.

Cap, P.-A. (1854). *Les Trois Règnes de la nature: le Muséum d'Histoire Naturelle*. Paris: L. Curmer.

Champollion, Jean-François (1868). *Lettres écrites d'Égypte et de Nubie en 1828 et 1829*. Paris: Didier et Cⁱᵉ.

Chassang, A. de (1862). *Philostrate, Apollonius de Tyane: sa vie, ses voyages, ses prodiges*. Paris: Didier et Cie. (repr. Paris: Éditions Sand, 1995).

Chesnel, A. de (ed.) (1862). *Dictionnaire des merveilles et curiosités de la nature et de l'art*, in *Nouvelle Encyclopédie théologique*, xlir Paris: J.-P. Migne.

Collin de Plancy, Jacques Auguste Simon (ed.) (1846). *Dictionnaire des sciences occultes et des idées superstitueuses*. 2 vols. Paris: J. P. Migne Editeur.

Creuzer, Frédéric (1825). *Religions de l'antiquité considérées principalement dans leurs formes symboliques et mythologiques*, trans. Frédéric Creuzer. Vol. i. Paris: Treuttel et Würtz.

—— (1829). *Religions de l'antiquité considérées principalement dans leurs formes symboliques et mythologiques*, trans. J. D. Guigniaut. Vol. ii/1. Paris: Treuttel et Würtz.

—— (1835). *Religions de l'antiquité considérées principalement dans leurs formes symboliques et mythologiques*, trans. J. D. Guigniaut. Vol. ii/2. Paris: Treuttel et Würtz.

—— (1838). *Religions de l'antiquité considérées principalement dans leurs formes symboliques et mythologiques*, trans. J. D. Guigniaut. Paris: Cabinet de Lecture Allemande de J.-J. Kosbühl.

Cuoq, Joseph (trans.) (1979). *Abd-al-Rahmân-al-Jabartî: Journal d'un notable du Caire durant l'expédition française (1798–1801)*, preface Jean Tulard. Paris: Albin Michel.

Cuvier, F. G. (1807). *Recherches anatomiques sur les reptiles regardés encore comme douteux par les naturalistes, faites à l'occasion de l'axolotl rapporté par M. de Humboldt du Mexique.* Paris: L. Hausmann.

Cuvier, Georges (1812). *Recherches sur les ossemens fossiles de quadrupèdes, où l'on rétablit les caractères de plusieurs espèces d'animaux que les révolutions du globe paroissent avoir détruites,* i: *Contenant le discours préliminaire de la géographie minéralogique des environs de Paris.* Paris: Deterville Libraire (repr. Brussels: Culture & Civilisation, 1969).

——(1831). *Zoologie de Pline,* trans. Ajasson de Grandsagne. Avec les recherches sur la détermination des espèces dont Pline a parlé par M. Le Bon G. Cuvier. 3 vols. Paris: C. L. F. Panckoucke.

—— (1841). *Histoire des sciences naturelles depuis leur origine jusqu'à nos jours: les siècles antériures au 16ᵉ siècle de notre ère.* Paris: Chez Fortin, Masson et Cⁱᵉ Libraires.

—— (1858). *Lettres de Georges Cuvier à C. M. Pfaff sur l'histoire naturelle, la politique et la littérature, 1788–1792,* trans. Louis Marchant. Paris: Librairie Victor Masson.

—— (1864). *Discours sur les révolutions de la globe: étude sur l' ibis et mémoire sur la Vénus Hottentote,* ed. and notes after Boitard. Paris: Passard Éditeur.

—— (1869). *Éloges historiques,* précédés de l'Éloge de l'auteur par M. Flourens. Paris: Paul Ducrocq.

—— (1969) *Recherches sur les ossemens fossiles de quadrupède, où l'on rétablit les caractères de plusieurs espèces d'animaux que les révolutions du globe paraissent avoir détruites.* 4 vols. Brussels: Culture & Civilisation (1st pub. Paris: Deterville Libraire, 1812).

—— (1999). *Anatomie des catastrophes: œuvres,* i: *Paléontologie.* Clermont-Ferrand: Éditions Paleo.

—— (2002). *Recherches sur les ossements fossiles: éléphants et mammouths.* Paris: Éditions Paleo (4th edn. Paris: Edmond d'Ocagne, 1834).

—— and Brogniart, Alexandre (1811). *Essai sur la géographie minéralogique des environs de Paris, avec une carte géognostique et des coupes de terrain.* Paris: Baudouin.

Denon, Dominique Vivant (1802). *Voyage dans la Basse et la Haute Égypte pendant les campagnes du général Bonaparte.* 2 vols. Paris: Didot.

Dictionnaire de mystique chrétienne ou Essai d'encyclopédisation historique et méthodique. (1858). Paris: J.-P. Migne Éditeur.

Du Camp, Maxime (1987). *Un voyageur en Égypte vers 1850: Le Nil de Maxime Du Camp,* introd. Michel Dewachter and Daniel Oster, preface Jean Leclant. Paris: Conti/Sand.

—— (1993). *Souvenirs littéraires 1822–1850.* Geneva: Slatkine Reprints.

Edmond, Charles (1867). *L'Égypte: l'Exposition Universelle de 1867*. Paris: Dentu.

Erdan, Alexandre (1855). *La France mistique: tableau des excentricités religieuses de ce tems*. Vols. i and ii. Paris: Coulon-Pineau.

Esquirol, Jean-Étienne-Dominique (1838). *Des maladies mentales, considérées sous les rapports médical, hygiénique et médico-légal*. 2 vols. Paris: J.-B. Baillière (repr. Paris: Frénésie, Ed. 8-T-19880, 1989).

Flourens, P. (1858). *Histoire des travaux de Georges Cuvier*. 5th edn. Paris: Garnier Frères.

Garnier, Adolphe (1852). *Traité des facultés de l'âme, comprenant l'histoire des principales théories psychologiques*. vol. i. Paris: Librairie de L'Hachette et Cie.

Geoffroy Saint-Hilaire, Étienne (1826). *Considérations générales sur les monstres, comprenant une théorie des phénomènes de la monstruosité*, extrait du *Dictionnaire classique d'histoire naturelle*. vol. ii. Paris: J. Tastu.

——— (2000). *L'Expédition d'Égypte: correspondance, 1798–1802*. Paris: Éditions Paleo.

Giraudet, Alexis (1843). *Nouveau Traité de géologie ou exposé de l'état actuelle de cette science, considéré dans ses rapports avec la minéralogie, l'agriculture, l'industrie, les arts et la tradition biblique*. Tours: A. Mame et Cie.

Gobineau, Arthur de (1984). *L'Inégalité des races*, précédé de 'La Révolution gobinienne' par J. G. Milliarakis. Paris: Éditions du Trident.

Haeckel, Ernest (1874). *Histoire de la création des êtres organisés d'après les lois naturelles*, trans. C. Letourneau. Paris: Reinwald.

Hello, Ernest (1897). *L'Homme: la vie, la science, l'art*. Paris: Librairie Académique Didier.

Humboldt, Alexandre de (1846). *Cosmos: essai d'une description physique du monde*. Vol. i, trans. H. Faye. Paris: Gide et Cie.

——— (1848). *Cosmos*. Vol. ii, trans. Ch. Galustey. Paris: Gide et J. Baudry Éditeur.

Jonquière, Clément de La (2003). *L'Expédition d'Égypte (1798–1801)*. 5 vols. Paris: Éditions Historiques Teissèdre.

Labarthe, Jules (1861). *Le Palais impériale de Constantinople et ses abords, Sainte-Sophie, le forum Augustéon et l'Hippodrome tels qu'ils existaient au dixième siècle*. Paris: Librairie de Victor Didron.

Laplace, Pierre-Simon (1821). *Précis de l'histoire de l'astronomie*. Paris: Mme Ve Courcier.

Le Poittevin, Alfred (1924). *Alfred Le Poittevin: Une promenade de Bélial et œuvres inédites* (1924), précédées d'une introduction par René Descharmes sur la vie et le caractère d'Alfred Le Poittevin. Paris: Les Presses Françaises.

Mariette, Auguste (1867). *Exposition Universelle de 1867: aperçu de l'histoire ancienne d'Égypte pour l'intelligence des monuments exposés dans le temple du parc égyptien*. Paris: Dentu Éditeur.

Matter, M. J. (1843). *Histoire critique du gnosticisme et de son influence sur les sectes religieuses et philosophiques des six premiers siècles de l'ère chrétienne.* 2nd edn. Vols. i–ii. Strasbourg: V. Levrault & Paris: P. Bertrand.

—— (1844). *Histoire de l'école d'Alexandrie comparée aux principales écoles contemporaines.* Vols. i–ii. Paris: Hachette.

—— (1862). *Saint-Martin: le philosophe inconnu, sa vie et ses écrits.* Paris: Didier et Cie.

Maunoury, A.-F. (1858). *Vie de saint Antoine par saint Athanase.* Paris: Dazobry, E Magdeleine & Cie.

Maury, L. F. Alfred (1848). *Des hallucinations hypnagogiques ou des erreurs des sens dans l'état intermédiaire entre la veille et le sommeil.* Extrait des *Annales médico-psychologiques.* Paris: Imprimerie de L. Martinet.

—— (1852). *Des ossements humains et des ouvrages de main d'homme—enfouis dans les roches et les couches de la terre pour servir à éclairer les rapports de l'archéologie et de la géologie.* Paris: Imprimerie de Crapelet.

—— (1857). *De certains faits observés dans les rêves et dans l'état intermédiaire entre le sommeil et la veille.* Extrait des *Annales médico-psychologiques.* Paris: Imprimerie de L Martinet.

—— (1860). *La Magie et l'astrologie dans l'antiquité et au moyen âge: étude sur les superstitions païennes qui se sont perpétuées jusqu'à nos jours.* Paris: Didier et Cie.

—— (1869). *La Terre et l'homme ou aperçu historique de géologie, de géographie et d'ethnographie générales.* Paris: Librairie l'Hachette et Cie.

Migne, Abbé J.-P. (1856). *Dictionnaire de mystique chrétienne ou essai d'encyclopédisation historique et méthodique.* vol. xxxvi. Paris: J.-P. Migne Éditeur.

Monuments de l'Égypte: édition impériale de 1809 (1988). Ed. Charles Coulston Gillispie and Michel Dewachter. Paris: Hassan.

Moreh, S. (ed. and trans.) (1975). *Al-Jabartî's Chronicle of the First Seven Months of the French Occupation of Egypt: Muharram-Rajab 1213, 15 June–Dec. 1798.* Leiden: E. J. Brill.

Olivet, Fabre d' (1823). *Caïn: mystère dramatique de Lord Byron.* Traduit en vers français et réfuté dans une suite de remarques philosphiques et critiques: précédé d'une lettre à Lord Byron, exposant les motifs et le but de cet ouvrage par Fabre d'Olivet. Paris: Chez Servier.

Pluquet, François-André-Adrien, Abbé (1817). *Mémoires pour servir à l'histoire des égarements de l'esprit humaine par rapport à la religion chrétienne, ou dictionnaire des hérésies, des erreurs et des schismes.* 2 vols. Besançon: Chez Petit.

Pouchet, Félix Andromède (1835). *Traité élémentaire de botanique appliqué.* Vol. i. Rouen: E. Legrand. Vol. ii. 1836.

—— (1841). *Zoologie classiques, ou histoire naturelle du règne animal.* 2nd edn. 3 vols. Paris: Librairie Encyclopédique de Roret.

Pouchet, Félix Andromède (1853). *Histoire des sciences naturelles du moyen âge ou Albert le Grand et son époque.* Paris: J. B. Baillière.

——(1859). *Hétérogénie, ou traité de la génération spontanée basé sur de nouvelles expériences.* Paris: J. B. Baillière et fils.

——(1861). *Générations spontanées: état de la question en 1860.* Paris: Félix Malteste et Cie.

——(1862). *Les Créations successives et les soulèvements du globe: lettres à M. Jules Desnoyers.* Paris: Félix Malteste et Cie.

——(1868). *L'Univers: les infiniment grands et les infiniment petits.* 2nd edn. Paris: L. Hachette et Cie.

Pouchet, Georges (1859). *Visite au Muséum d'Histoire Naturelle.* Rouen: A. Aillaud.

——(1893). *Conférence d'anatomie.* Enseignement spécial aux voyageurs. Paris: Administration des Deux Revues, 1–19.

Quinet, Edgar (1870). *La Création.* 2 vols. Paris: Librairie Internationale.

——(1982). *Ahasvérus.* Preface by Ceri Crossley. Geneva: Slatkine.

Renan, Ernest (1992). *Vie de Jésus (version intégrale).* Paris: Arléa (reprint of the 13th edn. published in 1864 by Michel Lévy).

Réville, Albert (1864). *La Vie de Jésus de M. Renan: devant les orthodoxies et devant la critique.* 2nd edn. Paris: Joël Cherbuliez Libraire-Éditeur.

——(1869). *Histoire du dogme de la divinité de Jésus-Christ.* Paris: Germer Baillière.

——(1870). *Histoire du Diable: ses origines, sa grandeur et sa décadence.* Strasbourg: Treuttel et Wurtz.

Simon, Jules (1845). *L'Histoire de l'École d'Alexandrie.* 2 vols. Paris: Joubert.

Staël, Madame de (1968). *De l'Allemagne.* 2 vols. Paris: Flammarion.

Vacherot, Étienne (1846–51). *Histoire critique de l'École d'Alexandrie.* 3 vols. Paris: Librairie Philosophique de Ladrange.

OTHER WORKS CONSULTED

Addison, Claire (1996). *Where Flaubert Lies: Chronology, Mythology and History.* Cambridge: Cambridge University Press.

Ancet, Pierre (2004). 'Le Problème du monstre humain: perception commune et histoire de la tératologie scientifique', in Pierre Guenancia and Pierre-François Moreau (eds), *Le Vivant et ses normes: Spinoza, Diderot, Saint-Hilaire.* Cahiers d'Histoire de la Philosophie No. 3. Bourgogne: Centre Gaston Bachelard, Centre de Recherches sur l'imaginaire et la rationalité de l'Université de Bourgogne: 105–25.

Appel, Toby A. (1987). *The Cuvier–Geoffroy Debate: French Biology in the Decades before Darwin*. New York: Oxford University Press.

Apuleius (1950). *The Golden Ass*, trans. and intrd. Robert Graves. London: Penguin.

Ardouin, Paul (1970). *Georges Cuvier: promoteur de l'idée évolutionniste et créateur de la biologie moderne*. Paris: Expansion Scientifique Française.

Ayres, Lewis (2006). *Nicaea and its Legacy: An Approach to Fourth-Century Trinitarian Theology*. Oxford: Oxford University Press.

Bardeau, Fabrice (ed.) (1977). *Le Livre des Gnostiques d'Egypte*. Paris: Éditions Robert Laffont.

Bart, Benjamin F. (1973). 'Psyche into Myth: Humanity and Animality in Flaubert's *Saint-Julien*', *Kentucky Romance Quarterly*, 20: 317–42.

—— (1977). *The Legendary Sources of Flaubert's Saint-Julien*. Toronto: University of Toronto Press.

Bartelink, G. J. M. (ed.) (1994). *Athanase d'Alexandrie: Vie d'Antoine*. Paris: Éditions de Cerf.

Baudat, Michel (1994). *De la Thébaïde à Montmajour: les reliques de Saint-Antoine Abbé*. Arles: Société des Amis du Vieil Arles.

Beausobre, M. de (1970). *Histoire critique de Manichée et du Manichéisme*. Vols. i–ii. Leipzig: B. R. Grüner. 1st pub. Amsterdam: Chez J. Frederic Bernard, 1734.

Beckett, Samuel (1952). *En attendant Godot*. Paris: Minuit.

Beer, Gillian (2000). *Darwin's Plots: Evolutionary Narrative in Darwin, George Eliot and Nineteenth-Century Fiction*. 2nd edn. Cambridge: Cambridge University Press.

Bem, Jeanne (2006). 'Flaubert adepte de la "rhétorique sémitique"?', in Logé Tanguy and Marie-France Renard (eds), *Flaubert et la théorie littéraire: en hommage à Claudine Gothot-Mersch*. Brussels: Facultés Universitaires Saint-Louis: 131–51.

Bernard, Jean-Louis (1994). *Apollonius de Tyane et Jésus*. Paris: Guy Trédaniel Éditeur.

Beyls, Pascal (1999). *Gabriel de Mortillet 1821–98, géologue et préhistorien*. Grenoble: Coll. Portraits de Meylan.

Bible, English: New International Version (1994). Lutterworth: Gideons International of the British Isles.

Blanckaert, Claude, Cohen, Claudine, Corsi, Pietro, and Fischer, Jean-Louis (eds) (1997). *Le Muséum au premier siècle de son histoire*. Paris: Éditions.du Muséum National d'Histoire Naturelle.

Bondeson, Jan (1999). *The Feejee Mermaid and Other Essays in Natural and Unnatural History*. Ithaca, NY: Cornell University Press.

Bourguet, Marie Noelle (1999). 'Des savants à la conquête de L'Egypte? Science, voyage et politique au temps de l'expédition de l'Egypte', in Bret (1999, 21–36).

Bowman, Frank P. (1973). *Le Christ romantique*. Geneva: Droz.

——(1987). *Le Christ des barricades, 1789–1848*. Paris: Éditions du Cerf.

Bret, Patrice (ed.) (1999). *L'Expédition d'Égypte: une entreprise des Lumières, 1798–1801*. Paris: Éditions Tec. et Doc.

Bricault, Gisèle (1992). *Saint Antoine l'Abbaye et l'ordre des Antonins*. Boulogne: Éds. du Castelet.

Brooke, John Hedley (1991). *Science and Religion: Some Historical Perspectives*. Cambridge: Cambridge University Press.

Brown, Andrew (1996). ' "Un assez vague Spinozisme": Flaubert and Spinoza', *Modern Language Review*, 91/4: 848–65.

Brown, Lee Rust (1997). *The Emerson Museum: Practical Romanticism and the Pursuit of the Whole*. Cambridge, MA: Harvard University Press.

Brown, Marshall (ed.) (2000). *The Cambridge History of Literary Criticism*, v: *Romanticism*. Cambridge: Cambridge University Press.

Buffetaut, Eric (2002). *Cuvier: le découvreur de mondes inconnus*. Paris: Belin.

Buisset, Christiane (1984). *Eliphas Lévi: sa vie, son œuvre, ses pensées*. Paris: Guy Trédaniel, Éds. de la Maisme.

Cahn, Théophile (1962). *La Vie et l'œuvre d'Étienne Geoffroy Saint-Hilaire*. Paris: PUF.

Cannuyter, Christian (2000). *L'Égypte copte: les chrétiens du Nil*. Paris: Découvertes Gallimard.

Cave, Tenrence (1990). *Recognitions: A Study in Poetics*. Oxford: Clarendon Press.

Chadwick, Henry (1999). *The Penguin History of the Church: The Early Church*. London: Penguin.

Chadwick, Owen (1998). *A History of the Popes, 1830–1914*. Oxford: Clarendon Press.

Chandler Smith, Joan (1993). *Georges Cuvier: An Annotated Bibliography of his Published Works*. Washington, DC: Smithsonian Institution Press.

Charlton, D. G. (1963). *Secular Religions in France, 1815–1870*. London: Oxford University Press.

Cholvy, Gérard (2001). *Christianisme et société en France au dix-neuvième siècle*. Paris: Éditions du Seuil (Points Histoire).

——and Hilaire, Yves-Marie (eds) (2000). *L'Histoire religieuse de la France 1800–1880: entre raison et révélation, un dix-neuvième siècle religieux?* Toulouse: Privat.

Clément d'Alexandrie (1954). *Les Stromates: Stromate 1*, introd. Claude Mondésert, trans, and notes Marcel Caster; *Stromate II*, introd. and notes P. Th. Camelot, trans. Claude Mondésert. Paris: Éditions du Cerf.

——(2001). *Stromate IV*, introd. Annewies Van Den Hoek, trans. Claude Mondésert. Paris: Éditions du Cerf.

Cohen, C., and Hublin, J.-J. (1989). *Boucher de Perches: origines romantiques de la préhistoire*. Paris: Belin.

Coilly, Nathalie, and Régnier, Philippe (2006). *Le Siècle des Saint-Simoniens: du Nouveau Christianisme au canal de Suez*. Paris: Éditions de la BNF.

Collaveri, François (1982). *La Franc-maçonnerie des Bonaparte*. Paris: Payot.

——(1986). *Napoléon: empereur franc-maçon*. Paris: Tallandier.

Cronin, Victor (1968). *Mary Portrayed*. London: Darnton, Longman and Todd Ltd.

Crossick, Geoffrey, and Jaumain, Serge (eds) (1998). *Cathedrals of Consumption: The European Department Store*. Aldershot: Ashgate.

Crossley, Ceri (1983). *Edgar Quinet (1803–1875): A Study of Romantic Thought*. Lexington, KY: French Forum Publishers.

——(1993). *French Historians and Romanticism: Thierry, Guizot, the Saint-Simonians, Quinet, Michelet*. London: Routledge.

——(2005). *Consumable Metaphors: Attitudes towards Animals and Vegetarianism in Nineteenth-Century France*. Bern: Peter Lang.

Culler, Jonathan (1974). *Flaubert: The Uses of Uncertainty*. London: Paul Elek.

Cunningham, Andrew, and Jardine, Nicholas (eds) (1990). *Romanticism and the Sciences*. Cambridge: Cambridge University Press.

Cunningham, Valentine (2006). 'The Necessity of Heresy', in Andrew Dix and Jonathan Taylor (eds), *Figures of Heresy: Radical Theology in English and American Writing*. Brighton: Sussex Academic Press: 1–18.

Dale, Andrew I. (1995). *Pierre-Simon Laplace: Philosophical Essay on Probabilities. Translated from the Fifth French Edition of 1825 with Notes by the Translator*. New York: Springer-Verlag.

Davy, Marie-Madeleine (1985). *Le Désert intérieur*. Paris: Albin Michel.

DeGrood, David H. (1982). *Haeckel's Theory of the Unity of Nature*. Amsterdam: B. R. Grüner Publishing Company.

Deligeorges, Stéphanie, Gady, Alexandre, and Labalette, Françoise (2004). *Le Jardin des Plantes et le Muséum National d'Histoire Naturelle*. Paris: Éditions du Patrimoine.

Descharmes, René (ed.) (1924). *Alfred Le Poittevin: Une promenade de Bélial et Œuvres inédites*. Paris: Les Presses Françaises.

Desportes, Matthieu (2002). 'Exemplaire familial: la circulation du souvenir à travers les dédicaces', in Yvan Leclerc (ed.), *Flaubert–Le Poittevin–Maupassant: une affaire de famille littéraire*. Rouen: Publications de l'Université de Rouen: 60–94.

Didyme l'Aveugle (1992). *Traité du Saint-Esprit*, Introd., trans., and notes Louis Doutreleau, SJ. Paris: Éditions du Cerf.

Dord-Crouslé, Stéphanie (1999), 'Savoir et ignorer dans *Bouvard et Pécuchet* de Gustave Flaubert', in Anne Balandard Méhon, Stéphanie Dord-Crouslé, and Michel Vanoosthuyse (eds), *Savoir et ignorer*. Paris: Belin: 93–181.

—— (2000). Bouvard et Pécuchet *de Flaubert: une 'encyclopédie critique en farce'*. Paris: Belin.

Dünne, Jörg (2003). *Asketisches Schreiben: Rousseau und Flaubert als Paradigmen literarisher Selbstpraxis in der Moderne*. Tübingen: Gunter Narr Verlag.

Dykstra, Darrell (1998). 'The French Occupation of Egypt, 1798–1801', in M. W. Daly, *The Cambridge History of Egypt: Modern Egypt from 1517-the End of the Twentieth Century*. Cambridge: Cambridge University Press: ii. 113–38.

El-Enany, Rasheed (2006). *Arab Representations of the Occident: East–West Encounters in Arabic Fiction*. London: Routledge.

Étienne, Bruno (1991). *L'Égyptomanie dans l'hagiographie maçonnique*, in *D'un Orient; l'autre*. Paris: CNRS.

Farmer, Hugh (ed.) (1992). *The Oxford Dictionary of Saints*. 3rd edn. Oxford: Oxford University Press.

Farrant, T. (2006). *Introduction to Nineteenth-Century French Literature*. London: Gerald Duckworth & Co.

Faure, Michel (1983). *Les Frères Montgolfier et la conquête de l'air*. Aix-en-Provence: Édisud.

Fischer, Jean-Louis (1997). 'Georges Pouchet (1833–1894): le mouvement, la forme et la vie', in Blanckaert et al. (1997, 363–73).

Fontenelle, Bernard Le Bovier de (1973). *Entretiens dur la pluralité des mondes; suivi de Histoire des oracles*. Verviers: Gérard.

Foucault, Michel (1966). *Les Mots et les choses: une archéologie des sciences humaines*. Paris: Gallimard.

—— (1969). *L'Archéologie du savoir*. Paris: Gallimard.

Fox, Robert (1992). *The Culture of Science in France, 1700–1900*. Aldershot: Variorum.

French, Roger, and Greenaway, Frank (eds) (1986). *Science in the Early Roman Empire: Pliny the Elder, his Sources and Influence*. London: Croom Helm.

Frye, Northrop (1957). *Anatomy of Criticism: Four Essays*. Princeton: Princeton University Press.

Georges Cuvier: de son temps au notre (n. d.). Langres: Expansion Éditeur.

Gibson, Ralph (1989). *A Social History of French Catholicism, 1789–1914*. London: Routledge.

Gillispie, Charles Coulston (1989). *Les Frères Montgolfier et l'invention de l'aéronautique*. Arles: Actes Sud.

—— (with the collaboration of Robert Fox and Ivor Grattan-Guinnes) (1997). *Pierre-Simon Laplace, 1749–1827, a Life in Exact Science*. Princeton: Princeton University Press.

Goulven, Laurent (1987). *Paléontologie et évolution en France, 1800–1860: de Cuvier–Lamarck à Darwin*. Paris: Éditions du Comité des Travaux Historiques et Scientifiques.

Gray, John (2004). *Heresies: Against Progress and Other Illusions*. London: Granta Books.

Green, Ann (1982). *Flaubert and the Historical Novel: Salammbô Reassessed*. Cambridge: Cambridge University Press.

—— (1986). '*Salammbô* and Nineteenth-Century French Society', in Lawrence M. Porter (ed.), *Critical Essays on Gustave Flaubert*. Boston: G. K. Hall & Co.: 104–19.

Green, Richard (1995). *The Thwarting of Laplace's Demon: Arguments against the Mechanistic World-View*. New York: St Martin's Press.

Guillemin, Henri (1963). *Flaubert: devant la vie et devant Dieu*. Paris: Nizet.

Guyader, Hervé Le (1998). *Étienne Geoffroy Saint-Hilaire, 1772–1844: un naturaliste visionnaire*. Paris: Belin.

Hahn, Roger (1994). *The New Calendar of the Correspondence of Pierre-Simon Laplace*. Berkeley and Los Angeles: University of California Press.

—— (2004). *Le Système du monde: Pierre-Simon Laplace: un itinéraire dans la Science*, trans. Patrick Hersant. Paris: NRF Gallimard.

Haig, Stirling (1986). *Flaubert and the Gift of Speech: Dialogue and Discourse in Four Modern Novels*. Cambridge: Cambridge University Press.

Harding, Sandra, and O'Barr, Jean F. (eds) (1987). *Sex and Scientific Enquiry*. Chicago: University of Chicago Press.

Hazlett, Ian (ed.) (1991). *Early Christianity: Origins and Evolution to AD 600*. London: SPCK.

Healy, John F. (1999). *Pliny the Elder on Science and Technology*. Oxford: Oxford University Press.

Heilbrun, J. L. (1999). *The Sun in the Church: Cathedrals as Solar Observatories*. Cambridge, MA: Harvard University Press.

Hesse, Mary B. (1966). *Models and Analogies in Science*. Notre Dame, IN: University of Notre Dame Press.

Hilaire, Yves-Marie (ed.) (2003). *Histoire de la papauté: 2000 ans de mission et de tribulations*. Paris: Tallandier.

Hoeges, Dirk (1980). *Literatur und Evolution: Studien zur französischen Literaturkritik im 19. Jahrhundert. Taine–Brunetière–Hennequin–Guyau*. Heidelberg: Carl Winter Verlag.

Hollier, Denis (ed.) (1989). *A New History of French Literature*. Cambridge, MA: Harvard University Press.

Isbell, John Clairbourne (1994). *The Birth of European Romanticism: Truth and Propaganda in Staël's De l'Allemagne*. Cambridge: Cambridge University Press.

Jacob, François (1970). *La Logique du vivant: une histoire de l'hérédité*. Paris: Gallimard.

Jaussaud, Philippe, and Brygoo, Édouard-Raoul (2004). *Du Jardin au Muséum en 516 biographies*. Paris: Publications Scientifiques du Muséum National d'Histoire Naturelle.

Jefferson, Ann (2007). *Biography and the Question of Literature in France*. Oxford: Oxford University Press.

Jordanova, Ludmilla J. (1984) *Lamarck*. Oxford: Oxford University Press.

Juden, Brian (1984). *Traditions orphiques et tendances mystiques dans le Romantisme française (1800–1855)*. 2nd edn. Geneva: Slatkine Reprints.

Karkoulis, Dimitri (2007). ' "They pluck'd the tree of Science / And sin": Byron's *Cain* and the Science of Sacrilege', *European Romantic Review*, 18/2: 273–81.

Kaufman, Suzanne K. (2005). *Consuming Visions: Mass Culture and the Lourdes Shrine*. Ithaca, NY: Cornell University Press.

Kay, Sarah, Cave, Terence, and Bowie, Malcolm (eds) (2003). *A Short History of French Literature*. Oxford: Oxford University Press.

Kearney, Richard (2003). *Strangers, Gods and Monsters*. London: Routledge.

Keller, Evelyn Fox (1985). *Reflections on Gender and Science*. New Haven: Yale University Press.

—— and Longino, Helen E. (eds) (1996). *Feminism and Science*. Oxford: Oxford University Press.

Kenner, Hugh (1962). *Flaubert, Joyce and Beckett: The Stoic Comedians*. Boston: Beacon Press.

Kristeva, Julia (1980). *Pouvoirs de l'horreur: essay sur l'abjection*. Paris: Seuil.

—— (1987). *Soleil noir: dépression et mélancholie*. Paris: Gallimard.

Kselman, Thomas A. (1983). *Miracles and Prophecies in Nineteenth-Century France*. New Brunswick, NJ: Rutgers University Press.

LaCapra, Dominique (1982). Madame Bovary *on Trial*. Ithaca, NY: Cornell University Press.

Laissus, Yves (1995). *Le Muséum National d'Histoire Naturelle*. Paris: Découvertes Gallimard.

—— (1998). *L'Égypte, une aventure savante: avec Bonaparte, Kléber, Menou (1798–1801)*. Paris: Fayard.

Laplace, Pierre-Simon (1776). *Mémoire sur l'inclinaison moyenne des orbites des comètes: sur la figure de la terre et sur les fonctions*, in *Mémoires de l'Académie Royale de Sciences de Paris, Savants étranges* (1773): vii. 503–434 and *Œuvres*, viii. 279–324.

Latour, Bruno (1999). *Pandora's Hope: Essays on the Reality of Science Studies*. Cambridge, MA: Harvard University Press.

Laurens, Henri (1989). *L'Expédition d'Égypte, une entreprise des Lumières, 1798–1801*. Paris: Colin.

——(1999). 'Les Lumières de l'Égypte', in Patrice Bret (ed.), *L'Expédition de l'Egypte, une enterprise des Lumières, 1798–1801*. Paris: Académie des Sciences. 1–6.

——Gillispie, Charles C., Golvin, Jean-Claude, and Traunecker, Claude (eds) (1989). *L'Expédition d'Egypte, 1798-*1801. Paris: Armand Colin.

Laüt-Berr, Sylvie (2001). *Flaubert et l'Antiquité: itineraries d'une passion*. Paris: H. Champion.

Leclerc, Yvan (1988). *La Spirale et le monument: essai sur* Bouvanrd et Pécuchet *de Gustave Flaubert*. Paris CDU/SEDES.

——(ed.) (2000). *Gustave Flaubert–Alfred Le Poittevin, Gustave Flaubert–Maxime Du Camp correspondances*. Paris: Flammarion.

——(2001). *La Bibliothèque de Flaubert: inventaires et critiques*. Rouen: Publications de l'Université de Rouen.

——(2002). *Flaubert–Le Poittevin–Maupassant: une affaire de famille littéraire*. Rouen: Publications de l'Université de Rouen.

Le Nain de Tillemont (1719). *Mémoires pour servir à l'histoire ecclésiastique des six premiers siècles*. vols iv, vii, viii. Brussels: Eugène Henri Fricx.

Levinas, Emmanuel (1979). *Le Temps et l'autre*. Paris: PUF.

Levy, David (1995). *Skywatching: The Ultimate Guide to the Universe*. London: HarperCollins.

Lima, Robert (2005). *Stages of Evil: Occultism in Western Drama*. Lexington, KY: Kentucky University Press.

Lórinszky, Ildikó (2002). *L'Orient de Flaubert: des écrits de la jeunesse à* Salammbô: *la construction d'une imagination mythique*. Paris: L'Harmattan.

McGrath, Alister (1999). *Science and Religion, an Introduction*. Oxford: Blackwell.

Maurel, Marie-Christine (1999). *August Weismann et la génération spontanée de la vie*. Paris: Éditions Kimé.

Miller, Michael (1981). *The Bon Marché: Bourgeois Culture and the Department Store, 1869–1920*. Princeton: Princeton University Press.

Miniac, Jean (ed. and trans.) (1992). *Saint Jérôme: vivre au désert: vies de Paul, Malchus, Hilarion 375–390*. Grenoble: Éditions Jérôme Millon.

Minois, George. (1990). *L'Église et la science: histoire d'un malentendu*, i: *De Saint Augustin à Galilée*. Paris: Fayard.

——(1991). *L'Église et la science: histoire d'un malentendu*, ii: *De Galilée à Jean-Paul II*. Paris: Fayard.

——(1998). *Le Diable*. Paris: PUF (Que sais-je?).

Monceaux, Paul (1901). *Histoire littéraire de l'Afrique chrétienne: depuis les origines jusqu'à l'invasion arabe*. Paris: Ernest Leroux.

Mours, Samuel, and Robert, Daniel (1972). *Le Protestantisme en France: du XVIIIᵉ siècle à nos jours, 1653–1970.* Paris: Librairie Protestante.

Moussa, Sarga (2004). *Le Voyage en Égypte: anthologie de voyageurs européens de Bonaparte à l'occupation anglaise.* Paris: Robert Laffont.

Neefs, Jacques (1987). 'De Flaubert à Perec', *Théorie littéraire d'enseignement,* 5: 35–49.

Neret, Gilles (ed.) (2001). *Description d'Égypte.* Cologne: Taschen.

Ogane, Atsuko (2006). *La Genèse de la danse de Salomé: l' 'appareil scientifique' et le symbolique polyvalente dans* Hérodias *de Flaubert.* Tokyo: Presses Universitaires de Keio.

Orr, Mary (1998b). 'Flaubert's Egypt: Crucible and Crux for Textual Identity', in Paul Starkey and Janet Starkey (eds), *Travellers in Egypt: Papers from the 1995 Durham Conference.* London: I.B. Tauris: 189–200.

—— (1999). 'Reversible Roles: Gender Trouble in Madame Bovary', in Tony Williams and Mary Orr (eds), *New Directions in Flaubert Studies.* Lewiston, NY: Edwin Mellen Press: 49–64.

—— (2003). *Intertextuality: Debates and Contexts.* Cambridge: Polity Press.

—— (2004). 'Death and the *Post mortem* in Flaubert's works', in Tim Unwin (ed.), *The Cambridge Companion to Flaubert.* Cambridge: Cambridge University Press: 105–21.

—— (2005). 'Hunting Legendary Monsters in Flaubert's *La Légende de saint Julien l'Hospitalier*', *FSB,* Summer: 15–19.

—— (2007). 'Keeping it in the Family: The Extraordinary Case of Cuvier's Daughters', in Cynthia Burek and Bettie Higgs (eds), *The Role of Women in the History of Geology.* London: Geological Society Special Publications 281: 277–86.

—— (2008a). 'Education, Education, Education: The Space of the Muséum as Showcase for Thinking its Public', in David Evans and Kate Griffiths (eds), *Institutions and Power.* Bern: Peter Lang.

—— (2009a). 'The Metamorphoses of Forms in Tournier's *Roi des Aulnes* and Pierrette Fleutiaux's *Métamorphoses de la reine*', in Lorna Milne and Mary Orr (eds), *Narratives of French Modernity: Themes, Forms and Metamorphosis.* Bern: Peter Lang.

—— (2009c). 'The Hidden Life of a Saint' . . . ' (under consideration).

Ortega, Maria Luia (1999). 'La Régénération de l'Egypte: le discourse confronté au terrain', in Bret (1999, 93–9).

Outram, Dorinda (1984). *Georges Cuvier: Vocation, Science and Authority in Post- revolutionary France.* Manchester: Manchester University Press.

Panagia, Davide (2006). *The Poetics of Political Thinking.* Durham, NC: Duke University Press.

Parisot, Roger (2002). *Hérésies*. Puiseaux: Pardès.

Paul, Harry B. (1979). *The Edge of Contingency: French Catholic Reaction to Scientific Change from Darwin to Duheim*. Gainesville, FL: University Presses of Florida.

Perrin, Claude (2000). *La Vie rocambolesque d'André Garnerin: pionnier du parachute*. Paris: Éd. Messene.

Poniatowski, Michel (1983). *Garnerin: le premier parachutiste de l'histoire*. Paris: Albin Michel.

Porter, Lawrence M. (1978). 'The Devil as Double in Nineteenth-Century Literature: Goethe, Dostoievsky, Flaubert', *Comparative Literary Studies*, 15 (Fall): 316–35.

—— (ed.) (2001). 'Critical Reception', in his *Encyclopedia of Flaubert*. Westport, CT: Greenwood Press: 77–90.

Raitt, Alan (1994). *Gustave Flaubert: pour Louis Bouilhet*. Exeter: Exeter University Press.

—— (2005). *Gustavus Flaubertus Bourgeoisophobus: Flaubert and the Bourgeois Mentality*. Bern: Peter Lang.

Régnier, Philippe (2006). *Le Siècle des Saint-Simoniens: du Nouveau Christianisme au canal de Suez*. Paris: BNF.

Retat, Laudyce (1977). *Religion et imagination religieuse: leurs formes et leurs rapports dans l'œuvre d'Ernest Renan*. Paris: Klincksieck.

Rottenberg, Elizabeth (2005). *Inheriting the Future: Legacies of Kant, Freud and Flaubert*. Stanford, CA: Stanford University Press.

Rudwick, Martin S. (1997). *Georges Cuvier, Fossil Bones and Geological Catastrophes: New Translations and Interpretations of the Primary Texts*. Chicago: University of Chicago Press.

Said, Edward W. (1978). *Orientalism*. London: Routledge and Kegan Paul.

Sartre, Jean-Paul (1971). *L'Idiot de la famille: Gustave Flaubert de 1821 à 1857*. 3 vols. Paris: Gallimard.

Schehr, Lawrence (1995). *The Shock of Men: Homosexual Hermeneutics in French Writing*. Stanford, CA: Stanford University Press.

—— (1997). *Rendering French Realism*. Stanford, CA: Stanford University Press.

Schiebinger, Londa (1993). *Nature's Body: Gender in the Making of Modern Science*. Boston: Beacon Press.

Schmidtt, Carl (ed.) (1978). *Pistis Sophia*, trans. and notes Violet MacDermot. Leiden: E. J. Brill.

Schor, Naomi (1985). *Breaking the Chain: Women, Theory and French Realist Fiction*. New York: Columbia University Press.

Schulz-Buschhaus, Ulrich (1995). *Flaubert: Die Rhetorik des Schweigens und die Poetik des Zitats*. Münster: Lit Verlag.

Seabrook, Michael (2007). 'Beyond the G(u)ilt Edge: Flaubert's Framing of the Bourgeois Mentality in *Bibliomanie*', in Lucy Bolton, Gerri Kimber, Ann Lewis, and Michael Seabrook (eds), *Fraued: Essays in French Studies*. Oxford: Peter Lang, 161–74.

Seznec, Jean (1993). *La Survivance des dieux antiques: essai sur le rôle de la tradition mythologique dans l'humanisme et dans l'art de la Renaissance*. Paris: Flammarion.

Smith, Annette (1984). *Gobineau et l'histoire naturelle*. Geneva: Librairie Droz.

Sochon, Serge (2004). *Pierre-Simon Laplace: un savant issu des Lumières*. Paris: Éditions Christian.

Solé, Robert (1997). *Égypte, passion française*. Paris: Seuil.

—— (1998). *Les Savants de Bonaparte*. Paris: Seuil.

Spary, E. C. (2000). *Utopia's Garden: French Natural History from Old Régime to Revolution*. Chicago: University of Chicago Press.

Starkey, Enid (1967). *Flaubert: The Making of the Master*. London: Weidenfeld & Nicolson.

—— (1971). *Flaubert the Master*. New York: Atheneum.

Steffan, Truman (1968). *Lord Byron's Cain: Twelve Essays and a Text with Variants and Annotations*. Austin, TX: University of Texas Press.

Stitt, Megan Perigoe (1998). *Metaphors of Change in the Language of Nineteenth-Century Fiction: Scott, Gaskell and Kingsley*. Oxford: Clarendon.

Surkis, Judith (2006). *Sexing the Citizen: Morality and Masculinity in France: 1870–1920*. Ithaca, NY: Cornell University Press.

Swerdlow, N. M. (1998). *The Babylonian Theory of the Planets*. Princeton: Princeton University Press.

Taguieff, Pierre-André (1998). *La Conleur du sang: doctrines racistes à la française*. Paris: Édition Mille et Une Nuits.

Tallett, Frank, and Atkin, Nicholas (eds) (1991). *Religion, Society and Politics in France since 1789*. London: Hambledon Press.

Taquet, Philippe (2006). *Georges Cuvier*. Paris: Odile Jacob.

Tarade, Guy (1999). *Les Chapelles alchimiques du sud-est: le grand secret des Antonins*. Le Coudray-Macouard: Cheminements.

Thiher, Allen (2001). *Fiction rivals Science: The French Novel from Balzac to Proust*. Columbia, MO: University of Missouri Press.

Tignor, Robert L. (ed. and trans.) (1995). '*The French View of the Events in Egypt: Memoirs by Louis Antoine Fauvelet de Bourrienne*', in *Napoleon in Egypt: Al-Jabarti's Chronicle of the French Occupation, 1798*. Princeton: Markus Wiener Publishing.

Todorov, Tzvetan (1970). *Introduction à la littérature fantastique*. Paris: Seuil.

Tooke, Adrianne (2000). *Flaubert and the Pictorial Arts: From Image to Text*. Oxford: Oxford University Press.

Tort, Patrick (ed.) (1983). *Geoffroy Saint-Hilaire. Cuvier: la querelle des analogues précédée de Goethe; dernière pages sur la philosophie naturelle.* Plan de la Tour: Éditions d'Aujourd'hui.

Tournier, Michel (1980). *Gaspard, Melchior et Balthazar.* Paris: Gallimard.

Uglow, Jenny (2002). *Lunar Men: Five Friends whose Curiosity Changed the World.* New York: Farrar, Straus and Giroux.

Vernay-Nouiri, Annie (2007). *Livres d'Arménie: collections de la BNF.* Paris: BNF.

Volney (Constantin-François Chasseboeuf) (1799). *Voyage en Syrie et en Égypte pendant les années 1783, 84 et 85.* 3rd edn. Paris: Chez Dugour et Durand Libraires (repr. ed. Anne Deneys-Tunney and Henry Deneys, Fayard, 1998).

Voragine, Jacques de (1998). *La Légende dorée.* Paris: Éditions du Seuil.

Wall, Geoffrey (2001). *Flaubert: A Life.* London: Faber and Faber.

Walter, Philippe (1996). *Saint Antoine: entre mythe et légende.* Grenoble: Ellug, Université Stendhal.

Ware, Timothy (1993). *The Orthodox Church.* New edn. London: Penguin.

Warner, Marina (1985). *Alone of All her Sex: The Myth and the Cult of the Virgin Mary.* London: Picador.

—— (2006). *Phantasmagoria: Spirit Visions, Metaphors, and Media into the Twenty-First Century.* Oxford: Oxford University Press.

Wiles, Maurice (1996). *Archetypal Heresy: Arianism through the Centuries.* Oxford: Oxford University Press.

Williams, Tony, and Orr, Mary (eds) (1999). *New Approaches in Flaubert Studies.* Lewiston, NY: Edwin Mellen Press.

Winchester, Simon (2002). *The Map that Changed the World: A Tale of Rocks, Ruin and Redemption.* London: Penguin.

Wright, M. Rosemary (1995). *Cosmology in Antiquity.* New York: Routledge.

Yanni, Carla (1999). *Nature's Museum: Victorian Science and the Architecture of Display.* London: Athlone Press.

Žižec, Slavoj (2001). *On Belief.* London: Routledge.

—— (2002). *Welcome to the Desert of the Real! Essays on September 11 and Related Dates.* London: Verso.

ELECTRONIC DOCUMENTS

<http://cerebro.xu.edu/math/Sources/Laplace/index.html> (accessed 25 Apr. 2007).

<http://www.chrysostompress.org/collection/1021 hilarion> (accessed 29 Jan. 2007).

<http://www.eastman.org/ne/cromer/m197900300003_ful.html> (accessed 17 May 2007).

<http://www-groups.dcs.st-and.ac.uk/~history/Biographies/Ptolemy.html>, 8pp. (accessed 30 Apr. 2007).

<http://www-groups.dcs.st-and.ac.uk/~history/Biographies/Laplace.html> (accessed 25 Apr. 2007).

<http://www.math.unicaen.fr/~reyssat/laplace>, 9 pp. (accessed 25 Apr. 2007)

<http://www.newadvent.org> (accessed 21 Dec. 2006).

<http://www.maths.tcd.ie/pub/HistMath/People/Laplace/RouseBall/RB_Laplace.html>, 5pp. (accessed 25 Apr. 2007).

<http://news.bbc.co.uk/2hi/africa/1971103.stm> (accessed 3 May 2007).

<http://flaubert.univ-rouen.fr>.

<http://flaubert.univ-rouen.fr/revue/revue4/03wulf.pdf> (accessed 4 Nov. 2007).

<http://www.soton.ac.uk/profiles/Orr.html>.

<http://www.soton.ac.uk/~bam2/col-index/fossi-Iindex/Forams/Eelco/Mediterranean/index.htm>.

Index